"In the Beginning . . ."

"In the Beginning..."
A Theology of the Body

EDUARDO J. ECHEVERRIA

Foreword by Janet E. Smith

◆PICKWICK *Publications* · Eugene, Oregon

"IN THE BEGINNING ..."
A Theology of the Body

Copyright © 2011 Eduardo J. Echeverria. All rights reserved. Except for brief quotations in critical publications or reviews, no part of this book may be reproduced in any manner without prior written permission from the publisher. Write: Permissions, Wipf and Stock Publishers, 199 W. 8th Ave., Suite 3, Eugene, OR 97401.

The Catholic Edition of the Revised Standard Version of the Bible, copyright 1965, 1966 by the Division of Christian Education of the National Council of the Churches of Christ in the United States of America. Used by permission. All rights reserved.

Scripture taken from the HOLY BIBLE NEW INTERNATIONAL VERSION®. NIV®. Copyright© 1973, 1978, 1984 by International Bible Society. Used by permission of Zondervan. All rights reserved.

Pickwick Publications
An Imprint of Wipf and Stock Publishers
199 W. 8th Ave., Suite 3
Eugene, OR 97401

www.wipfandstock.com

ISBN 13: 978-1-60608-648-3

Cataloging-in-Publication data:

    Echeverria, Eduardo J.

    "In the beginning ..." : a theology of the body / Eduardo J. Echeverria ; foreword by Janet E. Smith.

    xxviii + 340 p.; 23 cm. — Includes bibliographical references and index.

    ISBN 13: 978-1-60608-648-3

    1. Human body — Religious aspects — Catholic Church. 2. Homosexuality — Religious aspects — Christianity. 3. John Paul II, Pope, 1920–2005. Theology of the body. 4. Sex — Religious aspects — Catholic Church. I. Smith, Janet E., 1950- .

BX1795.B63 E25 2011

Manufactured in the U.S.A.

To my children

Michael, Genevieve, and Christine

Further let me ask of my reader, wherever, alike with myself, he is certain, there to go on with me; wherever, alike with myself, he hesitates, there to join with me in inquiring; wherever he recognizes himself to be in error, there to return to me; wherever he recognizes me to be so, there to call me back: so that we may enter together upon the path of charity, and advance towards Him of whom it is said, "Seek His face evermore" (Ps 105:4).

—St. Augustine *De Trinitate* I.3.5

Contents

Foreword by Janet E. Smith • *ix*

Acknowledgments • *xiii*

Introduction • *xv*

1. Biblical Revelation and Authority • 1
2. Catholic Biblical Hermeneutics and Ethics • 72
3. Experience and Revelation • 123
4. The Phenomenology of the Body • 166
5. Creation, Fall, Redemption, and Fulfillment • 205
6. The Theology of the Body and Homosexuality • 239
7. *Caritas in Veritate* • 306

Bibliography • *319*

Subject/Name Index • *335*

Foreword

Pope John Paul II's Theology of the Body, in spite of being a dense theological work, is much better known to popular audiences than to scholarly ones. Scholars, arguably, have been somewhat slow to mine the riches of the Theology of the Body. Eduardo Echeverria's "*In the Beginning*" provides a major contribution to our understanding of the Theology of the Body both for those with little theological background and for those with very sophisticated theological and philosophical training. It is of value not only for understanding what light the Theology of the Body has to shed on the issue of homosexuality; it is of value for those who want to know more about the philosophical and theological issues that undergird the Theology of the Body and that the Theology of the Body raises.

Readers of this book are in for an unexpected and unparalleled treat. They are going to meet not only a splendid application of John Paul II's Theology of the Body to the question of homosexuality, they are going to experience a marvelous mind at work, a mind that has amazing depth and scope. Echeverria's is a mind that loves a dispute and loves to engage in a dispute fairly. He uses the occasion of this book to argue for philosophical realism and theological propositionalism in a remarkably thorough way. A significant portion of this book is about neither homosexuality nor the Theology of the Body but is about questions regarding fundamental philosophical commitments and fundamental faith commitments, such as the authority and proper interpretation of scriptures.

Indeed, Echeverria does not really begin to treat the issue of homosexuality until mid-way through chapter 4. As Echeverria states in his introduction, he takes the "long route" to answering a series of questions. Personally, I always prefer the long version of any story, and that preference should be a principle when dealing with the complex issues that arise from the exercise of deriving truths from scripture. Echeverria is quite intimately aware of the kinds of presuppositions that underlie any hermeneutic and is not afraid to take on the project of explaining the fundamental principles that guide his hermeneutic. His wide-ranging erudition and patient pedagogy combined will likely dazzle readers and will certainly inform them. It is not often that the same person can justify his biblical hermeneutic, grapple with the legitimate role of experience in revelation, explain John Paul II's phenomenological method and personalism, and apply these to the sensitive issue of homosexuality. This book should become a standard textbook for graduate courses in moral theology; few other books provide the holistic approach that defines this work. Indeed, all graduate students in theology preparing for their comprehensive exams could well read this book as a marvelous review session—that will not only refresh their knowledge and help them synthesize it but enrich it.

Again, this book is remarkably rich in a number of surprising ways. The reader will likely be startled by a claim in the introduction: "This realist emphasis on the order of creation aligns Catholicism with the Dutch neo-Calvinist tradition of Reformed Christianity" (xxiv–xxv). Throughout the book, Echeverria draws upon resources of Reformed Christianity; he is intimately familiar with that tradition since for a period of time he belonged to it. Both the Catholic scholarly community and the Reformed scholarly community are likely to benefit greatly from being introduced to new thinkers who bring the best of their traditions to bear upon the issues Echeverria treats.

Perhaps there is no more controversial topic in our times than the question of homosexuality. Those who dare to raise the question of the morality of homosexuality risk being labeled as homophobic or intolerant even before the discussion begins. Whereas only a few decades ago, there was nearly widespread agreement that homosexuality was a form of sexual deviance, it has now become normalized to the point that it seems self-evident to many that homosexuality is a difference on the level of race and not a moral question at all. Echeverria intrepidly seeks to demonstrate that homosexual acts are immoral and does so by showing how the principles articulated in Pope John Paul II's Theology of the Body demonstrate the immorality of homosexual acts. He is, I believe, the first to do so.

Echeverria goes back to the very basics, as does John Paul II: he focuses his argument on the meaning of the body, of the body as an integral part of the person, as an external expression of the interior person. He speaks of the necessity of the person being integrated in body and soul.

He argues furthermore that the complementarity of the sexes is fundamental to the framework and substance of scripture and salvation history. With John Paul II he acknowledges that the body has meaning and that its meaning provides a limit or context for determining the morality of our choices. Sexuality, sexual differences, have a meaning—a meaning that involves the possibility of acts of self-giving that lead to union. Differences (not sameness) and procreativity are essential to achieving the union towards which sexuality drives.

Echeverria is an adroit dialectician. He knows who his critics are and how they argue; he gives them every consideration and respectfully assesses their claims. But he takes no prisoners. While he pays his opponents the compliment of reading them carefully and sometimes of presenting their positions more clearly than they do, he ruthlessly exposes the fallacies and contradictions that bedevil his opponents. Echeverria works out his position in respectful conversation with those, such as Luke Timothy Johnson, Margaret Farley, Andrew Sullivan, Stephen Pope, and Fr. Timothy Radcliffe, who maintain that homosexual acts are moral. Recognizing that philosophy is the handmaiden of theology, he enlists the careful thinking and argumentation of such philosophers as Germain Grisez, John Finnis, Robert George, and Michael Polanyi. Extremely helpful is his identification of six major justifications that have been advanced for the morality of homosexuality and then his patient and thorough response to each of those justifications.

Indeed, Echeverria's work is undeniably thorough and patient. He works through the issues and in the best Thomistic methodological tradition, lets all parties have their say. In turn, he justifies the hermeneutical principles that drive his own approach. This book is a splendid exercise in honest engagement of the issues that arise when trying to utilize John Paul II's Theology of the Body to explain and defend the Church's teaching on homosexuality. It is a model of how such an exercise should be conducted.

Janet E. Smith
Father Michael J. McGivney Chair in Life Ethics
Sacred Heart Major Seminary
Detroit, Michigan

Acknowledgments

I WISH TO EXPRESS my gratitude to the Academic Dean and Rector President of Sacred Heart Major Seminary, Fr. Todd Lajiness and Monsignor Jeffrey M. Monforton, who supported my Licentiate studies during which time I wrote the initial draft of this book. I would like to extend special thanks to Janet E. Smith, my friend and colleague, who gave me substantial feedback on that draft, encouraged me to revise it for publication, and also generously wrote the Foreword. I am also thankful to J. Daryl Charles and Hans Boersma for their thoughtful comments on the initial draft and for their encouragement. Their critical remarks, along with those of Janet Smith's, helped me to make this a better study of John Paul II's Theology of the Body than it otherwise would have been.

I am indebted and thankful to the late Pope John Paul II for his writings, especially but not only those that play a key role in this book. They were and continue to be an important stimulus to my own philosophical and theological work, my teaching, and, last but not least, the dynamics of an authentic Catholic understanding of true spirituality.

> May God grant that I speak with judgment and have thoughts worthy of what I have received, for he is the guide even of wisdom and the corrector of the wise. For both we and our words are in his hand, with all our understanding, too. (Wis 7:15–16)

Introduction

When we undertake the analysis of the "beginning" according to the dimension of the theology of the body, we do so by basing ourselves on the words of Christ with which he himself appealed to that "beginning." When he said, "Have you not read that from the beginning the Creator created them male and female?" (Matt 19: 4), he ordered us and always orders us to return to the depth of the mystery of creation. And we do so in the full awareness of the gift of original innocence, which belonged to man before original sin. Although an insurmountable barrier divides us from what man was then as male and female, through the gift of grace united to the mystery of creation, and from what both were for each other as a reciprocal gift, we are nevertheless *trying to understand that state of original innocence in its link with man's "historical" state after original sin, "the state of fallen and at the same time redeemed nature* [status naturae lapsae simul et redemptae]. (*MWTB*, 18.3)

Does John Paul II's *Theology of the Body* have anything to contribute to the debate about homosexuality?[1] In this book on the pope's theology of the body, I will argue that he has much to contribute to that debate, although he does not address that issue explicitly in *Man and Woman He Created Them: A Theology of the Body*.[2] Still, with the cur-

---

1. John Paul II, *Man and Woman He Created Them*. Furthermore references to this text will be cited parenthetically in the text as *MWTB*. Helpful for understanding the philosophical underpinnings of the *Theology of the Body* is the pope's pre-papal work, Wojtyla, *Love and Responsibility*. Also helpful is *The Acting Person*; and the pre-papal essays in Wojtyla, *Person and Community*, especially "Subjectivity and the Irreducible in Man," 209–17.

2. In his pre-papal work, *Love and Responsibility*, Wojtyla holds that same-sex attraction is a "deviation" from the "natural direction of the sexual urge ... towards a human being of the other sex" (49). Indeed, elsewhere in this book he speaks of same-sex attraction as belonging to a class of "perversions," or deviances, other members of that class being bestiality (extra-human sexual relations) or some kind of fetish with an inanimate object (105). Although Wojtyla doesn't say, I think we can distinguish a "sexual devi-

xv

rent consensus of the culture celebrating sexual diversity, which has led to the widely-held presupposition that the sexual difference of the two sexes is morally and theologically inconsequential, the pope's theology of the body is counter-cultural in affirming the normative significance of humanity's sexual difference in creation, after the fall, in redemption, and in the eschaton.[3]

The epigraph to this introductory chapter makes clear that the starting point of John Paul II's theology of the body is that sexual difference is grounded in the ontology of creation.[4] In other words, the sexual difference between male and female is a creational given such that all mankind is bound to the structures of creation. It is also a creational given that, at one and the same time, mankind is one and a bi-unity: male and female. John Paul explains:

> Let us enter into the setting of the biblical "beginning." In it the revealed truth concerning man as "the image and likeness" of God constitutes the immutable *basis of all Christian anthropology.* "God created man in his own image, in the image of God he created him; male and female he created them" (Gen 1:27). This concise passage contains the fundamental anthropological truths: man is the highpoint of the whole order of creation in the visible world; the human race, which takes its origin from the calling into existence of man and woman, crowns the whole work of creation; *both man*

---

ance" from "sexual dysfunctions [e.g., for men, premature ejaculation, impotency, and for women, vaginismus or orgastic dysfunction] in that [in the former] the object or action in which sexual satisfaction is sought is abnormal" (Ashley and O'Rourke, *Health Care Ethics*, 389).

3. In his fine study, *Creation and Covenant: The Significance of Sexual Difference in the Moral Theology of Marriage*, Christopher C. Roberts agrees with this assessment of John Paul II's theology of the body. Along with Karl Barth, John Paul II's "arguments about sexual difference seek to deepen and clarify the traditional premise that sexual difference has moral significance" (8). I have profited much from Roberts' study. See also Avila, "Sexual Difference and Marriage."

4. I am struck by the soundness of Paul Helm's observation and its relevance for understanding the pope's strategy: "Surely given the current penchant of the culture for pluralism, for celebrating difference, Christians need to celebrate sameness.... We cannot dodge our moral obligations by playing the cultural difference card. It is into this world of objective structures, though fallen and hence warped and bent, that the one Gospel comes. It is the Creator's Gospel.... The Gospel has the same kind of objectivity as the structures of creation do. It is the amazing grace of their Creator. Its claims are held to be true with the same kind of truth, not relative, subjective truth, but objective truth" ("Against Ideological Apologetics").

and woman are human beings to an equal degree, both are created in God's image.⁵

Indeed, the pope imitates Christ (see Matt 19:3–9) by appealing to the "beginning," to the creational ordinance for marriage, drawing on Genesis 1 and 2 for his understanding of the normative intent of a biblical ontology of creation, the objective structures of creation, in which the original meaning of the union of man and woman as willed by God from the beginning is grounded. His treatment of these foundational texts is ultimately theological, because grounded in an historical-redemptive dialectic of creation, fall, redemption, and fulfillment, but also philosophical—articulating a philosophical anthropology of the body-person, which in its broadest sense is man himself in the temporal form of existence of human life.⁶ I will lay out his philosophical anthropology of the body-person in chapter 4.

Additionally, John Paul's theology of the body is at once prophetic and evangelical. His theology draws on not only the nuptial symbolism of the prophets that "*portray the covenant as a marriage* established between God and Israel" (*MWTB*, 104.2), but also on "the definitive covenant in which Christ, having loved the Church and given himself for her, unites with her in a spousal way" (*MWTB*, 93.3), "which in turn allows us to understand marriage itself as a covenant between husband and wife" (*MWTB*, 104.2). Furthermore, his theology grounds marriage, according to the order of creation (Gen 2:24), in the sense that "in the common life of the couple ... the two, by being united in the conjugal act, become 'one-flesh'" (*MWTB*, 118.4). This "two-in-one-flesh union" is renewed in the sacrament of marriage. The sacramental theology of the Church defines a sacrament as "'a visible sign of an invisible reality' [Augustine], namely, of the spiritual, transcendent, and divine reality. In this sign—and through this sign [because the sacrament actually accomplishes what it

---

5. John Paul II, *Mulieris Dignitatem: On the Dignity and Vocation of Women*, no. 6. See also Barth: "In the whole reach of human life," writes Barth, "there is no abstractly human, but only concretely masculine or feminine being, feeling, willing, thinking, speaking, conduct and action, and only concretely masculine and feminine co-existence and cooperation in all these things" *Church Dogmatics* III/2, 286. Hans Urs von Balthasar echoes: "The polarity of man and woman can stand as the paradigmatic instance of the thoroughgoing communal character of humanity" (*Von Balthasar Reader*, 72).

6. On the development of a theological anthropology of the body person, see Martin, *Feminist Question*, 331–406.

signifies]—God gives himself to man in his transcendent truth and in his love." "The sacrament is a sign of grace," the pope adds, "and it is an *efficacious sign*. It does not merely *indicate* and express grace in a visible way, in the manner of a sign, but *produces* grace and contributes efficaciously to cause that grace to become part of man and to *realize and fulfill the work of salvation* in him, the work determined ahead of time by God from eternity and fully revealed in Christ" (*MWTB*, 87.5). It is in this pregnant sense, sacramentally speaking, that the theology of the body is evangelical because it proclaims the "*truth [about marriage] that comes from God*" (*MWTB*, 105.3).

Now, the doctrine of creation is an integral part of Christian revelation, but so too is a doctrine of sin. Man, savagely wounded by the Fall into sin, original sin (see Genesis 3), bears within himself this wound, which, as John Paul says, "constantly draws him towards evil and puts him in need of redemption."[7] The doctrine of sin, he adds, "has great hermeneutical value insofar as it helps one to understand human reality."[8] Yet, the deepest foundation of created reality is still what God made it despite the Fall.[9] The creation order continues to be upheld by God's common grace, which is a non-saving grace that limits the damaging effects of sin from having its full way with reality.[10] Dooyweerd is right: "A denial of this leads to the unscriptural conclusion that the fall is as broad as creation; i.e., that the fall destroyed the very nature of creation. This would mean that sin plays a self-determining, autonomous role over against God, the creator of all. Whoever maintains such a position robs God of his sovereignty and grants Satan a power equal to that of the origin of all

---

7. John Paul II, *Centesimus Annus*, no. 25. See also, "The Church's wisdom has always pointed to the presence of original sin in social conditions and in the structure of society: 'Ignorance of the Fact that man has a wounded nature inclined to evil gives rise to serious errors in the areas of education, politics, social action, and morals' [*Catechism of the Catholic Church*, no. 407]" (Benedict XVI, *Caritas in Veritate*, no. 34).

8. Ibid.

9. Nichols, *Shape of Catholic Theology*, 45.

10. Dooyweerd is right: "Relegating creation to the background is not scriptural. Just read the Psalms, where the devout poet rejoices in the ordinances that God decreed for creation. Read the book of Job, where God himself speaks to his intensely suffering servant of the richness and depth of the laws which he established for his creatures. Read the Gospels, where Christ appeals to the creational ordinance for marriage in order to counter those aimed at trapping him. Finally, read Romans 1:19–20, where the creational ordinances are explicitly included in the general revelation to the human race" (*Roots of Western Culture*, 59).

things."¹¹ Furthermore, the wounds affecting creation are healed through the saving work of Jesus Christ, redeeming and restoring from within this fallen world. John Paul II's view presupposes a theology of nature and grace in which its key theme is grace restoring and renewing nature. Later in chapter 5, I'll discuss in some detail the pope's theology. This theology is, for now, however briefly, well expressed by Etienne Gilson, "The work of creation is shattered, but the fragments remain good, and, with the grace of God, they may be reconstituted and restored."¹² Elsewhere he writes, "The true Catholic position consists in maintaining that nature was created good, that it has been wounded, but that it can be at least partially healed by grace if God so wishes. This *instauration*, that is to say, this renewal, this re-establishment, this restoration of nature to its primitive goodness by grace, is on this point the program of authentic Catholicism."¹³

In my judgment, this program of authentic Catholicism, as Gilson phrases it, has come to life in John Paul II's theology of the body, and hence it is indeed relevant to the condition and practice of homosexuality. It is relevant because the theology of the body-person provides not only a foundation for anthropology and sexual ethics in the ontology of creation, but also it brings God's healing grace to bear on "the condition [and practice] of a disordered sexuality that reflects the brokenness of our sinful world."¹⁴ Thus, this book is devoted to laying out the biblical, theological and philosophical foundations of the theology of the body in order to apply the insights of that theology to the vexing issue of homosexuality. I take the long route to that application:

---

11. Ibid., 60.
12. Gilson, *Spirit of Mediaeval Philosophy*, 127.
13. Gilson, *Christianity and Philosophy*, 21–22.
14. Belief Statement of the Christian Reformed Church on the condition of same-sex attraction and its expression in the practice of homosexual acts (such practice is called "homosexualism" by this Statement) is to the point because it sees clearly that the prior condition itself is objectively disordered and hence its sexual expression must also be intrinsically disordered. In short, referring to the condition itself as a sexual disorder means that no parity exists between heterosexual and homosexual men from the order of creation.

1. I consider the all-important question in this debate regarding the nature and authority of biblical revelation, its primacy and finality, for faith and practice, and its foundation in a doctrine of special revelation. In my treatment of biblical revelation, I also give a brief account of the relation of Scripture and Tradition.

2. I then turn to sketch the principles of a Catholic biblical hermeneutic especially as they pertain to the use of Scripture in ethics, and to the charge that such usage is arbitrary, reflecting a fundamentalist mindset.[15]

3. The issue of "experience" and whether it has any authority, even if not as a source of revelation, in my judgment, also raises questions of theological method and epistemology. The question regarding the place of "experience" is especially important because in some theological circles "experience" is treated as a separate source of authority and revelation, which is played off against Scripture itself. Do we give the last word to Holy Scripture as the supreme norm of faith or to our experience? I will briefly address this decisive question in this book.

4. Following that, I turn to the philosophical foundations of the theology of the body, especially to the pope's phenomenology of the Body. How should we understand the role of phenomenology in the philosophical infrastructure of that theology?

5. I then turn to the theology of nature and grace that informs John Paul's theological anthropology and its normative implications for sexual morality. In this context, I will also direct my attention to the biblical foundations of the theology of the body.

6. Finally, I apply those normative implications to the moral question of homosexuality in the last chapter of this book, wherein I will also address some of the usual objections to the Church's teaching concerning homosexuality.

The question could be raised by the reader as to why I take the long route to showing the relevance of the theology of the body for the homosexuality debate. Why am I discussing biblical authority, hermeneutics

---

15. I affirm the normative biblical hermeneutic as expressed in the Vatican II Constitution on Divine Revelation, *Dei Verbum*, nos. 7–10.

and ethics, experience and theological method *before* I explore the theology of the body and its normative implications?

Briefly, I want to reply in this book to critics of the orthodox Christian position regarding the significance of sexual difference in the moral theology of sexuality and, *a fortiori*, of marriage. I'm thinking of critics, such as Rowan Williams, who claim that the rejection of same-sex relations "must rely either on an abstract fundamentalist deployment of a number of very ambiguous biblical texts, or on a problematic and non-scriptural theory about natural complementarity, applied narrowly and crudely to physical differentiation without regard to psychological structures."[16] The thesis of my book is that John Paul II is neither fundamentalist in his biblical hermeneutic nor naturalistic in his anthropology. Indeed, both his hermeneutic and anthropology are deeply biblical in affirming the integrity of creation revelation as the foundation of the normative significance of humanity's sexual difference. As Christopher Roberts puts this point: "The same God whom we know in Christ has, in his goodness, created us as male and female. To be male or female, then, is to be blessed, for it is to be something that is good. To be this sexually differentiated creature is to be something that will be redeemed, *and redeemed as it was made and not as some other creature*; in other words, sexual difference itself will be present in our redemption. Sexual difference is something humans should embrace and welcome, for to do that is to honor creation and anticipate redemption."[17] In other words, redemptive grace does not render the goods of creation insignificant; rather grace presupposes nature, renewing and perfecting it, neither abolishing it nor leaving it untouched by grace's healing power, because it was *this* creation, in all its distinctness and particularity that God created, that fell into sin, and is redeemed in Christ, and no other.[18] In short, "Faith in redemption cannot be separated from faith in the Creator." Redemption, adds Joseph Ratzinger, "is an act of new creation, the restoration of creation to its true identity."[19]

Regarding fundamentalism, one might ask, "What is a fundamentalist?" It means, for some, someone who operates in his appeal to Scripture with the presupposition of *biblicism*. Dutch theologian Jochem Douma

16. Williams, "Body's Grace," 320.
17. Roberts, *Creation and Covenant,* 236; italics added.
18. Ibid., 208.
19. Ratzinger (Benedict XVI), *Spirit of the Liturgy*, 24, 34. See also, Hopko, *Christian Faith and Same-Sex Attraction*, 15–16.

gives a helpful definition of biblicism: "By *biblicism* we understand that appeal to Scripture which uses Bible texts in an atomistic (isolated) way by lifting them out of their immediate contexts or out of the whole context of Scripture." Let's call this atomistic appeal to Scripture the bad sense of using proof-texts. But there is a good sense of using biblical proof-texts, exegetically and scripturally. Otherwise, "It would be a hopeless situation," Douma correctly adds, "if by definition every appeal to Scripture were biblicistic. For then a pure appeal to Scripture in ethics [or theology] would be simply impossible."[20]

Following this definition of biblicism, John Paul is not a fundamentalist. Rather, in accordance with the biblical hermeneutic of Vatican II's *Dei Verbum*, and the Church's teaching regarding the unity and reliability of the Word of God, he gives "serious attention ... to the content and unity of the whole of Scripture" in developing the biblical foundation of the theology of the body.[21] His is a canonical exegesis, which involves placing the individual biblical texts in their immediate literary context,[22] within the unfolding history, from creation to eschaton, of God's revelation, the context of Scripture as a whole,[23] and the living tradition of the Church.[24] Indeed, the pope's view dovetails with the biblical hermeneutic of Richard B. Hays who holds that the theological consideration of homosexuality must take place in canonical context, "No theological consideration of homosexuality can rest content ... with a short list of passages that treat the matter explicitly. We must consider how Scripture frames the discus-

---

20. Douma, "Appendix: The Use of Scripture in Ethics," 363–64.

21. *Dei Verbum*, no. 12.

22. Ibid.: "To search out the intention of the sacred writers, attention should be given, among other things, to 'literary forms.' For truth is set forth and expressed differently in texts which are variously historical, prophetic, poetic, or of other forms of discourse. The interpreter must investigate what meaning the sacred writer intended to express and actually expressed in particular circumstances by using contemporary literary forms in accordance with the situation of his own time and culture."

23. Ibid.: "But, since Holy Scripture must be read and interpreted in the sacred spirit in which it was written, no less serious attention must be given to the content and unity of the whole of Scripture if the meaning of the sacred texts is to be correctly worked out." Nichols, *Shape of Catholic Theology*, 154. Ratzinger (Benedict XVI), *Jesus of Nazareth*, xix. For a similar emphasis, see also Anglican theologian, Ward, *Words of Life*, 122. For a summary statement on Catholic biblical hermeneutics, see Williamson, "Catholic Principles for Interpreting Scripture."

24. Ibid.: "The living tradition of the whole Church must be taken into account along with the harmony which exists between the truths of the faith ['analogy of faith']."

sion more broadly: How is human sexuality portrayed in the canon as a whole, and how are the few explicit texts treating homosexuality to be read in relation to this larger canonical framework?" Thus, adds Hays, "The normative canonical picture of marriage provides the positive backdrop against which the Bible's few emphatic negations of homosexuality must be read."[25]

Furthermore, John Paul II works with a hermeneutical schema that takes seriously the reality of general revelation in creation, for biblical revelation is not the whole of God's revelation to us. Rather, the structures or orders of creation are revelatory of God's ordained teleology of the world. So, John Paul does not succumb to biblicism in another sense of that word. In this second sense, biblicism is the view which holds that truly scriptural principles for any area of human activity must be derived strictly from explicit Bible texts. Dooyeweerd, along with John Paul, rejects this view. He writes:

> Is it not true that God revealed his whole law in the Ten Commandments? Is this revelation not enough for the simple Christian? I answer with a counterquestion: is it not true that God placed all the spheres of temporal life under his laws and ordinances—the laws that govern numerical and spatial relationships, physical and chemical phenomena, organic life, emotional feeling, logical thinking, language, economic life, and beauty? Are not all these laws grounded in God's creation order? Can we find explicit scriptural texts for all of them? If not, shall we not acknowledge that God gave man the task to discover them?[26]

The answer to the question raised by Dooyeweerd in the concluding sentence of this passage is, of course, affirmative. This, too, is the view of the Second Vatican Council in its teaching regarding "the autonomy of the various secular spheres."[27] The Council Fathers make clear in *Gaudium et Spes* that they reject, says Otto Semmelroth, "the false conception of autonomy which denies that things have their root in the divine will of the Creator and so abandons their use to the arbitrary will of man. This is said totally to overlook the fact that creatures are nothing without the Creator,

---

25. Hays, *Moral Vision of the New Testament*, 389–90.
26. Dooyeweerd, *Roots of Western Culture*, 58.
27. In what follows, I am citing Otto Semmelroth's commentary on chapter III, no. 36, of *Gaudium et Spes, Commentary on the Documents of Vatican II*, vol. 5, Pastoral Constitution on the Church in the Modern World, 191–92.

that their true pattern is obscured by the forgetfulness of the Creator."[28] That is, as Otto Semmelroth adds:

> Autonomy is entirely justified, if by autonomy we understand "that created things and societies themselves enjoy their own laws and values which must be gradually discovered, put to use and regulated by man" [*Gaudium et Spes*, no. 36]. The theological interpretation regards this autonomy as based on the "word" of creation. Because the world was created through the "word," all things are endowed with their own ontological consistency, truth, goodness, their own laws and orderly structure ("propria firmitate, veritate, bonitate propriisque legibus ac ordine"). The rationality of the whole world, i.e., all the laws of the physical, biological, mathematical, and logical realms of reality, as well as those of the world of artistic significance and those of personal existence and of man's social solidarity originate in the "word" of creation.[29]

In the above passage, it is correctly assumed that, in Holy Scripture, the "Word of God" also refers to divine speech that created and directs the world (Gen 1:3, 6, 9; Pss 33:6, 119:89–92, 147:15–18, 148:8). Of course, in Scripture, as John Frame adds, "'Word of God' applies not only to spoken and written revelation but also . . . to Jesus Christ himself as the supreme self-expression of the Father. Thus, God makes himself known to us, not only through the Bible, but through everything in creation. We ourselves, made in God's 'image,' constitute an especially important form of God's self-disclosure."[30] And since the human body shares in the dignity of that image, then it follows that the whole human person is an especially important form of God's creation revelation.[31]

Against this background, we can easily understand why John Paul is not a biblicist in this sense either: he grounds the theology of the body in God's creation revelation. Indeed, the pope's theology of the body is, in fact, a "realist theology," as Dominican theologian Romanus Cessario rightly calls this hermeneutical schema that takes seriously creational structures. It "seeks to contemplate an immanent wisdom in the universe . . . reflecting the ordered wisdom of the divine plan for creation."[32] Significantly, this

---

28. Ibid.
29. Ibid.
30. Frame, "Rationality and Scripture," 293–94.
31. *Catechism of the Catholic Church*, no. 364.
32. Cessario, "On Bad Actions, Good Intentions, and Loving God," 109.

realist emphasis on the order of creation aligns Catholicism with the Dutch neo-Calvinist tradition of Reformed Christianity.[33] Furthermore, John Paul takes these structures of creation as the normative starting point for developing not only the biblical and theological foundations of the theology of the body, instead of just individual biblical texts—although John Paul does appeal to biblical texts and premises to support ethical arguments—but also its normative moral requirements for discerning the sins of the body, especially but not only sexual sins.[34] In reply to the question Christ receives about marriage and divorce in Matt 19:3–8, Jesus refers us, says John Paul, to "the beginning," to "the first divine order." "This means that this order has not lost its force, although man has lost his primeval innocence." "*Christ's answer* is decisive and clear," adds John Paul. "For this reason, *we must draw the normative conclusions from it* [the normative order of creation], which have an essential significance not only for ethics, but above all for the theology of man and the theology of the body, which, as a particular aspect of theological anthropology, is constituted on the foundation of the Word of God who reveals himself" (*MWTB*, 3.4). Hence the title of my book, "In the Beginning," which signifies John Paul's reference to God's original order of creation, his good creation, an ontological foundation that explains the meaning and purpose of human sexuality, of human sexual difference.

Moreover, John Paul II is not naturalistic about complementarity, and he doesn't apply his theology of the body, indeed, his phenomenology of the body, merely to the physical body without regard to the unity of body and soul, of the whole man. In other words, as I shall show in chapter 4, the pope does not think of the human body as a mere abstract material body, but rather as the whole of man's temporal existence. Of course John

---

33. By "Reformed" I mean that version of Protestant Christianity arising from the Calvinist Reformation in sixteenth-century Europe. The term "neo-Calvinist" refers to a movement within Reformed Christianity that stems from the nineteenth-century Dutch educator, theologian, church leader, and politician Abraham Kuyper (1837–1920). Besides Kuyper, other genial spirits within this intellectual milieu include theologians Herman Bavinck (1845–1921) and Gerritt C. Berkouwer (1904–1996), and the philosopher, Herman Dooyeweerd (1894–1977). For an account of the notion of creation order in Dutch neo-Calvinism, especially the philosophy of Dooyeweerd, see Wolters, "Creation Order."

34. For an exposition of the pope's hermeneutical schema, see Kurz, "Scriptural Foundations of *The Theology of the Body*," and the reply by Stegman, "'Actualization': How John Paul II utilizes Scripture in *The Theology of the Body*."

Paul II addresses the problem regarding the unity of the human person in his theology of the body. According to José Noriega, "The problem is properly located in the relationship between corporal-anatomical identity and personal-relational identity, or, in other words, it is the question of the foundation of personal-relational identity, and what role the body plays in that identity."[35] According to the pope, then, the human person is a unified totality, existing as a whole, with body and soul being functionally inseparable, and thus we shall need to consider the question regarding the specifically human meaning of the body, its existential significance and not merely its biological significance, in conformity with the Creator's wise plan.[36] In short, what is John Paul II's understanding of the embodiment of the human person and, accordingly, the place of the body in moral action?[37]

One more introductory remark: my reflections in this book are interdisciplinary in nature, covering topics in systematic theology, moral theology, philosophical theology, and theological anthropology. Furthermore, this book is also an exercise in ecumenical theology, drawing on the best from both the Catholic and Reformed traditions—particularly, Dutch neo-Calvinism. Regarding ecumenism, searching for an ecumenical basis for cooperation among Christians where this is possible is an urgent necessity.[38] Indeed, as Herman Dooyeweerd correctly remarks, "In the face of the increasing dechristianization and spiritual uprooting of modern mankind this necessity is so evident that any further argument is superfluous."[39] Significantly, John Paul II argues in his 1995 Encyclical Letter, *Ut Unum Sint*, that the Church's unity is at the very heart of the proclamation of the Gospel, not only in the sense that it belongs to the very essence of Christ's body, and Christ cannot be divided, but also, and in particular, because disunity is a grave obstacle for proclaiming the Gospel credibly and authentically. Hence, as John Paul II rightly urges, "ecumenism is not only an internal question of the Christian

---

35. Noriega, "Homosexuality," 453.

36. Wojtyla, *Love & Responsibility*, 52. See also, John Paul II, *Veritatis Splendor*, nos. 46–51.

37. Crosby, "Estrangement of Persons from Their Bodies."

38. I develop a theological basis for ecumenical conversation in my book, *Dialogue of Love, Confessions of an Evangelical Catholic Ecumenist*.

39. Dooyeweerd, *New Critique of Theoretical Thought*, 3:543.

communities."[40] "At the same time," he adds, "it is obvious that the lack of unity among Christians contradicts the Truth which Christians have the mission to spread and, consequently, it gravely damages their witness."[41] In short, lack of unity among Christians compromises our witness to the world, contradicting the Gospel truth, such as the truth of the theology of the body, that Christians have the missionary mandate to live, proclaim, and defend.

This study is organized in the following way: I treat points 1–3 in the first three chapters, respectively, before turning to the theology of the body itself—its philosophical and theological underpinnings—in chapters 4 and 5, and its normative implications (points 4–6) for sexual ethics, particularity the ethics of homosexuality, in the book's penultimate chapter. In that chapter, I also deal with several objections to the Church's teaching on homosexuality. I conclude in the final chapter with a response to the pastoral objection to her teaching, namely, to the so-called "gap" that exists between Catholic sexual ethics and peoples' real lives.

40. John Paul II, *Ut Unum Sint*, no. 99.
41. Ibid., no. 98.

1

Biblical Revelation and Authority

CRITICS OF BIBLICAL AUTHORITY

THAT THE AUTHORITY OF the Holy Scriptures should be honored as the foundational court of appeal in moral matters is an ancient conviction of the Christian faith. Yet, the Bible's moral authority is rejected by many today, even by self-professing Christians, with the objection that appealing to its moral authority is selective and arbitrary. But is using the Holy Scripture as ultimate authority in moral matters arbitrary? A despiser like none other of the Christian tradition, Richard Dawkins thinks so:

> In practice no civilized person uses scripture as ultimate authority for moral reasoning. Instead, we pick and choose the nice bits of scripture (like the Sermon on the Mount) and blithely ignore the nasty bits (like the obligation to stone adulteresses, execute apostates and punish the grandchildren of offenders). The God of the Old Testament himself, with his pitilessly vengeful jealousy, his racism, sexism and terrifying bloodlust, will not be adopted as a literal role model by anybody you or I would wish to know. Yes, *of course* it is unfair to judge the customs of an earlier era by the enlightened standards of our own. But that is precisely my *point*! Evidently, we have some alternative source of ultimate moral conviction which overrides scripture when it suits us.[1]

---

1. This passage is found in Dawkins' commentary ("Obscurantism to the Rescue," 397–98) on John Paul II's 1996 address ("The Pope's Message on Evolution to the Pontifical Academy of Sciences") to the Pontifical Academy of Sciences. Dawkins is not alone among recent famous despisers of the tradition in this judgment about the moral authority of the Bible. Philosopher Simon Blackburn writes similarly: "Anyone reading the Bible might be troubled by some of its precepts. The Old Testament God is partial to some people above others, and above all jealous of his own pre-eminence, a strange

In the last sentence of the above passage, Dawkins alludes to an alternative source of ultimate moral conviction to which one allegedly appeals in rejecting Scripture. Luke Timothy Johnson, in a recent article, "Homosexuality & the Church," agrees with this claim.[2] That is, Johnson's position is representative of an approach to biblical authority that is widely influential today in the debates regarding homosexuality, namely, making an appeal on behalf of "experience" as that alternative source of moral conviction to override scriptural authority and hence the clear teaching of Scripture. Accordingly, I think a brief exposition of Johnson's position will raise several of the questions that I will address in the remainder of this chapter and the next.

First we must acknowledge that Johnson is not a despiser of the Christian tradition and of the Church's Scripture; indeed, he is a committed Catholic who holds that something normative is at work in the authority of Scripture and of the Church's tradition.[3] Nonetheless, he frankly dissents from explicit scriptural commands on homosexuality (see Lev 18:22; 20:13; Rom 1:18–32; 1 Cor 6:9–11; 1 Tim 1:10; Acts 15:28–29) and holds that "we must state our grounds for standing in tension with the clear commands of Scripture [regarding homosexuality], and include in those grounds some basis in Scripture itself." In evaluating Johnson's position on abandoning scriptural norms, I am seriously attentive to Rowan Williams' point that we must not assume that "revisionism on one question entails wholesale doctrinal or ethical relativism."[4] Still, in Johnson's case his rejection of those scriptural norms leads to a doctrinal dismissal of the orthodox doctrine of objective revelation, a confusion of objective

---

moral obsession. He seems to have no problem with a slave-owning society, believes that birth control is a capital crime (Genesis 38:9–10), is keen on child abuse (Proverbs 22:15; 23:13–14; 29:15), and, for good measure, approves of fool abuse (Proverbs 26:3). ... All in all, then, the Bible can be read as giving us a carte blanche for harsh attitudes to children, the mentally handicapped, animals, the environment, the divorced, unbelievers, people with various sexual habits, and elderly women. It encourages harsh attitudes to ourselves, as fallen creatures endlessly polluted by sin, and hatred of ourselves inevitably brings hatred of others" (*Being Good*, 10–11, 13). For a critique of the use of Scripture by Dawkins et al., see Paul Copan, "*Is Yahweh a Moral Monster?* The New Atheists and Old Testament Ethics."

2. Luke Timothy Johnson is the Robert R. Woodruff Professor of New Testament at the Candler School of Theology, Emory University. Besides "Homosexuality & the Church," Johnson made the same claims in an earlier article "Debate & Discernment."

3. See the book, Johnson and Kurz, *Future of Catholic Biblical Scholarship*.

4. Williams, "Knowing myself in Christ," 12.

revelation with the illuminating work of the Holy Spirit enabling us to grasp the full meaning of that revelation, and a denial that there exists fundamental revealed moral truth. I want now to support these claims.

What extra-scriptural grounds provide a basis, according to Johnson, for rejecting explicit scriptural commands? Briefly, he claims we should reject those commands because they reflect ethical precepts that are not only historically and culturally bound but also, indeed chiefly, morally wrong, and hence no longer acceptable to us today. Thus, regarding homosexuality, says Johnson, we must be intellectually honest. Says Johnson, "We are fully aware of the weight of scriptural evidence pointing away from our position." We must not twist Scripture to say something other than what it actually says, "through appeals to linguistic or cultural subtleties." Therefore, "The exegetical situation is," adds Johnson, "straightforward: we know what the text says. But what are *we to do* with what the text says" (italics added)? In other words, the issue is, says Johnson, not one of understanding what the Scripture *meant*, but rather with what it *means* for us today since our cultural situation is such that we cannot believe what they believed. Significantly, Johnson is not a moral relativist: he is saying that the biblical authors are wrong and we are right. So, then, what are we to do with the biblical text. He replies clearly although problematically:

> I think it is important to state clearly that we do, in fact, reject the straightforward commands of Scripture, and appeal instead to another authority when we declare that same-sex unions can be holy and good. And what exactly is that authority? We appeal explicitly to the weight of our experience and what the experience of thousand of others have witnessed to, which tells us that to claim our own sexual orientation is in fact to accept the way in which God has created us. By so doing, we explicitly reject as well the premises of the scriptural statements condemning homosexuality—namely, that it is a vice freely chosen, a symptom of human corruption, and disobedience to God's created order.[5]

Johnson thinks that there is historical precedence in the Christian tradition for rejecting straightforward scriptural commands. He asks, "Which Christians have ever observed the exhortation in Leviticus to stone psychics and put adulterers to death?" He agrees with Dawkins and others that Christians selectively, that is, arbitrarily, appeal to scriptural

---

5. Johnson, "Homosexuality & the Church."

commands. Here are some other examples one might give to illustrate Johnson's point. Christians appeal to God's prohibition against same-sex relations in Lev 18:22 ("You shall not have intercourse with a man as you would with a woman. It is an abomination."), but ignore the punishment of death for same-sex relations in Lev 20:13. They find scriptural warrant in the sixth commandment for rejecting adultery as wrong (Exod 20:14), but ignore the scriptural warrant that the punishment for committing adultery is death (see Lev 20:10). The fourth commandment tells us that we should honor our parents (Exod 20:12), but Exod 21:17 says that we should execute a son who swears at his father. Christians readily cite scriptural warrant for parental authority but none accept execution as a punishment for disrespecting parents.

Furthermore, says Johnson, the Old and New Testaments give "every indication that slaveholding was a legitimate, indeed God-ordained social arrangement, one to which neither Moses nor Jesus nor Paul raised a fundamental objection." "So how is it that now," adds Johnson, "in the early twenty-first century, the authority of the scriptural texts on slavery and the arguments made on their basis appear to all of us, without exception, as completely beside the point and deeply wrong?"

Johnson answers this question by appealing to human experience, namely, the experience of slavery and its horror, of the slaves' full humanity and the evil of their bondage, which over time reached a stage of critical consciousness and gradually entered into and took root in the popular conscience. As a result, "this nation could neither turn back to the practice of slavery nor ever read the Bible in the same way again." According to Johnson, our situation regarding homosexuality vis-à-vis the authority of Scripture is not unlike that of abolitionists in nineteenth-century America.[6]

---

6. There is a chorus of voices out there singing the same tune as Johnson's. For example, John D. Caputo writes: "In my view, even if there is a dominant view against homosexuality in the Scriptures and tradition—as a deconstructive reader, I would always insist on a full hearing for all the nondominant views, of which there are plenty—I would argue that on this point the Greeks were right and the dominant tradition among Jews and Christians is wrong, just as the Scriptures are wrong to underwrite slavery and the oppression of women" (*What would Jesus Deconstruct?*, 109). I argue in the text against the view that the Holy Bible underwrites slavery if that means that it is divinely ordained. Herman Ridderbos argues that Paul does not identify "the existing social order, especially slavery, with the divine order, or regards it as unalterable. To be sure, nowhere has a pronouncement been preserved in which he criticizes the institution of slavery and declares it to be contrary to the gospel. On the other hand, nowhere does he take it back

This charge is fairly common. How do we assess then Johnson's claim that our situation regarding homosexuality vis-á-vis the authority of Scripture is not unlike that of abolitionists in nineteenth-century America, and hence that just as Christians came to reject Scripture's stance on slavery so too we now may do the same with its stance on homosexual practice? There are very good reasons for rejecting Johnson's analogy of homosexuality and slavery.[7]

ANALOGY BETWEEN HOMOSEXUALITY AND SLAVERY

First, there is *no* Scriptural mandate for slavery, that is, no commandment to enslave others, nor is there is a penalty for releasing slaves. Rather, the Old Testament merely tolerates slavery as an institution and regulates it without approving it. What kind of slavery was actually being regulated? The enslaving of prisoners of war, of criminals, of people who sold themselves into slavery as a last-ditch way to avoid starvation,[8] or to advance their careers was permitted and regulated. As to regulating it, Robert J. Hutchinson writes, "while in the Code of Hammurabi anyone who harbors a runaway slave is to be put to death, the Old Testament law actually *commands* that such slaves be given refuge: 'You shall not turn over a slave [who has escaped] to his master. He shall dwell with you in your midst ... you must not ill-treat him' (Deut 23:16–17). Not only that, but anyone who abducts someone and sells him or her into slavery—as the

---

to a divine ordinance, as, for example, in the case of the subjection of the wife to the husband" (Ridderbos, *Paul, An Outline of His Theology*, 317). For an important critique of the claim that the Bible underwrites the oppression of women, see Martin, *Feminist Question*, 75–220.

7. I am heavily indebted to Gagnon, *Bible and Homosexual Practice*. On the question whether slavery is a good parallel for the homosexuality debate, see Gagnon, *Bible and Homosexual Practice*, 443–48. See also, Via and Gagnon, *Homosexuality and the Bible*. Gagnon develops his argument against several analogies in this more recent book: Gentile inclusion, slavery, women in ministry, divorce and remarriage (42–47). See also, Schmidt, *Straight and Narrow* and *Christian Anthropology and Homosexuality*. I will return to the vexing issue of homosexuality in Chapter 6.

8. On this, see Lev 25:39, "If one of your countrymen becomes poor among you and sells himself to you, do not make him work as a slave. He is to be treated as a hired worker or a temporary resident among you; he is to work for you until the Year of Jubilee. Then he and his children are to be released, and he will go back to his own clan and to the property of his forefathers. Because the Israelites are my servants, whom I brought out of Egypt, they must not be sold as slaves. Do not rule over them ruthlessly, but fear your God."

brothers of Joseph did in Genesis or the slave traders of the eighteenth century did—was to be put to death" (Exod 21:16). "What's more," adds Hutchinson, "when a Hebrew 'slave' was freed, the Bible says, 'you shall not send him away empty-handed, but shall weigh him down with gifts from your flock and threshing floor and wine press, in proportion to the blessings the Lord, your God, has bestowed upon you.'" Significantly, the biblical warrant for this treatment of slaves is as follows: "For remember that you too were once slaves in the land of Egypt, and the Lord, your God, redeemed you; therefore I command you this today" (Deut 15:12–18, esp. 13–15).[9] It is fair to state then that the Old Testament treatment of "slaves" is "revolutionary"[10] because "the overriding goal in Deuteronomy 15 is *that there be no slavery in the land at all.*"[11]

By contrast, there *is* a Scriptural mandate, in the Old and New Testament, to limit sexual unions to heterosexual ones. In addition there is a severe penalty having to do with a person's eternal standing before God or entrance into his Kingdom. Consider St. Paul: "Do you not know that the unrighteous will not inherit the kingdom of God? Stop deceiving yourselves: Neither sexually immoral persons [*pornoi*, i.e., like the incestuous man], nor idolaters, nor adulterers, nor 'soft men' [*malakoi*, i.e., men who feminize themselves to attract male sex partners], nor men who lie with a male [*arsenokoitai*, a term formed from the Levitical prohibition of male homosexual practice] . . . shall inherit the kingdom of God" (1 Cor 6:9–10).

Second, *pace* Johnson, slavery is *not* divinely instituted, a structure or mandate of creation, in short, a God-ordained social arrangement. By contrast, the institutions of civil authority, marital and parental relations are divinely instituted, creation structures. The latter are God-ordained, roles are divinely specified, and conduct is regulated. In particular, the biblical authors throughout the Scripture viewed heterosexual unions as normative structures of creation that are transculturally valid.

Third, there is tension within the biblical canon itself on the issue of slavery. This is evident from the trajectory within the Bible itself that critiques slavery. Some authors refer to this trajectory as the "unfolding

---

9. All the quotes in this paragraph are from Hutchinson, *Politically Incorrect Guide to the Bible*, 162–64. See also, Ashley, *Living the Truth in Love*, 290–93.

10. McConville, *Grace in the End*, 148, as cited in Copan, "Is Yahweh a Moral Monster?," 20.

11. Copan, "Is Yahweh a Moral Monster?," 19–20.

'redemptive-movement' of God's self-revelation to his people even within the OT."[12] As Gagnon summarizes this point, "We can discern a trajectory within the Bible that critiques slavery. Central in Israelite memory was the remembrance of God's liberation from slavery in Egypt (e.g., Exod 22:21; 23:9; Lev 25:42, 55; Deut 15:15).[13] Christian memory adds the paradigmatic event of Christ's redemption of believers from slavery to sin and people (e.g., 1 Cor 6:20; 7:23). Israelite law put various restrictions on enslaving fellow Israelites—even insisting that Israelites not be treated as slaves—while Paul regarded liberation from slavery as a penultimate good (1 Cor 7: 21–23; Phlm 16)." By contrast, adds Gagnon, "While Scripture shows unease with the institution of slavery, the only discomfort it shows toward same-sex intercourse is with the commission of the act, not with its proscription."[14]

Fourth, on the one hand, the Scripture is a countercultural witness regarding slavery, and indeed is rather liberating in relation to the ancient cultural norm. On the other hand, "The Bible's stance on same-sex intercourse moved in the opposite direction, against any accommodation. Simply put, Scripture nowhere expresses a vested interest in preserving slavery, whereas Scripture does express a vested interest in requiring a male-female dynamic in sexual relationships."[15] In sum, "Scripture itself does not provide the kind of clear and unequivocal witness *for* slavery that it exhibits *against* same-sex intercourse."[16]

Enough has been said here to rebut Johnson's argument from analogy, but I still must consider the relation between revelation and experience. I shall articulate my own position on this relation later in chapter 3 when I consider the question of experience and theological method. Although not a source of revelation, I shall argue, in that chapter, that

12. Paul Copan, "Is Yahweh a Moral Monster?," 29, who is indebted to Webb, "Redemptive-Movement Hermeneutic."

13. Hutchinson, *Politically Incorrect Guide to the Bible*, "[T]he overarching theme that runs throughout the Hebrew Bible—from the Torah through the Deuteronomic History and the prophets—concerns how God ransomed the children of Israel from slavery in Egypt. Over and over again, the Hebrew Bible insists that Israelites must not mistreat their *avadim* (servants/slaves) because 'you were once slaves [*avadim*] in the land of Egypt'" (165).

14. I borrow the apt phrase ("trajectory of critique") from Gagnon, *Homosexuality and the Bible*, 45.

15. Gagnon, *Homosexuality and the Bible*, 45.

16. Gagnon, "Authority of Scripture in the 'Homosex' Debate."

8   "IN THE BEGINNING"

human experience may act as a *corrective* of our interpretation of divine revelation, as it did when we became aware of the experience of slavery, the evil of bondage, and so forth, helping us to bring to its proper destination that Scriptural trajectory of critique, or redemptive-movement, regarding slavery in order to lay hold more fully of the Scriptural truth regarding human dignity.

BIBLICAL AUTHORITY, REVELATION, AND EXPERIENCE

What scriptural grounds provide a basis, according to Johnson, for rejecting explicit scriptural commands? How, then, does Johnson actually support his claim that the Christian is biblically warranted in rejecting scriptural commands on the grounds of authentic human experience that is putatively revelatory of the living God. He argues that appealing to human experience has scriptural warrant because the really normative thing about the Scripture, that is, the locus of biblical authority, is the self-revelation of the living God in people's lives or experience, and that experience provides criteria for interpreting the Bible. The Scriptural texts, says Johnson, "participate in revelation by their interpretation of experience."[17] So Scripture is the record of men's experiences. But this means that real authority, the real normative thing about Scripture, has shifted from the Scripture itself, from the objective revelation of God in deeds and words, in the communication of truth, to the historically reconstructed experience of the men and woman of the Old and New Testament. "Experience" itself is now seen as a separate source of authority, of revelation, and it is played off against Scripture itself.[18]

Accordingly, Johnson urges us to "place our trust in the power of the living God to reveal [himself] as powerfully through personal experience and testimony as through written texts." Of course he insists that by "experience" he does "not mean every idiosyncratic or impulsive expression

---

17. Johnson, "Participating in Revelation (1 Kg 19:9–18; Rom 9:1–5; Mt 14:22–33)," 731.

18. In this book, I take the Catholic faith as theologically normative. In that context, my own view of the role of "experience" in the doctrine regarding the sources of revelation, and hence in theological method and biblical hermeneutics, has been shaped decisively by Nichols, *Shape of Catholic Theology*, 235–47. Helpful also to me in this discussion has been Anglican bishop, Wright, "How can the Bible be Authoritative?" Idem., *Last Word*, especially 100–105.

of human desire."[19] But exactly what should count as a genuine instance of an experience responding to the divine initiative of revelation, revelatory of the work of the Holy Spirit, requires some sort of discernment of spirits (see 1 John 4:1–6), and I have trouble seeing what criteria Johnson uses. He dismisses the idea that an authentic revelatory experience, as he understands it, should be subject to the biblical revelation, the Word of God as proposed by the Church. When authentic experiences are a source of ongoing revelation that provides new insights, as Johnson claims, this view denies the principle of *canonicity*—the biblical text in its final form. He justifies the trust he invests in the belief that God's self-revelation continues in human experience and is not confined to God's written revelation by invoking "the basic Pauline principle that the Spirit gives life but the letter kills (2 Corinthians 3:6)" "And if the letter of Scripture cannot find room for the activity of the living God in the transformation of human lives," Johnson adds, "then trust and obedience must be paid to the living God rather than to the words of Scripture."[20] Of course, since he thinks that the weight of scriptural evidence is against him, it is understandable why he seeks to put his trust "in the continuing experience of God in the structures of human freedom."[21] But Johnson's position is not supported by his appeal either to Vatican II's *Dei Verbum* (no. 2.8) or to the Pauline principle of 2 Cor 3:6, "for the letter kills, but the Spirit produces life."

Regarding *Dei Verbum*, chapter II, par. 8, it does *not* support Johnson's belief that God's self-revelation continues through the work of the Holy Spirit and hence that revelation, in the objective and public sense, is not closed. Indeed, as *Dei Verbum*, chapter I, par. 4, states: "We now await no further public revelation before the glorious manifestation of our Lord Jesus Christ." What the document does express is, then, the conviction that the living God continues to work through the illuminating activity of the Holy Spirit. That is, the Holy Spirit has epistemological significance because it is he that makes objective revelation—that revelation consisting of acts and words, which are intrinsically bound up with each other, in the communication of revealed truth—not only known and appropriated by the believer but also aids the believer so as to be able to grow "in the understanding of the realities and words [of salvation history] that have

---

19. Johnson, "Homosexuality & the Church," 3.
20. Ibid.
21. Ibid.

been handed down." In other words, what grows is our understanding of the realities that God has objectively revealed in the truths of faith. The latter are "the propositions held to be true by the faith of the Church," as Germain Grisez rightly says. "In assenting to the truths of faith," Grisez adds, "those who share in the faith of the Church think the realities which God has revealed to be so—that is, as he has revealed them to be so."[22] And the Holy Spirit enables us to deepen our understanding of those truths so that they "may be more and more profoundly understood," and thus we will have a deeper grasp of those realities and words being passed on. Yet, as Herman Bavinck rightly says, the Holy Spirit's illuminating activity "is not a revelation in the sense that it adds a new element to objective revelation."[23] But this is precisely what Johnson thinks, namely, that God's continuing self-revelation in human experience gives us "access to what is revealed independently of the words and deeds which God used as his instrumentality in revealing."[24] But this is not what the Church teaches in *Dei Verbum* (no. 8). Indeed, it contradicts the faith of the Church. What the Church does teach is that the epistemological significance of the Holy Spirit's illuminating activity is that it "leads believers to the full truth," adds Vatican II, "and makes the Word of Christ dwell in them in all its richness (cf. Col 3:16)."

Johnson also appeals to the Pauline principle of 2 Cor 3:6, "for the letter kills, but the Spirit produces life" to justify his rejection of authoritative Scripture. In all honesty, I find it hard to believe that Johnson actually thinks that he can use this principle to defend his view that scriptural authority regarding homosexual practice is not normative. The Pauline principle contrasts letter and Spirit. The main point of this principle is that the letter or law kills because man in his sinfulness lacks power to keep the precepts of the law and that law itself is unable to effect the obedience of vital faith in sinners, which is something that only the Spirit can work in a man. In other words, the law is unable to give life; it fails to vanquish the power of sin, freeing man from his enslavement, and hence man is left with his inability to keep the law. Furthermore, the letter kills "because it enslaves one to the presumption that righteousness inheres in one's doing

---

22. Grisez, "On Interpreting Dogmas," 122.

23. Bavinck, *Gereformeerde Dogmatiek*, I, ET: *Reformed Dogmatics, Prolegomena*, vol. 1:348. Both sources will be cited throughout this book, first the original, followed by the pagination of the English in square brackets [ ].

24. Grisez, "On Interpreting Dogmas," 124.

of the law, when it is actually the case that true righteousness comes only as a gift from God."[25] For St. Paul, as Ernest Käsemann writes, "everything which forces us back on our own strength, ability and piety kills because it snatches the creature out of his creatureliness and this away from the almighty power of grace, of which we are in constant need."[26] Thus, the grace of the Holy Spirit is the effective agent who "gives life" by changing the human heart, which is given through faith in Christ, enabling us to keep the law out of an interior freedom that is expressed in the obedience of faith. Yes, for St. Paul, the law declares God's will. The moral law retains its meaning as, in St. Paul's words, "holy law" and as "holy and just and good" (Rom 7:12), and hence, *pace* Johnson, no disparagement of the moral law is intended.

At issue here is Johnson's idea of revelation.[27] Essentially, his view of revelation is such that, as he says, "revelation is open and ongoing in the world, specifically in human experience.... This is not a plea for the privileging of every private human experience. Not every human story reveals God. It is a plea to consider the theological implications of the millions of stories of believers (such as women and homosexuals) whom the church has persisted in regarding as 'objects' to be 'explained' rather than subjects, that is, persons through whose struggles the Holy Spirit speaks a word to the church."[28] But how does one know that an experience and its expression in words are revelatory of the Holy Spirit? How does experience, even supposing it is graced because of the Holy Spirit's presence, compare as a theological source with Scripture and the dogmatic tradition of the Church? Does not Johnson's view deny the objectivity of revelation? More expansively, does not his doctrine of continuing revelation conflict with

25. Paul Furnish, *II Corinthians*, 201. See also, Ridderbos, *Paul*, 214–18.

26. As cited in Furnish, *II Corinthians*, 201.

27. According to Avery Cardinal Dulles, Vatican II has been generally misunderstood by some to teach the idea of continuing revelation. This is one of twelve errors he identifies in post-Vatican II theology. He writes in "Vatican II: The Myth and the Reality": "A third error relating to revelation is the view that, according to the council, God continues to reveal himself in secular experience through the signs of the times, which therefore provide criteria for interpreting the Gospel. Vatican II, in fact, rejected the idea of continuing revelation. It taught that revelation became complete in Jesus Christ and that no further public revelation is to be expected before the end of time, when Christ returns in glory (DV, No. 4). In *Gaudium et Spes* the council spoke of the church's duty to interpret the signs of the times, but it specified that these signs are to be interpreted in the light of the Gospel" (*GS*, No. 4)

28. Johnson, "After the Big Chill: Intellectual Freedom & Catholic Theologians," 12–13.

"authoritative mediation of the content of faith through historical revelation, prophetic and apostolic testimony, Scripture, tradition, and the living Church [?]"[29] He suggests otherwise by claiming that taking with the same seriousness both God's self-disclosure in human experience and in Scripture "does not turn its back on tradition but recognizes that tradition must be constantly renewed by the powerful leading of the Spirit if it is not to become a form of falsehood."[30] But surely Johnson does turn his back on the entire authoritative biblical witness and thus the faith of the Church regarding homosexuality because, in his view, the contemporary experience of men and women renders that witness and faith false.

Johnson apparently thinks that the post-apostolic community has throughout the history of the Church been in a position to reinterpret Scripture in the way that Peter and Paul and James reinterpreted God's previous revelation in the Old Testament. Briefly, there is an important point to consider here in connection with the claim that a valid analogy may be drawn, in light of the working of the Holy Spirit, between the early church's openness to Gentile believers and the openness of Christians to same-sex marriages. Much as Acts 15 describes the movement of the Holy Spirit urging Jewish Christians to welcome Gentiles into the Church without binding them to Jewish ceremonial law, the Spirit is at work today urging Christians to be open to seeing same-sex relations as a blessing of creation rather than as an effect of the fall. But this analogy will not work for three basic reasons: "i) the inclusion of the Gentiles was the fulfillment of prophetic hopes (see for example Isaiah 2:2-4), while there is no such warranted Old Testament hope in the case of homosexual relations; ii) the opening to the Gentiles followed the decisive act of Christ at the turning of the ages. In the contrast to them, we should not presume ourselves apostles at a new turning of the ages; [and] iii) the Jerusalem Council specifically forbids porneia, that is, 'sexual immorality' [Acts 15:29]."[31]

---

29. Dulles, *Assurance of Things Hoped For*, 176.

30. Johnson, "Disembodied 'Theology of the Body,'" 7.

31. Goldingay, "Traditionalist Response," 71. For a fuller defense of the traditionalist biblical hermeneutic, see "Same-Sex Marriage and Anglican Theology: A View from the Traditionalists," 1–39. Regarding St. Paul's use of *porneia* and related notions such as *akatharsia* (sexual uncleanness) and *aselgeia* (licentiousness), he puts, Gagnon correctly notes, "same-sex intercourse at or near the top of a list of sexual offenses. Just as Paul correlated man-male intercourse with sexual immorality (*porneia*) in 1 Cor 6:9 (cf. 1 Tim 1:10), so too he treated same-sex intercourse as the prime example of 'sexual uncleanness' (*akatharsia*) in Rom 1:24–27" ("Immoralism, Homosexual Unhealth, and Scripture," VI.

Johnson's acceptance of this analogy as valid exposes his commitment to a doctrine of *continuing revelation* in human experience, meaning thereby that he claims that we can become aware of some new revelation in that experience.

In his critical article on John Paul's theology of the body, Johnson suggests that, *pace* John Paul, "revelation is not exclusively biblical but occurs in the continuing experience of God in the structures of human freedom."[32] He faults the pope for not taking "the self-disclosure of God in human experience with the same seriousness as it does God's revelation in Scripture."[33] I cannot let Johnson get away with this charge. For John Paul II, although Scripture is the Word of God, it is not the whole of God's revelation. The pope is a theological realist in affirming the ordering of everything that exists within creation, and this order is an expression of the ordered wisdom of the divine plan for creation. So, *pace* Johnson, we can speak here of a creation revelation in and through the created order, in which man and all things have been given their structure in the cosmos.

Of course John Paul does not identify, as Johnson does, this creation revelation with the doctrine of continuing revelation in human experience. In light of this identification, Johnson suggests that we should now adapt Gal 3:28 and reinterpret it to mean that "in Christ there is neither gay nor straight." Given that people participate in revelation by their interpretation of experience, according to Johnson, we may also have access to what is revealed, indeed, a fresh revelation, *independently* of the biblical pattern of words and deeds, divine events/actions and divinely-given interpretations of those events/actions, which God used as his medium in revealing himself in Holy Scripture.

That Johnson's view really embraces a doctrine of continuing revelation is evident from the following claim: "I suggest, therefore, that the New Testament provides impressive support for our reliance on the experience of God in human lives—not in its commands, but in its narratives and in the very process by which it came into existence. In what way are we to take seriously the authority of Scripture? What I find most important

---

Law versus Gospel). Further analysis of the argument that moral approval of homosexuality is analogous to the early Church's inclusion of gentiles is given by two recent articles: Richard Goldring, "Changing our corporate mind: reflections on paradigm shift in ethical thinking," and John Perry, "Gentiles and Homosexuals: A Brief History of an Analogy."

32. Ibid., 3.
33. Ibid., 7.

of all is not the authority found in specific commands, which are fallible, conflicting, and often culturally conditioned, but rather the way Scripture creates the mind of Christ in its readers, authorizing them to reinterpret written texts in light of God's Holy Spirit active in human lives. When read within the perspective of a Scripture that speaks everywhere of a God disclosing [him]self through human experience, our stories become the medium of God's very revelation."[34] In this passage, Johnson, first, works with a dichotomy between narratives versus commands, and he locates biblical authority in those narratives. He sets up here a false dichotomy that I will refute below. Second, Johnson is not "reinterpreting" Scriptural texts, but rather he is denying the biblical authority of texts pertaining to homosexual practice as false in view of God's *new* revelation, which, he alleges, surpasses God's written Word revelation, indeed, the historic faith of the Church.

I now want to make several objections to Johnson's position explicitly presented here. First, Johnson works with a false dichotomy of "narrative versus commands." Second, diminishing the authority of the law in the Bible, as his position suggests, results in a law/gospel segregation, which is a flawed view of the relation between "Gospel and Law." And third, as I have already argued above, Johnson espouses an unbiblical doctrine of continuing revelation, which is at odds with the historic Christian faith.

THREE OBJECTIONS TO JOHNSON'S POSITION

My first objection is, then, that Johnson works with a false dichotomy of "narrative versus commands." A narrative approach to Scripture attempts to counteract biblicism—bad "proof-texting"—as well as a tendency—particularly with respect to biblical morality—to treat Scripture as a mere system of general moral propositions. It locates the Christian moral life, and the responsibility to make choices that are worthy of the calling that we have received in Christ, within the context of the overarching biblical narrative of creation, fall into sin, redemption, and eschaton. So, yes, this authoritative biblical narrative is central for understanding the meaning and purpose of the moral life. Still, since the historic Christian faith teaches the Scriptures to be divinely authoritative for morals, then, we must still come to terms with the moral authority of specific moral directives, commandments, and rules. Working with a false dichotomy

---

34. Johnson, "Homosexuality & the Church."

of "narrative versus commands," Johnson leaves us confused about how to come to grips with the moral authority of the Bible. Does he actually deny "that there exist, in Divine Revelation, a specific and determined moral content, universally valid and permanent [?]"[35] Aren't there moral norms formulated in Scripture not only having the status of fundamental revealed moral truth but also are in themselves relevant for salvation? The New Testament moral teaching affirms not only the continuing validity of the Decalogue but also its perfection and superabundant fulfillment. As Grisez correctly emphasizes, "In the Sermon on the Mount, Jesus broadens and deepens several of the commandments and demands their interiorization (see Mt 5:21–37). All the synoptics, moreover, present Jesus as affirming the commandments as a necessary condition for entering eternal life (see Mt 19:16–20; Mk 10:17–19; Lk 18:18–21)."[36] St. Paul, too, adds Grisez "assumes the truth of the Decalogue and its permanent ethical relevance."[37] Indeed, following the pattern of Christ, St. Paul urges us to avoid self-deception regarding the inseparability of the moral choices we make that are worthy of the calling we have received in Christ and eternal life. Thus, he links fundamental moral decisions with admission to, as well as exclusion from, the Kingdom of God (see 1 Cor 6:9–11).[38]

Now, Johnson doesn't tell us why biblical authority is found primarily (exclusively?) in the Scripture's narratives rather than in its commandments. But I think we can surmise that it is because, as Johnson puts it, "specific commands ... are fallible, conflicting, and often culturally conditioned." Well, yes, concrete commands, such as, "Anyone who curses his father or mother must be put to death" (Exod 21:17), are culturally conditioned. But this concrete command is an *application* of a primary commandment that is absolute and universal: "Honor your father and your mother" (Exod 20:12).[39] Helpful here in distinguishing between commandments that are still valid from those that are not, is Lewis Smedes' distinction between "primary commandments" and "concrete command-

---

35. John Paul II, *Veritatis Splendor*, no. 37.
36. Grisez, *Way of the Lord Jesus*, vol. 1, *Christian Moral Principles*, 838.
37. Ibid.
38. Ratzinger, "Church's Teaching Authority—Faith—Morals."
39. On these distinctions, see Lewis Smedes' *Mere Morality*, especially chapter 1. Smedes develops these distinctions more fully in, "Bible and Ethics." Portions of this paper have been published in the first and last chapter of Smedes' *Mere Morality*. I will indicate when I cite from the conference paper.

ments." The former cover specific areas of life, such as human existence, property, communication, marriage, family. The latter demand or prohibit a specific act. At the root of each and every command is the "foundational commandment" that covers all of life, namely, the central commandment of Love: We are called to love God completely and to love our neighbor as we love ourselves.[40]

Again, this doesn't mean that "*all* the commandments in the Bible tell us what God wants us to do."[41] For instance, St. Paul makes a distinction between the ceremonial law and the moral law of the Old Testament. The Christian has transcended ritual concerns about "clean" and "unclean." Says St. Paul: "As one who is in the Lord Jesus, I am fully convinced that nothing is unclean in itself" (Rom 14:14). But neither does it mean that all the commands are culturally conditioned. How are we to tell the difference? As Paul Copan rightly notes, "Scripture itself (rather than twenty-first century critics) has the resources to guide us regarding what is ideal and normative and what is temporary and *sui generis* in the Bible."[42] Yes, the Holy Scripture has many literary styles and many ways of telling us what is God's will for us.[43] Still, Lewis Smedes is right that God's Word may be heard most urgently and clearly in his commandments. But in Johnson's move to justify his rejection of authoritative Scripture, in particular, stripping biblical commands of their divine authority, I dare say that he throws the baby out with the bathwater.

Does Johnson think that all the biblical commands are culturally conditioned such that there are no universally valid and permanent moral precepts? Aren't the biblical commandments against incest, bestiality (Exod 22:19), adultery (Exod 20:14), child sacrifice, prostitution (Lev 19:29; Deut 23:17–18), and rape (Deut 22:25–29), absolute and universally valid? Is it ever morally acceptable to oppress the poor? Commit idolatry (Exod 20:4; Deut 13:6–11)?[44] Bribery (Exod 23:8; 2 Chr 19:7)?

---

40. Helpful in understanding the central commandment of Love is Holwerda, "Jesus and the Law," 122–45.

41. Smedes, *Mere Morality*, 15.

42. In chapter 2, I develop Copan's point, with help from the late Reformed ethicist Lewis Smedes and Dutch Reformed theologian Jochem Douma, regarding the Scriptural resources for distinguishing the normative and temporary in the Bible itself.

43. On the claim that God's Word may be heard most urgently and clearly in his commandments, see Smedes, *Mere Morality*, 15–28.

44. Of course here, too, we have an instance of a concrete command ("Whoever sac-

Bearing false witness against one's neighbor (Exod 23:1-2)? Surely not.[45] Of course I'm not suggesting that Johnson thinks that any of these practices are morally acceptable. But it does seem to me that we cannot allow his position to pass without being challenged. By locating biblical authority primarily (exclusively?) in the Scripture's narratives rather than in its commandments he leaves us confused about how to come to terms with the Bible's authority for the moral life.

Furthermore, one does not need to choose between narratives or commands.[46] What is most important is that the Holy Scripture does not make such a choice. In the Gospels, for example, the moral commandments of the Mosaic Law continue to be authoritative for the Church. Indeed, the man who asks Jesus, "What must I do to inherit eternal life?" receives the reply, "You know the commandments: 'Do not murder, do not commit adultery, do not steal, do not give false testimony, do not defraud, honor your father and mother" (Mark 10:17-20; see Matt 19:16-30; Luke 18:18-30). St. Paul insists, "The law is holy, and the commandment is holy, righteous, and good" (Rom 7:12). Yes, the law does not save man, but it is, according to the New Testament, a necessary condition for the moral guidance of Christ's disciples, existing to correct, instruct, and lead to maturity. In fact, St. Paul exhibits his commitment to the authority of the Old Testament law, for example, "Beloved, never avenge yourselves, but leave it to the wrath of God; for it is written, 'Vengeance is mine, I will repay says the Lord'" (Rom 12:19; see Lev 19:18; Deut 32:35. See also 1 Cor 9:9; 10:1; 14:34; also 2 Cor 8:15; 9:9). In sum, the Mosaic Law is positive and constructive in the New Testament. "Freedom from the law as the road to salvation is simultaneously freedom for the law as a commandment with a specific content."[47] Of course, the Decalogue is not the only normative

---

rifices to any god other than the Lord must be destroyed" [Exod 22:20]) which is an application of a primary commandment from the Decalogue (Exod 20:1-6). The concrete command is contextually conditioned but not the primary command on which it is based.

45. Gagnon, "Are There Universally Valid Sex Precepts?"

46. There is no good reason to choose between, say, the themes of virtue and character and moral acts when reflecting on the Christian moral life. I address some aspects of this question in chapter 2, namely, the relation between virtue, a person's character, and moral principles that govern specific acts. For an important treatment of the relation between "narrative and commands," see Mouw, "Narrative, Character, and Commands," 116-49.

47. Forell, *History of Christian Ethics*, 1:24-25. I address the question of how the law and freedom are related more explicitly later in chapter 2.

source of biblical ethics, but it is a fundamental source. Indeed, as Grisez incisively says, "no reasonable reading of the Decalogue can deny it's status of fundamental revealed moral truth—a status always recognized by common Christian practice in moral instruction."[48]

My second objection to Johnson is this: if Johnson's antithesis between narrative and commands implies a law/gospel segregation, then how does he avoid antinomianism? What is antinomianism? "Even during the time when the New Testament was being written, the Apostles found it necessary to correct influences which were 'against the law'—tendencies to deny all law, to replace the law with the Spirit, or to oppose the law as revealed in the Old Testament. Some misleadingly suggested, out of a desire to magnify and emphasize the grace of God, that believers could continue in sin (e.g., Rom. 6:1-2). Others erroneously taught that the indwelling Holy Spirit (by whose ministry believers are begotten of God and have Christ abide in them) could be the compass of their behavior apart from God's commandments (e.g., 1 John 3:24; cf. vv. 4, 9). Still others thought of the Mosaic law as contrary to the promise God made to Abraham and fulfilled in Christ (e.g., Gal 3:21)."[49] Still others such as Johnson think that God reveals himself more fundamentally, indeed, most authoritatively in the stories of real people as they relate to God rather than in laws or commands.

But I dare say that this was not the stance of Jesus in the Gospels. Indeed, regarding several possible stances he might have taken with respect to the moral commandments—being against them, replacing them, and complementing them—"Jesus commands expose the true and positive meaning of the old commandments; they neither replace nor add to the moral teachings of the law, but tell us instead what the old law always asked of us."[50] What did the old law always ask for? That we love God above all and our neighbors as ourselves: this is the central Love commandment.

What then is the correct way to understand the relation between the Gospel and the Law? Johnson and others such as Paul Copan rightly insists that the meaning and purpose of biblical commands are to be understood in their broader narrative and, I would add with Copan, canonical

---

48. Grisez, *Way of the Lord Jesus*, 1:838.
49. Bahnsen, "Theonomic Antithesis to Other Law-Attitudes."
50. Smedes, *Mere Morality*, 257–58 n. 19.

contexts. As Copan rightly insists, "The Mosaic covenant (Exod 20—Num 10) is incorporated into the Pentateuch's larger narrative of God's dealings with the patriarchs and then the people of Israel. Additionally, if Christ is the end of the Law, both its fulfillment and its terminus (Rom 10:4), then we have an even wider canonical context available to assess OT ethical concerns."[51] The then Joseph Cardinal Ratzinger, now Pope Benedict XVI, provides a prime example of what Johnson and Copan argue about understanding biblical commandments in their narrative and canonical context.[52]

Benedict argues that the Torah itself is an integral whole and so "the worship of God is completely inseparable from morals, cult [ritual and juridical observances], and ethos [a spiritual environment or atmosphere]." Thus, given that it is something integral, adds Benedict, "one cannot simply separate out universally valid moral principles and transitory ritual and legal norms without destroying the Torah itself... which owes its existence to God's address to Israel. The idea that, on the one hand, there are pure morals that are reasonable and universal and, on the other, that there are rites that are conditioned by time and ultimately dispensable mistakes entirely the inner structure of the five books of Moses."[53] Benedict's point here is not about whether Scripture contains universally valid and permanent moral precepts. Of course he thinks it does. Rather, his point is about the *indivisible unity* of love of God and neighbor, that is, the inner structure of the Law being integrally related to the central commandment of Love, the worship of the one God of all men. "Hear, O Israel: The Lord our God, the Lord is one. Love the Lord your God with all your heart and with all your soul and with all your strength. These commandments that I give you today are to be upon your hearts" (Deut 6:4–6).

There is more: The faith of Israel is, says Benedict, directed universally to all men, from all nations, because the God of Israel is the one God of all men, and Israel is called to proclaim the glory of God among the nations (see Isa 66:19). Israel is called by the Lord to be a light to the nations. Benedict suggestively traces the universalistic promises of Scripture, through Genesis and Exodus, through the Psalms and into the Prophets (especially Isaiah). God's promises encompass the nations of

51. Copan, "Is Yahweh a Moral Monster?," *Philosophia Christi*, 10.
52. Joseph Ratzinger/Benedict XVI, *Many Religions—One Covenant, Israel, the Church and the World*, 21–46.
53. Ibid., 37–38.

the entire world. Arguably, the so-called Servant Songs in Isaiah refer to Israel. Of the Servant it is said, "I will keep you and will make you to be a covenant for the people, a light to the nations, to open eyes that are blind, to free captives from prison and to release from the dungeon those who sit in darkness" (Isa 42:6–7). In short, Israel is called to be a light to the nations.[54] Benedict XVI elaborates:

> The history of Israel should become the history of all. Abraham's sonship is to be extended to the "many." This course of events has two aspects to it: the nations can enter into the community of the promises of Israel in entering into the community of the one God, who now becomes and must become the way of all because there is only one God and because his will is therefore truth for all. Conversely, this means that all nations, without the abolishment of the special mission of Israel, become brothers and receivers of the promises of the Chosen People; they become People of God with Israel through adherence to the will of God and through acceptance of the Davidic kingdom.[55]

On the one hand, then, we have the faith of Israel that bears within itself the universalist promise of becoming the faith of all nations. On the other hand, we have the Law, says Benedict, in whom the faith of Israel in the one God of all men is expressed and his will, as expressed in the Law, is therefore truth for all. But this Law is particular because "concretely directed to Israel and its history." "It could not be universalized in this form," adds Benedict.[56] It will take Jesus Christ to fulfill the universalist promises of Scripture and hence the universality of the Law by putting it on an entirely new basis and bringing it to its fullness of meaning. In other words, as I said above, "Jesus exposed the true and positive meaning of the old commandments."[57]

---

54. On Israel's calling, see Kaiser, *Mission in the Old Testament*. See also, Köstenberger and O'Brien, *Salvation to the Ends of the Earth*, particularly chapter 2 on mission in the Old Testament. Their conclusion on mission in the OT is that the "final paragraph of Isaiah (66:18–24) [presents] an eschatological 'vision of staggering proportions,' in which God's gracious plan for the world is marvelously presented. The Lord himself is the missionary who gathers and rescues, not simply the dispersed of Israel, but also people from 'all nations,' in order that they may see his glory. The goal of mission is the glory of God, that he may be known and honored for who he really is" (52).

55. Ratzinger, *Many Religions—One Covenant*, 27–28.

56. Ibid., 38.

57. Lewis Smedes, *Mere Morality*, 258 n. 19.

We don't have the full picture yet, however. "Salvation is from the Jews" (John 4:22). God's salvific mission is a theme indivisibly binding the Old and New Testaments, Jesus and Israel, together. What this means, says Benedict, is "that there is no access to Jesus, and thereby there can be no entrance of the nations into the People of God, without the acceptance in faith of the revelation of God who speaks in the Sacred Scripture that Christians term the Old Testament."[58] Furthermore, Benedict argues, given the interrelation of both Testaments, that an inner continuity and coherence exists between the Gospel of Jesus Christ and the Law. "The whole Law, including the Prophets, depends on the twofold yet one commandment of love of God and love of neighbor (CCC [no.] 1970; Mt 7:12; 22:34–40; Mk 12:28–43; Lk 10:25–28; Jn 12:34; Rom 13:8–10). For the nations, being assumed into the children of Abraham is concretely realized in entering into the will of God in which moral commandments and profession of the oneness of God are indivisible, as this becomes clear especially in Saint Mark's version [Mark 12:29–31] of this tradition, in which the double commandment [of love of God and love of neighbor] is expressly linked to the "Shema Israel" [of Deut 6:4: "Hear, O Israel, the Lord our God, the Lord is one"], to the Yes to the one and only God. Man's way is prescribed for him."[59]

Moreover, Jesus came to fulfill not to abolish the Law. Jesus said, "Do not think that I have come to abolish the Law or the Prophets; I have come not to abolish but to fulfill" (Matt 5:17). In fulfilling the law, Jesus "opened up the Law," "broadened the law," says Benedict, "conscious of, and claiming to be, acting as Son, with the authority of God himself, in innermost unity with God the Father." "Only God himself," adds Benedict, "could fundamentally reinterpret the Law and manifest that its broadening transformation and conservation is its actually intended meaning." Thus, Jesus opened up the Law "not as a liberal reformer, not out of a lesser loyalty to the Law, but in strictest obedience to its fulfillment, out of his being one with the Father in whom alone Law and promise are one and in whom Israel could become blessing and salvation for the nations."[60] And the ground of that fulfillment is the life, passion, death, resurrection, and ascension of Jesus Christ. In sum:

---

58. Ratzinger, *Many Religions—One Covenant*, 28.
59. Ibid., 33–34.
60. Ibid., 39.

> That means then that all cultic ordinances of the Old Testament are seen to be taken up into his death and brought to their deepest meaning. All sacrifices are acts of representation, which, from symbols, in this great act of real representation become reality, so that the symbols can be dropped without one iota being lost. The universalizing of the Torah by Jesus, as the New Testament understands it, is not the extraction of some universal moral prescriptions from the living whole of God's revelation. It preserves the unity of cult and ethos. The ethos remains grounded and anchored in the cult, in the worship of God, in such a way that the entire cult is bound together in the Cross, indeed, for the first time has become fully real. According to Christian faith, on the Cross Jesus opens up and fulfills the wholeness of the law and gives it thus to the pagans, who can now accept it as their own in this its wholeness, thereby becoming children of Abraham.[61]

So Jesus Christ is the mediator of the universality of God: of the one God of all men and of his Law, which is expressive of his will, and which is the truth for all men.[62]

My third objection is that Johnson's position begs the question by assuming that the post-apostolic community is in the same position as the apostolic community who reinterpreted the previous Old Testament special revelation in the light of Jesus Christ's life, passion, death, resurrection, and ascension. But the apostolic community was in that unique position because of the foundational role of the apostles. Ridderbos explains: "When understood in terms of the history of redemption, the canon cannot be open; in principle it must be closed. That follows directly from the unique and exclusive nature of the power the apostles received from Christ and from the commission he gave them to be witnesses to what they had seen and heard of the salvation he had brought. The result of this power and commission is the foundation of the church and the creation of the canon, and therefore these are naturally unrepeatable and exclusive in character."[63] Therefore, that closure occurred, adds Yves M. J. Congar, "with the death of the last apostle in the sense that the witness borne to Christ, through and in whom the revelation of God's plan and

---

61. Ibid., 41.

62. I deal at length with the question of Jesus Christ being the fulfillment of the Law later in chapter 2.

63. *Heilsgeschiedenis en Heilige Schrift Van Het Nieuwe Testament*, 59; ET: *Redemptive History and the New Testament Scriptures*, 25.

his mystery was fulfilled, was secure and terminated at that moment."[64] Before that closure, then, the apostles received a fresh revelation, and we know that to be the case because it is authoritatively recorded in the written Word of God in Scripture. Johnson assumes that contemporary human experience is a vehicle for a fresh revelation, which somehow surpasses and improves upon God's revelation in Scripture. That assumption not only significantly diminishes and devalues Scriptural authority, but also conflicts with Catholic teaching—which rejects not only a doctrine of continuing revelation, unravels the confusion between objective, public revelation and revelation in the sense of an illumination of the Holy Spirit, and rejects the idea that the real place where God has revealed himself, namely, the real locus of authority and revelation, is in human experience rather than the objective revelation of God's written Word revelation.[65]

Still, Johnson's position raises the important question: If not "experience," then what is the locus of biblical authority and revelation? The Dogmatic Constitution of Divine Revelation, *Dei Verbum*, teaches in this regard that the "economy of revelation" takes place "by events and words intrinsically bound to each other" (no. 2). In reply to the question, in what form does the special revelation of Holy Scripture give us knowledge about God, *Dei Verbum* answers that the basic form is an account in words of divine actions and divinely-given interpretations of those actions. As the evangelical Anglican theologian, J. I. Packer, once succinctly put it, explaining why the words are a necessary part of God's special revelation:

> The biblical position is that the mighty acts of God are not revelation to man at all, except in so far as they are accompanied by words of God to explain them. . . . Moreover, the whole purposes of God's mighty acts is to bring man to know Him by faith; and Scripture knows no foundation for faith but the spoken word of God, inviting our trust in Him on the basis of what He has done for us. Where there is no word from God, faith cannot be. Therefore, verbal revelation—that is to say, propositional revelation, the dis-

---

64. Congar, *Word and the Spirit*, 57. Regarding the idea of a closed revelation with the death of the last apostle, Fr. Congar says that he is describing the view of Henri de Lubac, Karl Rahner, and Edward Schillebeeckx.

65. I make no pretense here of being exhaustive in my critical remarks of Johnson. In particular, I cannot address the matter of how the lengthy treatment of Catholic biblical scholarship he gives in the work he co-authored with William S. Kurz, SJ, *Future of Catholic Biblical Scholarship*, relates to the heterodox claims he makes throughout the articles I have been discussing in this chapter.

> closure by God of truths about Himself—is no mere appendage to His redemptive activity, but a necessary part of it. This being so, the inspiring of an authoritative exposition of His redemptive acts in history ought to be seen as itself one of those redemptive acts, as necessary a link in the chain of His saving purposes as any of the events with the which the exposition deals.[66]

In other words, special revelation takes place through events that have God as their origin in a singularly unique way, with the knowledge of those events reaching us in words that are inspired by God—hence the God-breathed character of propositional revelation—and which have a singularly unique capacity to mediate the true reality of the events.[67] Put differently, Holy Scripture is God's written revelation in which we find a pattern of event and interpretation, embracing both deeds and words, which are intrinsically bound up with each other (as Vatican II phrases it), such that "without God's acts the words would be empty, without his words the acts would be blind."[68] But Holy Scripture does more that merely reveal what the acts of God's signify. Holy Scripture is itself one of the redemptive acts that God uses to draw men into relationship with himself, Trinitarian communion—with the Father, in the Son, and through the power of the Holy Spirit. In the words of *Dei Verbum*:

> In His goodness and wisdom God chose to reveal Himself and to make known to us the hidden purpose of His will (see Eph 1:9) by which through Christ, the Word made flesh, man might in the Holy Spirit have access to the Father and come to share in the divine nature (see Eph 2:18; 2 Pet 1:4). Through this revelation, therefore, the invisible God (see Col 1:15; 1 Tim 1:17) out of the abundance of His love speaks to men as friends (see Ex. 33:11; John 15:14–15) and lives among them (see Bar. 3:38), so that He may invite and take them into fellowship with Himself. This plan of revelation is realized by deeds and words having in inner unity: the deeds wrought by God in the history of salvation manifest and confirm the teaching and realities signified by the words, while the words proclaim the deeds and clarify the mystery contained in them. By this revelation then, the deepest truth about God and the

---

66. Packer, *Fundamentalism and the Word of God*, 92. See also, Helm, *Divine Revelation*, 32–35.

67. On this, see Martin, "Some Directions in Catholic Biblical Theology," 67–68.

68. Vos, "Idea of Biblical Theology as a Science and as a Theological Discipline."

salvation of man shines out for our sake in Christ, who is both the mediator and the fullness of all revelation.[69]

What makes Scripture the revealed Word of God? Is Scripture a single, unified, authoritative Word of God? Does it possess canonical authority as an integrated whole because it is the inspired and inerrant Word of God? In the next section, I'll give a brief account of a Catholic understanding of special revelation, in particular of the God-breathed character of Scripture in attempting to answer briefly these questions.[70] In conclusion of this section and as a segue to the next, I set the stage with a citation from Berkouwer: "The gift of the God-breathed character of Scripture 'is granted only within the circle of revelation.' The God-breathed character is not separate from revelation, and for the church Holy Scripture is the revelation, that is, the only instrument 'by which the revelation of God in Christ can be known.' *Revelation* finds its end in *inspiration* and therefore cannot be explained by means of a general 'instrumentality,' because it is related to 'theophany, prophecy, and miracle,' which precede the God-breathed character itself."[71] In other words, Holy Scripture is *in* the redemptive economy of special revelation, that is, it is itself one of the redemptive acts of God's communicative act whereby in this revelatory activity he communicates himself and the mystery of his will to man.

---

69. *Dei Verbum*, no. 2.

70. Aside from the foundational Vatican II document *Dei Verbum*, which is normative for my theological understanding of special revelation, helpful to that understanding are the following sources: Grisez, *Way of the Lord Jesus*, vol. 1, particularly chapter 20, 477–505; idem., "On Interpreting Dogmas: A Preliminary Analysis." Dulles, *Models of Revelation*; Martin, *Sacred Scripture*; Bavinck, *Gereformeerde Dogmatiek*, 1:295–324, 348–465 [428–47, 459–65]. Berkouwer, *De Heilige Schrift* I–II; ET: *Holy Scripture*. Here, too, both sources will be cited throughout this book, first the original, followed by the pagination of the English in square brackets [ ]. Mavrodes, *Revelation in Religious Belief*; Webster, *Holy Scripture*.

71. Berkouwer, *De Heilige Schrift*, 2:50 [161]. The quote within the quote from Berkouwer is from Bavinck's *Gereformeerde Dogmatiek*, 2:396, 354 [426, 382]. Bavinck writes, "Divine inspiration is an element *in* revelation, a last act in which the revelation of God is concluded for this dispensation" (382). Similarly, Ridderbos writes in *Heilsgeschiedenis en Heilige Schrift Van Het Nieuwe Testament*, 120, "Daarom is dit getuigenis ook niet slechts een getuigenis aangáánde de openbaring, maar is het zelf mede in deze openbaring begrepen" [Therefore this witness is not only a witness to revelation but is itself a part of this revelation.] ET: *Redemptive History and the New Testament Scriptures*, 60.

SPECIAL REVELATION AND BIBLICAL AUTHORITY

General revelation is God's revelation of himself in, by and through the works of creation (Rom 1:19-20).[72] That is, God makes himself and his divine plan known to us, not only through the Holy Scripture, but also through his right ordering of everything in creation—nature, history, culture, society, and human existence in the world. As the *Catechism of the Catholic Church* succinctly states, "Because God creates through wisdom, his creation is ordered. . . . The universe, created in and by the eternal Word, the 'image of the invisible God,' is destined for and addressed to man, himself created in the 'image of God,' and called to a personal relationship with God."[73] The divine wisdom which orders and shapes human existence in the world is inseparably tied in with the preserving and providentially governing activity of God in the totality of relationships within cosmic reality. Since God has made this creation revelation to be known, corresponding to this divine wisdom through which the creation is ordered is "our human understanding, which shares in the light of the divine intellect, [and] can understand what God tells us by means of his creation, though not without great effort and only in a spirit of humility and respect before the Creator and his work."[74] In sum, as Albert M. Wolters puts it, "Creation makes itself known; there is a revelation in and through the created order."[75]

Against the background of the idea that God's creation is ordered, we can consider as an example of this ordered creation the God-ordained limits and responsibilities of marriage. According to the Catholic tradition, God himself is the author of marriage and hence marriage is grounded in

---

72. Martin, "Revelation as Disclosure." See also, Berkouwer, *De Algemene Openbaring*; ET: *General Revelation*. Bavinck, *Gereformeerde Dogmatiek*, 1:272-94, 324-48 [301-22, 355-76].

73. *Catechism of the Catholic Church*, no. 299. In *Caritas in Veritate*, Benedict XVI makes an important point about God's creation revelation: "*Nature expresses a design of love and truth*. It is prior to us, and it has been given to us by God as the setting for our life. Nature speaks to us of the Creator (cf. *Rom* 1:20) and his love for humanity. It is destined to be 'recapitualted' in Christ at the end of time (cf. *Eph* 1:9-10; *Col* 1:19-20). Thus it too is a 'vocation'. Nature is at our disposal not as 'a heap of scattered refuse', but as a gift of the Creator who has given it an inbuilt order, enabling man to draw from it the principles needed in order 'to till it and keep it' (*Gen* 2:15)" (no. 48).

74. Ibid.

75. "Creation Order," 40.

the order of creation.[76] Marriage is not a mere cultural or social artifact. Rather, there are common and permanent characteristics attached to the institution of marriage "despite the many variations it may have undergone through the centuries in different cultures, social structures, and spiritual attitudes." In addition, "Although the dignity of this institution is not transparent everywhere with the same clarity, some sense of the greatness of the matrimonial union exists in all cultures." One important factor that contributes to this lack of clarity is sin. In other words, marriage is also under the regime of sin. "As a break with God, the first sin had for its consequence the rupture of the original communion between man and woman." "Nevertheless, the order of creation persists, though seriously disturbed." Jesus Christ's redemptive work "restores the original order of creation disturbed by sin, [for] he himself gives the strength and grace to live marriage in the new dimension of the Reign of God."[77] The main point I want to make here now is about the prominent role of the special revelation of Holy Scripture: sin has also affected the human knower's capacity to grasp the original order of creation and God rectifies that fallen knower through Holy Scripture, bringing, in consequence, that ordered creation to clarity.[78] Thus, we now need to address the question of special revelation: chiefly, revelation in scripture, but also the relation between Scripture and Tradition.

The schema (S) I propose to use here to give an account of special revelation claims is as follows: (S) m reveals $α$ to n by means of (through, etc.) k.[79] This schema is about the origin, content, manner, and purpose of God's special revelation.[80] In other words, the agent of the revelation

76. *Catechism of the Catholic Church*, no. 1603.

77. The quotation in this paragraph are from the *Catechism of the Catholic Church*, 1603, 1607–1608, and 1615.

78. St. Bonaventure writes, "The world was like a damaged *[deletes]* book which God brought to perspicacity *[illuminavit]* and rectified by the book of Scripture" (as cited in Martin, "Revelation as Disclosure," 206 n. 3). Bonaventure's view is shared by John Calvin, *Institutes of the Christian Religion*, Book 1, chapter VI, no. 1, "Just as old or bleary-eyed men and those with weak vision, if you thrust before them a most beautiful volume, even if they recognize it to be some sort of writing, yet can scarcely construe two words, but with the aid of spectacles will begin to read distinctly; so Scripture, gathering up the otherwise confused knowledge of God in our minds, having dispersed our dullness, clearly shows us the true God" (70).

79. I am indebted to Mavrodes here for this schema. On this, see *Revelation in Religious Belief*, 88–94.

80. Genderen and Velema, *Concise Reformed Dogmatics*, 24–26.

is represented by *m*; α represents the content of the revelation, and *n* the recipient; *k* represents the manner or means of the revelation. I turn now to look at each of the elements in the schema.

The *agent* (*m*) of the revelation is God himself because revelation originates with God. "It pleased God, in his goodness and wisdom, to reveal himself and to make known the mystery of his will (cf. Eph 1:9)."[81] Furthermore, he is the essential foundation (*principium essendi*), the source, the primary efficient cause, of our knowledge of him. Without his divine self-communicative acts, his personal self-disclosures, we would not know anything of God at all. "He is knowable only because and insofar as he himself wants to be known."[82]

Moving on to the next item (α) in this schema, what is the content of revelation? Put differently, what is it that is revealed? In a fundamental sense, God reveals *himself*, and so we may say that the content of revelation is God's own proper reality, his own self, the gift of himself "as a communion of persons inviting human persons to enter into communion."[83] In the words of *Dei Verbum*, "His will was that men should have access to the Father, through Christ, the Word made flesh, in the Holy Spirit, and thus become sharers in the divine nature (cf. Eph 2:18; 2 Pet 1:4). By this revelation, then, the invisible God (cf. Col 1:15; 1 Tim 1:17), from the fullness of his love, addresses men as his friends (cf. Ex. 33:11; Jn 15:14–15), and moves among them (cf. Bar. 3: 38), in order to invite and receive them into his own company."[84] Indeed, *Dei Verbum* discloses that the purpose of God's self-revelation is coming to know him. "Now this is life eternal: that they may know you, the only true God, and Jesus Christ, whom you have sent" (John 17:3). We are invited, therefore, to Trinitarian communion with the Father, through the Son, Jesus Christ, the Word made flesh, in the power of the Holy Spirit. Revelation is, then, not the *mere* communication of truths but rather "the life-bestowing self-communication of the Trinitarian God, in which he addresses humans as friends," as *Dei Verbum* states.[85]

---

81. *Dei Verbum*, no. 2; see also no. 6.
82. Bavinck, *Gereformeerde Dogmatiek*, 1:183 [212].
83. Grisez, "On Interpreting Dogmas," 120.
84. *Dei Verbum*, no. 2.
85. Pottmeyer, "Tradition," 1123.

Yet, there is more to the content of revelation: God reveals himself in the economy of special revelation in his words and actions. *Dei Verbum* holds that the economy of revelation in Sacred Scripture consists of a pattern of deeds of God in history and words, of divine actions and divinely-given interpretations of those actions, that are inextricably bound together in that revelation.[86] That is, God's redemptive revelation of himself is accomplished through historical events as well as through written words. Thus: "the works performed by God in the history of salvation show forth and bear out the doctrine and realities signified by the words; the words, for their part, proclaim the works, and bring to light the mystery they contain."[87] In sum, "the most intimate truth which this revelation gives us about God and the salvation of man shines forth in Christ, who is himself both the mediator and the sum total of Revelation [see Matt 11:27; John 1:14, 17; 14:6; 17:1–3; 2 Cor 3:16, 4:6; Eph 1:3–14]."[88] This important emphasis on the *history* of salvation reaching its absolute zenith in the person and work of Christ, since God's revelation in him is perfect and definitive, means that there is a history of revelation, with revelation progressing through the history of salvation in phases.[89]

Moreover, God not only reveals himself, giving us himself in Trinitarian communion. Rather, at one and the same time, Holy Scripture is not only God's gift of himself, inviting humanity to share in his life, but also a disclosure of *revealed truths*. In other words, revelation, while involving a profound personal engagement with the revealing God, "also and necessarily has an irreducibly cognitive dimension."[90] The *Catechism of the Catholic Church* correctly captures both the personal and the propositional in its understanding of faith and revelation. "Faith is first of all a personal adherence of man to God. At the same time, and inseparably, it is a *free assent to the whole truth that God has revealed*."[91] In this connection, we should heed Paul Helm's point: "There is no antithesis between believing a proposition and believing a person if the proposition is taken

---

86. See also, Helm, *Divine Revelation*, 32–35.
87. *Dei Verbum*, no. 2.
88. Ibid.
89. Genderen and Velema, *Concise Reformed Dogmatics*, 25–26.
90. Guarino, *Vattimo and Theology*, 115.
91. *Catechism of the Catholic Church*, no. 150.

to be the assertion of some person."[92] Thus, we must reject the dichotomy between God revealing propositions and revealing himself, between the propositional and the personal,[93] if the propositions are understood to be assertions of God's self-communicative acts.[94] Indeed, Richard Swinburne

92. Helm, "Revealed Propositions and Timeless Truths," 135–36.

93. For an instructive account of the historical and theological origins of this dichotomy in the first half of twentieth-century, see Baillie, *Idea of Revelation in Recent Thought*. Baillie makes many sound points, but his analyses set up a false dichotomy between the personal and the propositional. For a far superior historical and systematic work, see the magisterial study by Dulles, *Assurance of Things Hoped For*. Early in the twentieth century, one of the first English-speaking theologians to eliminate the mediating role of propositions both from God's self-revelation to man and from man's faith in God was the Archbishop of Canterbury, William Temple (1881–1944). In a passage representative, I believe, of the thinking of much theology, then and now, Archbishop Temple declared in his Gifford Lectures: "There is no such thing as revealed truth. There are truths of revelation, that is to say, propositions which express the results of correct thinking concerning revelation; but they are not themselves directly revealed. . . . What is offered to man's apprehension in any specific Revelation is not truth concerning God but the living God Himself." To the Archbishop's credit, he conceded that "it is to be frankly recognized that [this conception] is by no means the traditional doctrine of Christendom" (*Nature, Man, and God*, Lecture XII, 301–27, and here at 317, 322, and 308, respectively). On the European continent just a few years earlier in 1929, Rudolph Bultmann, too, wrote as follows in reply to the following question, "What, then, has been revealed?" "Nothing at all," replied Bultmann, "as far as the question concerning revelation asks for doctrines—doctrines, say, that no man could have discovered for himself—or for mysteries that become known once and for all as soon as they are communicated" (Bultmann, "Concept of Revelation in the New Testament," 100). One could add to the list of those who reject propositional truth, and hence propositional revelation, and advocate a nonpropositional notion of faith, theologians such as Wilhelm Hermann, the early Barth, Emil Brunner, Paul Tillich, H. Richard Niebuhr, W. Cantwell Smith, Edward Schillebeeckx, Hans Küng, Rosemary Radford Ruether, and David Tracy, and philosophers like Ludwig Wittgenstein, R. B. Braithwaite, D. Z. Phillips, and last but not least, John Hick. Indeed, in 1966 Hick confidently declared that "in more recent times the notion of divinely revealed propositions has virtually disappeared from Protestant theology." He summarized the then and still, dominant view of revelation and faith as follows: "revelation is not a divine promulgation of propositions, nor is faith a believing of such propositions. The theological propositions formulated on the basis of revelation have a secondary status. They do not constitute the content of God's self-revelation but are human and therefore fallible verbalizations, constructed to aid both the integration of our religious experience into our own minds and the communication of religious experience to others" (Hick, *Faith and Knowledge*, 30, and 28–29.

94. This core certitude of the Christian faith does not exclude affirming that language has a variety of functions in revelation other than asserting: commanding, questioning, invitations, promising, praising, confessing, exhorting, and many others. There are also various literary genres: historical narrative, law, prophecy, poetry, proverb, romance, letter, apocalypse, and much else. Yet, the major point is that all these other ways that

is correct: "It is in any case very hard to see how God could reveal himself in history (e.g., in the Exodus or the life, death, and resurrection of Jesus) without at the same time revealing some propositional truth about himself. For events are not self-interpreting. Either God provides with the historical events its interpretation, in which there is a propositional revelation; or he does not, in which case how can anyone know that a revelatory event has occurred?"[95] As I have already shown above, this too is the view of *Dei Verbum* in affirming the inextricable connection between words and deeds in the economy of divine Revelation.

The dichotomy between the personal and the propositional extends so far in the thinking of Sandra M. Schneiders that she even applies it to the faith affirmation (to use her phrase) that the Bible is inspired. She compares the affirmation that the Bible is inspired with other faith affirmations, such as the "creation of the universe and the divinity of the human being Jesus of Nazareth." It is evident that by "affirmation" she does not mean that the believer, *qua* believer, is involved in holding certain propositions to be true about the world, Jesus Christ, and the Bible. In other words, such affirmations do not constitute genuine assertions and hence they make no claims about objective reality. A very telling example making clear that she does not think affirmations involve assenting to the truth of certain propositions is her claim that Jesus can be naturalistically explained by human generation. Now, of course she quickly adds in a note that this explanation would not be adequate from a theological perspective. Ok, but how does this help her get out of the quandary that her affirmation—"Jesus can be naturalistically explained by human generation"—does not logically exclude some possible state of affairs as false. For example, both the Apostles' and Nicene Creeds state that Jesus was conceived by the Holy Spirit and born of the Virgin Mary. This statement, if true, excludes as false that state of affairs in which Jesus could

---

God uses language in the special revelation of Holy Scripture "logically presupposes the straight propositional account" (Helm, *Divine Revelation*, 35). I shall return to the issue of literary genres, propositional truth, and inerrancy later in this chapter.

95. Swinburne, *Revelation*, 4. This, too, is the view of G. C. Berkouwer, "Sacrificium Intellectus?" 193–95. Berkouwer rejects the "simplistic dilemma" (his words) that pits God's personal self-communication over against revelation as "information-bearing," as "declarative, as disclosive of information of all sorts of 'truths'" (193–94, my translation). Similarly, Avery Cardinal Dulles, "Orthodox Imperative," 33: "A non-propositional understanding of revelation contradicts the tenor of Holy Scripture and the earliest confessions of faith, which describe particular historical events of crucial importance for faith."

be completely explained by human generation. Schneiders apparently disagrees. She suggests that "faith affirmations are more akin to poetic discourse," quickly assuring us that "[t]his does not mean that faith affirmations," she adds, "are a mere reading into reality of what cannot be seen by others because it is not really there." Schneiders insists that "faith [affirmations] bears upon reality."[96] That may very well be the case for her, but it is hard to see how that can be the case, since her view of faith affirmations do not logically exclude certain states of affairs as false because they seem to assert nothing.

Furthermore, our understanding of divine revelation is not free from ambiguity if we speak, as Catholic theologians O'Collins and Farrugia do, of divine revelation being "*primarily* God's self-revelation, which invites the personal response of faith," and "*secondarily* the communication of truths about God and human beings that would otherwise remain unknown.... In revelation we primarily meet God and not divinely authorized truths."[97] The chief problem with this formulation is that it does not seem to grasp propositions as an integral part of the interpersonal relationship of divine revelation and faith, of God's self-communicative act and hence as an authentic mediation of his self-revelation.[98] In other words, this formulation leaves it unclear that faith itself is propositional, that is, that one assents primarily to God himself but as mediated in and through determinate propositions. Due to a lack of clarity the danger looms large that this formulation sets up a false dichotomy between the personal and the propositional. More accurately stated, in one and the very same act, God reveals himself but he also reveals a set of truths, that is to say, propositional revelation, disclosing truths about himself and his plan of salvation (e.g., that the Kingdom is at hand, that Jesus is the Christ, the Incarnate Word, the Son of the living God, that Jesus Christ died for our sins on the cross, and that God raised Jesus from the dead, that Jesus will return, and so forth). Revelation necessarily has both aspects: the personal and the propositional. This point is so important that I need to develop it a bit further.

Aidan Nichols writes, "Whatever else doctrines are, they are propositions, and no account of revelation which would exclude propositions

---

96. The quotations in this paragraph are from Schneiders, *Revelatory Text*, 49–50.

97. O'Collins and Farrugia, *Catholicism: The Story of Catholic Christianity*, 97; italics added.

98. Grisez, *Way of the Lord Jesus*, vol. 1:503 n. 8.

wholly from its purview could do justice to the role of doctrines in Catholic Christianity."⁹⁹ Consider, for instance, Michael Lawler's heterodox view that denies the integral role of propositions in his conception of revelation. He says, "Revelation is not the communication of objective knowledge *about* God, but the communication of a subject-*God* to human subjects as to friends. God does not reveal books or propositions or words; God reveals [him]self."¹⁰⁰ There is a false dichotomy in Lawler's view between the personal and the propositional. Furthermore, he claims that Vatican II rejected the idea of revealed truth, of propositional revelation, but he is mistaken: that Vatican II affirmed propositional revelation is entirely supportable from the council's teaching. Its teaching is summarized by the *Catechism of the Catholic Church:* "Faith is first of all a personal adherence of man to God. At the same time, and inseparably, it is a *free assent to the whole truth that God has revealed.*"¹⁰¹ Hence, it is crucial to be clear about the epistemological significance of theological propositions in grasping the truth about reality.

Aquinas understood this matter well. Yes, he does say, "Actus autem credentis non terminator ad enuntiabile sed ad rem" [The believer's act (of faith) does not terminate in the propositions, but the realities [which they express].¹⁰² While it is true to say that the *ultimate object of faith* is not a set of theological formulas that we confess, but rather God himself, it is also the case that for Aquinas articles of faith are necessary for knowing God. In other words, one assents primarily to God himself but as mediated in and through determinate propositions. Propositions are an authentic mediation of God's self-revelation because faith involves belief, and to have a belief means that one is intellectually committed, or has mentally assented, to the truth of some proposition or other. Faith involves belief, says Aquinas, and "belief is called assent, and it can only

---

99. Nichols, *From Newman to Congar,* 175. See also, Guarino, *Vattimo and Theology,* We may not equate "doctrine simply with propositional truth" and eviscerate "the vital, personalistic, engaging elements of religious experience" (103). Still, "Christianity insists that revelation, while a profoundly multi-faceted reality, also and necessarily has an irreducibly cognitive dimension" (115).

100. Lawler, *What is and what ought to be: The Dialectic of Experience, Theology, and Church,* 78. Sandra M. Schneiders also rejects propositional revelation in her study, *Revelatory Text,* 53–55.

101. *Catechism of the Catholic Church,* no. 150.

102. Aquinas, *Summa Theologia,* II-II, q. 1, a. 2, ad. 2.

be about a proposition, in which truth or falsity is found."[103] As Charles Cardinal Journet also puts it, "The object of faith is both the statement so far as this touches reality, and reality so far as this is shown in the statement. It is both the statement to which faith assents, and reality which becomes open to it by its assent, towards which it tends, and in which it terminates."[104] Furthermore, the *Catechism of the Catholic Church* puts this point accurately: "We do not believe in formulas, but in those realities they express, which faith allows us to touch. 'The believer's act [of faith] does not terminate in the propositions, but in the realities [which they express]' [St. Thomas Aquinas, *STh* II-II, 1, 2, ad. 2]. *All the same*, we do approach these realities with the help of formulations of the faith which permit us to express the faith and to hand it on, to celebrate it in community, to assimilate and live on it more and more."[105]

Moreover, that assent to some definite propositions is essential to faith is clear from the New Testament itself (see Acts 2:41; Rom 10:9–17; 1 Cor 15:1–8; 1 Tim 4:6; 2 Tim 3:14; 4:1–5; and many other places). Mindful of Nichols' point that whatever else doctrines are, they are propositions, we may put this last point by stating that the Gospel, then, is also a teaching, meaning thereby "an *instructive* communicating of facts and events of salvation, or an instructive interpretation of the Holy Scripture of the Old Testament."[106] In this connection, Geiselmann correctly states that the "New Testament itself calls the gospel a doctrine, *didachē* (Rom 16:17, Acts 2:42), *didaschalia* (Rom 12:7; pastoral letters, *passim*). To preach the word of God is also paraphrased with *didaschein* (2 Thess 2:15; Col 2:7; Eph 4:21; 1 Tim 4:11; Acts 5:42; 18:11; 28:31). The announcer of the word of God may also be honored by the title of teacher (*didaschalos*) (1 Tim 2:7; 2 Tim 1:11)."[107]

---

103. Aquinas, *Disputed Questions on Truth*, q. 14, art. 8, ad. 12

104. Journet, *What is Dogma?* 11–12.

105. *Catechism of the Catholic Church*, no. 170, italics added. See also, Guarino, *Vattimo and Theology*, 103–18, for a defense of propositional revelation and faith's knowledge of God as mediated through determinate propositions.

106. Heinrich Schlier, *Wort Gottes. Eine neutestamentliche Besinnung*, 39, as cited by Geiselmann in "Scripture, Tradition, and the Church," 53–54. Schlier adds, "The notion of 'teaching' points out that the gospel may be present in a fixed tradition, as the expression *hygiainousa didaschalion* (2 Tim 4:5, *et al.*) already suggests."

107. Geiselmann, "Scripture, Tradition, and the Church," 53. Elsewhere Geiselmann writes, "The Gospel of Jesus Christ of necessity assumes in the Church's paradosis the form of *didaskalia*, of doctrine, just as, of course, [St] Paul himself in his writings was

SCRIPTURE AND TRADITION[108]

Now, the Church takes with utmost seriousness the task of preserving the apostolic *parathêkê* (deposit), which is the living deposit of faith once for all delivered to the saints (Jude 3): the single deposit of faith that is given to be handed down from one generation to another. Vatican II teaches that "God has graciously arranged that the things he had once [for all] revealed for the salvation of all peoples should remain in their entirety, throughout the ages, and be transmitted to all generations."[109] Indeed, the apostolic *paradosis* (tradition, "what is handed on"), which is the form in which the Gospel of Jesus Christ originally comes to us, is transmitted to the Church "under the double form of living kerygma and its written expression in Scripture (cf. 1 Tim 6:20; 2 Tim 1:12 and 14; 2 Tim 3:15)."[110] In particular, Geiselmann correctly notes, "Holy Scripture is the *paradosis* of the apostolic kerygma, become writing."[111] Alternatively put, "New Testament Scripture is the written counterpart of apostolic tradition."[112] In its being so transmitted the apostolic *paradosis* "becomes the *parathêkê*, the apostolic bequest which is committed to the Church's safe-keeping."[113] "The Scriptures were given to the Church," adds Geiselmann, "so that it could preserve the Gospel entrusted to it."[114] Furthermore, this apostolic *paradosis* is itself divine in origin because it is what God himself hands on. As Ratzinger explains:

---

conscious, in view of the false teachings arising in the Church, and in view of the false gnosis invading it (1 Tim 6:20), that he was no longer solely an apostle and herald of the message of Christ, but also a teacher of the gentiles (2 Tim 4:17)" (*Meaning of Tradition*, 31).

108. My discussion of Scripture and Tradition that follows in the next few pages is indebted, chiefly, to several sources: *Dei Verbum*, nos. 7–10; Geiselmann, *Meaning of Tradition*; idem., "Scripture, Tradition, and the Church"; Ratzinger, "Revelation and Tradition"; Nichols, *Shape of Catholic Theology*, 165–80; *Fourth World Conference on Faith and Order*; Congar, *Meaning of Tradition*; idem., *Tradition and Traditions*.

109. *Dei Verbum*, no. 7.

110. Geiselmann, *Meaning of Tradition*, 23.

111. Geiselmann, "Scripture, Tradition, and the Church," 55.

112. Geiselmann, *Meaning of Tradition*, 23; see also 24.

113. Ibid. Geiselmann adds, "Holy Scripture as the guardian of the Gospel is the dowry of the Holy Spirit to the Bride of Christ, the most precious jewel in which the *Spiritus creator* endowed her subsequent life with the word of Christ" (37).

114. Ibid., 37.

> At the beginning of all tradition stands the fact that the Father gives the Son over to the world and that the Son for his part allows himself to be given over to the "nations"—as a sign. This original *paradosis*, in its character as judgment and salvation, is constituted in the abiding presence of Christ in his Body, the Church. To that extent the whole mystery of Christ's continuing presence is primarily the whole reality which is transmitted in tradition, the decisive fundamental reality which is antecedent to all particular explicit expressions of it, even those of Scripture, and which represents what has in fact to be handed down.[115]

In other words, the apostolic tradition has its ultimate source in the "original *paradosis*," namely, in God's revelatory self-communication, which revelation culminates in God the Father's handing over his own Son, Jesus Christ, to man, indeed, for us all "because of our offenses" (Rom 4:25; see also 8:32). Here we must emphasize, as Ratzinger himself does in the above passage, that Christ himself is present and engaged for his part in the fact that the Father hands over the Son to the world by simultaneously handing himself over (Eph 5:2).[116]

Furthermore, this apostolic tradition is *the* Tradition (with a capital *T*), because it is revelation itself.[117] By Tradition, then, "is meant the Gospel itself, transmitted from generation to generation in and by the Church, Christ himself present in the life of the Church."[118] Tradition or *paradosis* in this sense has a New Testament pedigree. It is revelation-in-its-transmission. In St. Paul, Tradition is revelation itself because what is handed down is the Christian faith, God's self revelation and self-giving in Christ. "For what I received I passed on to you as of first importance: that Christ died for our sins according to the Scriptures, that he was buried, that he was raised on the third day according to the Scriptures, and that he appeared to Peter, and then to the Twelve" (1 Cor 15:3–5). Later St. Paul urges us to "stand firm and hold fast to the traditions that you were taught by us, either by word of mouth or by our letter" (2 Thess 2:15). Indeed, he also commands us in the name of the Lord Jesus Christ to live "according to the tradition" by "keeping away from believers who are living in idleness and not according to the tradition that they received

---

115. Ratzinger, "Revelation and Tradition," 46.
116. Pottmeyer, "Tradition," 1124.
117. Nichols, *Shape of Catholic Theology*, 169.
118. *Fourth World Conference on Faith and Order*, 50.

from us" (2 Thess 3:6). Of course the Tradition that comes down from the apostles, the apostolic tradition, is authoritative for the faith and life of the Church. "Our starting point is that we are all living in a tradition which goes back to our Lord and has its roots in the Old Testament, and are all indebted to that tradition inasmuch as we have received the revealed truth, the Gospel, through its being transmitted from one generation to another. Thus we can say that we exist as Christians by the Tradition of the Gospel (the *paradosis* of the *kerygma*) testified in Scripture, transmitted in and by the Church through the power of the Holy Spirit."[119]

Moreover, if it is true that the *paradosis* of the apostolic kerygma is its written expression in Holy Scripture, it is equally the case that "Scripture and tradition are combined in the idea of *parathêkê* [deposit]."[120] The two, then, are related by mutual dependence, says Geiselmann, confirming the observation of J. A. Möhler that "Church, Gospel and tradition always stand and fall together."[121] Möhler's point is true not only because the deposit of faith is entrusted to the Church for safe-keeping, guarded by a living teaching authority[122], but also "the apostolic paradosis [is] perpetuated in the form of the Church's paradosis. In this way ecclesiastical paradosis joined sacred Scripture as the second form, independent of Scripture, of the *parathêkê* entrusted to the Church."[123] On this view, the Gospel of Jesus Christ has been proclaimed to us in the apostolic tradition. Significantly, it is the single source of all truth of salvation and morality, with Scripture and the Church's living tradition being "the different modes of existence

---

119. Ibid., 52.

120. Ibid.

121. Möhler, *Die Einheit in der Kirche*, (1825), 80, as cited by Geiselmann, *Meaning of Tradition*, 23.

122. Nichols explains the responsibility of this "living teaching authority: originally the apostles, then 'apostolic men' such as Timothy and Titus, at once apostolic delegates and the presiding figures of local Churches—what Luke portrays in Acts as 'presybter-bishops'. Finally, in the generation following the age of the New Testament, the guardians of the deposit [*parathêkê*] are identified with the bishops of the Catholic episcopate. The task of such people is to secure the deposit against attempts to corrupt it; and this desire to protect orthodoxy, the integrity of the gospel, against what would later be called heresy is already there in the New Testament. But the job does not stop with the largely negative business of defending something from attack. It goes beyond this to include the duty of transmitting the tradition to one's contemporaries across space and to one's successors across time" (*Shape of Catholic Theology*, 168).

123. Geiselmann, *Meaning of Tradition*, 27.

within the Church of the gospel of Jesus Christ."[124] Geiselmann explains, "The Church's paradosis is the mode in which apostolic paradosis exists in the post-apostolic Church and exercises together with Scripture a necessary function in preserving the Gospel of Jesus Christ entrusted to the Church. For without the Church's paradosis the unity of faith and the uniform understanding of faith by the community of the faithful would be impossible and the Church as the one apostolic and Catholic teaching would be at an end."[125] Geiselmann's explanation affirms the interdependency of Scripture and the Church's tradition, indeed, the necessity, even the inevitability of that tradition for preserving and deepening our understanding of Scripture. His explanation, therefore, raises the question of the relation between the written expression of the apostolic paradosis, the *parathêkê* (deposit of faith), and the Church's tradition, which is itself the unfolding of the apostolic tradition. In short, it raises the question of the relation between Scripture and tradition.

Three possible answers have been given to this question. First, we have the view that has been called "Tradition 0" and which is opposed to the idea that tradition is indispensable to the preservation and understanding of the Scriptures. In sum, one can understand the Scriptures without benefit of tradition, namely, councils, creeds, confessions, in short, the Church's tradition.[126] Scripture is hermeneutically sufficient to be interpreted correctly, and hence in that sense it is "self-interpreting." Critics of this view, such as Kevin Vanhoozer call it "solo" *scriptura* in order to distinguish it from the Reformational biblical hermeneutic of *sola scriptura*.[127]

The latter represents an alternative view, one which Heiko Obermann describes as "Tradition I."[128] On this second view of the relation between

---

124. Geiselmann, "Scripture, Tradition, and the Church," 50.

125. Geiselmann, *Meaning of Tradition*, 27.

126. This nomenclature, "Tradition 0," is from Alister McGrath, *Reformation Thought*, 144–45. In his book, *Shape of Sola Scriptura*, Keith A. Mathison argues that proponents of Tradition 0 include the radical reformers of the sixteenth century, eighteenth-century American Christians, and contemporary Evangelicals influenced by the modern idea of individual autonomy.

127. Vanhoozer, *Drama of Doctrine*, 154.

128. Obermann, *Forerunners of the Reformation*, 58. In his book, *Recovering the Reformed Confessions*, R. Scott Clark defends Tradition I as the confessional Reformed approach to tradition (7–17), which approach had as its proponents the Protestant Reformers Luther and Calvin, and in the twentieth-century theologians such J. Gresham Machen (1881–1937) and John Murray (1898–1975).

Scripture and tradition, there is only "one-source" of revelation, namely, the Scriptures, and tradition "transmits the one, same word of God as that contained in the Scriptures."[129] According to Obermann, Vanhoozer, and McGrath, the Reformational hermeneutic of *sola scriptura* "preserves an important role for tradition; hence it does not entail Tradition 0."[130] Tradition I affirms the hermeneutical insufficiency of the Scriptures,[131] and so there is no question of rejecting tradition outright, because tradition is required as an aid to its correct understanding. However, since we cannot presume that the Church's tradition has always rightly interpreted the Scriptures, tradition as such must be properly located "within the economy of salvation and the pattern of divine authority." Vanhoozer explains, "the church's interpretation is to be preferred because it is *right*—in accordance with the Scriptures—not simply because it comes from the church." "We cannot take for granted," adds Vanhoozer, "that the content of the apostolic tradition is found in the teaching of the church. To presume such a coincidence is altogether too naïve."[132] Given that post-apostolic traditions of the Church may be in error, it then becomes necessary—and this is the argument of the Protestant Reformers—for the Church to affirm *sola scriptura*, meaning thereby specifically that "Scripture stand over against her, a superior norm."[133] Ultimately, the Reformational hermeneutic of *sola scriptura* is about affirming the authority of the Scripture over tradition, indeed, over the teaching office of the Church.

---

129. Vanhoozer, *Drama of Doctrine*, 156 n. 21.

130. Ibid., 156.

131. Vanhoozer, *Drama of Doctrine*, 160: "Neither Spirit nor tradition can be left out of an account of how Scripture functions authoritatively in the church." See also, Velema and Van Genderen, *Concise Reformed Dogmatics*: "[T]he confession of the sufficiency of Scripture does not imply that all traditions must be considered useless. The churches of the Reformation also recognize elements of tradition.... [T]raditions are both useful and necessary. We agree with Bavinck that tradition is the means by which all the treasures and possessions of our ancestors are transmitted to present and future. There is indeed a variegated reformed tradition. There is tradition in our confession, in our worship service, in preaching, in theology, in devotional literature that is nurtured by Scripture" (105).

132. Vanhoozer, *Drama of Doctrine*, 164. Again, Velema and Van Genderen, *Concise Reformed Dogmatics*: "The stream of tradition must always lead us back to the source that is normative: Holy Scripture.... The Reformation only recognizes *a tradition that is based on Scripture and derives from Scripture*" (105).

133. Cullmann, "New Direction: Divine Revelation and the Virgin Mary," 48.

There is a third view to consider, which Obermann calls "Tradition II."[134] Proponents of this view hold that not everything the church needs to know is found in Scripture and hence they reject the material sufficiency of Scripture. Accordingly, "tradition—in this context, the handing on of oral apostolic teaching—becomes a second source of revelation that provides supplementary information."[135] Tradition II then is the view that tradition supplements Scripture such that revealed truth has two separate sources. This view is known as the two-source theory of revelation, these two sources being Scripture and tradition and, arguably, as Aidan Nichols rightly notes, it is the dominant [theory] in the period between the [sixteenth-century] Council [of Trent] and the nineteenth century."[136] "On this view," Nichols adds, "there are (alongside Scripture) confessional, liturgical, and ethical traditions in the Church deriving from ancient times and testifying to revelation."[137] Now, whether or not Trent taught this dual-source theory of revelation raises complex historical questions that are beyond the scope of the present work. Three further points are, however, apt.

First, Trent closed off three approaches to the issue concerning the relation of Scripture and tradition. One, it closed off, says Nichols, the "Protestant position in its Lutheran or Calvinist form." Now, the Rome-Reformation conflict was, in part, over the idea that tradition expressed a mode of transmitting revelation additional to that of Holy Scripture.[138] It was also a conflict over the teaching authority of the Church, which is a question of the magisterium. Judging from the context in which Nichols makes this statement about Trent he must think that the Reformers emphasis on freedom of interpretation, private judgment, albeit Spirit-led, for the resolving of disputed interpretation of Holy Scripture, unleashed a "church-dissolving" dynamic, which severed religious subjectivity from the life and faith of the Church, indeed, the authority of the teaching office. Given this view of the Reformers, we can well understand why Trent closed off the Protestant position.

---

134. Obermann, *Forerunners of the Reformation*, 58.

135. Vanhoozer, *Drama of Doctrine*, 154.

136. Nichols, *Shape of Catholic Theology*, 176. For support of Nichols' claim, see Geiselmann, "Scripture, Tradition, and the Church," 39–40; idem., "Scripture and Tradition in Catholic theology."

137. Nichols, *Shape of Catholic Theology*, 176.

138. Ratzinger, "Revelation and Tradition," 26.

Two, Trent also closed off "the late medieval concept of post-apostolic revelation made to the Church." Doctrinal development is not synonymous with continuing revelation because the Church holds that God's public revelation was completed once and for all in Christ. Three, adds Nichols, Trent "disposed of the idea of an esoteric, non-public apostolic tradition coming out of the closet from time to time."[139]

The second point I want to make is this: Trent taught neither the material sufficiency of Scripture, nor the dual-source theory of revelation. Geiselmann correctly stresses this point: "One cannot emphasize enough that nothing, absolutely nothing, was decided at the Council of Trent concerning the relation of Scripture and Tradition."[140] This judgment is endorsed by Reformed theologian Berkouwer, who writes,

> Trent did not say, to be sure, that all the truth concerning salvation is revealed in Scripture. But since Trent did not make a pronouncement on this matter and was content to contradict the Reformation with an expression of great respect for tradition, the relationship between Scripture and tradition is a completely open matter. Indeed, the matter is so open that it is now argued that the text of Trent's decree is not in conflict with the notion that tradition is not a source of revelation on the same level with Scripture, but is only an *interpretative source*. Trent, it is argued, leaves Catholics free to identify themselves with the very ancient tradition of the Church according to which *all the truth of salvation is contained in Scripture*.[141]

We can conclude from Geiselmann and Berkouwer's judgment that Trent left open the two-source theory of revelation. But we can also conclude about Trent, as Nichols does, that it "can coexist with what may be called the 'classical view' of the High Middle Ages, namely, that all revelation is virtually contained in Scripture, requiring, however, the Church's in-

---

139. Nichols, *Shape of Catholic Theology*, 176.

140. Geiselmann, "Scripture, Tradition, and the Church," 47–48.

141. Berkouwer, *Vatikaans Concilie en Nieuwe Theologie*, 114 [ET: 96–97]. To cite again Reformed theologians, Velema and Van Genderen, from their work, *Concise Reformed Dogmatics*: Dutch theologian "B. Wentsel concluded correctly that the substantive [material] sufficiency of Scripture was not proclaimed. Neither did the council support the view that tradition is of a complementary nature as taught by the theory of two sources. Neither was it said that tradition plays an exclusively interpretive role" (103 n. 31). In short, all these possibilities were left open, as Geiselmann, Berkouwer, and Nichols claim.

terpretation, leaning on apostolic tradition, for its explication."[142] Finally, Trent kept open one other possibility:

> Trent cannot be said to exclude what has become in the Modern period perhaps the favored view of Catholic theologians: the view that sees Tradition (now spelt with a capital *T* and distinguished from traditions in the plural) as theologically prior to the Bible, and defines that Tradition as the life and consciousness of the Church, of which Scripture forms an essential part.[143]

In light of this third possibility concerning the relation of Scripture and Tradition, I would like to make a third point by answering the question left hanging in Nichols above passage regarding the claim that although Tradition, as the life and consciousness of the Church, is necessarily a reality at once larger than the Bible, it is inclusive of it and, indeed, forms an essential part of Tradition. What, then, is the normative significance for the Church and, indeed, her teaching office, of the Holy Scriptures that are entrusted to her as a *parathêkê*? Can Scripture still be regarded as "the supreme norm of faith, the *norma [normans,] non normata* [that is, the normative standard that has no norm above itself]"[144] for the Church and also for her teaching office, the Magisterium?

This question becomes particularly important when we understand and appreciate that the *parathêkê* was entrusted to the Church for safekeeping, but "that did not mean that the Church was to preserve the Gospel of life as a lifeless treasure. . . . The treasure of apostolic paradosis was not a mummy which after embalming was locked in a tomb and guarded. The striving for an ever deep understanding of the Gospel within the Church, and the tendencies hostile to the Gospel which forced their way into the Church from outside, confronted those to whom the Gospel was entrusted with perpetually new situations and consequently with perpetually new tasks."[145] The upshot of this claim is that the Gospel of Jesus Christ transmitted by the apostolic paradosis assumes the mode of existence, not only in Holy Scripture, which is that paradosis's "literary concretization" (in Karl Rahner's wonderfully apt phrase[146]), but also in

---

142. Nichols, *Shape of Catholic Theology*, 176.
143. Ibid., 176–77.
144. Ibid., 177.
145. Geiselmann, *Meaning of Tradition*, 29.
146. Rahner, *Foundations of Christian Faith*, 363.

the ecclesiastical paradosis, meaning thereby in the "teaching, liturgy, and life of the Church, and in the hearts of the faithful" (2 Cor 3:3; 1 Thess 4:9; 1 John 2:28)."[147] Tradition in this sense encompasses the way of life and faith of the whole Church—the institutions, liturgy, sacraments, councils, creeds, catechisms, and practices as well as the supreme rule of faith, which is the Holy Scripture. "Tradition as the Christian religion itself, the life and consciousness of the Church considered as a reflection of the word of God, of God's self-communication, is necessarily a reality at once larger than the Bible and inclusive of it."[148] Again, how does Scripture function in this Catholic view as the supreme norm of faith?

The brief answer to this question here must be that to read, study, and interpret the Scriptures in the proper context of the life and faith of the Church "is not to appeal away from Scripture to something other than Scripture."[149] That is, adds Nichols, it "is not, *pace* Protestant fears, to submit the Bible to an alien authority, but rather to identify and declare what is the Bible's own deepest reality" as it is expressed in the Church's tradition, "in the entire range of articulations of the life of faith that the past has bequeathed to us."[150] Elsewhere Nichols speaks of these "articulations" as "perennially valid sources from which insight and illumination flow down to us in the life of faith."[151] Nichols elaborates:

> If someone writes a book on the Eucharist, for example, and we are asked what we think of it, we should judge it in the light of the sources, monuments, or criteria that come to us from Tradition. So for instance we should ask, How does the book stand in relation to Scripture's witness on the Eucharist? How does its sense of the Eucharist match up to what is found in the texts and rubrics of

---

147. Pottmeyer, "Tradition," 1124.

148. Nichols, *Shape of Catholic Theology*, 169.

149. Ibid., 177.

150. Ibid., 177, 179. Yes, we must add, in the words of Ratzinger's commentary on *Dei Verbum*, "not everything that exists in the Church must for that reason be also a legitimate tradition.... Consequently, tradition must not be considered only affirmatively, but also critically; we have Scripture as a criterion for this indispensable criticism of tradition, and tradition must therefore always be related back to it and measured by it." Still, adds Ratzinger, "on this point Vatican II has unfortunately not made any progress, but has more or less ignored the whole question of the criticism of tradition. By doing this, it has missed an opportunity for ecumenical dialogue.... That this opportunity has been missed can only be regarded as an unfortunate omission" ("Dogmatic Constitution on Divine Revelation," 185, 193).

151. Ibid., 178.

the Church's liturgies? In her art and architecture? In the writings of the Fathers? In the teachings of the councils? All of these are expressions of the Church's life and self-understanding, and so all of them are highly pertinent to judging the Catholicity of a piece of theological writing.[152]

Since Nichols holds that Scripture is the supreme norm of faith, then all these others sources are subordinate norms. This means that Scripture sets the norm for subsequent expressions of the Church's life and faith in her traditions, and hence it can therefore be described as (with words of *Dei Verbum*) "the supreme rule of faith."[153] To that extent," as Ratzinger puts it, "there exists something like a certain independence of Scripture as a separate, and in many respects perfectly unambiguous, criterion in face of the Church's magisterium." He adds, "What can be unambiguously recognized from Scripture, whether by scientific methods or by simple reading, has the function of a real criterion, the test of which even the pronouncements of the magisterium itself have to meet."[154] Yes, the Lord himself has delivered the Word of God to the Church, but at the same time she has the responsibility, indeed, the urgent task, "of guarding the purity of the testimony *once* given, and of defending" that Word "against the caprice *of gnosis* which perpetually seeks to establish its own autonomy" and rob it entirely of its binding normative authority.[155]

PROTESTANT CRITICS

Pace Protestant critics, the Church confesses the Scriptures to be, in the words of John Paul II, "the highest authority in matters of faith" while tradition is "indispensable to the interpretation of the Word of God."[156] So, as it stands the following statement by Reformed theologians, for example, Van Genderen and Velema, is simply false: "The Roman Catholic Church declared: All authority that Scripture has among us depends on the authority of the church."[157] I am not exactly sure why, but Protestant critics of the Catholic Church almost invariably miss this point that the

---

152. Ibid., 178–79.
153. *Dei Verbum*, no. 21.
154. Ratzinger, "Revelation and Tradition," 48–49.
155. Ibid., 49, 31.
156. John Paul II, *Ut Unum Sint*, no. 79.
157. *Concise Reformed Dogmatics*, 84.

Church does not "create the normative value of Scripture," as Yves Congar puts it, but "it can only recognize it." "One cannot say," adds Congar, "that Scripture takes its authority from the Church, or even its canonicity, fundamentally."[158] *Pace* Timothy Ward, the Catholic tradition does locate Scripture properly within the redemptive economy and the pattern of divine authority. It too ties "Scripture to God as a key part of his redemptive and revelatory activity, since that is precisely what he himself has done. ... In this sense the doctrine of Scripture ought to be a subsection within our doctrines of God, of redemption and of revelation."[159] Furthermore, *pace* Kevin Vanhoozer, ecclesiology is not first theology for the Catholic tradition. If Vanhoozer means to suggest that the primary principle or supreme rule of faith is the Magisterium of the Church, then *Dei Verbum* explicitly affirms the opposite. "The "Magisterium is not superior to the Word of God, but is its servant."[160] Unlike Cullmann, Ward and Vanhoover completely overlook this claim of *Dei Verbum*, namely, "the teaching office serves Scripture: *Magisterium verbum Dei ministrant*."[161] In other words, the teaching office of the Church must be a servant and not master of the Word of God "in order that the full and living Gospel might always be preserved in the Church through the bishops as the successors of the apostles."[162]

As Yves Congar also says, "The Magisterium is simply the servant, the purveyor of the rule. ... The Magisterium enjoys no autonomy with regard to the deposit [of faith]. There is no moment of its activity as Magisterium ... when it is exempt from referring to the deposit and to its statements, since the former is merely a witness to the latter." There is more: "The grace promised to the Magisterium is not one of *inspiration*, but of *assistance*. It is not a gift of invention, but of discernment. ... The Magisterium does not have an autonomous value: it receives assistance only when it keeps, interprets and defines the *Revelation*, of which it has been made a witness. Similarly, the Church has no power to create truth."[163]

---

158. Congar, *Tradition and Traditions*, 419. Berkouwer, *Vatikaans Concilie en de nieuwe theologie*, 105–33; ET: *The Second Vatican Council and the New Catholicism*, 89–111.

159. Ward, *Words of Life*, 95.

160. *Dei Verbum*, no. 10.

161. Cullmann, "New Direction," 48. Obermann, *Forerunners of the Reformation*, 58.

162. *Dei Verbum*, no. 7.

163. Congar, *Meaning of Tradition*, 70–71, 81.

And if it still isn't clear that the Church is not a source of revelation in Catholic teaching, Congar forcefully states:

> To imagine that the Church, at a given moment in its history, could hold as of a faith a point which had *no* statable support in Scripture, would amount to thinking that an article of faith could exist without bearing any relation to the centre of revelation, and thus attributing to the Church and its magisterium a gift equivalent to the charism of revelation, unless we postulate, gratuitously, the existence of an esoteric oral apostolic tradition, for which there exists no evidence whatsoever. It is an express principle of Catholic teaching that the Church can only define what has been revealed; faith can only have to do with what is formally guaranteed by God.[164]

Furthermore, both Vatican I and II gave the same reply when asked why the Church honors as sacred and canonical the books of the Old and New Testaments, whole and entire, with all their parts. In the words of the Fathers of Vatican II, "The divinely revealed realities, which are contained and presented in the text of sacred Scripture, have been written down under the inspiration of the Holy Spirit. For Holy Mother Church relying on the faith of the apostolic age, accepts as sacred and canonical the books of the Old and New Testaments, whole and entire, with all their parts, on the grounds that, written under the inspiration of the Holy Spirit (cf. Jn 20:31; 2 Tim 3:16; 2 Pet 1:19–21; 3:15–16), they have God as their author, and have been handed on as such to the Church herself."[165] The 1870 Dogmatic Constitution on the Catholic Faith of Vatican I similarly affirms the Holy Scripture's plenary inspiration: the "books of the Old and New Testament are to be received as sacred and canonical, in their integrity, with all their parts."[166] Why, then, does the Church hold the books of the Old and New Testaments to be sacred and canonical? Well, "not because, having been carefully composed by mere human industry, they were afterwards approved by her [the Church's authority], nor merely because they contain

---

164. Congar, *Tradition and Traditions*, 414.

165. *Dei Verbum*, no. 11. In view of the teaching of Vatican I and II, as cited in the text, on the relationship between inspiration and canonicity, Sandra M. Schneiders is simply wrong to claim "that the Church never considered inspiration the grounds or criterion for including a writing in the canon but, once a book was canonized, it was regarded as inspired" (*Revelatory Text*, 47).

166. Vatican I, 1870, *Decreta Dogmatica Concilii Vaticani de Fide Catholica et de Ecclesia Christi*, Chapter II, *Of Revelation*, 241.

revelation, with no admixture of error; *but because, having been written by the inspiration of the Holy Ghost, they have God for their author, and have been delivered as such to the Church herself.*"[167] Thus, the Scriptures are canonical because they are inspired, God-breathed, not vice-versa: inspired because they are canonical. In fact, as Benedict XVI has recently argued, "since Scripture is inspired, there is a supreme principal for its correct interpretation without which the sacred writings would remain a dead letter of the past alone: Sacred Scripture 'must be read and interpreted with its divine authorship in mind' (*Dei Verbum*, no. 12)."[168]

Of course the Church does play an irreplaceable role in the theology of Holy Scripture since we have to ask how the canon was arrived at, and hence how the Church's act of canonization is to be theologically described. But we need a theological account of the Church's action that can be consistent with Vatican I and II and thus that can be seen as the "'accepting', the *recipere* of the canon."[169] In other words, in the act of canonizing, the Church's act is a receptive rather than an authorizing act. Put differently, Yves Congar reiterates this very point: "It is not that the Church and her Magisterium actually create the canon; even less do they endow Scripture with its authority, as mistakenly rather than intentionally certain Catholic apologists have sometimes maintained. With this dogma, as with others, Church and Magisterium simply recognize the truth established by *God's* action, [and] submit to it."[170]

Timothy Ward misses precisely this point in the contrast he draws between Protestants and Catholics: for the former the act of canonization is a receptive act, but for the latter it is an act of creating the canon according to the Church's own authority. I take Ward to mean that he thinks the Catholic tradition holds that the Scriptures are inspired, and hence have authority, because they are canonical. By contrast, for Protestants

---

167. Ibid., 242.

168. "Address of His Holiness Benedict XVI to the Participants in the Plenary Assembly of the Pontifical Biblical Commission."

169. Berkouwer, *De Heilige Schrift*, I, 89 [72]. Reformed theologian Berkouwer is more in tune with the Catholic teaching of Vatican II's *Dei Verbum* than is Catholic theologian Michael G. Lawler who writes that "[scriptural] authority... is social and socially approved authority, derived not from scripture itself but from the community of believers, for that community has, first, canonized and, then, accepted scripture as its classical representation of the God encountered in the immediate experience of Jesus, and established it as a secondary revelation" (*What Is and What Ought to Be*, 84).

170. Congar, *Meaning of Tradition*, 110.

the compilation of the canon is "an act in service of his [the Holy Spirit's] original authorship of Scripture by which he brought the church, through a complex historical process, to recognize which books he had in effect authored and which he had not.... Through the Spirit the church therefore did not create the canon of Scripture, but came to recognize it."[171] But this is precisely what Vatican I and II affirm, as I showed above. So Ward is mistaken in claming that Roman Catholics believe that the Holy Spirit speaks "through the official teaching institution of the church in Rome . . . *in order to give Scripture its authority*."[172]

The basic point that the Church's act of canonization is a receptive act is also clearly made by Aidan Nichols when he criticizes the view of inspiration, the so-called approbation theory, explicitly rejected by Vatican I, which reduces inspiration to canonicity. This theory forgets, he says, that "when the Church declares a book to be part of the canon she does not render it inspired but, on the contrary, claims that God has already been operative in its making, that 'merely giving one's approval to what someone else has written does not make one the author of the canon.' So this theory down by claiming for the Church something the Church has never dared to claim for itself."[173] In sum, the Church's act of canonization has noetic but not ontological force, acknowledging what Scripture is, but not making it so.[174] As Ward correctly says, "This is an aspect of God's faithfulness to and consistency with his Word, bringing about human recognition of what he had already performed in the breathing out of Scripture."[175] So the formation of the canon is the reception and acceptance of the authority of Scripture, of what Scripture *is*, not the conferral

---

171. Ward, *Words of Life*, 92. Unlike Ward, philosopher Richard Swinburne understands the point that the Church holds the Scripture to be canonical because inspired, not vice-versa. He writes: "The First Vatican Council affirmed that the Church recognized books as Scripture in virtue of their prior inspiration; the inspiration existed prior to its recognition" (*Revelation*, 175 n. 12). In addition, Swinburne says, "What the Church proclaimed with respect to the Bible was not just 'here is a book which we have found and recognized as true,' but 'here is a book which we have found and recognized as inspired by God and so as true'" (175).

172. Ibid., 110; emphasis added.

173. Nichols, *Shape of Catholic Theology*, 120.

174. This, too, is the view of Kevin Vanhoozer, "The Bible is not Scripture simply because an interpretative community decides to use it as such.... The church acknowledges what the Bible is—divine discourse—but this acknowledgment does not make it so" ("Scripture and tradition," 165).

175. Ward, *Words of Life*, 92.

by the Church of such authority on Scripture. Nevertheless, such an act of reception is still an "extension of Christ's active, communicative presence in the Spirit's power through the commissioned apostolic testimony" of Peter and his apostolic successors."[176]

The agent or subject of transmission of the deposit of faith is the Church, the whole Church, the People of God, the Body of Christ, but in a singularly unique way the chief subject of tradition is the Church's teaching office, or Magisterium, the hierarchy, whose delegated authority, given to Peter and his successors by Christ the Lord himself is located in the power of the keys (see Matt 16:17–19)—keeping faithfully, judging authentically and defining infallibly the content of the deposit.[177] The Holy Scripture is the supreme rule of faith, and the Magisterium is simply its servant, not herself the rule of faith; rather she is, says Congar, "the purveyor of the rule, but it acts by authority coming from God and, when the need arises, makes use of this authority." Yes, adds Congar, "the *rule* of faith is inherent to the *object* of faith; the Magisterium is 'normative' for the believer in that it transmits the object of faith, that is, the norm."[178]

Furthermore, the Tradition of the Gospel, promised by the prophets, truly, fully, and unsurpassably disclosed in Jesus Christ, and proclaimed by the apostles, is the singularly unique source of all truth, indeed, all that is necessary for salvation. Tradition in this sense is theologically *prior* to both Scripture and tradition and "flow out from the same divine wellspring," from the "single sacred deposit of the Word of God, which is entrusted to the Church."[179] In other words, "the saving Gospel is contained entirely in the Scriptures, as it is also contained entirely in tradition."[180] Scripture, God's written revelation, and unwritten traditions are *not* two independent sources of divine revelation, meaning thereby that each is incomplete and insufficient without the other. In short, on this view, revelation does not come in two separate sources.

Still, the two source theory of revelation is certainly the view that Bavinck knew, criticizes, and rejects.[181] The two source theory is distin-

---

176. Webster, *Holy Scripture*, 59.
177. Congar, *Meaning of Tradition*, 45, 64–67. See also, *Dei Verbum*, no. 10.
178. Ibid., 70.
179. *Dei Verbum*, nos. 9–10.
180. Congar, *Meaning of Tradition*, 42.
181. Bavinck, *Gereformeerde Dogmatiek*, I, 455–65 [485–94].

guished from the view that revelation in its transmission, the Tradition of the Gospel, comes to us in two different ways. In other words, Scripture and tradition are two modalities by which the Tradition of the Gospel, the whole Gospel, one and the same revelation, is communicated to men. Regarding Holy Scripture, which is the "literary concretization" (to use again Rahner's wonderfully apt phrase[182]) of the Tradition of the Gospel, *Dei Verbum* writes, "Sacred Scripture is the speech of God as it is put down in writing under the breath of the Holy Spirit." And in regard to tradition, it "transmits in its entirety the Word of God which has been entrusted to the apostles by Christ the Lord and the Holy Spirit." "It transmits it to the successors of the apostles so that," *Dei Verbum* adds, "enlightened by the Spirit of truth, they may faithfully preserve, expound and spread it abroad by their preaching."[183]

There remains to say on the question of Scripture and tradition, first, that the same value should not be attributed to them. Congar rightly states, "Scripture has an absolute sovereignty; it is of divine origin, even in its literary form; it governs tradition and the Church, whereas it is not governed by tradition or by the Church."[184] "If tradition or the Magisterium," adds Congar, "claimed to teach something contradicting the Holy Scriptures, it would certainly be false, and the faithful ought to reject it."[185] But someone may object. Doesn't *Dei Verbum* make the opposite point that Congar is making about the value of Scripture and tradition by putting both on the same level? It says, "Both Scripture and Tradition must be accepted and honored with equal feelings of devotion and reverence."[186] What does this passage mean? Is it affirming the two-source theory of revelation, or, alternatively, simply the hermeneutical insufficiency of Scripture and hence the interpretative function of tradition?

I want to make a second point now in answering this question. That is, I don't think that *Dei Verbum* is affirming the two-source theory. Although I cannot argue the point fully here, *Dei Verbum* is not putting Scripture and tradition on the same level of authority. Even Bavinck acknowledges that "the Roman Catholic Church" holds "that Scripture

---

182. Rahner, *Foundations of Christian Faith*, 363.
183. *Dei Verbum*, no. 9.
184. Congar, *Tradition and Traditions*, 422.
185. Congar, *Meaning of Tradition*, 100.
186. *Dei Verbum*, no. 9.

is complete, constitutes an organic whole, and that the canon is closed. However highly it esteemed tradition, in theory it never ventured to put the decisions of the church on a par with Scripture. It still makes a distinction between the word of God and the word of the church."[187] If we read this just cited passage from *Dei Verbum* in context we shall see that *Dei Verbum* is expressing a point about the necessary relationship between Scripture and tradition such that the Church cannot come to understanding and certainty of revealed truth from Scripture alone. In other words, it is affirming the hermeneutical insufficiency of Holy Scripture, "according to which Scripture requires supplementation by tradition only as an aid to its correct understanding."[188] Using *Dei Verbum*'s own words, "The Church does not draw her certainty about all revealed truths from the holy Scripture alone."[189] As Nichols correctly explains, this means that Scripture is taken to be an interpretative source rather than a source of revelation. He adds, "It can be said that tradition is more a medium than it is an object. Though tradition has its own *loci* [including liturgy, council, creeds, *sensus fidelium*], it is more an environment or context or atmosphere in which we read Scripture than an object set side by side with Scripture."[190]

Bavinck's complaint, then, that the Church holds to the insufficiency of Scripture doesn't mean that the Church wants to "augment [Scripture] with tradition," as he claims.[191] Rather, the Church in *Dei Verbum* is, partly, saying what Bavinck said in 1895. "Therefore, a tradition is needed that preserves the connectedness between Scripture and the religious life of our time. Tradition in its proper sense is the interpretation and application of the eternal truth in the vernacular and life of the present generation. Scripture without such a tradition is impossible."[192] Therefore: "there is not a single point of belief that the Church holds by tradition alone, without any reference to Scripture; [and vice-versa] just as there

---

187. Bavinck, *Gereformeerde Dogmatiek*, I, 459 [489].
188. Pottmeyer, "Tradition," 1123.
189. *Dei Verbum*, no. 9.
190. Nichols, *Shape of Catholic Theology*, 22.
191. Bavinck, *Gereformeerde Dogmatiek*, I, 460 [489].
192. Ibid., 464 [493].

is not a single dogma that is derived from Scripture alone, without being explained by tradition."[193]

One third and final point I want to make about the relation between Scripture and tradition is that there is no interpretation and understanding of Holy Scripture not only without tradition, but also without the Church. On this matter of the relation between Scripture and the Church, Bavinck stresses their reciprocal interrelationship even while affirming the subordination of the latter to the former. In other words, Bavinck seems to affirm that Scripture and the Church are interrelated and joined together such that one cannot maintain itself without the other. He writes eloquently:

> In applying [objective] revelation, illumination and regeneration, Scripture and church are linked to each other.... Revelation in this dispensation is continued jointly in Scripture and in the church. In this context the two are most intimately connected. Scripture is the light of the church, the church the life of Scripture. Apart from the church, Scripture is an enigma and an offense. Without rebirth no one can know it. Those who do not participate in its life cannot understand its meaning and point of view. Conversely, the life of the church is a complete mystery unless Scripture sheds it light upon it. Scripture explains the church; the church understands Scripture. In the church Scripture confirms and seals its revelation, and in Scripture the Christian—and the church—learn to understand themselves in their relation to God and the world, in their past, present, and future.[194]

Elsewhere in his *magnum opus*, *Gereformeerde Dogmatiek*, Bavinck develops a Scriptural view of tradition in which he affirms that "tradition preserves the connectedness between Scripture and the religious life of our time." "Tradition in its proper sense is," he adds, "the interpretation and application of the eternal truth [of God's Word] in the vernacular and life of the present. *Scripture without such a tradition is impossible*."[195] In light of Bavinck's claims about Scripture, tradition and the Church, we can say that the three realities of Sacred Tradition, Sacred Scripture and Magisterium of the Church exist in reciprocal interrelations with each other such that, *Dei Verbum* rightly says, "one of them cannot stand

---

193. Congar, *Meaning of Tradition*, 48–49; see also, 106.
194. Bavinck, *Gereformeerde Dogmatiek*, I, 356 [384].
195. Ibid., 464 [493].

without the others."[196] "Scripture's sovereign character does not prevent it from being *just one component* of God's redemptive work, a work which demands in addition the Church and Tradition. Nor does it mean that there do not hold between these three realities certain reciprocal interrelations which make it impossible to isolate them completely from one another, still less to actually oppose them."[197] Scripture, tradition and Magisterium work together, "each in its own way under the action of the one Holy Spirit," so that "all [may] contribute effectively to the salvation of souls."[198]

OBJECTIVE AND SUBJECTIVE REVELATION

Returning now to the remaining elements of the schema (S) that I have been using here to give an account of special revelation—(S) m reveals a to n by means of (through, etc.) k—I turn to the variable n, which refers to the recipient of the revelation. God's special revelation in the Scriptures is redemptive revelation. God reveals himself in Scripture not only to increase man's knowledge but to bring us the knowledge of the eternal salvation of mankind in Jesus Christ. "By divine revelation, God chose to show forth and communicate himself and the eternal decrees of his will concerning the salvation of mankind. He wished, in other words, 'to share with us divine benefits which entirely surpass the powers of the human mind to understand.'"[199]

According to Vatican II, then, Scripture is a manifestation of God's revelatory activity in the history of redemption. It thus has a salvific purpose and, indeed, a distinctive kind of power. For the gospel is the "power of God unto salvation" (Rom 1:16; see also, 2 Tim 3:15, John 6:63). Of course, then, the Scripture informs us by giving knowledge of God's revealed truth, but they not only gives us the truth "needed to reform, to sanctify our lives, we also find there the *ability* to do so; for the Holy Spirit of God works in and with the Word, and he works in saving power [1

---

196. *Dei Verbum*, no. 10.
197. Congar, *Tradition and Traditions*, 422.
198. *Dei Verbum*, no. 10.
199. *Dei Verbum*, no. 6. The quote within the quotation is from Vatican I, 1870, *Decreta Dogmatica Concilii Vaticani de Fide Catholica et de Ecclesia Christi*, chapter 2, *Of Revelation*, in *Creeds of Christendom*, 241.

Thess 1:5; see also 2:13]."[200] "The Word of God is living and active" (Heb 4:12), and his Word has grace and power that "is able to build you up and to give you the inheritance among all those who are sanctified" (Acts 20:32). We may even say, according to Congar, that the Holy Scripture "is a sort of sacrament conveying the Gospel so that we may live by it." He explains:

> The divine Scriptures are regarded as a kind of sacrament: a grace-bearing sign that effectively realizes communion with God, and salvation, when it is used in the right condition. These conditions are obviously spiritual humility, purity of heart, a true desire to seek God and a strong love of the Gospel. . . . [Thus] it requires that we place ourselves in God's plan, in the framework of his Covenant, in the perspective of the communication he himself wishes to make to us, that is, in the fellowship of his people. The Scriptures do not surrender their meaning by the bare text; they surrender it to a mind that is living, and living in the conditions of the Covenant. This mind, or living subject, . . . is the Church, God's People, the Body of Christ and Temple of the Holy Spirit.[201]

Since Holy Scripture has a redemptive focus with the gospel message of integral salvation, we can, therefore, understand why the recipient of this redemptive revelation is *fallen humanity*. "But this soteriological character must then be understood scripturally, i.e., in the sense that the whole person has been tainted by sin and must therefore also be wholly saved and redeemed by grace in Christ. Errors, lies, darkness of intellect are all constituents of sin; hence the revelation of salvation ought not to consist only in a communication of life but also in the announcement of truth. Christ has become for us wisdom and righteousness (1 Cor 1:30). He is the complete Savior, the Savior of the whole person and the whole world."[202] Furthermore, I contend that, as far as humanity is concerned, the Church, which is the new and reborn humanity in Christ, is the soteriological goal of the Kingdom —of the people elected and called by God to share in the joy of the Kingdom. But the Kingdom of God is broader than the Church. It is the saving plan of God that is realized in and through

---

200. Frame, "Rationality and Scripture," 298.

201. Congar, *Meaning of Tradition*, 102, 90; idem., *Tradition and Traditions*, 388–89, 403–6. I am indebted to Hans Boersma for suggesting that I think of the written Word of God as a kind of sacrament.

202. Bavinck, *Gereformeerde Dogmatiek*, I, 318 [345].

Christ, encompassing the whole of creation. In this connection, Bavinck is right,

> God's aim in special revelation is both much deeper and reaches farther. It is none other than to redeem human beings in their totality of body and soul with all their capacities and powers; to redeem not only individual, isolated human beings but humanity as an organic whole. Finally, the goal is to redeem not just humanity apart from all the other creatures but along with humanity to wrest heaven and earth, in a word, the whole world in its organic interconnectedness, from the power of sin and again to cause the glory of God to shine forth from every creature. Sin has spoiled and destroyed everything: the intellect and the will, the ethical and physical world. Accordingly, it is the whole person and the whole cosmos at whose salvation and restoration God is aiming in his revelation. God's revelation, therefore, is certainly soteriological, but the object of that salvation is the cosmos, and not only the ethical or the will to the exclusion of the intellect, and not only the psychological to the exclusion of the somatic and physical, but everything in conjunction. For God has consigned all human beings under sin that he might have mercy upon all (Rom 5:15f.; 11:32; Gal 3:22).[203]

I turn now to the last variable in the schema, k, which pertains to the mode or means of revelation. We spoke above of special revelation as an act of God by which he communicates himself and the mystery of his will to man. In this connection, we need to understand that this communicative act of God reaches us in two ways, and hence I will distinguish between the external and the internal principle of knowing (*principium cognoscendi externum* and *internum*), the external and the internal word, objective revelation and subjective illumination. Francis Martin gives an account of these two ways in the following[204]:

> There is first God's activity in history that is accomplished through intimately connected words and deeds, culminating in Jesus Christ, who is both the mediator and fullness of revelation [*principium cognoscendi externum*]. Second, there is the activity, also historical and also mediated by Jesus Christ, by which God moves and assists someone to believe, that is to commit himself ... to God, yielding to and accepting the divine self-communication [*princi-*

---

203. Ibid., 319 [346].
204. His account is based on *Dei Verbum*, particularly nos. 2–6.

pium cognoscendi internum]. While the first activity was brought to completion by the resurrection of Jesus Christ, the second is still continuing. This second dimension is always present as the Holy Spirit brings each person into living contact with the Father's self-revelation in Jesus Christ from the dead. In a mysterious interaction of divine initiative and human freedom, the Holy Spirit leads those who assent to his action from the first act of yielding in faith to its consummation in a transforming vision of God. Only then does God completely manifest and communicate himself, which allows us to obtain a clear knowledge of the eternal mystery of his will. Revelation actually exists only when both dimensions of the divine activity are present: the words and deeds culminating in Christ and the personal appropriation of these realities.[205]

Everything hangs inseparably together in this doctrine of revelation: corresponding to the objective revelation of God occurring outside of ourselves in acts, in historical events culminating in the person and work of Christ, who is the fullness and mediator of all revelation, there is the subjective revelation of the Spirit working in order than man may acknowledge and accept that revelation. In sum, corresponding to this external principle of knowing there is an internal principle, to this objective revelation there is a subjective revelation or illumination—all are part of the one activity we call revelation.

Undoubtedly, Fr. Martin agrees that objective revelation, which consists in acts, in the events of history culminating in the person and work of Christ, but also in words, in the communication of truth, *exists independently* of the believer's personal appropriation of those realities. Of course he is correct to insist on an internal revelation or illumination of the Spirit. As Bavinck puts it, "objective revelation in Christ is not sufficient, but there needs to be added a working of the Spirit in order that human beings may acknowledge and accept that revelation of God and thereby become the image of the Son." Most significant, Bavinck adds, "[S]o external and objective revelation demands an internal revelation in the subject. . . . But it can come into its own only if it is positioned in relation to the objective revelation granted in Christ. Detached from or elevated above this revelation, it loses its criterion and corrective and opens the door to all sorts of arbitrariness and fanaticism. Even the very concept of subjective revelation is determined and controlled by that of

---

205. Martin, *Feminist Question*, 2–3.

objective revelation."²⁰⁶ Bavinck's point that an external and objective revelation demands an internal revelation in the subject is made also by Ratzinger: "Revelation is in fact fully present only when, in the addition to the material statements which testify to it, its own inner reality is itself operative in the form of faith. Consequently, revelation to some degree includes its recipient, without whom it does not exist. Revelation cannot be pocketed like a book one carries around. It is a living reality which calls for the living man as the location of its presence."²⁰⁷

Furthermore, it is in the context of the second dimension, of the *principium cognoscendi internum*, of God's active self-presence as the Holy Spirit, of subjective revelation, that we can see a positive role for "experience": this is the context within which we hear Scripture, and hence the context in which the Scripture exercises its normative authority (*principium cognoscendi externum*).²⁰⁸ I will turn to develop the relation between revelation and experience in chapter 3.

NORMATIVE AUTHORITY OF SCRIPTURE

Now, something further must be said, even if only briefly, about the fundamental doctrine that the self-revelation of God is deposited in Holy Scripture. Scripture is one of God's redemptive acts and hence as such the instrumental efficient cause of the knowledge of divinely revealed realities. How then does the gift of Holy Scripture stand with respect to divine revelation? We must avoid two extremes here: either completely allowing revelation to *coincide* with the whole of God's revelation to us, ignoring either creation revelation, or, more particularly, the history of revelation—

---

206. Bavinck, *Gereformeerde Dogmatiek*, I, 320 [347–48].

207. Ratzinger, "Revelation and Tradition," 36. Ratzinger is opposing here a view of biblical revelation in which the word revelation is seen as a lifeless treasure, a mere collection of doctrines, rather than as a "dynamic process between God and man, which consistently becomes reality only in an encounter" ("Biblical Interpretation in Conflict," 122). Yes, Ratzinger affirms the full validity of the teaching that the "reality of revelation is a reality of the word—that in the word, the proclamation of the reality of revelation comes to me.... It nonetheless remains true that the mere word before us, available to us, is not yet itself the reality of revelation, which is never just 'available' to us. What is said here is simply intended to point to the difference between the word and the reality that occurs within it, a difference not abolished by the nature of revelation as word [the verbal character of revelation]" ("Revelation and Tradition," note 12, 70).

208. For a brief but helpful discussion of this place for "experience," see Wright, *Last Word*, 102–3.

creation, fall, redemption, eschaton—that is an antecedent and broader reality necessary for understanding the unique and distinctive revelational and redemptive act of God in divinely inspiring his written word, the Holy Scriptures. *Dei Verbum* correctly understands divine inspiration of the Holy Scriptures to be an element in revelation. In sum, Ridderbos is right, "Scripture has a history. It is a product of God's revelatory activity in the history of redemption. Therefore the revelatory character of the Bible should not be separated in a mechanical fashion from the history of redemption in which it came into being, for its revelatory character is neither an isolated phenomenon nor derived only from formal statements of Scripture concerning its authority."[209]

Alternatively, we must avoid completely *detaching* revelation from Scripture, letting Scripture stand by itself, construing Scripture deistically, such that it becomes a mere human record or witness to revelation of Spirit-empowered humans, rather than one of God's redemptive acts, and hence a part of the economy of revelation in which the Bible is understood to be God speaking.[210] Bavinck focuses our attention on the various acclamations that often accompany this view of Scripture. "'Not the letter but the Spirit'; 'not the Scripture but the person of Christ'; . . . And Lessing managed to produce the familiar petition: 'O Luther, you great and holy man! You have delivered us from the yoke of the pope but who will deliver us from the yoke of the letter, the paper pope'? This view is no less wrong but even more dangerous than the other. For in many cases revelation and divine inspiration do coincide. . . . Those who deny divine inspiration and despise Scripture will also in large part lose the revelation; they will have left nothing but human writings. In addition the revelation, even where in fact or word it preceded its recording, is known to us solely from Holy Scripture. We literally know nothing of the revelation of God in the time of Israel and in Christ except from Holy Scripture. There is no other primary principle."[211] The Holy Scripture is, then, the primary principle, or

---

209. Ridderbos, *Heilsgeschiedenis en Heilige Schrift Van Het Nieuwe Testament*, 9; ET: *Redemptive History and the New Testament Scriptures*, ix.

210. Seerveld, *How to Read the Bible to Hear God Speak*, 79. Seerveld writes, "The history-telling of holy Scriptures is never just archival data because the script is God-speaking about certain actualities (indicative) and what God's deeds and the human responses inscribed mean for us readers today on how to respond to the Lord (imperative)" (80).

211. Bavinck, *Gereformeerde Dogmatiek*, I, [381–82].

supreme rule of faith. God made it so through divine inspiration, which is an element in the drama of God's redeeming and communicative self-giving in the economy of revelation. In the words of *Dei Verbum*, "For since [the Scriptures] are inspired by God and committed to writing once and for all time, they present God's own Word in an unalterable form, and they make the voice of the Holy Spirit sound again and again in the words of the prophets and apostles. It follows that all the preaching of the Church, as indeed the entire Christian religion, should be nourished by sacred Scripture."[212] This means that the doctrine of Holy Scripture is, as a matter of first principle, according to *Dei Verbum*, an aspect of the doctrine of God, of his redemptive self-revelation in the economy of revelation, rather than of the doctrine of the Church.

INERRANCY

Now, since Holy Scripture is the supreme norm of faith, the *norma normans, non normata* [the normative standard that has no norm above itself], "Scripture can contain no error in its identification of divinely revealed truth."[213] With this claim we come to the issue of inerrancy. The Catholic tradition sees inerrancy to be the consequence of the Bible's divine authorship and inspiration. "*God is the author of Sacred Scripture.* 'The divinely revealed realities [of salvation history], which are contained and presented in the text of Sacred Scripture, have been written down under the inspiration of the Holy Spirit.'"[214] *Dei Verbum* expands, "Since, therefore, all that the inspired authors, or sacred writers, affirm should be regarded as affirmed by the Holy Spirit, we must acknowledge that the books of Scripture firmly, faithfully and without error, teach that truth which God, for the sake of our salvation, wished to see confided to the sacred Scriptures."[215] The biblical doctrine of inerrancy is evidently an implication of the authority of Scripture. However briefly, I must say something about inerrancy because, not only does Vatican II reaffirm the inerrancy of Scripture, taking inerrancy to be a natural implication of divine inspiration, of the Holy Spirit's work of inspiring the whole of

---

212. *Dei Verbum*, no. 21.

213. Grisez, *Way of the Lord Jesus*, 1:836.

214. *Catechism of the Catholic Church*, no. 105. The quote within the quote is from *Dei Verbum*, no. 11.

215. *Dei Verbum*, no. 11.

Scripture and, in consequence, making no false assertions. But also inerrancy is a consequence of the full trustworthiness of Scripture and hence of "the speech act of a God who cannot lie," as Ward puts it, "and who has chosen to reveal himself to us in words."[216]

There are three points I want to make about the passage on inerrancy from *Dei Verbum*, no. 11.[217] First, we must get it straight that the adjectival clause, "for the sake of our salvation," does not qualify the truth that God reveals but rather God's purpose in revealing himself. They are mistaken who interpret this passage to mean that the sort of truth that is taught in Scripture is salvific truth, and hence that Vatican II espoused a version of limited inerrancy, in the sense that scripture is without error only regarding matters of faith and morals and facts bound up with the history of salvation. In other words, *Dei Verbum* is stating that our salvation is the purpose for which God gave us biblical truth. Rather than restricting biblical inerrancy to "some subset of the assertions contained in it," such as those assertions that bear upon matters of faith and morals, the most relevant sources *Dei Verbum* refers to in footnote 5, namely, the encyclicals of Leo XIII and Pius XII, *Providentissimus Deus* (1893) and *Divino afflante Spiritu* (1943),[218] respectively, "exclude altogether the possibility

---

216. Ward, *Words of Life*, 135.

217. I am much indebted here to Nichols, *Shape of Catholic Theology*, 131–40; Grisez, *Way of the Lord Jesus*, 1:835–39; Harrison, "Truth and Salvific Purpose of Sacred Scripture according to *Dei Verbum*, Article 11"; idem. "Does Vatican II allow for errors in Sacred Scripture?" Helpful, too, was Ward, 137–38, and also Frame, "Rationality and Scripture," 293–97.

218. The encyclicals by Leo and Pius are found in *The Scripture Documents: An Anthology of Official Catholic Teachings*, 37–61, and 115–39, respectively. Leo states, "But it is absolutely wrong and forbidden either to narrow inspiration to certain parts only of Holy Scripture or to admit that the sacred writer has erred. For the system of those who, in order to rid themselves of these difficulties, do not hesitate to concede that divine inspiration regards the things of faith and morals and nothing beyond, because (as they wrongly think) in a question of truth or falsehood of a passage, we should consider not so much what God has said as the reason and purpose in saying it—this system cannot be tolerated.... And so far is it from being possible that any error can coexist with inspiration, that inspiration not only is essentially incompatible with error but excludes and rejects it as absolutely and necessarily as it is impossible that God himself, the Supreme Truth, can utter that which is not true" (55). Pius similarly states: "When, subsequently, some Catholic writers, in spite of [Vatican I's] solemn definition of Catholic doctrine, by which such divine authority is claimed for the 'entire books [of Scripture] with all their parts', as to secure freedom from any error whatsoever, ventured to restrict the truth of Sacred Scripture solely to matters of faith and morals, and to regard other matters, whether in the domain of physical science or history, as *obiter dicta* [incidental references] and—as

of error from all assertions in Scripture."[219] What is more, the recent 1998 *Doctrinal Commentary on the Concluding Formula of the Professio Fidei*, issued by the then Joseph Cardinal Ratzinger, Prefect for the Congregation of the Doctrine of the Faith, states that "the Church proposes as divinely and formally revealed and, as such, as irreformable," meaning thereby as infallible truth, "the absence of error in the inspired sacred texts."[220] Furthermore, the importance of the inerrancy of Scripture was made clear in the recent 2008 synod of Catholic Bishops on the "Word of God" that declined to accept article 15 of the *Instrumentum Laboris* (working document). This article deals with the topic of inerrancy and seems to suggest a notion of restricted or limited inerrancy. Instead of accepting this article, the bishops proposed Proposition 12 to the Synod for further study: "The Synod proposes that the Congregation for the Doctrine of the Faith clarify the concepts of the Bible's inspiration and truth, together with their reciprocal relationship, so as to enable a better understanding of *Dei Verbum*, #11. In particular, there is a need to bring out clearly the originality of Catholic Biblical hermeneutics in this field."[221] Clearly, then, forty years after Vatican II's *Dei Verbum* the inerrancy of Scripture is of such importance that the bishops are asking for clarification.

The second point I wish to make follows *Dei Verbum* in arguing for the relevance of the genre or literary form of Scripture in determining "that meaning which God has thought well to manifest through the medium of [the sacred writers'] words." Understanding literary form will help us to see the sense in which "truth is differently presented and expressed in the various types of historical writing, in prophetical and poetical texts, and in other forms of literary expression."[222] The point I am trying to make

---

they contended—in no wise connected with faith, our predecessor of immortal memory, Leo XIII . . . justly and rightly condemned these errors and safeguarded the studies of the divine books by most wise precept and rules" (116).

219. Grisez, *Way of the Lord Jesus*, 1:839.

220. Ratzinger, *Doctrinal Commentary on the Concluding Formula of the Profession Fidei*, no. 11.

221. The translation of Proposition 12 is by Fr. Brian Harrison, "Does Vatican II allow for errors in Sacred Scripture?"

222. *Dei Verbum*, no. 12. Regarding literary genre and the historicity of the fall, see Henri Blocher: "The real issue when we try to interpret Genesis 2-3 is not whether we have a historical account of the fall, but whether or not we may read it as the account of a historical fall. The problem is not historiography as a genre narrowly defined—in annals, chronicles, or even saga—but correspondence with discrete realities in our or-

here is that Scripture is going to speak truly and hence error-free in all that it affirms when interpreted according both to the intended sense of its sacred writers and the corresponding literary form. In this connection, it is also important to clarify that inerrancy is compatible with the writers of Scripture "lacking modern technical precision, irregularities of grammar or spelling, observational descriptions of nature, the [truthful] reporting of falsehoods [not the truth of the propositions themselves], the use of hyperbole and round numbers, the topical [and not strictly chronological] arrangement of material, variant selections of material in parallel accounts, or the use of free citations."[223] That Scripture does not err in everything it affirms is compatible with these everyday features of ordinary language.[224] Indeed, Ward correctly notes, "it is by taking full account of these features that we shall be able to discern what in fact God is and is not asserting in Scripture."[225]

---

dinary space and sequential time" (*Original Sin*, 50). Karl Rahner makes a similar point as Blocher, distinguishing between "the historical content and the historical mode of expression," and asking whether "Adam's individuality belongs to the mode of expression or the (historical) content of ... the first chapters of Genesis." That is, is the literary genre of these chapters itself historical in the modern sense or is it just "a statement the *content* of which ... is constituted by an historical state of affairs" ("Theological Reflections on Monogenism," 252–53). See also, T. C. O'Brien, O.P., who writes, "Original sin is taken on the level of a *history* of salvation, and the state and the sin of Adam are treated as real events and parts of a divine plan, *economy*, for man. To regard the first sin and the fall as a mere symbol or mythological representation of men's collectivity in their sinful condition is incompatible with Catholic teaching, which envisages a real situation of a real person, namely a 'sin' actually committed by an individual together with its consequences for him." Again: "All the literary forms are shaped and directed to bring out as history God's plan of man's creation, fall and redemption. There is a real link between past events, under whatever literary form they appear, and the conditions present to the author and explained in the light of these origins. Unlike the ancient myths these Biblical accounts are not a symbolic expression of some universal truth; they are an account of an actual situation in terms of its causes: the present is seen in the past, the past in the present" (Appendix 3, "Thematic Conspectus of Catholic Teaching," and 4, "Old Testament," respectively, in vol. 26, *Original Sin*, of St. Thomas Aquinas, *Summa Theologiae* 1a2ae. 81–85, at 115 and 121).

223. This citation is from Article XIII of the 1978 Chicago Statement on Biblical Inerrancy (Online: http://www.reformed.org/documents/index.html?mainframe=http://www.reformed.org/documents/icbi.html), but the same point is made by Nichols, Grisez, Harrison, Ward, and last but not least, *Dei Verbum*, no 12. Also, Hodge and Warfield, *Inspiration*, 28–29.

224. Ward, *Words of Life*, 133.

225. Ibid.

Biblical Revelation and Authority 63

The third and final point I wish to make about inerrancy regards the relation between the salvific purpose of Holy Scripture and the presupposition that the Bible contains no assertions of false propositions. In what sense is the inerrant truth of Scripture focused on its relevance to man's salvation? Aidan Nichols gives one plausible answer to this question. "This means that the absolute, unconditional inerrancy of the Bible is a formal, not a material, inerrancy; inspiration has the effect of rendering Scripture inerrant under one formal perspective only, that of relevance to human salvation."[226] The formal perspective, or specific focus, of Scripture's inerrancy is, then, soteriological, having the overall objective that is directed toward teaching us about God's revelatory and redemptive actions toward us, rather than other needs, such as arise in the enterprises of science (e.g., a formula for converting mass in energy) or history for their own sakes (e.g., chronology). "In regard to history," as Harrison observes, "the sacred writers sometimes select and condense their material, relate events in an order which is not strictly chronological, give incomplete accounts, and so on. In a work dedicated to setting out the facts as clearly and methodically as possible in the interests of technically precise history, these might be judged as defects or errors."[227] Well, that judgment would be made only if we fail to observe differences in literary conventions or standards of precision between the times of the Bible and our own times.

Of course this conclusion does not mean that we can deduce *a priori* from the formal perspective, or redemptive focus, of Scripture as a whole that Scripture has no bearing on science and history, and as if we're saying that the Bible is inerrant only in matters of faith and morals. That would mean that we've returned to a restricted or limited view of inerrancy, which, as Aidan Nichols reminds us, has been "rejected by the papal teaching office from Leo XIII onwards."[228] Besides, such an *a priori* approach cannot be the case since facts about historical events that took place in space-time history are necessary to the biblical revelation itself for its own coherence. Nichols refers, in this connection, to historical events

---

226. Nichols, *Shape of Catholic Theology*, 138.
227. Harrison, "Truth and Salvific Purpose of Sacred Scripture According to *Dei Verbum*, Article 11," 17.
228. Nichols, *Shape of Catholic Theology*, 138.

such as the original sin of Adam and Eve,[229] biblical history of Israel,[230] the life, passion and death of Jesus Christ, the empty tomb, the resurrection, and the founding of his Church on the apostles, as well as the filling of the Church with the Holy Spirit, are facts bound up with the history of salvation, matters bearing directly upon revealed truth.[231] In other words, says Nichols, "If it could be shown that these events, or sequences (and clusters) of events, never happened, or that they happened in such a form

---

229. On this, see Nichols, *Epiphany*, 175–76: "The story of the Fall could be read as a symbolic account of human rebelliousness against God, of how all our cultural developments (as for the Genesis writer, clothing, metal-working, city-building) are spoilt by an element of vengefulness and pride. *Yet sin must have entered human life at some historical moment*, whether identifiable or not. For unless evil marred the creation of humanity contingently (i.e., historically), it could only have done so essentially (i.e., by God's own creative act), which is unthinkable. In claiming Adam (with Eve) as historical figures, the Church is confirmed by the New Testament, especially by Paul's appeal to Adam's fall as the act which Christ's redemptive act inverted. *Revelation presents both as historical events with metahistorical meaning*" (italics added). See also, *Catechism of the Catholic Church*, no. 390: "The account of the fall in *Genesis* 3 uses figurative language, but affirms a primeval event, a deed that took place *at the beginning of the history of man*. Revelation gives us the certainty of faith that the whole of human history is marked by the original fault freely committed by our first parents." John Paul II upholds the essential historicity of the Fall in Vol. II of *A Catechesis on The Creed*: "The description of the first sin, which we find in the third chapter of Genesis, acquires a greater clarity in the context of creation and of the bestowal of gifts. By these gifts, God constituted man in the state of holiness and of original justice. This description hinges on the transgression of the divine command not to eat 'of the fruit of the tree of the knowledge of good and evil.' This is to be interpreted by taking into account the character of the ancient text and especially its literary form. However, while bearing in mind this scientific requirement in the study of the first book of Sacred Scripture, it cannot be denied that one sure element emerges from the detailed account of the sin. It describes a primordial event, that is, a fact, which according to revelation took place at the beginning of human history" (27). Paul VI also proclaims Adam's historical fall in *The Credo of the People of God*, reaffirming the teaching of the Council of Trent, Fifth Session, June 17, 1546, on Original Sin.

230. Nichols gives us some idea of what that biblical history would include, for example, "the call of Abraham; the Exodus from Egypt; the Sinai experience of Moses; the establishment of the Davidic dynasty with its messianic promises; the Exile and restoration of Israel from Babylon" (*Shape of Catholic Theology*, 80).

231. Frame, "Rationality and Scripture," 296–97, "These events are crucial to any account of history, 'scientific' or otherwise." Furthermore, adds Frame, "the gospel message is a message of cosmic importance about the creation, fall and redemption not only of man, but of all things, and that it makes a demand upon all areas of human life including, of course his science. If Scripture is 'the Word of God written', then surely what God teaches us therein must be accepted, not only in its central thrust, but also in its *obiter dicta*. It is blasphemous for us to tell God that we honor only what we regard as the 'main drift' of his words."

that the Jewish and Christian interpretations of them are effectively excluded, then manifestly the claims of the Judeo-Christian religion would fall to the ground."[232] For, adds Nichols, "a revelation given in history, and bearing on the destiny of both history and cosmos, will necessarily entail some factual assertions about both."[233]

Moreover, in concluding my remarks about inerrancy, let me say something, however briefly, about what Nichols calls the "holistic aspect of inerrancy."[234] This aspect of inerrancy requires one to ask about the relevance of a particular biblical teaching to the perspective of the Bible as a whole, of what it means in the larger canonical context and its ultimate relevance to salvation. Of particular relevance to this book is the biblical teaching regarding the normative significance of sexual difference for a theology of marriage, of the embodiment of the human person and, accordingly, the place of the body in sexual morality, of the two-sex prerequisite of the "one flesh" union (Gen 2:24) for normative human sexual behavior. St. Paul, for one, regarded the significance of male-female differentiation in the context of marriage and the corresponding two-sex prerequisite in sexual ethics to be relevant truths tied to our salvation, to making choices worthy of the calling that we have received in Christ (see 1 Cor 6:19).[235] Nichols would rightly see these truths as inerrant given the message of the Bible as a whole. The question that remains to be asked, in light of this holistic treatment of inerrancy, is whether these salvifically relevant truths of biblical revelation are free from error under another formal perspective than simply that of salvation. For example, are these salvifically relevant truths free from error from the perspective of a rational sexual ethics grounded in the natural moral law? The answer to this question, says Nichols, "will depend ... on *a posteriori* considerations of its consonance with what is known of reality from other sources, such as those of natural law." In this connection, one may consider the philosophically relevant arguments of Germain Grisez, John Finnis, of Robert George and Patrick Lee on sex and marriage. Their arguments clearly sup-

---

232. Nichols, *Shape of Catholic Theology*, 80–81.
233. Nichols, *Epiphany*, 49.
234. Nichols, *Shape of Catholic Theology*, 138.
235. Gagnon, "Scriptural Perspectives on Homosexuality and Sexual Identity," 298–99.

port these salvifically relevant truths regarding marriage and sexual ethics to be free from error from the perspective of a rational sexual ethics.[236]

Of course there is much more that can be said about biblical inerrancy, but these three points must suffice for the purpose of setting out a Catholic doctrine of special revelation.

BIBLICAL AUTHORITY AND THE TEACHING OFFICE

Finally, in conclusion of this chapter and in preparation for the next, I want to return briefly to the question of Scriptural authority. Bavinck is a more careful interpreter of the Church's teaching on the doctrine of Scriptural authority than is either Ward or Vanhoozer. Unlike them, he at least begins by acknowledging that, according to Vatican I, "The church, by its recognition, does not make Scripture inspired, canonical, authentic, and so forth." Says Bavinck, "The Vatican Council (1870), after all, recognized the books of the Old and the New Testament as canonical precisely 'because, *written under the inspiration of the Holy Spirit, they have God as their author* and as such have been entrusted to the church.'"[237] Indeed, he even acknowledges that "Roman Catholic theologians distinguish between the authority of Scripture with respect to itself (*quoad se*) and with respect to us (*quoad nos*)."[238] The point of this distinction is to make clear that Scripture's canonical authority with respect to itself is grounded in its being divinely inspired, having divine authorship, and hence entrusted to the Church by the Holy Spirit, "as a divine deposit committed to the spouse of Christ to be faithfully protected and infallibly promulgated" (in the words of Vatican I). Thus, scriptural authority is not established *quoad nos*. Yet, Bavinck still insists that Rome faces a "powerful contradiction." "On the one hand, in the doctrine of Scripture they attempt to prove its inspiration and authority from Scripture itself. On the other, having come to the doctrine of the church, they attempt to weaken those proofs and to demonstrate that only the witness [or authority] of the church offers

---

236. Grisez, *Way of the Lord Jesus*, vol. 2, *Living a Christian Life*, 633–56. Finnis, "Law, Morality, and 'Sexual Orientation'"; idem., "Good of Marriage and the Morality of Sexual Relations: Some Philosophical and Historical Observations," 97–134; idem., "Reason, Faith and Homosexual Acts," 61–69. Lee and George, *Body-Self Dualism in Contemporary Ethics and Politics*, 176–217.

237. Bavinck, *Gereformeerde Dogmatiek*, I, 426 [457].

238. Ibid.

conclusive certainty [of Scripture's canonical authority]."²³⁹ Where exactly is the "powerful contradiction" here?

I dare say that it is, in Bavinck's eyes, a conflict between two views of ultimate authority; between the authority of Scripture and the Church's authority. And at the root of this conflict is the issue of Scripture being self-interpreting ("Scripture interprets Scripture") versus the Church's authority, exercised by the Church apostolic office of teaching, of preserving the deposit of faith. Of course Bavinck himself recognizes that the act of canonization is itself an act of the Church receiving, recognizing, confessing, and interpreting the Bible as Holy Scripture, as the written Word of God. But, in Bavinck's view, he thinks that Rome arrogates to itself an authority in this act of canonization that elevates it above the Word of God, making the Church's authority, rather that written Word of God, the final ground of faith. And Bavinck objects, "The Church can only recognize that which is; it cannot create something that is not." At least that is how Bavinck sees it, but I think he is mistaken.

As I argued above in laying out the relation between Holy Scripture, tradition and Magisterium, *both* Vatican I and II teach that the Church's authority is derived from Jesus Christ and hence is exercised in his Name. Vatican I states regarding the Church's authority, "And so in the performance of our supreme pastoral office, we beseech for the love of Jesus Christ and we command, by the authority of him who is also our God and savior, all faithful Christians, especially those in authority or who have the duty of teaching, that they contribute their zeal and labor to the warding off and elimination of these errors from the Church and to the spreading of the light of the pure faith." Vatican II is even clearer. "The task of giving an interpretation of the Word of God . . . has been entrusted to the living teaching office of the Church alone. Its authority in this matter is exercised in the name of Jesus Christ. *Yet this Magisterium is not superior to the Word of God, but is its servant.* It teaches only what has been handed on to it. At the divine command and with the help of the Holy Spirit, it listens to this devotedly, guards it with dedication and expounds it faithfully. All that it proposes for belief as being divinely revealed is drawn from this single deposit of faith."²⁴⁰

---

239. Ibid., 426 [458].
240. *Dei Verbum*, no. 10; italics added.

Still, given Bavinck's view regarding the self-attested authority, and hence self-interpreting nature, of Scripture, he thinks it follows from declaring the church to be subordinate to the Word of God, that this subordination rescues the freedom of Christians, meaning thereby the freedom of private judgment over the Tradition and Magisterial teaching office of the Church.[241] This Protestant principle of private judgment gives to all men "the freedom to understand that Word," and by implication, the Creeds and Confessions of the Church, "personally as he interprets it." Bavinck explains this freedom: "Morally, of course, we are bound in this connection to Christ, and we will all have to give an account of how we have understood the word of Christ and put it into practice. But vis-à-vis our fellow humans and fellow Christians, we are completely free." But doesn't this leave the interpretation of Scripture up to our own subjectivity, and with that the church then basically ceases to exist as an independently existing reality?

Of course, Bavinck notes, the Catholic Church has, on this score, consistently charged "Protestantism with individualism, subjectivism, and sectarianism." In rejoinder, he adds, that this charge reflects the weakness of Rome "inasmuch as it must maintain itself by hierarchical means." Admittedly, says Bavinck, "It is perfectly true that, if the Word is the mark of the Church and is put into all men's hands, by that very token everyone has received the right to make judgments concerning the church and, if one sees fit, to separate from it. But we must completely respect this freedom, and no state or church must curb it."[242] This understanding of freedom unleashed upon the Church a "church-dissolving" (as Bavinck phrases it) element within Protestantism and, over time, has resulted in its suicide. Still, we can imagine Bavinck replying to this charge of epistemological suicide by saying (in the words of Karl Rahner) "that in fact the Spirit of God will prevent religious subjectivity from robbing scripture and the letter of scripture of its authority." In rejoinder, the Catholic "would have to say [that] according to the Catholic understanding of the church and of faith . . . we believe that the word of God and scripture are capable of exercising such a power to form faith." Rahner explains:

> But for us Catholics the precise question is *how* this takes place in the concrete, and how in the concrete this power of God in the

---

241. Bavinck, *Gereformeerde Dogmatiek*, I, 427 [459].
242. Ibid., IV, [318].

church and in the witness of scripture can be understood. This does not dethrone scripture. It does not cease to be the *norma non normata* for the church and also for its teaching office. We did not discover the Bible somewhere by our own curiosity, but rather, as something which awakens faith and brings faith and communicates the Spirit, it comes to us only in the preaching of the concrete church. And this says to us: here is the word of God, a word which it gives witness to in such a way that according to the Catholic understanding of the faith too it can manifest itself by its own power. . . . However, faith's living understanding of scripture, and scripture's transposition into faith's really pneumatic experience of the reality which scripture means are processes whose place scripture itself cannot take, and the process of faith's living understanding of scripture has itself an ecclesial structure. It is not simply and merely an affair of the individual's religious subjectivity. Rather it is more originally an affair of the church as such, and affair of the single community of believers within which the individual Christian acquires his concrete understanding of the faith. This community of faith is not only the sum of individual religious subjectivities, but rather it really has a structure, a hierarchical constitution, and an authoritative leadership through which the church's single understanding of the faith receives its unambiguous meaning and its binding character.[243]

Indeed, with Bavinck's emphasis on freedom, private judgment, for the resolving of disputed interpretation of Holy Scripture, he severs religious subjectivity from the life of the Church. Although I cannot fully argue the point here, I think that Bavinck's emphasis on private judgment is inconsistent, or at the very least in tension, with his view of the reciprocal interrelationships between Scripture, tradition, and the church, as I briefly explained earlier. Furthermore, as Rahner states admirably well in the passage above regarding the formative process of faith's understanding of divine revelation, of salvation, of sin, the cross and grace, and so much more, it only comes ecclesially, by being a member of Christ's historic Church. And this ecclesial structure is hierarchically constituted, with the official and public teaching office of the Church, the Magisterium, grounded in an authentic episcopacy.

The nature and function of the Magisterium is ultimately grounded, biblically speaking, in the three offices of prophet (teacher), priest, and king that Jesus Christ united and fulfilled in himself. As Dulles explains,

243. Rahner, *Foundations of Christian Faith*, 364–65.

"Before his Ascension Jesus conferred a share of all these functions on the Church and its leaders. According to the final verses of Matthew's Gospel he commissioned the Eleven to teach, to baptize, and to issue commands. The Apostles and their successors have the power to teach all nations the way of Christ, to sanctify the faithful through sacraments and other forms of worship, and to exercise pastoral government over the community of Christian believers."[244] Dulles draws on the work of Monsignor Robert Sokolowski to support his claim that the teaching office of the Church holds a certain primacy over the sanctifying and governing office. He elaborates: "The priorities among the three tasks of the hierarchy are mutual. The sanctifying office has priority in the order of final causality, since it is the goal of the others. Governance is primary in the sense that it is a condition of possibility for the exercise of all ecclesial activities. But the prophetic or teaching office holds primacy in the sense that it gives meaning to the other two.... 'It establishes the space in which sanctification and governance can take their place, and it makes clear what the sanctification and governance really are.'"[245]

Significantly, Vatican II teaches that magisterial authority is not only exercised in the name of Jesus Christ but also that it is "is not superior to the Word of God, but is its servant."[246] The hierarchical teaching office, the Magisterium, of the Church is exactly what is needed to counteract the "church-dissolving" element that seems to be inherent to Protestantism, especially because of its principle of private judgment, and so that we can distinguish between true and false reform in the Church. Therefore, although I cannot argue the point here, the task of this hierarchical teaching office is to implement the authority of the normative sources—Scripture, Creeds and Confessions—of the faith by listening to these sources devoutly, guarding them with dedication, and expounding them faithfully.[247] In the words of Vatican II, "All that it proposes for belief as being divinely revealed is draw from this single deposit of faith," namely, the Word of God.[248]

---

244. Dulles, *Magisterium, Teacher and Guardian of the Faith*, 1.

245. Ibid., 2. The quote within the quote is taken from Robert Sokolowski, *Christian Faith & Human Understanding*, 117.

246. *Dei Verbum*, no. 10.

247. Braaten, *Mother Church*, 96.

248. *Dei Verbum*, no. 10.

Furthermore, this magisterial authority cannot be given without ordination since to teach with authority, to be teachers of the Church, is a gift of the Holy Spirit that is received by ordination. This is the teaching of the Catholic Church and, remarkably, of evangelical catholic Lutheran theologian, Carl Braaten. He is very critical of the legacy of Protestantism in which the link between ordination and magisterium is severed. It seems obvious to me that Braaten is right in his assessment that Protestantism suffers from a "magisterial vacuum" because "it possess no concrete official and public locus of authority."[249] In sum, says Braaten, "Neither orthodoxy nor episcopacy alone can deal with the crisis of authority in the church. Orthodoxy without episcopacy is blind; episcopacy without orthodoxy is empty."[250] Braaten point is decisive for understanding the rule of faith that includes Sacred Tradition, Sacred Scripture and Magisterium. As Dulles puts it, "These three elements are so intimately conjoined that they constitute a single composite norm."[251] This, too, is the teaching of Vatican II. "It is clear, therefore, that sacred Tradition, sacred Scripture, and the Magisterium of the Church, in accordance with God's most wise design, are so linked and joined together that one cannot stand without the others, and that all together and each in its own way under the action of the one Holy Spirit, contribute effectively to the salvation of souls."[252]

I turn now to the next chapter where I develop a biblical hermeneutic as well as address the question regarding the moral authority of Sacred Scripture.

---

249. Avery Cardinal Dulles, sympathetic review of Braaten's *Mother Church*.
250. Braaten, *Mother Church*, 97.
251. Dulles, *Magisterium*, 8.
252. *Dei Verbum*, no. 10. Dulles correctly stresses, "The Magisterium does not have the power to proclaim new revelations, still less to impose its own version of the truth. The popes and councils teach very clearly that the Magisterium is not an original source of revelation, but a witness to a revelation handed down from the past" (*Magisterium*, 6).

2

Catholic Biblical Hermeneutics and Ethics

CONTOURS OF A CATHOLIC BIBLICAL HERMENEUTIC

I BEGIN THIS CHAPTER by drawing out some of the hermeneutical implications of the doctrine of special revelation that I sketched in the second part of the first chapter.[1] Pared down for my purpose here, I will sketch some of the basic ingredients in a biblical hermeneutic as it bears on the question of biblical morality and, in turn, John Paul II's theology of the body.

First, since exegesis without presuppositions is not possible, then, we explicitly state our commitment to the Bible as authoritative Scripture, along with *Dei Verbum*, and the "control beliefs" that direct our biblical hermeneutic.[2] Therefore, the starting point of a Catholic biblical hermeneutics is, as Ashley rightly states, "divine faith that the Bible [as a whole] . . . understood [as a divinely inspired authority] in the Sacred Tradition of the Church is God's Word guiding us to union with him."[3] Since God communicated his message through the medium of words, of a verbal revelation, then the interpreter of the Bible intent upon getting at what God intends to communicate to us, should carefully interpret the literal sense of the biblical text, meaning the "sense that the author intended and

---

1. Helpful in drawing out these implications is Ashley, "Bible Gap."

2. Nicholas Wolterstorff first introduced the notion of "control beliefs" in his 1976 book, *Reason within the Bounds of Religion*, to refer to the "religious beliefs of the Christian scholar" that function as control "within his devising and weighing of theories" (76). In this chapter, I am applying the religious control beliefs that derive from the Catholic doctrine of special revelation I sketched in the last chapter to a biblical hermeneutic that comports well with those beliefs.

3. Ashley, "Bible Gap."

expressed in language."[4] As Aquinas says, "the literal sense is that which the author intends."[5] Pius XII agrees: "the exegete . . . must search out and expound the literal meaning of the words, intended and expressed by the sacred writer."[6] But the meaning of Holy Scripture is not reducible to its literal meaning, its historical-grammatical meaning.[7] Still, as Nichols puts it, "the literal sense must be the primary sense of Scripture in the sense of being the necessary foundation for any other senses that Scripture may carry." Thus, the literal sense is the foundational sense. And yet, to get to the spiritual sense of the text, the Catholic exegete must interpret the canonical sense. In other words, he must heed the hermeneutical principle found in *Dei Verbum* describing his responsibility to determine the canonical meaning of a book or particular text by attending to the content and unity of the whole of Scripture.[8] Here, then, is the rule that Nichols calls the hermeneutical golden rule: "interpret every text of Scripture on the understanding that it forms part of a larger whole."[9]

Furthermore, the canonical sense is the bridge to the spiritual sense of the text: Christological typology, moral (tropological) sense, and eschatological (anagogical) sense.[10] To quote Nichols again, "These three senses

4. Nichols, *Shape of Catholic Theology*, 142.
5. Aquinas, *Summa Theologiae*, I, q. 1, a. 10.
6. Pius XII, *Divino Afflante Spiritu*, no. 26.
7. The then Joseph Cardinal Ratzinger writes, "Also from the complex nature of the literary genre 'Bible' comes the fact that the meaning of its individual texts cannot be confined to the historical intention of the first author—for the most part established in a hypothetical manner. All of the texts are actually found in a process of continual rewriting, in which their potential richness of meaning is always being more fully disclosed, and therefore no text belongs simply to a single historical author. Since the text itself has a developmental character, it is not permissible, even based upon its literary genre, to confine it to a determined historical moment and to keep it there; in this case it would be confined to the past, while to read the Scripture as Bible means precisely that the present is found in the historical word, opening up a future" ("Current Doctrinal Relevance of the *Catechism of the Catholic Church*").
8. *Dei Verbum*, no. 12.
9. Nichols, *Shape of Catholic Theology*, 155.
10. Ratzinger, "Current Doctrinal Relevance of the *Catechism of the Catholic Church*": "The doctrine of the multiple meanings of Scripture, which was developed by the Fathers and in the Middle Ages was given a systematic form, based today upon this particular concept of the formation of the text is again recognized as scientifically satisfactory. The *Catechism* therefore briefly illustrates the traditional understanding of the four senses of Scripture—it would be better to say, of the four dimensions of the meaning of the text. There is first of all the so-called literal sense, that is, the historical-literary meaning,

together make up, then, the spiritual or traditional sense of Scripture. When combined with the literal sense, they compose the classic hermeneutic scheme found in the Catholic reading of the Bible.... The spiritual sense entails the claim that the literal sense can point beyond itself: first to Christ, who is the center of Scripture as of faith; second, to the individual person in his or her religious existence; and finally, to humanity's ultimate destiny."[11] This means that the Catholic exegete must thereby take a next hermeneutical step toward discovering the further or deeper meanings found by the Church in light of the total movement of redemptive history and, accordingly, in light of that history's concentration point, the historical revelation of God in Christ, who is the fullness and mediator of all revelation (as *Dei Verbum* phrases it). Moreover, we have to take one last hermeneutical step of discovering the *sensus plenior*: "The *sensus plenior* is that additional, deeper meaning, intended by God but not clearly intended by the human author, which is seen to exist in the words of a biblical text (or group of texts, or even a whole book) when they are studied in the light of further revelation or development in the understanding of revelation."[12] I will return to these four hermeneutical steps later in this chapter. For now I want to draw out a second hermeneutical implication.

Second, the fundamental hermeneutical focus of the normative text of Scripture is, as *Dei Verbum* says, "what God wanted to put into the sacred writings for the sake of our salvation." As I argued in the last chapter, this redemptive focus does not limit the truth that God reveals; rather, it merely gives Scripture a centrality by indicating God's purpose in revealing. Ashley describes this focus admirably well.

> What we need for our salvation is to know God as he reveals himself to be and how we are to respond to him in our own lives,

which an exegete seeks to re-present as the expression of the historical moment of the origin of the text. There is the so-called 'allegorical' sense; unfortunately this discredited term prevents us from grasping exactly what it means. In the word, once you take it out of an earlier limited historical context, it actually contains a method of faith, which inserts this text within the whole of the Bible, and beyond that time directed as is every time, coming from God and going to God. There is also a moral dimension—the word of God always gives direction for the journey, and, finally, there is the eschatological dimension, transcending the here and now, and moving toward what is definitive; tradition calls this the 'anagogical sense.'"

11. Nichols, *Shape of Catholic Theology*, 161.

12. Brown, *Sensus Plenior of Sacred Scripture*, 92. See also, Nichols, *Shape of Catholic Theology*, 162.

> not merely as individuals but as a Church which he has chosen in Christ and called to be his witness to the world. The Bible cannot be read, therefore, simply as a collection of documents with a variety of sources written on the different occasions and expressing the authors' contrasting insights. It must be read as ultimately a unified revelation of who God is and a consistent and sufficient guide for Christian living. This is not to deny the polyphony of biblical voices, but to show that they form a harmonious composition not a cacophony.[13]

In sum, the Holy Scripture, given its unity and reliability as the Word of God, is a canonically unified whole centered on Jesus Christ.

Third, the reciprocal relationship between Scripture and Tradition are joined in a hermeneutical circle. Scripture and tradition are two modalities by which the Tradition of the Gospel, one and the same revelation, is communicated to men in and throughout the life and consciousness of the Church. Holy Scripture is the "literary concretization" (to use Rahner's apt phrase) of divine revelation and the supreme norm of faith, and the Word of God is mediated through the unwritten traditions, or witnesses, of the liturgy, the councils, creeds, catechisms, and so forth. In other words, these traditions testify to the Word of God, but they are also "the proper context in which to read, study, and expound the Scriptures." As Nichols explains, "Tradition as the Christian religion itself, the life and consciousness of the Church considered as a reflection of the Word of God, of God's self-communication, is necessarily a reality at once larger than the bible and inclusive of it." On this view, Nichols adds, "Scripture can still be called the supreme norm of faith, the *norma non normata*, in the sense that to appeal to Tradition to interpret Scripture aright is not to appeal away from Scripture to something other than Scripture.... To judge the Bible on the basis of Tradition as expressed in traditions is not, *pace* Protestant fears, to submit the Bible to an alien authority, but rather to identify and declare what is the Bible's own deepest reality."[14] Moreover, given that the Scripture is the supreme norm of faith, the highest authority in matters of faith (as John Paul II phrases it[15]), then, the tradition, too, as well as the Church, stands under the Scripture's judgment. "The

---

13. Ashley, "Bible Gap."
14. Nichols, *Shape of Catholic Theology*, 169, 177, respectively.
15. John Paul II, *Ut Unum Sint*, no. 79.

Catholic exegete's task, therefore, is not completed until this hermeneutic circle is closed and Scripture and Tradition confirm each other."[16]

Fourth, "Who will defend Scripture when the Church is confronted by two or more contradictory interpretations of Scripture?"[17] Are we thrown back on our private judgment? Let us recall that Bavinck tried to block the move to hermeneutical individualism, subjectivism, and sectarianism (meaning thereby "sect" in the Troeltschian sense where the church is understood as a voluntary association of like-minded individuals), and the corresponding "church-dissolving" element of Protestantism, by invoking the Spirit of God in the work of defending religious subjectivity from the loss of the authority of Scripture. How's Bavinck's approach working? Not at all, I would say, if we are to judge by the "church-dissolving" brought about by the two or more contradictory interpretations of Scripture on homosexuality. David Lyle Jeffrey once said, "The loss of the Church's teaching authority has led to the loss of the authority of Scripture."[18] In short, it is the Church that must defend the authority of Scripture. So in reply to the question, "Who speaks for the Scripture?" I must say: "Only the Church, guided and inspired by the Holy Spirit, can properly read and interpret those writings that were written under the inspiration of the Spirit and which have been collected together in the one canon by the action of the Spirit. The Bible, as Bible, only teaching anything because the Church teaches on the basis of the Bible and tells us what it means—or perhaps better, because God guides the Church to discern and express what he means in and by his Word."[19]

I turn now to develop these hermeneutical principles in somewhat more detail so as to answer, however briefly and tentatively, how the Church gets at the true meaning of Scripture. Following that, I'll show how some of these principles help us in addressing the criticism that Christians arbitrarily use the Scripture as ultimate authority in moral matters.

---

16. Ashley, "Bible Gap."

17. Kimel, "Sola Scriptura."

18. Jeffrey, "Houses of the Interpreters, Spiritual Exegesis and the Retrieval of Authority," 30. Similarly, Braaten writes, "The authority of the Bible is not autonomous. When people cease to believe in the church, they will soon cease to believe in the Bible" (*Mother Church*, 148).

19. Kimel, "Sola Scriptura."

CATHOLIC HERMENEUTICAL PRINCIPLES

The fundamental commitment of the Catholic faith to the view that God's special revelation, the Holy Scriptures, discloses matters that are true is, as I see it, the basic motive behind "the imperative of interpreting the normative text—and getting it right" (as the late Jaroslav Pelikan phrased it[20]). As John Paul II puts it regarding the relation between meaning and truth of the biblical text,

> As does every other text, so also do the sources with which the theologian deals, before anything else communicate a meaning which needs to be illuminated and explained. Furthermore, this meaning displays itself as the truth about God, which is given to the sacred text by God himself. This means that the Word of God which communicates this truth is expressed in human language, by means of that amazing "condescension" which reflects the logic of the Incarnation. Therefore in interpreting the sources of Revelation theologians must remind themselves of the depth and appropriateness of the truth that the passages of Scripture desire to open up, even within the limits imposed by human language. The truth of the biblical texts, and of the Gospels in particular, is certainly not restricted to the narration of simple historical events or the statement of neutral facts, as historicist positivism would claim. Beyond simple historical occurrence, the truth of the events which these texts relate lies rather in the meaning they have *in* and *for* the history of salvation. This truth is elaborated fully in the Church's constant reading of these texts over the centuries, a reading which preserves intact their original meaning. There is a pressing need, therefore, that the relationship between fact and meaning, a relationship which constitutes the specific sense of history, be examined also from the philosophical point of view.[21]

The pope is making, chiefly, two points in this passage. First, he is expressing in his own terms the relation between the various meanings of Scripture in a hermeneutical schema where the canonical and spiritual meaning of Scripture cannot be restricted to the literal sense alone, that is, the historical-grammatical meaning of the biblical text. Why? The truth of the historical events to which these biblical texts are referring must not be restricted to mere historical narratives, but rather is found in the meta-historical meaning (canonical and spiritual meaning) of these historical

---

20. Pelikan, *Interpreting the Bible & the Constitution*, 39.
21. John Paul II, *Fides et Ratio*, no. 94.

events, meaning thereby "the depth and appropriateness of the truth that the passages of Scripture desire to open up," which is "the meaning they have *in* and *for* the history of salvation." As Nichols explains: "Thus we can appreciate not only the immediate bearings of a scriptural text, the literal sense; not only its reference to Christ as the center of revelation, the Christological sense; nor only its implications for our existence, the moral sense. We can also use Scripture as a vehicle for our own entry into the mystery of God. And it is characteristic of the mystical sense to approach the Bible in just this way."[22] Of course John Paul argues that the truth regarding the meta-historical meaning of these events, that is, the deeper meaning of a biblical text elaborated by the Church, and which is beyond the literal sense, is reached only *through* the literal sense, indeed is based on its historical-grammatical meaning, and presupposes it. In the following example of Aidan Nichols, I think he illustrates how the pope's hermeneutical schema may illuminate:

> The story of the Fall could be read as a symbolic account of human rebelliousness against God, of how all our cultural developments (as for the Genesis writer, clothing, metal-working, city-building) are spoilt by an element of vengefulness and pride. Yet sin must have entered human life at some historical moment, whether identifiable or not. For unless evil marred the creation of humanity contingently (i.e., historically), it could only have done so essentially (i.e., by God's own creative act), which is unthinkable. In claiming Adam (with Eve) as historical figures, the Church is confirmed by the New Testament, especially by Paul's appeal to Adam's fall as the act which Christ's redemptive act inverted. *Revelation presents both as historical events with metahistorical meaning.*[23]

Two, John Paul II is also affirming that God's Word written contains, as Canadian Jesuit philosopher Bernard Lonergan puts it, realism about truth, that is, the Holy Scripture "tells us of things as in fact they are."[24] In other words, Lonergan adds, "realism [about truth] consists in this, that the truth that is acknowledge in the mind corresponds to reality." He explains: Scripture is true in a realist sense "both because [what it asserts to be the case] is to be believed and not contradicted, and also because it is a true word, telling of things as in fact they are. For realism consists in this,

---

22. Nichols, *Shape of Catholic Theology*, 160.
23. Nichols, *Epiphany,* 175–76; italics added.
24. Lonergan, *Way to Nicea*, 128.

that the truth that is acknowledged in the mind corresponds to reality. But whoever believes the true word of God certainly acknowledges truth in his mind—indeed his adherence to this truth is so complete that he banishes from his thoughts even the slightest suspicion that things might be other than as God has revealed them to be."[25] There is more: How does the pope understand the relation between meaning and truth? Well, he takes the truth of a proposition to be closely connected with its meaning. Again, Lonergan explains that "meaning of its nature is related to what is meant, and what is meant may or may not correspond to what is in fact so." If it corresponds," Lonergan adds, "the meaning is true. If it does not correspond, the meaning is false." Lonergan then correctly notes the disastrous implication of denying the correspondence view of truth, meaning thereby the realist notion of truth in which a proposition is true if and only if objective reality is the way the proposition says it is; otherwise, the proposition is false. He writes:

> To deny correspondence is to deny a relation between meaning and meant. To deny the correspondence view of truth is to deny that, when the meaning is true, the meant is what is so. Either denial is destructive of the dogmas.... If one denies that, when the meaning is true, then the meant is what is so, one rejects propositional truth. If the rejection is universal, then it is the self-destructive proposition that there are no true propositions. If the rejection is limited to the dogmas, then it is just a roundabout way of saying that all dogmas are false.[26]

Now, let me illustrate the self-destructive consequence of denying propositional truth, but now in the practical context of preaching.[27] Let us agree that Scripture functions in a way that mediates its cognitive meaning in a realist sense. Says Lonergan, "In so far as meaning is cognitive, what is meant is real."[28] Let us also agree that Scripture "is mediated by meaning in its communicative function inasmuch as it is preached."[29] In addition, Scripture "is mediated by meaning in its constitutive function

---

25. Ibid., 128–29.

26. Lonergan, "Dehellenization of Dogma," 14–15, 16, respectively.

27. Helpful here are Fr. Lonergan's distinctions between functions of meaning: cognitive, constitutive, communicative, and effective or transformative (*Method in Theology*, 76–78, and 356).

28. Ibid., 356.

29. Lonergan, "Origins of Christian Realism," 244.

inasmuch as it is a way of life that is lived. It is mediated by meaning in its effective function inasmuch as its precepts are put into practice."[30] Thus, the meaning of Scripture is at once cognitive, communicative, constitutive, and effective. Lonergan explains:

> The Christian church is the community that results from the outer communication of Christ's message and from the inner gift of God's love. Since God can be counted on to bestow his grace, practical theology is concerned with the effective communication of Christ's message. The message announces what Christians are to believe, what they are to become, what they are to do. Its meaning, then, is at once cognitive, constitutive, effective. It is cognitive inasmuch as the message tells what is to be believed. It is constitutive inasmuch as it crystallizes the hidden inner gift of love into overt Christian fellowship. It is effective inasmuch as it directs Christian service to human society to bring about the kingdom of God. To communicate the Christian message is to lead another to share in one's cognitive, constitutive, effective meaning. Those, then, that would communicate the cognitive meaning of the message, first of all, must know it.... Next, those that would communicate the constitutive meaning of the Christian message, first of all, must live it. For without living the Christian message one does not possess its constitutive meaning; and one cannot lead another to share what one oneself does not possess. Finally, those that communicate the effective meaning of the Christian message, must practice it. For actions speak louder than words, while preaching what one does not practice recalls sounding brass and tinkling symbol.[31]

Recall now John Paul's point above that "[textual] meaning presents itself as the truth about God which God himself communicates through the sacred text." I have unpacked his meaning in terms of a realist—propositional, or cognitive—view of truth. Suppose now that we diminish or entirely eliminate Scripture's functioning in a way that mediates its cognitive meaning in a realist sense, and that we insist on this especially when we are preaching the Gospel to a church in conflict. The ecclesial community in conflict is precisely the Anglican communion, and its internal conflict, more accurately, brokenness and self-destruction, over the morality of homosexuality and, consequently, biblical authority.

---

30. Ibid.
31. Ibid., 361–62.

Well, this is precisely what is going on Lorraine Cavanagh's essay, "Truth and Meaning: Preaching the Gospel from a Church in Conflict." Her aim is to outline the dynamics of preaching in a situation where the emphasis is "to communicate meaning and the reality of the possibility of transformation to those who need to hear the truth of the Gospel [of reconciliation]." That is, preaching is about communicating meaning "for the good of the worshipping community as a whole." It is "a public discernment of the truth," says Cavanagh, "where truth is allowed to be uncoupled from fixed readings of scripture." The chief enemy of her understanding of preaching, which promotes a dynamic understanding of Scriptural truth, is "static absolutes," approaches to Scripture that "conflate issues [like the morality of homosexuality] with scriptural truth and proclaimed in absolute terms," "static thinking," and, most clearly, the notion of truth that means "the propositional truth of scripture, as 'true or false.'" All this is "in contrast to the deeper truthfulness which exists in the movement and in the transforming power of God's Spirit." "Where truth is disconnected from the continuing process of thinking and praying theologically," Cavanagh adds, "which includes discerning the Holy Spirit 'working' in the breadth of history and in the continuity of tradition, the lines of thought which convey meaning to the listener are 'short-circuited.'" She explains:

> That is to say, the preacher is constantly brought back, in a rational and intellectual sense, to his or her own point of departure (in itself a static thought situation) and risks failing to connect with his or her own deeper experience of God in prayer and with the life experience, as well as experience of God, which others have. This is a static, or non-dynamic, situation which can lead to sermons being impoverished by consideration of objective, or propositional, veracity instead of being enriched by them.[32]

The dilemma posed by Cavanagh is specious. First, Christian revelation is both personal and propositional; it is not either of God revealing himself, or by God's revelation of propositional truth. Rather, propositional revelation is an integral part of God's self-revelation. Put differently, without propositional truth, it doesn't seem to me that Scripture can say *something*, never mind something that is somehow biblically *authoritative*.

---

32. The quotations in the above paragraph are all from "Truth and Meaning: Preaching the Gospel from a Church in Conflict," 293.

Second, the ontology of meaning that informs a biblical hermeneutic of preaching should be at once cognitive, communicative, constitutive, and effective, as Lonergan clearly explained. Diminishing or eliminating altogether the cognitive meaning of Scripture in preaching leaves the hearer at a loss as to what is to be believed, namely, the *fides quae*, the faith which the Church believes to be the objective content of revealed truth. Cavanagh's approach to preaching leaves us confused, as did Luke Timothy Johnson, about how to come to grips with the moral authority of the Bible. The same question I posed to Johnson, I also ask of Cavanagh: Does she actually deny "that there exist, in Divine Revelation, a specific and determined moral content, universally valid and permanent [?]"[33] Aren't there moral norms formulated in Scripture not only having the status of fundamental revealed moral truth but also are in themselves relevant for salvation?

Third, Cavanagh suggests that her approach to preaching promotes a dynamic presence of the Holy Spirit working to deepen our understanding of the truth of Scripture, and that the Spirit's works "in the breadth of history and in the continuity of tradition." As her formulation stands, it seems consistent with *Dei Verbum*. "For there is a growth in the understanding of the realities and the words [of salvation history] which have been handed down. This happens through the contemplation and study made by believers, who treasure these things in their hearts (see Luke 2:19, 51) through a penetrating understanding of the spiritual realities which they experience, and through the preaching of those who have received through Episcopal succession the sure gift of truth. For as the centuries succeed one another, the Church constantly moves forward toward the fullness of divine truth until the words of God reach their complete fulfillment in her."[34]

Yet, the crucial difference between Cavanagh and the Catholic Church is fundamental: the Church's promotes a dynamic understanding of the truth of Scripture that presupposes a propositional view of truth.[35] The propositional truths of faith and morals are one thing, while the mode in which they are expressed is another. In their new expressions that purport to deepen our understanding of what God wants Scripture

---

33. John Paul II, *Veritatis Splendor*, no. 37.
34. *Dei Verbum*, no. 8.
35. For a defense of this claim, see Echeverria, *Dialogue of Love*, 19–34.

to say, however, they must keep the same meaning and same judgment, and only a propositional view of truth can make that possible. Otherwise, the preacher will not *"say the same thing* that a scriptural text or texts say." Thus, Robert W. Jenson correctly adds, "As Scripture directly controls our homiletical discourse, it says what God wants it to say."[36] Furthermore, as Vatican I put it, making a point directly relevant to the matter of propositional truth, but now with respect to dogma: "Hence, too, that meaning of the sacred dogmas is ever to be maintained which has once been declared by Holy mother Church, and there must never be any abandonment of this sense under the pretext or in the name of a more profound understanding. May understanding, knowledge and wisdom increase as ages and centuries roll along, and greatly and vigorously flourish, in each and all, in the individual and the whole Church: but this only in its own proper kind, that is to say, in the same doctrine, keeping the same meaning, and the same judgment."[37]

Fifth, the Church teaches "that in matters of faith and morals, belonging as they do to the establishing of Christian doctrine, that meaning of Holy Scripture must be held to be the true one, which Holy mother Church held and holds, since it is her right to judge of the true meaning and interpretation of Holy Scripture." The role of the teaching authority of the Church has been totally lost in Cavanagh's biblical hermeneutic that she employs to support her view of preaching.

I want now to move on to ask, in light of the understanding of the relation between meaning and truth shared by John Paul II and Bernard Lonergan: What is it that the interpreter is trying to get right? Well, the text represents the communicative act of a communicative agent. That is, an author produces a text in order to communicate *something* to someone; thus interpretation is a process of coming to understand the truth of what is said—the determinate meaning embedded within the text and to which the interpreter is fundamentally accountable. A realist and reconstructive hermeneutics of biblical textual meaning holds that there is a meaning in the text, that this textual meaning is knowable, that is, fundamentally identifiable and recoverable, and that interpreters should strive to grasp

---

36. Jenson, "Hermeneutics and the Life of the Church," 92.

37. Vatican Council I, *Decreta Dogmatica Concilii Vaticani de Fide Catholica et de Ecclesia Christi* (1870), Chapter IV: Faith and Reason.

this determinate meaning.[38] Thus, the goal of interpretation is to recover the meaning of the text.

What is the original meaning of the text? The original meaning is the literal sense which is the sense intended by the author and expressed in language. In other words, the literal sense is properly described as the sense conveyed by the words. "The literal sense of Scripture is that which has been expressed directly by the inspired human authors. Since it is the fruit of inspiration, this sense is also intended by God, as principal author. One arrives at this sense by means of a careful analysis of the text, within its literary and historical context. The principal task of exegesis is to carry out this analysis, making use of all the resources of literary and historical research, with a view to defining the literal sense of the biblical texts with the greatest possible accuracy.... To this end, the study of ancient literary genres is particularly necessary."[39] The literal sense is often communicated as resting foremost on authorial intention—and of course it does, because any author uses actual words with an intended meaning. Now, we must not separate authorial intention from what the writer actually wrote because not only is what he wrote evidence for what he intended but also his intention helps us to determine the meaning of what he wrote.[40] This holds true for interpreting any text.

In the case of the Bible, however, recovering original meaning involves various literary genres such as historical narrative, law, prophecy, poetry, proverb, parable, romance, letter, and apocalypse. Moreover, interpretation, biblical or otherwise, however, does not limit the original meaning to the intent of the original human author, because "the logical implications of the text are not to be restricted to what the original writer intended."[41] In the case of the biblical text, however, the matter of authorial intention is more complex than just logical implication because the Bible has dual authorship: the intention of God and the intention of the human author. Indeed, Scripture has not only human authors but also God as its primary author. God himself, in a manifestation of divine providence, is the author of the whole Bible and hence of its multiple complex senses, that is, the

---

38. On this, see Vanhoozer, *Is There a Meaning in this Text?* See also, Lonergan, *Method in Theology*, chapter 7, Interpretation, 153–73; Guarino, *Foundations of Systematic Theology*, chapters 5–6.

39. *Interpretation of the Bible in the Church*, II. Hermeneutical Questions, B. 1, The Literal Sense.

40. On this, see Helm, *Divine Revelation*, 101.

41. Ibid.

literal sense, canonical sense (which is the bridge to the spiritual sense), and the plenary sense.[42] Furthermore, the divine authorial intention at the level of the canon as a whole supervenes rather than contravenes the intention of the human author, and thus must be considered part of the literal sense of Scripture.

The spiritual sense, by contrast, although it is still enveloped within God's authorship and divine intention, is the sense that is not contained or expressed explicitly in the words of the text. Since the Spirit is the inspirer of Scripture and of history, not only words but also events can be pointers to other words and events. But this is not at the level of the literal meaning of the words but rather at the level of the spiritual sense of the text, which is in some sense enveloped in and supervenes on the literal sense.[43] "While there is a distinction between the two senses, the spiritual sense can never be stripped of its connection with the literal sense. The latter remains the indispensable foundation. Otherwise one could not speak of the "fulfillment" of Scripture. Indeed, in order that there be fulfillment, a relationship of continuity and of conformity is essential. But it is also necessary that there be transition to a higher level of reality."[44] Fr. Bernard Lonergan gives a good description of this process of supervenience. Using the term "sublation" to describe the relation between the different levels of meaning, Longergan writes: "What sublates goes beyond what is sublated, introduces something new and distinct, yet so far from interfering with the sublated or destroying it, on the contrary needs it, includes it, preserves all its proper features and properties, and carries them forward to a fuller realization within a richer context."[45]

Kevin Vanhoozer gives an example of the intended meaning of the divine author supervening on the intention of the human author: "the canon does not change or contradict the meaning of Isaiah 53 but supervenes on it and specifies its referent. In speaking of the Suffering Servant,

---

42. On this, see Davis and Hays, "Nine Theses on the Interpretation of Scripture," 1–5. See also, *Interpretation of the Bible in the Church*, II. Hermeneutical Questions, B. The Meaning of Inspired Scripture, nos. 1–3.

43. Vanhoozer, *Is There a Meaning in this Text?*, 265. I am indebted to Kevin Vanhoozer for his insight that the divine authorial intention supervenes the intention of the human author.

44. *Interpretation of the Bible in the Church*, II. Hermeneutical Questions, B. The Meaning of Inspired Scripture, 2. The Spiritual Sense.

45. Lonergan, *Method in Theology*, 241.

Isaiah was referring to Christ (viz., God's gracious provision for Israel and the world)."[46] Another example: Moses was inspired to raise up the bronze serpent by God (see Num 21:8–9), and to record this under the Spirit's inspiration. But the interpretation of this event in John 3:14 as referring to Christ—clearly part of God's intention—is not an interpretation of Numbers 21 according to the literal sense, but rather according to the spiritual sense, that is, Christological typology.

According to the *Catechism of the Catholic Church*, typological exegesis "discerns in God's works of the Old Covenant prefigurations of what he accomplished in the fullness of time in the person of his incarnate Son."[47] That is, "Christians therefore read the Old Testament in the light of Christ crucified and risen. Such typological reading discloses the inexhaustible content of the Old Testament. . . . Typology indicates the dynamic movement toward the fulfillment of the divine plan."[48] Thus, to understand God's intention in and through the words of Scripture, particularly its Christological meaning, requires knowing the whole unity of God's salvific plan in Christ. In sum, this means that the divine author's intention when considered in light of Scripture as a canonical whole must be taken to be part of the plenary sense of Scripture.[49] Let us here recall briefly the aim of the tropological or moral sense of the Bible. Explains Nichols, "By this is meant the implications a biblical text for the behavior of the reader—called 'tropological' from the Greek word for behavior, *tropos*.'"[50] Last, there is the anagogical or eschatological sense of the biblical text. "Here what is being said is that any given text of Scripture may well be relevant to the overall end and purposes of Scripture—the final destiny of humanity in God. Thus the anagogical sense enables us to rise up, *anagogein*, toward the God who is the *eschaton*, the final goal of our lives."[51]

What then are the principles by which we should interpret normative texts such as Holy Scripture? Briefly, recovering the literal sense of

---

46. Vanhoozer, *Is There a Meaning in this Text?* 265.

47. *Catechism of the Catholic Church*, no. 128.

48. Ibid., nos. 129–30.

49. This conclusion will be essential to John Paul II's hermeneutical schema. On this, see, Kurz, "Scriptural Foundations of *The Theology of the Body*," 29. I'll return to this point in chapter 5.

50. Nichols, *Shape of Catholic Theology*, 158.

51. Ibid., 160.

biblical texts requires attending to the following directives given in *Dei Verbum* no. 12:

> To search out the intention of the sacred writers, attention should be given, among other things, to "literary forms." For truth is set forth and expressed differently in texts which are variously historical, prophetic, poetic, or other forms of discourse. The interpreter must investigate what meaning the sacred writer intended to express and actually expressed in particular circumstances by using contemporary literary forms in accordance with the situation of his own time and culture. For the correct understanding of what the sacred author wanted to assert, due attention must be paid to the customary and characteristic styles of feeling, speaking and narrating which prevailed at the time of the sacred writer, and to the patterns men normally employed at that period in their everyday dealings with one another.

Being the inspired interpretative record of redemptive *history*, the literal-historical sense of the biblical text is foundational to the other senses of Scripture. Indeed, *Dei Verbum* no. 2 speaks of the "economy of revelation" taking place "by events and words intrinsically bound to each other." In short, the historical realities of redemption are inseparably connected to God's verbal communication of truth. "In this context," to quote Francis Martin, "we may say that in order to participate more fully in the *realities* mediated by the words . . . it is of great importance that we grasp what, in terms of his own context, the author 'wants to say.'"[52] In other words, "without God's acts the words would be empty, without His word the acts would be blind."[53]

In addition, *Dei Verbum* no. 12, lists three imperatives[54] for reading and interpreting Holy Scripture "in the same Spirit in which it was written in order rightly to draw out the meaning of the sacred texts." The first imperative enjoins us to attend "to the content and unity of the whole of Scripture"—the divine economy of creation, fall into sin, redemption, and consummation, which unifies all the individual books of the Bible as well as the Old and New Testaments: what may rightly be called the *canonical*

---

52. Martin, "Some Directions in Catholic Biblical Theology," 67–68.

53. As Geerhardus Vos says in his address, "Idea of Biblical Theology as a Science and as a Theological Discipline."

54. *Catechism of the Catholic Church* lists the three criteria of *Dei Verbum* no. 12 as imperatives (nos. 112–14).

sense of the Holy Scripture as a whole. This imperative is particularly important toward counteracting an atomizing and pluralizing understanding of the Scriptures under the influence of historical criticism, which contributed to the surrendering of the unity of Scripture. That is, this hermeneutical imperative is particularly important in light of the fact that "With the advent of historical study and increased attention to the author and the author's intention, the tendency has been to consider a book or part of a book as an isolated entity." "Thus," as Francis Martin adds, "we have the modern phenomenon of studies devoted to 'the theology of Jeremiah,' or Mark, or Deutero-Isaiah.... Such studies are valuable since they allow us to grasp the teaching of individual authors as these are embedded in the concrete consciousness and energy of any one person. [Yet] There are other procedures that are not as useful, and, in fact, are wrong. *These consist in trying to determine a more primitive layer of composition, attempting to discern its theological direction, and then attributing to the final and more 'orthodox' redaction a different direction. The orientation of most of this work is to consider that the 'orthodox' layer was superimposed upon a more primitive and less exclusive way. The multiplicity of opinions resulting from this procedure is evidence enough of its shaky foundation and it often betrays a theological bias on the part of the investigator.*"[55] This approach has led to the loss of the canonical meaning of Scripture and that

---

55. On this see Martin, "Some Aspects of Biblical Studies since Vatican II: The Contribution and Challenge of *Dei Verbum*," 233, italics added. Benedict XVI makes a similar point, November 9, 2006, in his "Discourse to the Swiss Bishops": "Our exegesis has progressed by leaps and bounds. We know truly a great deal about the development of texts, the subdivision of sources, etc. We know what words would have meant at that time. But we are increasingly seeing that if historical and critical exegesis remains solely historical and critical, it refers the Word to the past, it makes it a word of those times, a Word which basically says nothing to us at all; and we see that the Word is fragmented, precisely because it is broken up into a multitude of different sources. With *Dei Verbum*, the Council told us that the historical-critical method is an essential dimension of exegesis because, since the faith is a *factum historicum*, it is part of the nature of faith. We do not merely believe in an idea; Christianity is not a philosophy but an event that God brought about in this world, a story that he pieced together in a real way and forms with is as history. For this reason, in our reading of the Bible, the serious historical aspect with its requirement must be truly present; we must effectively recognize the event and, precisely in his action, this 'making of history' on God's part. *Dei Verbum* adds, however, that Scripture, which must consequently be interpreted according to historical methods, should also be read in its unity and must be read within the living community of the Church. These two dimensions are absent in large areas of exegesis."

loss has considerable implications for the authority of Scripture. In other words, as Calvin Seerveld puts it,

> In my judgment it is a mistake to treat nuanced features of narratives as if they be fragments from heterogeneous sources, and then deconstruct a masterfully told tale into a mix of certified facts and literary flourishes of disparate pre-texts. . . . Higher-critical reading of Scripture can have the dispassionate seriousness of a good dentist drilling in teeth to fix cavities; we need dependable dentistry in order to have a good bite and to develop normative mouth hygiene. Such assiduous professional attention uncovers and certifies important historical facts and literary nuances for reading aright. But to treat the biblical text *first of all* as an archaeological dig in which you must discover, date and identify each fascinating piece of rubble but *neglect to get at the artifact in its integrality is a lamentable failing of such scholarship*. A person can learn a lot in following this method, but unless you use it propadeutically as supplement, you can miss the pearl of great price: hearing God speak.[56]

Thus without this hermeneutical imperative of attending to the content and unity of the whole of Scripture, guiding the work of exegesis, we will not be properly disposed for interpreting, say, the relation between the Old Testament and New Testament, but it will also have serious consequences for dogmatics as well as moral theology.

The second imperative enjoins us always to read the Holy Scripture in and with the Church's ongoing Tradition—"the living Tradition of the entire Church." Scott Hahn correctly notes: "Reading scripture within the mainstream of *tradition* means reading it as salvation *history*—and thus reading it *typologically*, as it appears in the liturgy and in the lectionary."[57]

---

56. Seerveld, *How to Read the Bible to Hear God Speak*, 63; italics added. Similarly, as Douma correctly says, "Faith in the one, multifaceted, but therefore still internally consistent Word of God was exchanged for the conviction that the Bible is a collection of human documents containing a plurality of mutually contradictory theologies. . . . Obviously, this had consequences not only for doctrinal reflection, but for ethical reflection as well" (Douma, "Use of Scripture in Ethics," 359; idem., *Responsible Conduct: Principles of Christian Ethics*, 55–111).

57. Hahn, *Letter and Spirit: From Written Text to Living Word in the Liturgy*, 164. Regarding the unity of the two testaments, *CCC* states, "The Church, as early as apostolic times, and then constantly in her Tradition, has illuminated the unity of the divine plan in the two testaments through typology, which discerns in God's works of the Old Covenant prefigurations of what he accomplished in the fullness of time in the person of his incarnate Son (no. 128).

Of course the living Tradition of the Church includes as well the Church Fathers, both East and West, Ecumenical Councils, Creeds,[58] and the *sensus fidelium*—"insofar as the faithful have been reflective of proper Catholic teaching through their own faith, prayer, and devotion."[59]

The third imperative—"*Be attentive to the analogia fidei*"—i.e., the analogy of faith, which expresses an integrative aim in biblical interpretation enjoining us to see the Bible, with its internal diversity, as a unity, viz., a unified act of communication structured by the divine authorial intention of the Holy Spirit. So here the interpreter focuses on "the coherence of the truths of faith among themselves and within the whole plan of Revelation."[60] Two implications of this principle of harmony helpful in dealing with cruxes of interpretation are as follows: one, Scripture should not be set against Scripture because "each part of the sacred text must be understood as compatible with others,"[61] and two, "the secondary and obscure in the Scripture should be interpreted in the light of what appears primary and plain."[62]

What about the great tradition of spiritual exegesis for determining the spiritual sense of the biblical text? According to the Pontifical Biblical Commission, spiritual exegesis is built on the foundational literal-historical sense of the biblical text; "otherwise, one could not speak of the 'fulfillment' of Scripture."[63] But scriptural meaning is not restricted to the literal sense, to conscious intentions of the human author expressed in language. Sacred Scripture has dual authorship, divine and human, with God as its primary author, and hence the divine author's intention is part of the literal sense of Scripture. "Because Scripture carries the word of God, its message is open to fulfillment in ways broader and deeper

---

58. In his magisterial study, *Credo: Historical and Theological Guide to Creeds and Confessions of Faith in the Christian Tradition*, Jaroslav Pelikan states, "At least as important a function of creeds and confessions in relation to Scripture is to define rules of biblical hermeneutics" (143), Section 5.4. Confessional Rules of Biblical Hermeneutics (142–57) is devoted to a discussion of this thesis.

59. Guarino, "Catholic Reflections on Discovering the Truth of Sacred Scripture," 81. On who the "fideles are and what their 'sense' tells us about the Church's teaching on contraception," see especially Janet E. Smith's essay, "*Sensus Fidelium* and *Humanae Vitae*." I will return to the role of the sensus fidelium in discerning revelation later in chapter 3.

60. *Catechism of the Catholic Church*, no. 114.

61. Martin, "Some Directions in Catholic Biblical Theology," 68.

62. Packer, "Biblical Authority, Hermeneutics and Inerrancy," 149.

63. *Interpretation of the Bible in the Church*, II. B, no. 2.

than such conscious intentions."[64] Yet, spiritual exegesis like typological exegesis does not ignore the literal-historical sense of the text; quite to the contrary, spiritual exegesis means interpreting the Holy Scripture in the light of redemptive history, the historical revelation of God in Christ, who is the fullness and mediator of all revelation. "The spiritual sense," the Commission writes, "results from setting the text in relation to real *facts* which are not foreign to it: the paschal event [the death and Resurrection of Christ], in all its exhaustible richness, which constitutes the summit of the divine intervention in the history of Israel, to the benefit of all mankind" (emphasis added). Aidan Nichols explains:

> *So in principle the whole of the Old Testament revelation could be reapplied in a unique way to Christ himself.* The central events and images of the Jewish Scriptures were so many types or foreshadowings of the life, death, and resurrection of Christ. Such Christological typology is the most characteristic form of interpretation of the Old Testament in the New. Sometimes it is quite conscious, being introduced by a New Testament author with a phrase like "according to the Scriptures," or "as it is written," or "in order to fulfill the Scriptures." On other occasions, it is unconscious or at least never made explicit, as when St. Matthew presents Jesus as a new Moses giving the new Law not on Sinai but on the Mount of the Beatitudes. Its most systematic realization is to be found in the Letter to the Hebrews with its Christocentric reading of the Old Testament priesthood and cultus. This is the earliest and still the most important form of spiritual interpretation of the Bible. Perhaps the best-known example of this type of exegesis, reading the Jewish Scriptures as having a reference to Jesus Christ, is the application to Jesus of the poems about a 'suffering servant' in Second Isaiah. In terms of the literal sense, the subject of these poems was either the people of Israel in the sixth century before the Christian era, or part of that people, a spiritual elite centering perhaps on the prophet's own disciples; or again, some devout individual, possibly Jeremiah, or the last king of Judah, Jehoiachim. In terms of the spiritual sense, however, a variety of New Testament references present the subject of these poems as Jesus himself, in whom their language finds its fulfillment in a way that surpasses anything their makers could have grasped.[65]

---

64. Nichols, *Shape of Catholic Theology*, 156.
65. Ibid., 157; italics added to the first sentence.

The first sentence of the above quotations may strike some as an over-statement: not everything in the OT is Christological and typological. That is how it struck my colleague J. Daryl Charles: "If everything is Christological and typological, then we may as well, as did Origen, allegorize everything in the OT. But this cripples a proper historical exegesis. Christ is NOT in everything, even when he fulfills everything. The Song of Songs is not a love story to or about Jesus; it is an ancient Near Eastern love poem."[66] I agree with Charles that the meaning of Scripture is its historical-grammatical meaning, its literal sense. Yet, the canonical meaning of any biblical text cannot be restricted to its historical-grammatical meaning. We need to consider its canonical meaning. And, as Congar correctly stresses, "The deeper meaning of a text was beyond the literal sense, although only to be reached *through* the literal sense."[67] Put differently, "The canonical sense of a book or passage," says Aidan Nichols, "the transformation of its literal sense, which results from placing that literal sense in the context of Scripture as a whole."[68] Furthermore, Nichols is aware of the danger that Charles refers to. He writes:

> Modern scholars tend to distinguish sharply between Christological allegory and Christological typology. The difference is that in allegory an exegete is not looking for what we can major correspondence in Scripture but for any reference—however alight—which can be related—however obscurely—the person and work of Christ. Thus the red girdle that the prostitute Rahab used to guide the Israelites to safety, as described in the Book of Joshua, could be interpreted in terms of the Christological allegory as referring to the blood of the cross. But the scope for arbitrariness in this sort of exegesis is so endless that contemporary exponents of the spiritual sense of the Bible understandably fight shy of it. The Christological sense as typology rather than allegory is taken much more seriously, not least because its basic principles are already found within the Bible itself. Internally, within the biblical text we can find evidence of the practice of typological exegesis, and in the New Testament such typological exegesis takes on a specifically Christological character.[69]

---

66. J. Daryl Charles, private email to me, Tuesday, June 3, 2008.

67. Congar, *Tradition and Traditions*, 388.

68. Nichols, *Shape of Catholic Theology*, 154.

69. Ibid., 155–56. See also *Catechism of the Catholic Church*, "It is on this harmony of the two Testaments that the Paschal catechesis of the Lord is built, and then, that of the

In fact, the Commission argues against separating the literal and spiritual senses; rather the spiritual sense is already enclosed in an anticipatory sense within the literal sense in the light of the history of God's revelation in Christ, who is the fullness and mediator of all revelation. "When a biblical text relates directly to the paschal mystery of Christ or to the new life which results from it, its literal sense is already a spiritual sense. Such is regularly the case in the New Testament. It follows that it is most often in dealing with the Old Testament that Christian exegesis speaks of the spiritual sense."[70] Furthermore, the spiritual sense is, as I have already indicated, divided by the Fathers and theologians of the Middle Ages such as Thomas Aquinas into three main categories: allegorical or Christological sense, because the whole Bible must be read in the light of Christ; the tropological (from the Greek word for behavior, *tropos*) or moral sense, drawing out the implications of Scripture as a whole for human acting; and the anagogical or eschatological sense, revealing man's final destiny in God and the glory of eternal life.[71]

Thomas Aquinas is helpful here in clarifying how the multiple complex senses of Scripture can be based on the literal sense; indeed, presuppose the sense which the author intends. Since the primary author of Holy Scripture is God, the Holy Spirit, says Aquinas, he "has it within his power to signify his meaning, not by words only (as a person also can do), but also by things [persons and events] themselves." In other words, meaning may be conveyed by those things that are meant by the words themselves. Aquinas explains: "the things referred to by the words also themselves have a reference. Therefore that first kind of referring, in which words refer to things, belongs to the first sense: the historical or literal. That second kind of referring, in which things referred to by

---

Apostles and the Fathers of the Church. This catechesis unveils what lay hidden under the letter of the Old Testament: the mystery of Christ. It is called 'typological' because it reveals the newness of Christ on the basis of the 'figures' (types) which announce him in the deeds, words, and symbols of the first covenant. By this re-reading in the Spirit of Truth, starting from Christ, the figures are unveiled. Thus the flood and Noah's ark prefigured salvation by Baptism, as did the cloud and the crossing of the Red Sea. Water from the rock was the figure of the spiritual gifts of Christ, and manna in the desert prefigured the Eucharist, 'the true bread from heaven'" (no. 1094).

70. *Interpretation of the Bible in the Church*, II. B, no. 2.

71. On these three senses, see Nichols, *Shape of Catholic Theology*, 154–62. See also, Aquinas, *Summa Theologiae* 1.1.10, "Whether in Holy Scripture a word may have several senses?"

words also have a reference, is called the spiritual sense, which is based on the literal, and presupposes it." "The multiplicity of these senses does not produce equivocation or any other kind of multiplicity," Aquinas adds, "for these senses are not multiplied because one word signifies several things, but because the things signified by the words can themselves be signs of other things."[72] Illustrative of Aquinas' point is typological exegesis, in particular, Christological typology. In this connection, Nichols argues, in addition, that such exegesis presupposes both a providential connection between the persons and events of biblical history as well as divine consistency in God's communication with us. Thus: "If divine providence worked self-consistently in the biblical history, then something like typology must be true. The principal events and persons of Scripture must be related by significant correspondences, and these will come to a supreme intensity in the figure [that] is . . . the center of God's self-revelation, Jesus Christ."[73]

With the canonical and spiritual senses of Scripture, we have already moved in the direction of the *sensus plenior*: the plenary sense of Scripture, the text's deeper meaning, the whole unity of God's salvific plan in Christ, according to the intention of its divine author.[74]

JOHN PAUL II'S HERMENEUTICAL PRINCIPLES

Against the background of these principles, I want to describe briefly how some of these principles of Catholic hermeneutics are at work in John Paul II's own hermeneutical presuppositions.

First, the pope assumes a hermeneutical approach to Scripture that treats it *as a whole*, a canonical whole. This assumption is evident in his treatment of Gen 1–2 and Mt 19:3–12: the creation narrative is indispensable framework for interpreting the New Testament teaching of Jesus and Paul on homosexuality, that is, same-sex relations are contrary to the order of creation.[75] In this connection, he assumes a basic unity of content

---

72. Aquinas, *Summa Theologiae*, I., q. 1, a. 10.
73. Nichols, *Shape of Catholic Theology*, 158.
74. On this, see *Interpretation of the Bible in the Church*, II. B, no. 3, The Fuller Sense.

75. This hermeneutical approach is common to Christians' faithful to the historic Christian faith, Protestant or Catholic. For a Protestant who agrees with John Paul II, see the James Harrison Buchanan Professor of New Testament at the Southern Baptist Theological Seminary, Louisville, Kentucky, Schreiner, "New Testament Perspective on Homosexuality."

in biblical teaching of such fundamental matters as the meaning of the body-person, sex, and marriage, the moral life. Given that presupposition that Scripture is a unified and canonical whole, the biblical revelation manifests a God who will not fundamentally contradict himself. In *Homosexualitatis problema* (1987), the Congregation for the Doctrine of Faith identifies as one of the major causes for confusion regarding homosexuality a "new exegesis of Sacred Scripture which claims variously that Scripture has nothing to say on the subject of homosexuality or that it somehow tacitly approves of it or that all of its moral injunctions are so culture-bound that they are no longer applicable to contemporary life." The Congregation holds that these views are "gravely erroneous" (no. 4). Although the Congregation acknowledges the historical distance between now and the time the Scriptures were written, "There is nonetheless a clear consistency within the Scriptures themselves on the moral issue of homosexual behavior. The Church's doctrine regarding this issue is thus based not on isolated phrases [verses] for facile theological argument, but on the solid foundation of a constant biblical testimony."[76]

Second, the pope's hermeneutical schema assumes the unity of historical exegesis and theological interpretation. This is possible because he assumes Scripture has two authors: divine and human; and hence he can defend the claim that the divine author's intention when considered in light of Scripture as a canonical whole must be considered part of the literal sense of Scripture. The unity of historical exegesis and theological interpretation means that Scripture possesses a "multivalent potential of meaning."[77]

Third, the unifying principle of the Scripture as a canonical whole is Christ. As Aidan Nichols puts it, "Though we cannot pick and choose as to what in the Canon *we shall have*, nonetheless *the Canon itself has* a centre. Here as everywhere in revelation, Christ is the centre."[78] Thus, Scripture is to be read and interpreted Christocentrically, because the revelation

---

76. *Homosexualitatis problema*, nos. 4 and 5. Perhaps the most definitive defense of this "constant biblical testimony," using the methods of historical biblical criticism, is that of Robert A.J. Gagnon, Professor of New Testament at Pittsburg Theological Seminary, *Bible and Homosexual Practice: Texts and Hermeneutics.*

77. Stegman, "'Actualization': How John Paul II Utilizes Scripture in *The Theology of the Body*," 48.

78. Nichols, "Reclaiming the Bible," 167.

of Christ, who is the fullness and mediator of all revelation, "*holds the interpretive key to unlocking the meaning of the biblical witness.*"[79]

Fourth, Scripture is to be interpreted in and with the mind of the Church, and, given the Scripture's hermeneutical relevance, appropriated in the *ongoing* life of the Church. The Pontifical Biblical Commission's *Interpretation of the Bible in the Church* calls this "actualization," which means that the interpreter is showing the hermeneutical relevance of the Scripture. There is no doubt that John Paul II is convinced that authoritative Scripture, indeed, the Word of God, is hermeneutically relevant to our present condition. Thomas D. Stegman, distinguishes the principles that ground the process of actualization as follows:

> 1) [B]iblical texts contain a wealth of meaning that gives them value for all time and all cultures; 2) these texts are historically conditioned, thus necessitating a hermeneutical process to bring their essential message to bear on the present, actual situations; and 3) the living tradition of the Church stimulates the task of actualization. In implementing the process of actualization, the key is to draw—from the fullness of meaning *contained in* the texts—those elements that speak to the present situation in order to convey the saving will of God in Christ. Observe two critical elements of the preceding statement. First, actualization is grounded in what is contained in the biblical text itself. Second, the goal of actualization is to allow Scripture to speak afresh to new situations.[80]

Against the background of these hermeneutical principles, I turn now to give a theological interpretation of the resources that Scripture itself gives us for discerning "what is ideal and normative and what is temporary and *sui generis* in the Bible."[81]

CHRIST THE FULFILLMENT OF THE LAW[82]

In the previous section of this chapter, we learned that Scripture has different levels of meaning, in particular, the canonical and spiritual sense, and that we have various principles for discovering Scripture's that mean-

---

79. Stegman, "'Actualization': How John Paul II Utilizes Scripture in *The Theology of the Body*," 48.

80. Ibid., 50.

81. Copan, "Is Yahweh a Moral Monster?" 17.

82. Portions of this section were previously published in "Moral Life in Biblical Perspective," 28–32, 48–49.

ing. How does the canonical and spiritual sense of the biblical text help us to discover which moral truths are binding? As we have seen, some thinkers argue that the Church's appeal to the Bible's moral authority is selective and arbitrary. The point of this objection to using scripture in ethics is clear—because Christian appeal to scriptural warrant is selective and arbitrary the Scripture is unreliable as the authoritative and foundational court of appeal for ethics.

Yet, in my judgment, the objection fails to persuade. The use of Scripture as morally authoritative, though selective, is not arbitrary. Undoubtedly, it is impossible to take over everything that Scripture, from Genesis to Revelation, commands and forbids. But the key to determining which moral teachings are binding lies in Scripture itself since we can identify what ceremonial laws and civil laws, including the penal code, are no longer binding. To understand the reason why not everything accurately recorded in Scripture has normative authority for our faith and conduct, but only has historical authority, that is, it has authority for the people of the time, we need to think through the implication of the principle that the economy of revelation was given in the form of a history, passing through a succession of periods, culminating in Jesus Christ, who is both the mediator and fullness of revelation.[83] In other words, as Bavinck succinctly put it, "The revelation contained in Scripture is a historical and organic whole." He explains:

> Much of what was commanded and instituted by God, or prescribed and enjoined by prophets and apostles, no longer applies to us directly and pertained to persons living in an earlier age. The command to Abraham to offer up his son, the command to Israel to kill all the Canaanites, the ceremonial and civil laws in force in the days of the OT, the decrees of the synod of Jerusalem, and many more things, while indeed useful for instruction and correction as history, cannot and may not any longer be obeyed by us. Furthermore, the record of revelation not only includes the good works of the saints but also the evil deeds of the ungodly. Frequently words and actions are recorded in Scripture, therefore, that, while they are represented as historically true, are not pre-

---

83. Millard Erickson offers a set of criteria to distinguish what is "historically authoritative" and "normatively authoritative": (1) constancy across cultures, (2) universal setting, (3) a recognized permanent factor as a base, (4) indissoluble link with an experience regarded as essential, and (5) final position within progressive revelation" (*Christian Theology*, 130–34).

sented as normative. . . . Also the sins of the saints, of Abraham, Moses, Job, Jeremiah, Peter, etc., are given as a warning, not as models for our conduct.[84]

Perhaps it would be helpful for understanding Bavinck's point about the difference between historical and normative authority to distinguish two senses of "reveal."[85] First, there is the sense of "reveal" that means the "*recording* or *reporting* sense." "Revelation in this sense is simply the accurate recording of the often mistaken and wicked beliefs and opinions of men. It is revelation to us in that without these opinions and views being recorded it is highly probable that we would be ignorant of them. This is probably the case also with the recording of certain historical events."[86] There is a second of "reveal" that means the "*disclosing* or *endorsing* sense." "If God reveals in this sense then his disclosure of whatever the matter is is a necessary and sufficient condition for that matter being true or right." In other words, in the disclosing or endorsing sense of "reveal" what is revealed does correspond to what God himself regards as being true. Now, the difference between these two senses of "reveal" has the following implications. First, there are false beliefs, opinions and the like that are accurately recorded or reported in the Bible, but that does not count against identifying the Bible with God's special revelation because what is revealed, in the recording or reporting sense of "reveal," does not correspond to what God himself regards as true, and is therefore false. Thus, "if the Bible in its entirety is God's revelation it does not follow that every sentence of the Bible is God's revelation [in the second sense of 'reveal'], any more than it follows that because a poem rhymes every word in the poem rhymes." There is a second important implication that follows from this distinction. That is, Paul Helm concludes, "this distinction imposes a considerable hermeneutical burden on any would-be interpreter of the special revelation. For he has to determine the exact limits of each kind of revelation, otherwise it may happen that the mistaken beliefs of men would be equated with the special revelation of God's will."[87] There remains to ask whether

---

84. Bavinck, *Gereformeerde Dogmatiek*, I, 428–29 [459].

85. I am following Paul Helm's illuminating distinction between the two senses of "reveal" in his book, *Divine Revelation*, 68–70.

86. Ibid.

87. Ibid.

there is a way to ease the hermeneutical burden on the would-be interpreter of special revelation. I want to suggest the following criteria that Robert A. J. Gagnon stipulates for anyone who takes Scripture to be the primary authority for faith and practice. Gagnon writes:

> If that primacy counts for anything, it must count for core values. Core values are values that are held 1. pervasively throughout Scripture (at least implicitly), 2. absolutely (without exceptions), and ... 3. strongly (as a matter of significance). This applies all the more to instances in which: 4. such values emerged in opposition to contrary cultural trends and ... 5. have prevailed in the church for two millennia. *Such a [core] value is the biblical limitation of sex to intercourse between male and female, with its attendant opposition to same-sex intercourse.* If the authority of Scripture means anything, those who seek to overturn its core values must meet an extraordinary burden of proof. The evidence must be so strong and unambiguous that it not only makes the witness of Scripture pale by comparison but also directly refutes the reasons for the Bible's position.[88]

One point of clarification here may be needed. Gagnon's criteria are helpful perhaps even in some sense necessary for determining why certain "core values" of Scripture still have authority for us. Yet, they are not sufficient to explain what makes Scripture the revealed Word of God, at least not according to Catholic teaching. As I argued in chapter 1, the only sufficient explanation for biblical authority is that the Bible is the inspired and inerrant Word of God, possessing canonical authority because divinely inspired, having divine authorship, and hence entrusted to the Church by the Holy Spirit. In other words, Scripture is an integrated whole, a single, unified, authoritative Word of God, which means that the whole of Scripture, in light of its God-breathed character, has canonical authority. In that sense all of Scripture is normative. Hence, we cannot *abstractly separate* in Scripture the authority of history and normative authority. So I reject the dualistic construal of the distinction between historical and normative authority that leads to the process of sifting and separating the Word of God and the word of men. The point I am making then—in line with Bavinck and Berkouwer—should not be interpreted as dualism.[89] Rather, the question has to do with distinct kinds of scrip-

---

88. Via and Gagnon, *Homosexuality and the Bible, Two Views*, 42; italics added.
89. Berkouwer, *De Heilige Schrift*, II, 110–11 [190–92].

tural authority, namely, that not all Scriptural authority is the authority of a law enacted by a legislature. For God's Word has historical contours. Against that background, we can easily understand why Bavinck judges that the sins of the saints in Scripture, although given as a warning, still have authority for us. He elaborates: "Even in the deceptive words of Satan and the evil deeds of the ungodly, God still has something to say to us. Scripture is not only useful for teaching but also for warning and reproof. It teaches and corrects us, both by deterrence and by exhortation, both by shaming and by consoling us." Still, adds Bavinck, the distinction between historical and normative authority "does make clear that Scripture cannot and may not be understood as a fully articulated code of law. Appeal to a text apart from its context is not sufficient for a dogma. The revelation recorded in Scripture is a historical and organic whole. That is how it has to be read and interpreted. A dogma that comes to us with authority and intends to be a rule for our life and conduct must be rooted in and inferred from the entire organism of Scripture. The authority of Scripture is different from the authority of an act of parliament or congress."[90]

Let us recall here the hermeneutical rule that the unifying principle of the Scripture as a canonical whole is Christ. That means that the revelation contained in Scripture is a historical and organic whole that finds in unity in Christ. We come now to the notion of the law's fulfillment in Christ. The revelation of Christ is the "goal" of the law. He is not the law's termination, but rather that toward which it moves (Rom 10:4), neither absorbing nor superseding it; instead Christ has perfected the law. Following Francis Martin, I will appeal to Lonergan's use of the notion of sublation to explain the sense in which Christ fulfills the old Covenant and "love is the fulfilling of the law" (Rom 13:10).[91] "What sublates goes beyond what is sublated, introduces something new and distinct, yet so far from interfering with the sublated or destroying it, on the contrary needs it, includes it, preserves all its proper features and properties, and carries them forward to a fuller realization within a richer context."[92] In this light, I argue now that Christ is the interpretive key to unlocking the meaning of the law.

This is the view of John Paul II in *MWTB*:

90. Bavinck, *Gereformeerde Dogmatiek*, I, 429 [460].
91. Martin, "All Israel will be Saved."
92. Lonergan, *Method in Theology*, 241.

> Jesus brings about a *fundamental revision of the way of understanding and carrying out the moral law of the Old Covenant*....Especially significant are the words ... Jesus declares, "Do not think that I have come to abolish the Law or the Prophets; I have not come to abolish but to fulfill" (Mt 5: 17). In the sentences that follow, Jesus explains the meaning of this antithesis and the necessity of the "fulfillment" of the law for the sake of realizing the kingdom of God.... *The fulfillment of the law is the* underlying *condition* for [the] reign [of God's Kingdom] in the temporal dimension of human existence. It is a question, however, of a fulfillment that fully corresponds to the meaning of the law, of the Decalogue, of the single commandment. Only such a fulfillment *builds the righteousness that God, the Legislator, has willed*. Christ, the Teacher, urges us not to give the kind of human interpretation of the whole law, and of the single commandments contained in it, that does not build the righteousness willed by God, the Legislator. "Unless your righteousness exceeds that of scribes and Pharisees, you will never enter the kingdom of heaven" (Mt 5:20). (*MWTB*, 24.1)

John Paul II is making several important points here. First, Jesus neither replaces nor adds to the moral teachings of the Law, but rather he exposes its true and positive, indeed, fullest meaning in light of the central Love commandment: that we love God completely and love our neighbor as ourselves. In that sense Jesus interiorizes the demands of the law because fulfillment of the law must be measured by that central commandment to love. Indeed, the *Catechism of the Catholic Church* teaches that the central commandment to love expresses the "fundamental and innate vocation of every human being."[93] Second, Jesus does not merely call for an increased rigor in obeying the Law. If it were merely the latter, then our righteousness would not exceed that of the scribes and Pharisees, and we would be trapped in legalism, in fact, works-righteousness. Rather, the pope's stress on the fulfillment of the law as being the precondition for the reign of God's Kingdom in temporal existence is made possible by Jesus' life, death, resurrection, and ascension. The saving grace of God precedes and makes possible the demand for righteousness that God has willed. Thus, righteous living in God's Kingdom is built on the foundation of fulfillment in Christ.[94]

---

93. *Catechism of the Catholic Church*, no. 1604.
94. Holwerda, "Jesus and the Law," esp. 115–17.

Third, against this background, we can appreciate Douma's correct conclusion: "When we take into account this *fulfillment in Christ*, it is impossible to view the Mosaic legal code in its totality as still being the guide for today. Moreover, the unity of Holy Scripture presupposes that in our moral reflection we will always use the *entire canon* of Scripture."[95] This is the first hermeneutical imperative of *Dei Verbum*, no. 12: to attend to the canonical sense of the Scripture, which is arrived at by interpreting the literal sense in the context of the whole Bible. In light of this imperative, we can develop the notion of the law's fulfillment in Christ.

The Gospel of Christ is "a law of freedom, because it sets us free from the ritual and juridical observances of the Old Law."[96] Civil, criminal, and cultic (ritual) Old Testament Laws are no longer binding for us. Laws regarding temple sacrifices, ritual cleanliness, and diet, like forbidding unclean meats, whose point is holiness and forgiveness of sins, have been fulfilled by the sacrificial death of Jesus on the cross. His atoning death both perfected and transformed the OT sacrificial system, because He makes a full and perfect sacrifice for sin on our behalf. "We have been sanctified through the offering of the body of Jesus Christ once for all . . . For by one offering He has perfected forever those who are being sanctified" (Heb 10:10, 14). Again:

> But Christ came *as* High Priest of the good things to come, with the greater and more perfect tabernacle not made with hands, that is, not of this creation. Not with the blood of goats and calves, but with His own blood He entered the Most Holy Place once for all, having obtained eternal redemption. For if the blood of bulls and goats and the ashes of a heifer, sprinkling the unclean, sanctifies for the purifying of the flesh, how much more shall the blood of Christ, who through the eternal Spirit offered Himself without spot to God, cleanse your conscience from dead works to serve the living God? And for this reason He is the Mediator of the new covenant, by means of death, for the redemption of the transgressions under the first covenant, that those who are called may receive the promise of eternal inheritance (Heb. 9:11–15).

Now to our primary question: Is the biblical prohibition against homosexuality to be classified along with the other temporary ceremonial laws that are no longer binding because of Christ's perfect sacrifice for sin on

---

95. Douma, "Use of Scripture in Ethics," 389.
96. *Catechism of the Catholic Church*, no. 1972.

our behalf? Some critics of using Holy Scripture as morally authoritative claim that prohibiting homosexuality today would be like forbidding unclean meats, and since we don't accept the latter prohibition, it would be inconsistent to accept the former. This argument is unconvincing, however for several reasons.

First, the ceremonial laws of the Old Testament point to or prefigure Christ and these laws have been fulfilled by Christ's obedience. The same cannot be said for the biblical prohibition against homosexuality. Second, the death penalty demanded for homosexuality puts it in the moral realm and not in the ceremonial laws. The primary character of the holiness code is moral, prohibiting incest, adultery, child sacrifice, oppression of the poor, slander, hatred, unjust weights and measures, and these precepts are still binding today. In sum, as Greg L. Bahnsen correctly argues:

> Christ himself appealed [to the contents of Lev 18-20] as summarizing all the law and the prophets (Lev 19:18; cf. Matt 22:39-40).
> ... The defender of homosexuality must produce a viable criterion for distinguishing between moral and ceremonial laws, or else consistently reject them all (contrary to the emphatic word of Christ). We have the New Testament warrant for discontinuing obedience to the sacrificial system (Heb 10:1-18).
> ... However, the Scriptures never alter God's revealed law regarding homosexuality, but leave us under its full requirement (cf. Deut 8:3; 12:32; Matt 4:4). Indeed, the Bible repeatedly condemns homosexuality, the New Testament itself stressing that it is contrary to God's law (1 Tim 1:9-10), bringing God's judgment and exclusion from the kingdom (Rom 1:24ff.; 1 Cor 6:9-10). Therefore, the prohibition against homosexuality cannot be viewed as part of the ceremonial system prefiguring Christ or as temporary in its obligation.[97]

---

97. Bahnsen, *Homosexuality*, 40-41. Bahnsen's study on homosexuality is valuable in its defense of biblical authority, the biblical assessment of homosexuality, the act/condition distinction and the causes of homosexuality. His pastoral compassion and sensitivity to the difficulties homosexuals may encounter from their condition, which constitutes a "trial" (cf. *Catechism of the Catholic Church*, no. 2358), is also commendable. My basic disagreement with Bahnsen, however, is with his understanding of the relation between the laws given to Israel in the Old Testament, especially the penal code that he expects the state to prescribe and implement today, and the New Covenant. Thus, I reject Bahnsen's defense of homosexual acts as criminal and therefore punishable, which he, as a theonomist, defends as biblically warranted (see chapter 5, "The Response of Society: Homosexual Acts as Criminal," 99-124).

Furthermore, the penal code of the Mosaic Law no longer possesses juridical authority. This code stipulates capital punishment for more than twenty crimes such as disrespecting parents, adultery, and homosexuality (Lev 20:9–10, 13). Moreover it was directed toward the civil society of Israel and thus this criminal code, not the moral principles behind it, lost its validity when Israel ceased to be a theocratic nation. Hence the OT penal code is no longer binding for us. Moreover, as Dutch Reformed theologian Jochem Douma correctly notes, "Christ is directing His teaching not toward the external civil order, but toward the internal spiritual and moral meaning of the law."[98]

Certainly, Christians must still accept as binding the moral commands prohibiting, for example, adultery, homosexuality, and disrespecting parents. The moral laws, whose core is the Ten Commandments, retain their direct and unchanging validity. Moreover, even these commandments receive a new foundation in the Gospel.[99] "The Law of the Gospel 'fulfills,' refines, surpasses, and leads the Old Law to its perfection."[100]

Indeed, the key to understanding what happens to the whole law (cultic, civil and moral) of the Old Testament is Jesus Christ. Jesus said, "Do not think that I have come to abolish the Law or the Prophets; I have come not to abolish but to fulfill" (Matt 5:17). On the one hand, Christ's fulfillment of the law means that we are free from the law as a means of salvation. Because of sin, which the law cannot remove, sins remain a form of bondage from which Christ sets us free. Thus, we are justified through the saving work of Jesus Christ. We are no longer under God's law, but under His grace. On the other hand, that the law is fulfilled in Christ does not mean that the gospel has no further relation to the law.

---

98. Douma, "Use of Scripture in Ethics," 378. See also, Douma, *Responsible Conduct*, 55–111.

99. It is impossible to pause here—though I must admit I am very tempted—to examine another set of claims that has contributed to the erosion of biblical authority, that is, the rejection of universally valid moral precepts, sexual or otherwise, through the influence of cultural relativism, existentialistic personalism, nominalism, and occasionalism—all of which contributed to some sort of situation ethics that renders impossible a direct appeal to Biblical texts that are universally valid. For an instructive study on the theological and philosophical basis of situations ethics both twentieth-century century century Protestant and Roman Catholic theologians, see Gustafson, *Protestant and Roman Catholic Ethics*, esp. 30–137. See also, Gagnon, "Are there Universally Valid Sex Precepts? A Critique of Walter Wink's Views on the Bible and Homosexuality."

100. *Catechism*, no. 1967.

Although we are freed from bondage to the law as a way of salvation, the moral law remains God's will for the life of the Christian. I argued in chapter 1 that Johnson obscures the importance of this point by locating the authority of the Bible primarily in narratives and not as well in God's commandments.

In what sense does the moral law remain God's will for the Christian when he has been called to freedom in Christ? To answer this important question, we turn to the Doctor of the Church, and great theologian and philosopher, St. Thomas Aquinas. Aquinas' distinction between the *obliging* and *compelling* forces of the moral law is helpful here.[101] Some key texts are found in St. Paul. St. Paul says, "Now the Lord is the Spirit, and where the Spirit of the Lord is, there is freedom" (2 Cor 3:17). Elsewhere he writes: "But if you are led by the Spirit, you are not under the law" (Gal 5:18). St. Paul here is talking of the interior freedom of those who are moved by the Spirit. But those who are moved by the Spirit would not be against the moral laws expressed in the second table of the Decalogue for they have an *obliging* force. "All the faithful are under the Law, because it was given to all—hence it is said: 'I have not come to abolish the law but to fulfill it.'"[102] *Pace* antinomians, moral laws do tell us what one is allowed or not allowed to do, permitted or forbidden. Yes, "For freedom Christ has set us free" (Gal 5:1). But our freedom in Christ does not mean that we are no longer obliged to be faithful in marriage (and not commit adultery), to protect human life (and not commit murder), to honor our parents, keep our promises, tell the truth (and not bear false witness against our neighbor), and the like. Being free in Christ does not mean that we're *above* the law. Christians are not antinomians. This is evident from St. Paul's description of those persons who "walk by the Spirit." "Walk by the Spirit and you will certainly not carry out [the] desires of the flesh. . . . If you are being led by the Spirit you are not under [the jurisdiction] of the law. Now the works of the flesh are evident: sexual immorality [*porneia*], [sexual] impurity [*akatharsia*; a term used of same-sex intercourse in Rom 1:24–27], [sexual] licentiousness [*aselgeia*] . . . I warn you, just as I warned you beforehand, that those who do such things will not inherit the kingdom of God. . . . And those who belong to Christ [Jesus] [have] crucified the flesh with its passions and its desires. If we live by the Spirit, let us also

---

101. Aquinas, *Commentary on Saint Paul's Epistle to the Galatians*, chapter 5, lecture 5, 172.

102. Ibid., 172.

walk by the Spirit" (Gal 5:16–25). So those who are moved by the Spirit are not under the law—and thus are not constrained by it—means that they have the interior freedom to choose the good out of love for God, with the dynamism of the Holy Spirit in them being their inspiration. "If you love me, you will keep my commandments," says Jesus (John 14:15). "For charity inclines to the very things that the Law prescribes. Therefore, because the just have an inward law, they willingly do what the Law commands and are not constrained by it."[103]

Therefore he who would do evil but is led back by a sense of shame or by fear of the law is compelled to keep the law, and thus experiences the moral law as a form of bondage, imposing moral precepts unrelated to his good. This man is still *under* the law, and hence not free in a Pauline sense. On true freedom, then, Aquinas writes: "A person is free when he belongs to himself; a slave, on the contrary, belongs to his master. In the same way, he acts freely who acts spontaneously, while he who receives his impulse from another does not act freely. Therefore, he who avoids evil not because it is evil but because of a commandment of God is not free. But he who avoids evil because it is evil is free. Now it is precisely this that the Holy Spirit brings about, for he perfects our spirit interiorly, giving it a new dynamism, and thus the person refrains from evil out of love, as if the divine law commanded it of him. He is free, therefore, not in the sense that the divine law no longer holds for him, but in the sense that his interior dynamism moves him to do what the divine law prescribes."[104]

Aquinas' concluding point that the divine law still holds for the man of Pauline freedom is clear because both Jesus and the Apostles appeal to the Ten Commandments (Matt 19:18; Rom 13:9; Eph 6:2; James 2:11). The moral law retains its meaning as, in St. Paul's words, 'holy law' and as "holy and just and good" (Rom 7:12). Thus, on the one hand, Jesus fulfills the law cannot mean that Christians can break with the moral law. On the other hand, as the former Joseph Ratzinger, now Benedict XVI, correctly explains, "universalizing of the Torah by Jesus, as the New Testament understands it, is not the extraction of some universal moral prescriptions from the living whole of the God's revelation. It preserves the unity of cult

---

103. Ibid. The Psalmist speaks of the man of God as one who has delight in the law and commandments, who loves the law, with the law being true and life-giving (see Psalm 119).

104. Aquinas, *Commentary on Saint Paul's Second Epistle to the Corinthians*, chapter 3, lesson 3.

and ethos. The ethos remains grounded and anchored in the cult, in the worship of God, in such a way that the entire cult is bound together in the Cross, indeed, for the first time has become fully real."[105] Thus, as the law's fulfiller, Jesus takes up the Law into His death and brings it to its deepest meaning by perfecting and transforming it (see Matt 5:17–20). The *Catechism* clearly articulates the relation of the Old Law to the New Law:

> The Law of the Gospel *fulfills the commandments* of the Law. The Lord's Sermon on the Mount, far from abolishing or devaluing the moral prescriptions of the Old Law, releases their hidden potential and has new demands arise from them: it reveals their entire divine and human truth. It does not add new external precepts, but proceeds to reform the heart, the root of human acts, where man chooses between the pure and the impure, where faith, hope, and charity are formed and with them the other virtues. The Gospel thus brings the Law to its fullness through imitation of the perfection of the heavenly Father, through forgiveness of enemies and prayer for persecutors, in emulation of the divine generosity.[106]

Jesus fulfills the law by bringing out its fullest and complete meaning. He fulfills it also by bringing the finishing or capstone revelation—He radicalizes the law's demands by going to its heart and center, which is that we love God above all and our neighbors as ourselves.[107] In Matt 22:40, Jesus says, "On these two commandments hang all the Law and the Prophets." That is, as God's expressed will, love of God and love of neighbor is the root of the Ten Commandments.

As John Paul II explains, "Jesus brings God's commandments to fulfillment . . . by interiorizing their demands and by bringing out their fullest meaning. Love of neighbor springs from a loving heart." Because the love of God has been poured out in our hearts by the grace of the Holy Spirit, given to us through faith in Christ (Rom 5:5), not only does His love now indwell in, and act through, us, but God's law is placed within our hearts (Jer 31:33f.; Heb 10:16).

Because love of God and neighbor is the heart of the law, Jesus shows that the commandments prohibiting murder and adultery mean more than the letter of the law states. Jesus is not an ethical minimalist, a view which associates the law with mere formality and externalism in

---

105. Ratzinger/Benedict XVI, *Many Religions—One Covenant*, 41.
106. *Catechism*, no. 1968.
107. Ibid.

morals, but rather an ethical maximalist.[108] A maximalist, and Christ was a maximalist, refers to the dimension of interiority. Christ appeals to the inner man. As I argued above, Jesus neither replaces nor adds to the moral teachings of the Law, but rather he exposes its true and positive, indeed, fullest meaning in light of the central Love commandment: that we love God completely and love our neighbor as ourselves. In that sense Jesus interiorizes the demands of the law because fulfillment of the law must be measured by that central commandment.

John Paul II in the *Theology of the Body* makes precisely the claim we are supporting here; that Christ does not abandon the Old Law, but introduces another element of the law, the interior perspective that opens up and fulfills the whole meaning of the law. He states, "The casuistry of the books of the Old Testament, which was preoccupied with investigating what, according to external criteria, constituted such an 'act of the body,' and was at the same time oriented toward fighting adultery, opened various legal 'loopholes' for adultery. In this way, on the basis of many compromises 'because of hardness of ... heart' (Mt 19: 8), the meaning of the commandment willed by the Legislator [Creator] suffered deformation. One was concerned with the legalistic observation of the formula, which did not 'superabound' in the inner righteousness of hearts. *Christ shifts the essence of the problem into another dimension* when he says, 'Whoever looks at a woman to desire her has already committed adultery with her in his heart.'" So Christ calls us, at one and the same time, to enter "into the depth *of the norm itself and descend into the interior of man, the subject of morality*" (*MWTB*, 24.4, 24.3). Interiority is important because the standard of the Christian life is an interior state: holiness, or sanctification, and "we are sanctified by God to God."[109] Obedience to the commandments is then a moral and spiritual journey, in Christ and through the grace of the Holy Spirit, toward perfection, shown in faith working through love (cf. Col 3:14). In this light, John Paul adds, "the commandment 'You shall not murder' becomes a call to an attentive love that protects and promotes the life of one's neighbor. The precept prohibiting adultery becomes an invitation to a pure way of looking at others.... 'You have heard that it was said to men of old, You shall not murder, and whoever murders will be liable to judgment. But I say to you that whoever is angry with his brother shall be

---

108. Nichols, *Epiphany*, 391–432.

109. Webster, *Holiness*, 90.

liable to judgment ... You have heard that it was said, You shall not commit adultery. But I say to you that whoever looks at a woman lustfully has already committed adultery with her in his heart' (Matt 5:21–22)."[110]

Thus, Jesus does not merely call for an increased rigor in obeying the Law. If it were merely the latter, then our righteousness would not exceed that of the scribes and Pharisees, and we would be trapped in legalism, in fact, works-righteousness. Rather, the pope's stress on the fulfillment of the law as being the precondition for the reign of God's Kingdom in temporal existence is made possible by Jesus' life, death, resurrection, and ascension. The saving grace of God precedes and makes possible the demand for righteousness that God has willed. In other words, the moral and spiritual journey of obedience to the commandments, that is, righteous living in God's Kingdom, is built on the foundation of fulfillment in Christ.[111]

I shall have more to say about the interiority of morality below. Here I shall resume the discussion of hermeneutics and ethics in light of several models of revelation.

> Moral guidelines (norms) can and must be *deduced* from the Bible as the revealed Word of God:
>
> Variant (a): they can be deduced directly because Revelation= Word=Scripture=text;
>
> Variant (b): they can be deduced directly but not without taking account of the *historical distance* between the biblical writers and our time. This is done by factoring the difference in situation into the formation of a judgment;
>
> Variant (c): they can be deduced *indirectly* by way of an appeal to central biblical motifs (covenant, view of man, view of the body, the love-command), etc.).
>
> (2) One can indeed deduce guidelines for action from the Bible, not primarily because their moral validity is rooted in the fact that they are laid down in Scripture, but because, from an ethical viewpoint, they are good for people. Consequently we find them also in the Bible. To "deduce" means one can also trace them to Scripture. In the Bible, though morality often turns out to be crucial in the

---

110. *Veritatis Splendor*, no. 15
111. Holwerda, "Jesus and the Law," 115–17.

end, it is not the central issue. God's design is to continue to teach us even through a fallen nature, culture, and history.

(3) Central to our agenda must be the doing of God's will. That does not consist in following rules but is discovered in seeing what God is concretely doing in history. The church has found that God's action is liberating. The Bible is the story of liberation from oppression. For that reason we must not automatically do the same today as what God's people did in earlier times. The church must understand the Bible in light of its concrete experience with liberation and oppression.[112]

As I see it, model (1), in all its variants, has been consistently used by Christians throughout the centuries in appealing to the authority of Scripture—but only as long as the unity of Scripture and its reliability as the Word of God was accepted as a first principle of the moral life as well as in doctrinal matters, indispensable and decisive. Model (2), which is compatible with (1), should be understood in terms of natural law, which purports to defend the universal claims for biblical morality. On this Model (2), Scriptural moral norms are the Creator's norms, and they are expressions of his design for human life. In order to work out the relation between Models (1) and (2) we need to discuss the larger question of how Christ relates creation and the will of God. "Is Christ in continuity with creation? Or is Christ in disjunction with creation?" In other words, what is the relation between redemption and creation? This theological question is fundamental to understanding John Paul II's in the *Theology of the Body*. The pope states that Genesis 2 and 3 theologically gives us an "account that is a description of events" that makes clear "the essential difference *between the state of man's sinfulness and that of his original innocence*." That is, there are "two different states of human nature, '*status naturae integrae*' (state of integral nature) and '*status naturae lapse*' (state of fallen nature) (*MWTB*, 3.3). Yet, John Paul argues that the order of creation is the essential continuity between creation, fall into sin, and grace in Christ. He writes, "*Christ's words* [in Mt 19:3–8], which appeal to the 'beginning,' *allow us to find an essential continuity in man and a link* between these two different states or dimensions of the human being ['*status naturae integrae*' and '*status naturae lapsae*,' that is, the state of integral nature and the state of fallen nature]" (*MWTB*, 4.1). Redemption,

---

112. On these models, see Pronk, *Against Nature? Types of Moral Argumentation regarding Homosexuality*, 283–84.

then, is about the restoration of the fallen creation. In short, grace restores or renews nature, meaning thereby that God's grace in Christ restores all life to its fullness, penetrating and perfecting and transforming the fallen creation from within its own order, bringing creation into conformity with His will and purpose.[113]

As the *Catechism of the Catholic Church* puts it: "Jesus came to restore creation to the purity of its origins."[114] Elsewhere in the *Catechism* we read: "In his preaching Jesus unequivocally taught the original meaning of the union of man and woman as the Creator willed it from the beginning. . . . *By coming to restore the original order of creation disturbed by sin*, [Jesus] himself gives the strength and grace to live marriage in the new dimension of the Reign of God."[115] This question is raised against the background of a fallen creation. Given the fallen creation, does new life in Christ oppose creation? Put differently: does grace replace fallen nature? "Nature" here has the chief meaning of ontological rather than physical or biological. So when we ask about the relation between nature, sin and grace, we are asking in what manner and to what extent sin and grace affect the essence or structure of reality. On the one hand, are the structures of creation so corrupted that grace, no longer able to transform them, merely replaces them altogether by adding the spiritual realm over and above creation, a *donum superadditum*? On the other hand, does grace leave nature untouched, merely completing or supplementing it, with nature taken to be unaffected by the Fall or, in turn, by Redemption internally, which effectively limits the scope of sin and redemption to the supernatural realm and results in naturalism on the level of nature.[116]

In the early twentieth century, the great French Catholic thinker, Jacques Maritain, wisely noted that it is erroneous to ignore that there is a distinction between nature and grace as well as a union.[117] How then

---

113. I will return to this fundamental question in chapter 5.

114. *Catechism of the Catholic Church*, no. 2336.

115. Ibid., nos. 1614–1615; italics added.

116. On this point, see De Lubac, *Catholicism: Christ and the Common Destiny of Man*, 313–14. My thinking on the relation between nature and grace is heavily indebted to Dutch neo-Calvinist philosopher Herman Dooyeweerd (1894–1977). For a brief introduction to his thought, see his Harvard Lectures, *In the Twilight of Western Thought*.

117. Jacques Maritain, *Clairvoyance de Rome*, 222 (italics added), "There is one error that consists in ignoring the distinction between nature and grace. There is another that consists in ignoring their union," as cited in De Lubac, "Apologetics and Theology," *Theological Fragments*, 91–104, and this citation at 103, note 28.

should we understand the union-in-distinctness of nature and grace? In particular, how do we understand the Thomistic dictum that grace does not abolish nature but presupposes it? The brief answer to this question must be that *grace restores or renews nature*, meaning thereby that God's grace in Christ *restores all life to its fullness, penetrating and perfecting and transforming the fallen creation from within its own order*, bringing creation into conformity with His will and purpose.[118] In the words of Henri de Lubac, "The supernatural does not merely *elevate* (this traditional term is correct, but it is inadequate by itself) ... [Rather] it *transforms it* ... 'Behold, I make all things new!' (Rev 21:5). Christianity is 'a doctrine of transformation' because the Spirit of Christ comes to permeate the first creation and make of it a 'new creature.' What is true of the final great transformation, on the occasion of the 'Parousia' at which there will arise 'new heavens and a new earth' (Revelation 21), is already true now, according to St. Paul, of each one of us."[119] Thus, the key idea here is that *grace restores nature*. "Faith in redemption cannot be separated from faith in the Creator." Redemption, adds Joseph Ratzinger, now Benedict XVI, "is an act of new creation, the restoration of creation to its true identity."[120]

What is the import of this latter understanding of nature and grace for understanding Model (2) as well as for the claim that Scriptural moral norms are the Creator's norms, that is, expressions of his design for human life? We can briefly respond to this question in the words of Lewis Smedes:

> Christ is continuous with creation, the restorer of creation's original intent. It comes to a universal claim for the morality taught by Jesus: it is the way all persons should live. The morality of the Bible is not an esoteric way of life for a relatively few disciples; it is the human way of life. But is it a way of life which ordinary people can be persuaded to accept? The continuity between Christ's law and God's original purpose with his creatures does not entail an ability of sinful people either to tune into it or live by it. Jesus' moral teachings assume that a conversion is necessary in the hearts of those who hear them, a personal conversion that includes both a new vision of God and new power to will to do his will. So, even though the special morality of the Gospel is—in the deepest sense—valid

---

118. This theological understanding of the relation between nature, sin and grace is fundamental to John Paul II's *TOB*. I argue for this claim in chapter 5.

119. De Lubac, *Brief Catechesis on Nature and Grace*, 81–82.

120. Ratzinger/Benedict XVI, *Spirit of the Liturgy*, 24, 34.

for all people, it is—in terms of its feasibility—applicable only to those who are prepared by the Spirit to accept it. Still, it is important that when one does accept Jesus' moral law, he is accepting, not an odd, esoteric, enclave morality, but the morality of the truly human existence.[121]

The *Catechism of the Catholic Church* illustrates Model (2) in its understanding of marriage. God himself is the author of marriage and hence the latter is grounded in the order of creation. Marriage is under the fall into sin and hence marital "union has always been threatened by discord, a spirit of domination, infidelity, jealousy, and conflicts that can escalate into hatred and separation." This brokenness "does not stem from the *nature* of man and woman, nor from the nature of their relations, but from *sin*. . . . Nevertheless, the order of creation persists, though seriously disturbed." The redemptive work of Christ is, however, continuous with the order of creation, with God's original intent for marriage, because he came "to restore the original order of creation disturbed by sin." Furthermore, Christ himself "gives the strength and grace to live marriage in the new dimension of the Reign of God. It is by following Christ, renouncing themselves, and taking up their crosses that spouses will be able to 'receive' the original meaning of marriage and live it with the help of Christ. This grace of Christian marriage is a fruit of Christ's cross, the source of all Christian life."[122] In short, redemption restores the creation to its true identity.

As to Model (3), its popularity arose with the surrender of the unity and reliability of Scripture under the influence of historical critical investigation (see chapter 2 above), but also with the denial that there exists in Holy Scripture, as a special revelational act of God, fundamental revealed moral truth. With this denial came the acceptance of the claim that "the revelation of the will of God is not given in the form of immutable and universally valid ethical norms."[123] What encouraged this acceptance was the rejection of revealed truth, that is, propositional revelation. "It is for this reason that there is among scholars, across the Christian traditions, a movement away from what we might call a 'biblical rules' approach to

---

121. Smedes, "Bible and Ethics."

122. The quotations in this paragraph are from the *Catechism of the Catholic Church*, nos. 1603, 1606, and 1615.

123. Typical of this acceptance is a statement adopted by the Reformed Ecumenical Council, Athens 1992, *Hermeneutics and Ethics*.

theology. 'Realizing the impossibility of transposing rules from biblical times to our own, interpreters look for larger themes, values, or ideals which can inform moral reflection without determining specific practices in advance.'"[124] So on this Model (3) biblical authority can be ascribed to themes like love, justice, freedom even though their concrete applications brings one into open conflict with biblical commandments, as in the view of Luke Timothy Johnson. This is not the view of the Catholic Church, or for that matter of any orthodox Christian rooted in the historic moral teaching of Christianity. I continue now with a sketch of the application of Model (1).

SCRIPTURE FUNCTIONS IN A VARIETY OF WAYS

Looking back to variant (b) of Model (1), we can take account of the *historical distance* between the biblical writers and our time without a wholesale abandonment of Scriptural norms. According to Jochem Douma, Scriptural revelation functions in a variety of ways as a moral authority—it functions as *guide, guard, compass*, and *example*.[125] Helpful here in distinguishing these various functions is Lewis Smedes' distinction between "primary commandments" and "concrete commandments." The former cover specific areas of life, such as human existence, property, communication, marriage, family. The latter demand or prohibit a specific act in the context of applying a primary command.

First, Scripture functions as a *guide* telling us specifically and concretely what is good and evil. There are primary commands against murdering my neighbor, against stealing or lying, or against committing adultery, and disrespecting parental authority in the family. These commands are meant to safeguard respect for persons. They are universal—they are always and everywhere valid, because it is true of all men that they should not kill, steal, lie, dishonor their parents, or commit adultery. Of course not all men heed these commandments, but all men should. Yet, while these commands stand above cultural relativities—children should obey their parents is universally valid—some specific applications

---

124. Lawler, *What Is and What Ought to Be*, 84. The quote within the quote is from Cahill, "Is Catholic Ethics Biblical?" 5–6. For a similar view that rejects propositional revelation and hence claims "the futility of attempting to derive specific moral solutions from particular biblical texts or even combination of texts," see Schneiders, *Revelatory Text*, 63 n. 35; see also 54, 58–59.

125. Douma, "Use of Scripture in Ethics," 367–76.

of these commands, so-called concrete commands—executing a son who swears at his father—are not accepted now as binding. Such commands are now understood to be a cultural rather than an absolute norm expressed in a primary commandment.

Biblical revelation also functions as a *guard*. This is especially the case when a direct appeal to Scripture is not possible because of the difference in situation between the biblical time and now. We're all aware of, and have been influenced by, cultural developments that have led to changes in, for example, the relationships between husbands and wives, parents and children, government and citizens. For instance, we cannot directly appeal to Scripture to justify the rise of human rights, democracy, freedom of religion, and better forms of government. In other words, Scripture cannot function as a direct guide (in the above stated sense of telling us specifically and concretely what is good and evil) on these and other related matters. This is not to say that the biblical revelation is irrelevant, say, for the notion of human rights.

Nonetheless, the Biblical revelation has played a crucial and authoritative role as guard for various cultural changes and developments in human rights issues like the abolition of slavery, child labor, and colonialism. That man is created in the "image and likeness of God" (Gen 1:26–27) is an inherent indication of human worth and, with it, personal dignity. Furthermore, the Biblical insistence that justice be done for the powerless, especially the poor, widows, orphans, and strangers, suggests that respect is due to them on the basis of their inviolable dignity. Moreover, the saving revelation of the Father's love in Jesus' death on the cross reveals to man, as John Paul II says, "not only the boundless love of God who 'so loved the world that He gave His only Son' (Jn 3:16), but also the *incomparable value of every human person*."[126] In connection with the pope's point, we can easily understand what Douma rightly says about the function of Scripture as guard: "Scripture is ... a guard that warns against corrupt developments. Old Testament prophets left behind no blueprint for political and social relationships, but they certainly denounced abuses where God was not being honored and people were not being respected. Scripture does not choose for or against democracy and other matters that we today value highly. But the Bible does sharpen our vision for seeing where people are abused and oppressed, regardless of political or economic system."

---

126. John Paul II, *Evangelium Vitae*, no. 2.

Biblical revelation also functions as a *compass* indicating the general direction we should go for finding an answer to the question of what is good or evil in a universally valid sense. For example, we could appeal to the universally valid Scriptural prohibitions or primary commands against homosexual relations (see Rom 1:21–27; 1 Cor 6:9–10), but we can also use Scripture as a compass for dealing with the question of the biblical validity of such relations. Consider the biblical account of God's original creation of sexual differentiation from the beginning ("male and female He created them" states Gen 1:27), of His ordaining sexual relations to be in the form of male-female union, because man and woman were created for one another in full complementarity (Gen 2:18–23), of man and woman—Adam and Eve—becoming "one flesh," one reality (Gen 2:24), and last but not least, the procreative openness to new life that is divinely enjoined, "be fruitful and multiply" (Gen 1:28).

The creation account in God's Word presents the constant principles for sexual activity that remain valid in every age—sex belongs within the context of marriage, marriage is exclusively heterosexual in nature, whose rationale is the full complementarity of the man-woman relationship as well as procreative openness to new life. This creation account is reaffirmed in the New Testament by Jesus Christ (Matt 19:4–6), as well as St. Paul (Eph 5:31), as the original design of the Creator. Thus, in light of creation, there is no biblical defense for homosexuality, because it belongs to the realm of man's fall into sin and not to the divine order of creation. The Bible gives us, then, constant principles that help us to discover what we should think and do, and in this sense it can be used as a compass.

Let's consider, however briefly, the objection that the literal sense of Scripture does not support the historic Christian teaching on homosexuality. Let us summarize what I have been arguing in the previous paragraphs. Homosexual practice is a violation of God's intentional creation of human beings as "male and female" (Gen 1:27) and the normative structure of marriage as a union between a man and a woman (Gen 2:24). Jesus Christ himself gives normative priority (see Matt 19:4–6; Mark 10:6–9) to these two texts from the creation narrative in Genesis as does St. Paul in his opposition to homosexual practice in Rom 1:24–27 and 1 Cor 6:9. Regarding Jesus, it is not surprising since, as Robert A. J. Gagnon points out, "The supposition of a Jesus supportive of, or even neutral toward, committed homosexual unions is without historical analogue in Jesus' immediate cultural environment. It is revisionist history at its worst."[127] "Moreover," adds Gagnon, "although we have no extant saying of Jesus that loosened the Law's demand for sexual purity, we do have sayings where Jesus closed remaining loopholes in the Law's sexual commands by *further intensifying* God's demand (adultery of the heart; divorce and remarriage) and warning people that sexual impurity could get one thrown into hell full-bodied (Matt 5:27–32). The trend of Jesus' teaching on sexual ethics is not toward greater license but toward fewer loopholes." Gagnon's theological exegesis dovetails with the interpretation I gave earlier of John Paul II's view of the moral law and interiority. I argued that Jesus is not an ethical minimalist, a view which associates the law with mere formality and externalism in morals, but rather an ethical maximalist.[128] A maximalist, and Christ was a maximalist, refers to the dimension of interiority. Christ appeals to the inner man. As I argued above, Jesus neither replaces nor adds to the moral teachings of the Law, but rather he exposes its true and positive, indeed, fullest meaning in light of the central Love commandment: that we love God completely and love our neighbor as ourselves. In that sense Jesus interiorizes the demands of the law because fulfillment of the law must be measured by that central commandment.

We should now add, as Gagnon correctly states, that every single scriptural text (whether narrative, law, proverb, poetry, and moral exhortation) treating the issue of homosexual practice treats it as an offense of great abhorrence to God. In short, all these texts presuppose a male-female prerequisite. In other words, as Gagnon puts it, "the male-female prerequisite is the foundational prerequisite for defining most other sexual norms." How so?

Well, the scriptural norm of marital monogamy and indissolubility are based on the foundational principle of the male-female prerequisite. The two-in-oneness of the sexes ordained by God at creation is the foundation limiting the number of persons in a conjugal bond. We must pause here to consider the objection, especially with respect to Jesus, that he "had no interest in maintaining a male-female requirement for sexual relations." In reply to this objection, Robert Gagnon persuasively writes: "What the evidence *really* shows: Jesus believed that a male-female requirement for sexual relations was foundational, a core value of Scripture's

127. In this paragraph and the next, I am closely following Gagnon, "What the Evidence *Really* Says."

128. Nichols, *Epiphany*, 391–432.

sexual ethics on which other sexual standards should be based, including the 'twoness of a sexual union.'"[129] He elaborates:

> The male-female prerequisite is the foundation or prior analogue for defining other critical sexual norms. Jesus himself clearly predicated his view of marital monogamy and indissolubility on the foundation of Gen 1:27 and 2:24, texts that have only one thing in common: the fact that an acceptable sexual bond before God entails as its first prerequisite (after the assumption of an intra-human bond) a man and a woman (Mark 10:6-9; Matt 19:4-6). Jesus argued that the "twoness" of the sexes ordained by God at creation was the foundation for limiting the number of persons in a sexual bond to two, whether concurrently (as in polygamy) or serially (as in repetitive divorce and remarriage). The foundation can hardly be less significant than the regulation predicated on it; indeed, it must be the reverse.... The principle by which same-sex intercourse is rejected is also the principle by which incest, even of an adult and consensual sort, is rejected. Incest is wrong because, as Lev 18:6 states, it involves sexual intercourse with "the flesh of one's own flesh." In other words, it involves the attempted merger with someone who is already too much of a formal or structural same on a familial level. The degree of formal or structural sameness is felt even more keenly in the case of homosexual practice, only now on the level of sex or gender, because sex or gender is a more integral component of sexual relations, and more foundationally defines it, than is and does the degree of blood relatedness. So the prohibition of incest can be, and probably was, analogically derived from the more foundational prohibition of same-sex intercourse.[130]

In sum, following Douma, I have been arguing that Scriptural revelation functions in a variety of ways as a moral authority—it functions as *guide*, *guard*, *compass*, and *example*. I have already briefly shown how it functions in the first three senses. I now want say something about how it functions as an *example*: the Bible also provides the example that Christ and others have given. As a *model*, we have the lives of the saints in the Old and New Testament (Luke 4:25-27; 1 Cor 10:1-5; Phil 3:17; 2 Thess 3:9; Heb 6:12; Heb 11—12:1; James 5:17-20). No doubt, following Christ, who is our great example, is even more essential to the Christian moral life (Matt 16:24; 19:21; John 13:15; 1 Cor 11:1; 1 Peter 2:21). Following

---

129. Gagnon, "What the Evidence *Really* Says."
130. Gagnon, "What Should Faithful Lutherans in the ELCA Do?"

Christ involves holding fast to His very person, indeed it is abiding in a living relationship with Him. Thus, following Christ is not an outward imitation, but the existential reality of being in love with God, because Christ dwells by faith in the heart of the believer (see Eph 3:17). In short, following Christ means being conformed to Him, which is the effect of grace, of the active presence of the Holy Spirit in the believer's life.[131]

Thus, being in love with Christ moves us to live differently than unbelievers. In the words of Jochem Douma, "The Christian must walk differently from the pagan, not (only) because the Ten Commandments require this of him, but because he has learned to know Christ (Eph 4:20). He must have an attitude of forgiveness, even as God in Christ has forgiven him (Eph 4:32). He must find out what is pleasing to Christ (Eph 5:10). In their marriage, husband and wife must reflect the relationship between Christ and His church (5:22). Christians must flee fornication because their bodies are members of Christ (1 Cor 6:3ff.)."[132]

Yet, there is more. The Sermon on the Mount and, with it, the Beatitudes (Matt 5:3–12), are at the heart of Jesus Christ's moral teaching. The Beatitudes reveal the perfect charter for the Christian life, which includes the moral life—thus the Fathers of the Church like St. Augustine, the great medieval Christian thinkers like St. Thomas Aquinas, and most recently, John Paul II. The Beatitudes are poverty of spirit, humility, docility before the Word of God, sorrow for sin or penitence, hunger and thirst for justice, the practice of mercy, and purity of heart.

St. Augustine and St. Thomas Aquinas saw the Sermon on the Mount as the heart and center of the New or Evangelical Law, perfecting and fulfilling the Old Testament Law of Moses for Christians. Recall that the Old Law is not abolished by Christ (see Matt 5:17); it is maintained in its essentials, with its best elements conserved and brought to perfection. The New Law, at its core, is an interior law that God has placed within our hearts (Jer 31:33; Heb 10:16); it is not a law written on tablets of stone or on paper, like the Ten Commandments. Rather, it is an interior law inscribed in hearts. As Aquinas puts it, "It is the grace of the Holy Spirit, given through faith in Christ, which is preeminent in the Law of the New Covenant and that whereby its power exists. So before

---

131. John Paul II, *Veritatis Splendor*, nos. 19–20.
132. Douma, "Use of Scripture in Ethics," 374.

all else the New Law is the very grace of the Holy Spirit, given to those who believe in Christ."[133]

In the Beatitudes, we find the goal of human existence, the ultimate end of human life, which is to know, to love, and to serve God in this life and to be happy forever with Him in the next. God calls us to His own beatitude--the supernatural reality of eternal life, which the Holy Bible expresses as the Kingdom of God, the joy of the Lord, God's rest, and the vision of God. "Blessed are the pure in heart, for they shall see God" (Matt 5:8; see 1 John 2; 1 Cor 13:12). God's own Beatitude is a gift of His grace to us, and the Beatitudes of the Sermon on the Mount are God's answer to man's natural desire for happiness. In the words of the late Belgian moral theologian, Servais Pinckaers, O.P., "Linked with the desire for happiness, the teaching of the Sermon penetrates to our inmost souls and responds to our deepest aspirations, purifying them and directing them to the crowning happiness of the loving vision of God."[134]

But what is the connection of the Sermon on the Mount with the moral life? Well, the moral life is not just about obligations or commandments, merely about do's and don'ts. Unmistakably, God commands us to respect our parents, and prohibits adultery, homosexuality, stealing, lying, and so forth. Yet, at one and the same time and inseparably, the moral life is, in light of man's final end, about a loving union with God. Our final end is to become co-lovers with God, entering by grace into the eternal exchange of love of Trinitarian communion, Father, Son, and Holy Spirit.[135] This love is God's own love flooding our hearts through the Holy Spirit given to us through faith in Jesus Christ (Rom 5:5; 8:9). Hence the moral life is relational in this way. And so there is no opposition between the commandments and the Beatitudes, because both aspects of the moral life are about happiness, about the deliberate ordering of our moral actions to God, to eternal life. As John Paul II correctly explains:

> The *Beatitudes* are not specifically concerned with certain particular rules of behavior. Rather, they speak of basic attitudes and dispositions in life and therefore they *do not coincide exactly with the commandments*. On the other hand, *there is no separation or opposition* between the Beatitudes and the commandments; both refer to the good, to eternal life. The Sermon on the Mount be-

---

133. Aquinas, *Summa Theologiae*, I–II, q. 108, a. 1.
134. Pinckaers, *Pursuit of Happiness—God's Way*, 28–29.
135. See *Catechism*, no. 221.

gins with the proclamation of the Beatitudes, but also refers to the commandments (cf. Matt 5:20–48). At the same time, the Sermon on the Mount demonstrates the openness of the commandments and their orientation toward the horizon of the perfection proper to the Beatitudes. These latter are above all *promises*, from which there also indirectly flow *normative indications* for the moral life. In their originality and profundity they are a sort of *self-portrait of Christ*, and for this very reason are *invitations to discipleship and communion of life with Christ*.[136]

In short, God is the supreme good in whom man finds his full and perfect happiness. And both the Ten Commandments and the Beatitudes give us the way to fulfill this desire for happiness. "This desire is of divine origin: God has placed it in the human heart in order to draw man to the One who alone can fulfill it."[137]

The promises revealed by the Beatitudes make clear that the happiness God promises does not come without a spiritual struggle; they refer to life's trials, overturning many of our human ideas about happiness. For example, says Fr. Pinckaers, "The beatitude of the poor runs counter to a concept of happiness based on the pursuit of sensible goods, riches and honors. The beatitude of the meek countervails the idea that happiness is to be found in the gratification of the irascible passions, anger and the instinct to dominate. Thirdly, the beatitude of those who mourn reverses the theory that happiness consists in pleasure and sensual delight."[138] So Jesus' Sermon on the Mount challenges us to find true happiness, beyond false appearances, by practicing the Gospel virtues, from humility to purity of heart. And the heart and center of Gospel morality are these promises of happiness and of the joy of the Trinitarian life expressed by the Beatitudes. "The beatitude we are promised confronts us with decisive moral choices. It invites us to purify our hearts of bad instincts and to seek the love of God above all else. It teaches us that true happiness is not found in riches or well-being, in human fame or power, or in any human achievement—however beneficial it may be—such as science, technology, and art, or indeed in any creature, but in God alone, the source of every good and of all love"[139]

---

136. *Veritatis Splendor*, no. 16.
137. *Catechism*, no. 1718.
138. Pinckaers, *Pursuit of Happiness—God's Way*, 30.
139. *Catechism*, no. 1723.

In biblical perspective, then, the *magna charta* of the Christian moral life is the Sermon on the Mount. In short, living the Beatitudes, which is faith working through love, is the pursuit of happiness—but God's way.

3

Experience and Revelation

IS EXPERIENCE A SOURCE OF REVELATION?

IS HUMAN EXPERIENCE A *source* of revelation? That is, is an individual's experience "a *final arbiter* of truth and falsehood in the Church [?]"[1] In other words, can we extend to experience the status of a foundation and cognitive source of Christian truth?[2] Is this turn to individual experience "no more acceptable than any of the other historically recurring attempts to make of private inspiration a supreme court for adjudicating the gospel [?]"[3] Yes, replies Nichols. "It is not experience we should trust but the transmutation of experience by Scripture and Tradition."[4] Alternatively, Bavinck asks whether experience is such that "it only brings us into union with the existing truth, and makes us recognize as truth what formerly was for us only an empty sound, or even was denied and opposed by us [?]" Yes, answers Bavinck to this question, and he develops this point:

> Experience comes into being only when, first, there exists, something to experience, and afterwards this something is really experienced; it cannot otherwise exist. Religion is without doubt a matter of the heart; but it cannot be separated from all objective knowledge of God through his revelation in nature and history, in

---

1. Nichols, "Reviving Doctrinal Consciousness," 41.
2. According to liberal Catholic theologian Roger Haight, S.J., a new style of doing theology emerged in American Catholic theology between 1965 and 1975, and one of its chief characteristics is "a turn to experience, whether it be transcendental experience or a more historically concrete set of experiences, as a point of departure for theological reflection" ("Liberal and Catholic," 23).
3. Nichols, "Reviving Doctrinal Consciousness," 41.
4. Ibid.

> Scripture and conscience. A subjective religion is always preceded by an objective religion, whatever this may be. Just as language presupposes the capacity for speech in the child, but yet is learned from the mother, so also religious experience arises out of preceding revelation. Every child grows up in the religion of its parents, and thereby develops its own religious life; the pious teaching and example of the mother awaken piety in the heart of the child. No less than in sensation, science, and art, does this take place also in religion. Man is never self-sufficient and independent of the outside world; he needs the earth to feed and clothe him, light to see, sound to hear, the phenomena of nature or the facts of history to observe and to know, and in the same way revelation to awaken and strengthen his religious life. The heart cannot be separated from the head, nor faith as trust from faith as knowledge. Even those who look upon dogmatics as an exposition of pious feelings [such as F. Schleiermacher] recognize that these feelings nevertheless are due to the external influences, as, for example, from the person of Christ. Experience does not come first, after which interpretation follows, but revelation precedes, and is experienced in faith.[5]

Although I cannot fully argue the point here, experience is *not* a foundation, a source of revelation, a final arbiter of truth and falsehood in the Church, from which the belief-content (*fides quae*) of the historic Christian faith can be inferred and known. Rather, as Bavinck puts it in the concluding sentence of the above passage, "revelation precedes, and is experienced in faith." This epistemic order of things is grounded in the fact that experience is not a source of knowledge, but an organ of knowledge. "For though the eye may be the indispensable organ for the perception of light, it is not its source.... Similarly, faith, regeneration, or experience cannot be the source of our religious knowledge, or the first principle of our theology."[6] In presuming its objectivity, Bavinck says that it is in and through experience that revelation can be received. Bavinck elaborates:

> We experience certain religious-ethical feelings of guilt, repentance, forgiveness, gratitude, joy, and the like, but all the other things that occur in a historical religion, strictly speaking, fall outside of experience. In none of the twelve articles of [in the Apostles' Creed] can "I believe" be replaced by "I experience." That God is the Creator of heaven and earth, that Christ is God's only begotten Son, conceived by the Holy Spirit and born of the Virgin Mary,

---

5. *Wijsbegeerte der Openbaring*, 176. ET: *The Philosophy of Revelation*, 239.
6. Bavinck, *Gereformeerde Dogmatiek*, I, 533 [564–65].

are things that cannot, in the nature of the case, be experienced. Although there certainly are effects in the church that directly proceed from its glorified head in heaven, that Christ arose from the dead, ascended to heaven, and is now seated at the right hand of God are things we know only from Holy Scripture. Our heart can most certainly bear witness to all these facts and experience their power, but as facts they are firmly established to our mind only by the testimony of the apostles. If denying this, people want to deduce and construct these facts from Christian experience, they do violence to that experience.... Experience cannot bear the burden laid on it; the truth of historic Christianity cannot rest on experience as its ultimate ground.[7]

The experience of faith (*fides qua*) cannot bear the burden laid upon it by an experiential model of revelation. The latter merges revelation and experience in such a way that it unduly subordinates the content of revelation, the objective content of faith (*fides quae*) to that experience, as though the former were always derived from the latter. The rejection of that model is compatible with the acceptance of the idea that revelation is communicated within an experience.

But that does not mean that experience is constitutive of revelation. Rather, the knowledge of faith itself does include some experience of its own without implying that in the absence of an experience there is no revelation. For instance, as Nichols correctly notes (echoing a point that Bavinck makes in passing in the above passage), "the main historical events of God's saving intervention in the world are unlimited in their efficacy and so can form the basic pattern for the personal life of each Christian may be a corrective in our understanding of revelation. They are reproduced over and over again, refracted in a myriad of souls." The German mystical writer, Angelus Silesius, adds Nichols, wrote, "'Were

---

7. Ibid., 503–4 [534–35]. See also, Bavinck, *Certainty of Faith*, 71–72: "The inadequacy of the method of experience is abundantly clear because at various times everything or nothing can be deduced from it [experience], and not without justification. All religions awaken religious emotions and experiences. If they give us the right to conclude to the truth of that faith and of its content, in philosophical language, if judgments of value are the ground and proof of judgments of being, then the Buddhist can conclude to the truth of nirvana from his experience, the Muslim mystic similarly to the reality of his sensible heaven and the Roman Catholic to the light of the cult of the Virgin Mary. All of them could agree with Zinzendorf, giving this ultimate ground for their faith: *Es ist mir so, mein Herz sagt mir das* [It is so to me; my heart tells me]." For a critique of the theological method of feminist theology in which experience is treated as a foundation or source of revelation, see Martin, *Feminist Question*, 168–220.

Christ to be born a thousand times in Bethlehem, but not in you, you would be lost forever." Furthermore, "In baptism we die and rise again with Christ, and this act must be lived out in many small dyings and risings in a progressive 'imitation of Christ.' In these ways, we can and must vindicate the Church's dogma in our own experience."[8] Nevertheless, the content of revelation (*fides quae*) "may not be cast without remainder in terms of experience. Experience needs to be supplemented by such things as the prior tradition, the Scriptures themselves as a relatively independent norm, and the deliverances of those commissioned to teach authoritatively in the Christian community."[9] In short, these media of God's revelation of truth stand as norm over against all experience.[10]

John Paul II, too, resists opposing revelation and experience. He says, "*human experience is in some way a legitimate means for theological interpretation*." That is, he argues that the authority of God's Word revelation does not exclude experience, but rather it is *in* the experience itself that the authority is acknowledged and confessed. Furthermore, he adds,

> When, in the context of the theology of bodily man ... we reflect about the *method* of further analyses of the revelation of the "beginning" [orders of creation], in which the appeal to the first chapters of Genesis is essential, we must immediately turn our attention to a factor that is particularly important for theological interpretation—important, because it consists in the relation between revelation and experience. In the interpretation of the revelation about man, and above all about the body, we must, for understandable reasons, appeal to experience, because bodily man is perceived by us above all in experience.... *[O]ur human experience is in some way a legitimate means for theological interpretation* and that, in a certain sense, it is an indispensable point of reference to which we must appeal in the interpretation of the "beginning." (*MWTB*, 4.4)

The crux of this important passage from John Paul II is that reflection on human experience is theologically legitimate because the starting point of his theology of the body is that sexual difference is grounded in the ontology of creation. As I said in the introductory chapter, the pope works with a hermeneutical schema that takes seriously the reality of

---

8. Nichols, *Epiphany*, 63.
9. Ibid., 63–64.
10. Genderen and Velema, *Concise Reformed Dogmatics*, 22.

general revelation in creation, for biblical revelation is not the whole of God's revelation to us. Rather, the structures or orders of creation are revelatory of God's ordained teleology of the world. Still, since sin has also affected the human knower's capacity to grasp the original order of creation, God rectifies that fallen knower through biblical revelation, bringing, in consequence, that creation revelation into focus and clarity.

Earlier in chapter 1, I argued that Luke Timothy Johnson accepted a doctrine of continuing revelation, indeed, that he took the real locus of authority and revelation to be in human experience. So Johnson thinks experience is constitutive of revelation. I think there are serious problems with positions like Johnson's, namely, overemphasizing the importance of human experience leads to thinking that the belief-content (*fides quae*) of Christian faith fluctuates with the historical changes experience undergoes, which makes anthropological determination the criterion for revelation. I argued this point earlier in Chapter 1. Johnson would probably reply to my criticisms of his view that it one-sidedly emphasizes the role that he thinks experience, even putatively revelatory of God at work in human experience, plays to the neglect of the normative texts of canonical Scripture, creeds and the Church's teaching authority. So perhaps we should add the moment of correlation or mediation between such texts, creeds, councils, on the one hand, and contemporary human experience on the other.[11]

Johnson advocates what I will call a "dialogical authority of Scripture": the normative value of Scripture emerges from its continuing religious value for the Church which confers authority upon its claims after deciding whether those claims warrant assent or not.[12] This view of authority stands in contrast to the Catholic view of biblical authority, as normatively expressed in *Dei Verbum*, where Scripture's canonical authority is grounded in its divine authorship and inspiration. That Johnson accepts a "dialogical authority of Scripture" is clear from his own words: "hermeneutics involves the complex task of negotiating normative texts and continuing human experience. Within this faith community, this means an openness to the ways in which God's revelation continues in human experience as well as a deep commitment to the conviction that

11. Johnson, "Debate & Discernment."
12. I owe this phrase to Cornelius Trimp, *Betwist Schriftgezag*, 1970, as cited by Genderen and Velema, *Concise Reformed Dogmatics*, 92–93. But Schneiders also uses it in describing her own position in *Revelatory Text*, 55–59.

such revelation, while often, at first, perceived as dissonant with the symbols of Scripture, will, by God's grace directing human fidelity, be seen as consonant with those symbols and God's own fidelity."[13] Moreover, adds Johnson, "Scripture does not characteristically speak with a single voice." Rather, "[Scripture] contains an irreducible and precious pluralism of 'voices' shaped by literary genre, theme, and perspective. The authority of these texts, furthermore, is most properly distinguished in terms of their function. . . . Responsible hermeneutics claims the 'freedom of the children of God' authorized by the New Testament, and seeks to negotiate the various 'voices/authorities' within the texts in an effort to conform to that 'mind of Christ' (1 Cor 2:16) that is the authentic form of Christian identity which those texts are, through the power of the Holy Spirit, capable of 'authoring.'"[14]

Johnson then goes on to apply these hermeneutical principles to the specific case of homosexuality. In sum, says Johnson, the Bible unequivocally condemns homosexual practice (Lev 18:22; Wis 14:26; Rom 1:26–27; 1 Cor 6:9) as a vice and hence as incompatible with life in the Kingdom of God. In this judgment he is joined by other New Testament biblical theologians, such as Richard B. Hays[15] and Robert A. J. Gagnon. Still, unlike Hays and Gagnon, Johnson rejects the biblical commandments condemning homosexual practice. He claims that compared with other practices the Bible's extensive and detailed condemnation of, for example, economic oppression, there is the "relative paucity of passages" condemning homosexual practice, plus its off-handed rejection, appears "instinctive and relatively unreflective." There is also the question of its being offensive to God's creation order given that "for gay persons the acceptance of their homosexuality is an acceptance of creation as it applies to them. It is emphatically not a vice that is chosen. If this conclusion is correct, what is the hermeneutical implication?"[16]

I think we have said enough about Johnson's hermeneutical approach to negotiating normative texts and continuing human experiences. I would like to give some reasons why his biblical hermeneutic is theologically unacceptable, in addition to the criticisms I have already made in chapter 1.

13. Johnson, "Debate & Discernment."

14. Ibid.

15. Hays, *Moral Vision of the New Testament*, 389: "The biblical witness against homosexual practices is univocal."

16. Ibid.

First, although he speaks of his biblical hermeneutic as consisting of a normative triad of canonical Scripture, creed, and teaching authority, his doctrine of God's continuing revelation in human experience can be said to act foundationally since it is the ultimate arbiter against which all the other normative elements of that triad is judged.[17] To be fair to Johnson, however, he does distinguish his hermeneutical discernment of revelatory experience from the theologically meaningless, because the former practice does not "appeal to some populist claim such as 'everyone does it,' or 'surveys indicate.'" Despite that disclaimer, Johnson leaves us with the idea that the homosexual is justified in accepting his homosexuality by virtue of his claim that his homosexuality is an acceptance of creation as it applies to him. Put differently, the unacceptable hermeneutical implication of Johnson's claim that a homosexual's acceptance of his condition is an acceptance of creation as it applies to him is that "each human being is the norm for creation rather than creation . . . is the norm for each human being."[18] In this light, we can understand the rationale behind Johnson's claim that a committed homosexual union is an indication of "homosexual holiness," as he puts it, or "homosexual covenantal love," as he also says.

Still, as Gagnon critically remarks, the "problem with such a rationale . . . is that it begs the question of whether a homosexual orientation is a good thing." Indeed, adds Gagnon, "It does so by assuming that deeply engrained, biologically related impulses are necessarily moral."[19] Furthermore, the fact remains that human experience, according to Johnson, should override the canon of Scripture that speaks in a single voice about the immorality of homosexual practice. As Gagnon correctly says, and apparently Johnson does not disagree, "Every narrative, law, proverb, exhortation, metaphor, and poetry that has anything to say about sexual relations at least implicitly presupposes a male-female requirement." Indeed, *pace* Johnson, "an opposite-sex prerequisite for sexual relations is [therefore] not an isolated or insignificant view in the canon of Scripture."[20] Thus, we cannot equate the relative paucity of passages explicitly condemning homosexual practice with importance. Gagnon correctly notes, "Bestiality is

17. In chapter 6, I will deal with the general question of the embodiment of the human person and, accordingly, the place of the body in moral action.
18. Levering, "Knowing What is 'Natural,'" 141 n. 68.
19. Gagnon, "Scriptural Perspectives on Homosexuality and Sexual Identity," 283.
20. Ibid., 301.

mentioned even less in the Bible than homosexual practice and incest gets only comparable treatment, yet who would be so foolish as to argue that Jews and Christians in antiquity would have regarded sex with an animal or sex with one's mother as inconsequential offenses? *Infrequency of mention is often an indicator that the matter in question is foundational rather than insignificant.*"[21] The upshot is this: "Scripture—and here the views of Jesus are definitely to be included—presents a two-sex prerequisite for sexual behavior as the most sacred and inviolable structural dimension of God-ordained human sexual behavior."[22]

Second, with all due respect to Johnson, however, rightly knowing, discerning what the will of God is (Rom 12:2) with the mind of Christ, "Christ thinking" (*nous Christou*, 1 Cor 2:16), as St. Paul calls it, which involves "the mode of thinking governed and illumined by Christ in which the pneumatic [spiritual] man is distinguished from the physical [natural],"[23] cannot legitimate rejecting a clear statement of Scripture, especially one that expresses a core value of biblical sexual ethics, a value that "Scripture holds . . . pervasively, absolutely, strongly, and counter-culturally."[24] Third, the claim that a person's acceptance of his homosexuality is an acceptance of creation as it applies to them ("God created me this way") grants such latitude to a person's judgment regarding his involuntary impulses, however deeply ingrained, that one does not know why such a criterion would exclude "polysexuals" (experiencing sexual desire for more than one man or woman concurrently) or "pedosexuals" (experiencing sexual desire for children). Again, Johnson begs the question by assuming that such deeply ingrained impulses are necessarily moral. Moreover, suppose we grant that the condition of homosexuality is not one that is merely chosen, but that there are multiple causative factors for homosexuality—indirect congenital influences, postnatal biological influences, macro- and microcultural influences from one's environment, and personal psychological predispositions—surely that is nevertheless consistent with Gagnon's claim that "choices . . . involv[ing] responses to socio-cultural stimuli . . . may, down the end of a long road, lead to greater or lesser likelihood of homosexual identification."[25]

---

21. Gagnon, "What the Evidence *Really* Says."
22. Gagnon, "Scriptural Perspectives on Homosexuality and Sexual Identity," 298.
23. Ridderbos, *Paul*, 228.
24. Gagnon, "Scriptural Perspectives on Homosexuality and Sexual Identity," 301.
25. Gagnon, "Sexual Orientation," email Correspondence, July 8, 2009.

Fourth, on the question of impulses that we didn't choose to experience, adds Gagnon, "whether an individual chooses an impulse or not is not a moral argument. All of us are loaded with sinful impulses that we did not ask to experience. The fact that an impulse is involuntary does not disqualify the impulse from being sinful or immoral." Thus, *pace* Johnson, no hermeneutical implications follow about the immorality of homosexuality from not having chosen the impulses associated with same-sex attraction. Indeed, Pauline anthropology, as expressed in Romans 7: 14–25, describes the struggle between the old man and the new man (reminiscent of Gal 5:17), of an internal conflict with myself, "the 'I-myself' (v. 25!) and the flesh, the law of God and the law of sin." Ridderbos rightly remarks, "In the struggle between those parties the victory is to the flesh and sin, and the ego finds itself, despite all that it would will and desire, in absolute bondage and the situation of death."[26] Nowhere does St. Paul suggest that these impulses should be trusted for their goodness, as indices of how God made me. On the contrary, "If then, any man is in Christ, he is a new creature. The former things have passed away; behold, all things are made new" (2 Cor 5:17).

Elsewhere St. Paul expresses the same teaching. He describes the "new *man*" as one "who is renewed in knowledge according to the image of Him who created him" (Col 3:10). Thus, adds St. Paul, "those who belong to Christ Jesus have crucified the flesh with its [sinful] passions and desires" (Gal 5:25). As Gagnon pointedly puts it, "nothing less than death of the self is required."[27] Now, even though we have are a "new man" in Christ, a spiritual battle still wages in our life, "the desires of the flesh" continue to tempt us, and hence we are exhorted by St. Paul, "If we live by the Spirit, let us also walk by the Spirit" (Gal 5: 25).

Now the crucial question for any theological hermeneutic, such as Johnson's, that emphasizes correlation or mediation between two or more sources is this: How does contemporary human experience compare as a theological source with Scripture and the dogmatic tradition of the Church? Does correlation mean absolute equality between the authority of Scripture and the authority of experience? Let us now look at a few examples of theologians who have dealt with this question. I will argue that

---

26. Ridderbos, *Paul*, 127.
27. Gagnon, "Scriptural Perspectives on Homosexuality and Sexual Identity," 294.

they have been unsuccessful in their efforts to enlist human experience as a theological source.

SENSUS FIDELIUM

Some theologians have attempted to link the notion of experience as a source of revelation with the Catholic theme of the *sensus fidelium*. Australian Catholic theologian Ormond Rush is one such theologian. His attempt fails, as I will now show.

Rush appeals to a total of five "mutually critical criteria for judging faithful receptions of revelation (God's self-communication through Jesus Christ in the Spirit)."[28] According to him, revelation is not only a communication of individual truths about God and man, but also "fundamentally . . . God's loving self-communication to humanity through Christ in the power of the Holy Spirit."[29] "God's offer of salvation through Christ in the Spirit": this seems to be, in Rush's view, the constitutive content of "the great *traditio*,"[30] as he phrases it. Furthermore, I would add, the apostolic tradition (*paradosis*) is transmitted to, or handed on to, the Church in its written expression in Scripture. "Holy Scripture is the *paradosis* of the apostolic kerygma, become writing."[31] In other words, it is the "literary concretization" (Karl Rahner) of the Tradition of the Gospel. *Dei Verbum* writes, "Sacred Scripture is the speech of God as it is put down in writing under the breath of the Holy Spirit." And in regard to tradition, it "transmits in its entirety the Word of God which has been entrusted to the apostles by Christ the Lord and the Holy Spirit." "It transmits it to the successors of the apostles so that," *Dei Verbum* adds, "enlightened by the Spirit of truth, they may faithfully preserve, expound and spread it abroad by their preaching."[32] In its being so transmitted the apostolic *paradosis*, the Tradition of the Gospel, "becomes the *parathêkê*, the apostolic bequest which is committed to the Church's safe-keeping."[33] Moreover, as I put it earlier in chapter 1, the apostolic *paradosis* is itself divine in origin because it is what God himself hands on. That is, it is God's revelatory

---

28. Rush, *Still Interpreting Vatican II, Some Hermeneutical Principles*, 66.
29. Ibid., 65–66.
30. Ibid., 66.
31. Geiselmann, "Scripture, Tradition, and the Church," 55.
32. *Dei Verbum*, no. 9.
33. Ibid.

self-communication, which revelation culminates in God's handing over his own Son, Jesus Christ, to man for us all "because of our offenses" (Rom 4:25; 8:32). Here we must observe that Christ himself is present and engaged for his part in the fact that the Father hands over the Son to the world by simultaneously handing himself over (Eph 5:2).[34]

The criteria used for judging whether or not the reception of revelation, God's offer of salvation through Christ in the Spirit, of the apostolic *paradosis*, is faithful are scripture, tradition, magisterium, contemporary theological scholarship, and *sensus fidelium*. It is puzzling why Rush does not identify Scripture and Tradition as revelation's normative "sources" of revealed truth and the starting-point of theological knowledge; instead, he calls all of these criteria "witnesses to salvific revelation."[35] Although he says that "each is a distinctive authority in its own way," presumably to avoid being misunderstood to be saying that these "witnesses" are equally weighted, he doesn't avoid that misunderstanding. Indeed, he never explains the distinctive manner in which each of these witnesses is authoritative vis-á-vis each other. Given that he uses the phrase "mutually critical" to describe the relation between these criteria, I get the sense that there exists parity, an equal authoritative weight among them. So, rather than ranking the authority of Scripture and Tradition as primary sources of revealed truth, indeed constitutive sources of Tradition, because without them the life and faith of the Church is unthinkable, whereas the others would be subordinate to those sources, Rush speaks of these five witnesses as "mutually critical criteria for judging faithful receptions of revelation."[36] Are they then equally weighted authorities for Rush? If they are, his biblical hermeneutic is inconsistent with the normative teaching of *Dei Verbum*, meaning thereby with the "authoritative mediation of the content of faith through historical revelation, prophetic and apostolic testimony, Scripture, tradition, and the living Church."[37]

To be sure, it is right to hold that the apostolic *paradosis* "is attested to in Holy Scripture, in the teaching, liturgy, and life of the Church, and in the hearts of the faithful [*sensus fidelium*] (2 Cor 3:3; 1 Thess 4:9; 1 John

---

34. Pottmeyer, "Tradition," 1124.
35. Rush, *Still Interpreting Vatican II, Some Hermeneutical Principles*, 66.
36. Ibid.; see also, 78.
37. Dulles, *Assurance of Things Hoped For*, 176.

2:28)."[38] But isn't there something less authoritative about a "witness" than a "source?"[39] In particular, is Holy Scripture merely a witness, or attestation, to God's revelation? Alternatively, is the Bible itself, in addition to being among the attestations to the apostolic *paradosis*, revelatory of the one true God, indeed being itself not only one of God's redemptive acts but also the primary norm for subsequent ecclesiastical tradition, possessing canonical authority, because it is as such the instrumental efficient cause of the knowledge of divinely revealed realities? As I showed earlier in chapter 1, *Dei Verbum* teaches the latter when saying that the sacred Scriptures not only contain the Word of God, but also, "since they are inspired, really are the Word of God."[40] Clearly, according to *Dei Verbum*, the sacred Scriptures are not only a witness to revelation but are themselves a part of this revelation. That is, the Scriptures are "God's own Word, a Word communicated personally to men and women for their salvation, for the sake of leading them to eternal life."[41]

Rush is therefore mistaken when he says that *Dei Verbum* speaks of Scripture as a mere witness. His position leaves unclear the principle of *canonicity*. That way of thinking about Holy Scripture diminishes the normative testimony of the prophets and apostles as God's Word revelation, which testimony has been written down and is believed in by the Church as the special work of the Holy Spirit. Indeed, the Council describes Scripture as the "supreme rule" of the Church's faith. "For, since they are inspired by God and committed to writing once and for all time, they present God's own Word in an unalterable form, and they make the voice of the Holy Spirit sound again and again in the words of the prophets and apostles. It follows that all the preaching of the Church, as indeed the entire Christian religion, should be nourished and ruled by sacred Scripture."[42]

Now, contemporary theological scholarship, in short, theological reflection, and the magisterium are also among the criteria of Christian thought enumerated by Rush. Significantly, these criteria are not only not equally weighted, but also they are not theological *sources*. Scripture and

38. Pottmeyer, "Tradition," 1124.

39. For an insightful discussion of this distinction and its application to Holy Scriptures, see Trimp, "Witness of the Scriptures," 172–84.

40. *Dei Verbum*, no. 24.

41. Guarino, *Vattimo and Theology*, 105.

42. Ibid., no. 21.

tradition are each in its own way "a perennially valid source from which insight and illumination flow down to us in the life of faith."[43] Theological reflection and the teaching office of the Church, the magisterium, are "aids or helps in the evaluation of these sources."[44] They are not equally weighted, however, since the Magisterium is an authoritative guide to the meaning and truth of divine revelation, because commissioned by Christ to speak to the Church in his name. Still, they help each other. "Magisterium and theologians share a common service to Christian truth," as Nichols says, "bound as they are by the Word of God in Scripture and Tradition."[45] Theologians, by fulfilling their own unique gift as teachers, are called on to assist the magisterium, providing, in the words of Paul VI, "the help which the magisterium needs in order to fulfill its mission as light and norm for the Church."[46] Nichols adds: "The magisterium, by fulfilling its own functions, aids the theologian to identify the content of revelation—through the efforts of the bearers of magisterium to maintain the unitary consistency of Christian faith—and to preserve the historic continuity of the faith today with the faith of all preceding Catholic generations and, ultimately, of the apostles themselves."[47]

One final criteria enumerated by Rush is the "sense of the faithful" (*sensus fidelium*).[48] I think this criterion is a theological source because it is an expression of the unfolding apostolic tradition in the life and faith of the Church. Now, the function of the *sensus fidelium* as an expression of the Church's tradition is, first, to react "against anything that is not in accordance with the apostolic paradosis." Furthermore, adds Geiselmann, "in the past it has also made a positive contribution to the continually advancing understanding of the apostolic paradosis and will continue to do so."[49] So, it is not only the "teaching Church" (*Ecclesia docens*) that is of theological interest, epistemologically speaking, but also the *Ecclesia*

---

43. Nichols, *Shape of Catholic Theology*, 178.
44. Ibid., 234.
45. Ibid., 259.
46. As cited in Nichols, *Shape of Catholic Theology*, 259.
47. Ibid.
48. For some historical background to the origins of this notion in Melchior Cano, and with him the Spanish theologians Valencia, Suarez, and others, see Geiselmann, *Meaning of Tradition*, 19–23. See also, Nichols, *Shape of Catholic Theology*, 221–31. See also, Congar, *Lay People in the Church*, 288–94.
49. Geiselmann, *Meaning of Tradition*, 22.

discens, the "learning Church," and hence " is itself for theologians a *locus* of teaching authority."[50]

Rush picks out the *sensus fidelium* as a criterion against the background of correctly insisting that the primary addressees, or receivers, of the Word of God, the Holy Scripture and Tradition, are the whole People of God, the whole Church, not the hierarchy alone but the whole body of the faithful. In the words of *Lumen Gentium*, the whole body means "from the Bishops down to the last of the lay faithful [St. Augustine]."[51] They are the subjects of the *sensus fidei fidelium* [the sense of the faith of the faithful]. This is true, I would add, because the whole Church is a servant of the Word of God, subject to its authority. With this conclusion we can resist compartmentalizing the distinction between the "teaching Church" (*Ecclesia docens*) and the "learning Church" (*Ecclesia discerns*), as if the hierarchy alone is the teaching Church and the laity alones listens. Rather, as Ratzinger correctly says, "in the last analysis the whole Church listens, and, *vice versa*, the whole Church shares in the upholding of true teaching."[52]

Notwithstanding Rush's correct view that the *sensus laicorum* [the sense of the faith pertaining to the laity] is not the fullness of the *sensus fidelium*, given that the latter comprises the whole body of the faithful, "from the Bishops down to the lay faithful," he still ascribes a unique place to the laity's "sense of the faith" as "a crucial source and criterion for discerning the signs of the times."[53] He says, "the *sensus laicorum* is a vital source and criterion for discerning the *sensus fidelium*."[54] This conclusion follows, says Rush, from Christ's prophetic office being fulfilled not only through the hierarchy but also through the laity.

Yes, Vatican II taught that every Christian is called to be a witness to the faith and to that extent a teacher. For the prophetic office of Christ is fulfilled "not only through the hierarchy who teach in his name and by his power, but also through the laity whom he constitutes his witnesses and equips with a sense of the faith (*sensus fidei*) and a grace of speech precisely so that the power of the gospel may shine forth in the daily life

---

50. Nichols, *Shape of Catholic Theology*, 221.
51. *Lumen Gentium*, no. 12.
52. Ratzinger, "Dogmatic Constitution on Divine Revelation," 197.
53. Rush, *Still Interpreting Vatican II*, 83.
54. Ibid., 83.

of family and society."⁵⁵ Still, Christ's lay faithful, while they do teach, do not do so in virtue of apostolic authority; the hierarchy alone teaches with such authority, expounding and maintaining the continuity and consistency of Christian belief, indeed, of the deposit of faith by way of authoritative judgment. In contrast, the laity "teach in virtue of the faith within, through all the activities of life and mind that it stimulates and develops," says Congar. "More exactly still," Congar adds, "all the richness of the deposit confided to the Church that can be revealed to a life of active faith objectively ruled and supervised by the apostolic hierarchy—it is through that that the faithful teach."⁵⁶

Unfortunately, Rush incorrectly concludes from the truth that every Christian is called to be a witness to the faith and to that extent a teacher that a certain *parity* exists in regard to the teaching function of both the *sensus fidelium* and the magisterium. In this connection, he speaks of the need for "more participatory and reciprocal structures of reception and dialogue"⁵⁷ in the governing of Church life. This conclusion leads him to the blur the difference between the magisterium and the laity. The magisterium of the Church is ultimately charged with determining what the normative substance of Christian believing is, that is, authentic Catholic teaching, because "decisive authority is located in the power of the keys, given to Peter by Christ the Lord himself."⁵⁸ In Rush's view, I don't see any place for the distinctive teaching office of the Church, and this stems from a misinterpretation, as I will now argue, of the *sensus fidei* [sense of the faith].

First, Rush assigns systematic theological significance to the order of treatment in *Lumen Gentium* of the People of God and the hierarchy. That is, since the former is treated before the latter, Rush claims that Vatican II's treatment "marks a shift to greater emphasis on the *sensus fidelium* [sense of the faithful] as a source, criterion, and target of church teaching."⁵⁹ I sense logical slippage here in Rush's claim. I agree that *Lumen Gentium* in its first two chapters on the mystery of the Church and the People of God subordinates an ecclesiology in which the institutional element is

---

55. *Lumen Gentium*, no. 35.
56. Congar, *Lay People in the Church*, 293.
57. Rush, *Still Interpreting Vatican II*, 83.
58. Nichols, *Shape of Catholic Theology*, 257.
59. Rush, *Still Interpreting Vatican II*, 40.

treated as primary and integrates that element into an ecclesiology where the Church cannot be viewed apart from the *corpus Christi mysticum*, a Mystical Communion with the living Christ, the Body of Christ, which is the radical communion of the new and reborn humanity in Jesus Christ. The Church is a Sacrament, a Herald of the Gospel, and a Servant of the Word of God, yes, but also the visible Church, the bodily, historical, organized institution.

Still, it is one thing to affirm this rich ecclesiology; it is quite another thing to suggest that this marks a greater emphasis on the *sensus fidelium*, particularly when that emphasis is taken to mean that Vatican II affirms a certain parity between the teaching function of the *sensus fidelium* and the magisterium. Yet, this is precisely what Rush is suggesting. He says that because the *sensus fidelium* can be a mark of the infallibility of a teaching, as *Lumen Gentium* notes, it follows that a "relationship of reciprocity" exists between that source of truth, its infallibility, and the "infallibility *in docendo* [teaching] of the magisterium," since what the whole People [of God] have received and believe must be what the church teaches."[60] No such relationship is posited by *Lumen Gentium*. We find in that Vatican II document a view that is more adequately represented by Congar:

> When . . . all infallibility in the Church is expressly referred to the working of the Holy Spirit which Jesus promised should enable his Church to live in the truth, then the prospect widens out. In that case, each [hierarchy and faithful] is acted on in view of an infallibility (finally one) according to his place in the body, receiving the infallibility that belongs to him in function of the infallibility of the infallibility of the total organism, rather as each of man's various powers receives its part and pertinent energy from the soul. The episcopal body, heir to the apostolical body, has the help of the Holy Spirit lest it err in discharging its teaching office; it forms a college in whose midst, like Peter amidst the other apostles, the Bishop of Rome, Peter's heir and successor, has the help of carrying out his part as the final criterion of unity and orthodoxy; the faithful people has the help of the Holy Spirit to be faithful people, that is, to cleave to God with a living faith in him, but a faith whose objective determinations are, in accordance with the divine economy, brought to the people by the teaching of its hierarchs.[61]

---

60. Ibid., 40.
61. Congar, *Lay People in the Church*, 290.

Most significant, Rush attempts to provide additional justification for this so-called relationship of reciprocity, as he calls it, between the *sensus fidelium* and the magisterium in his interpretation of Vatican II's calling to the laity, in *Sacrosanctum Concilium*, the constitution on the Sacred Liturgy. He misinterprets that calling and, in consequence, continues to blur the difference between the teaching office of the Church, which teaching is exercised in virtue of apostolic authority, and the laity. We read there "that all the faithful should be led to that full, conscious, and active participation in liturgical celebrations which is demanded by the very nature of the liturgy."[62] The liturgy, indeed, the "Eucharistic sacrifice, is the source and summit of the Christian life,"[63] and hence "it is the primary and indispensable source from which the faithful are to derive the true Christian spirit."[64] Why is the Church's liturgy the source and summit of the Christian life? Briefly, Vatican II teaches that the Church's liturgy is the deepest point of entry into the redeeming acts of God in Christ, his passion, death, resurrection, and ascension, which acts constitute the mystery of man's salvation, and a profound personal engagement with the revealing God. Rush overlooks this profound truth. Instead, he takes the calling of the laity to "full, conscious, and active participation" to be a matter of providing the laity with a "vital source and criterion," a hermeneutical standpoint, for not only "discerning the *sensus fidelium*," but also "for interpreting the 'spirit' of the Council and therefore the 'letter' of its documents."[65] Rush's misinterpretation of this calling is at the root of his insistence that the Church needs "more participatory and reciprocal structures of reception and dialogue"[66] in her governing life. It is, chiefly, responsible for his blurring of the difference between the magisterium and the laity.

Still, Rush's claims raise many questions. What is the *sensus fidei*? In what sense, if any, is the *sensus fidei* an authentic theological source? Why does it have any authority in establishing Church teaching? What are the limits of its authority? Last but not least, who are the *fideles* (faithful)? As Janet Smith asks regarding this last question, "Is being a *baptized* Catholic

---

62. *Sacrosanctum Concilium*, no. 14.
63. *Lumen Gentium*, no. 11.
64. *Sacrosanctum Concilium*, no. 14.
65. Rush, *Still Interpreting Vatican II*, 82.
66. Ibid., 83.

sufficient to qualify as one of the faithful? Does one need to be a *practicing* Catholic? Does one need to *believe* the central *dogmas* of the Faith? Are there any other qualifying criteria?"[67]

Consider now the succinct definition of the concept of *sensus fidei* given in a joint statement of the Anglican-Roman Catholic International Theological Commission: "In every Christian who is seeking to be faithful to Christ and is fully incorporated into the life of the Church, there is a *sensus fidei*. This *sensus fidei* may be described as an active capacity for spiritual discernment, an intuition that is formed by worshipping and living in communion as a faithful member of the Church."[68] This active capacity of the faithful for spiritual discernment, as Geiselmann puts it, "a special Christian tact or flair, a deep and sure feeling which guides and directs into all truth, a deep inner sense,"[69] is generally more acute in proportion to a Christian's personal faith and holiness. Significantly, an independent status should not be ascribed to the sense of faithful, "isolating it from the enduring testimony of the successors of the apostles in the Church. The 'sense' always remains linked to the witness borne by the apostolic ministry and is an organic part of the testimony of the Church as a whole."[70] Therefore, insofar as the faithful have been reflective of proper Catholic teaching through their own faith, prayer, and devotion they have theological primacy in answering the question, "Who are the *sensus fidelium*?" For "by their faith, hope, and love they will have penetrated the mysteries of faith more deeply than others," says Nichols.[71]

But this may push the question one step back: "Who are the devout?" Well, as Nichols adds, "clearly it cannot include people who practice their faith irregularly, or people not sharing the already defined faith of the Church, the already established sense or drift of tradition."[72] What then is the *nature* of this active capacity, Christian tact or flair, for spiritually discerning what is compatible with the revelation of the Gospel and what is not? Janet Smith nicely answers this question and she is guided by the Thomistic understanding of the virtue of prudence.

---

67. Smith, "*Sensus Fidelium* and *Humanae Vitae*," 279.
68. *Gift of Authority*, no. 29.
69. Geiselmann, *Meaning of Tradition*, 20.
70. Ibid.
71. Nichols, *Shape of Catholic Theology*, 230.
72. Ibid.

Prudence is that virtue or *habitus* possessed by the person who has authentic and reliable knowledge of the reality to which some moral precept applies, as well as, of course, an understanding and acceptance of the precept as well. The understanding of the precept is not the understanding of the philosopher or the expert; it is the understanding that can be described as the acceptance of the truth of the precept as corresponding to the truth of reality. Aquinas's concept of connaturality is applicable here; as an analogy we might speak of the horse trainer who knows horses so well that he can judge quickly when a horse is ill or out of sorts and knows how to remedy its condition; or the connoisseur of wine who can identify to what region and year a wine belongs. These individuals know a great deal about horses and wines generally and also of horses and wines in particular. The person who possesses prudence is one who has lived a virtuous life and has extensive knowledge of the realm of life in which he must make his moral judgment. The faithful spouse needs not only to know that adultery is wrong, but [also] must know what presents a temptation to infidelity for him or herself, and also have the virtues to avoid or extricate one's self from such situations. Connaturality is also reliable in matters of faith, but requires knowledge both of general principles and experience of relevant lived realities. [For example] That the bishops consulted the faithful about Mary's Immaculate Conception makes sense only if they believed that the faithful had an intimate knowledge of Mary acquired, one supposes, through having acquired a knowledge of Mary's role in [the history of] salvation, most likely through instruction and through prayerful practice of Marian devotions.[73]

Thus far, I have been using interchangeably *sensus fidei* and *sensus fidelium*. They do presuppose a common basis, which Congar nicely formulates thus:

> [T]here is a gift of God (of the Holy Spirit) which relates to the twofold reality, objective and subjective of faith (*fides quae creditur; fides qua creditur*), which is given to the hierarchy and the whole body of the faithful together ... and which ensures an indefectible faith to the Church. This gift, we say, relates to the objective reality of faith, that is, the deposit of notions *and of realities* which constitute tradition; correlatively, it relates to subjective reality, that is, to the grace of faith in the *fidelis*, or religious subject, the quasi-

---

73. Smith, "*Sensus Fidelium* and *Humanae Vitae*," 282.

instinctive ability that faith has to see and adhere to its object (at least within certain limits).⁷⁴

As we can see from Congar's description in the above passage, the *sensus fidei* includes two related realities. On the one hand, the *sensus fidei* is a quality of religious subjectivity (*fides qua creditur*). The supernatural gift of God's grace is infused in the subject with faith, love, and the gifts of the Holy Spirit (wisdom, understanding, counsel, fortitude, knowledge, piety, and fear of the Lord⁷⁵), conferring that subject with the active capacity for spiritual discernment between the truth of faith and its denial. On the other hand, Congar speaks of that objective reality of faith that the religious subject holds to be true, to which objective content of truth is what the faithful assent, believe and confess (*fides quae creditur*), and which can be known objectively.⁷⁶

Pié-Ninot helpfully explains that the second of these two notions underwent development and was then regarded as the *sensus fidelium*. Therefore, there is a distinction to be made between *sensus fidei* and *sensus fidelium*; the terms are not exactly equivalent. What, then, is the difference? The International Anglican-Roman Catholic Commission answers this question. It states, "when this capacity [*sensus fidei*] is exercised in concert by the body of the faithful we may speak of the exercise of the *sensus fidelium*." In other words, "The exercise of the *sensus fidei* by each member of the Church contributes to the formation of the *sensus fidelium* through which the Church as a whole remains faithful to Christ."⁷⁷ In other words, the difference here is that the notion of universality was added to

---

74. Congar, *Lay People in the Church*, 288.

75. *Catechism of the Catholic Church*, no. 1831.

76. Salvador Pié-Ninot, "Sensus Fidei," 992–93. Pié-Ninot explains the biblical roots of the *sensus fidei*: "An effort to base the *sensus fidei* theologically finds in the NT clear testimonials to the reality of an organ of faith, in each of the baptized, as well as in the entire church. Thus, in various texts, we read of 'the mind of Christ' (1 Cor 2:16), 'spiritual insight' (Col 1:9), and 'innermost vision' (lit. 'enlightened eyes of the heart', Eph 1:18; cf. John 14:17; 16:13; Phil 1:9; etc.). On this basis, patristic and theological tradition frequently speaks of the 'eyes of the heart', 'the eyes of the spirit', or the 'eyes of faith'. Suffice it to recall Augustine's expression: *Habet namque fides oculos suos* ("After all, faith has its eyes," *Epist*. 120.2.8); as well as the words of Aquinas: *Per lumen fidei vident esse credenda* ("Through the light of faith, they see that these [things] are to be believed," *ST* 2-2, q. 1, a. 5, ad 1) and *occulata fide* with reference to Jesus' resurrection ("by a faith endowed with eyes," *ST* 3, q. 55, a. 2, ad 1)" (993).

77. *The Gift of Authority*, no. 29.

the assent involved in the *fides quae creditur*. This, says Pié-Ninot, "refers to the situation in which the entire body of believers, 'from the bishops down to the last member of the laity' . . . maintain the same faith. It is in this situation, Vatican II asserts, that the whole people of God cannot err." Adds Pié-Ninot,

> An assertion of this infallibility is legitimate, then, when the content of the proposition under consideration fulfills the following four conditions: [1] when it is a matter of universal consent, [2] when it refers to revelation, [3] when it is a work of the Holy Spirit, and when it is recognized by the magisterium (cf. *Dei Verbum*, 8, 10; *Lumen Gentium*, 12, 25).

Now, then, why is the *sensus fidelium* "a vital aspect of theological epistemology in Catholicism [?]"[78] Here we must turn to the *Lumen Gentium* (no. 12) for an answer:

> *The entire body of the faithful, anointed as they are by the Holy One (1 Jn. 2:20, 27), cannot err in matters of belief.* They manifest this special property by means of the whole people's supernatural discernment [*sensus fidei*] in matters of faith when *"from the bishops to the least of the lay faithful"* they show universal agreement [*universalem suum consensum*] *in matters of faith and morals.* That discernment in matters of faith [*sensus fidei*] is aroused and sustained by the Spirit of truth. *It is exercised under the guidance of the sacred teaching authority (magisterium),* in faithful and respectful obedience to which the people of God accepts that which is not just the word of men but truly the Word of God. Through it, the people of God adheres unwaveringly to the faith given once and for all to the saints, penetrates it more deeply with right thinking, and applies it more fully in its life.[79]

For my purpose here, the most important thing in this passage would be ignored if we simply emphasize that the laity itself is for theologians a source of teaching authority; an authentic source for discerning what is and what is not compatible with the biblical revelation. Rather, most important, and therefore inconsistent with Rush's claim, is that their sense of the faith is *not* in isolation, however, from the "*guidance of the sacred teaching authority (magisterium).*" This means that only that laity

---

78. My discussion of the *sensus fidelium* is indebted not only to Janet Smith and Yves Congar, but also to Nichols, *The Shape of Catholic Theology*, 221–31.

79. *Lumen Gentium*, no. 12; italics added.

who understand and concretely live what the Church teaches are reliable interpreters of the faith. As John Paul II puts it, "In the community of the faithful—which must always maintain Catholic unity with the Bishops and the Apostolic See—there are great insights of faith. The Holy Spirit is active in enlightening the minds of the faithful with his truth, and in inflaming their hearts with his love. But these insights of faith and this *sensus fidelium* are not independent of the magisterium of the Church, which is an instrument of the same Holy Spirit and is assisted by him. *It is only when the faithful have been nourished by the Word of God, faithfully transmitted in its purity and integrity, that their own charisms are fully operative and fruitful.*"[80]

Treating then the matter of the Church's teaching authority later in *Lumen Genitum* than that of the People of God, as *Lumen Gentium* does, has no bearing, therefore, on when the magisterium exercises its authority. Rush is wrong to suggest otherwise. Vatican II does not teach that reciprocity exists between the laity and the magisterium. *Pace* Rush, *Lumen Gentium* does not teach that there is a "reciprocal relationship" between the laity and the magisterium as if to suggest some kind of mutual submission. This is clear from the role the magisterium plays in "guaranteeing the Church's unity in the truth of the Lord." *Donum Veritatis*, the 1990 Instruction on the Ecclesial Vocation of the Theologian, makes this point abundantly clear, It is worthy of being cited at some length:

> Dissent sometimes also appeals to a kind of sociological argument which holds that the opinion of a large number of Christians would be a direct and adequate expression of the "supernatural sense of the faith." Actually, the opinions of the faithful cannot be purely and simply identified with the "*sensus fidei*." The sense of the faith is a property of theological faith; and, as God's gift which enables one to adhere personally to the Truth, it cannot err. This personal faith is also the faith of the Church since God has given guardianship of the Word to the Church. The "*sensus fidei*" implies then by its nature a profound agreement of spirit and heart with the Church, "*sentire cum Ecclesia*." Although theological faith as such then cannot err, the believer can still have erroneous opinions since all his thoughts do not spring from faith. Not all the ideas which circulate among the People of God are compatible with the faith. This is all the more so given that people can be swayed by

---

80. John Paul II's address during the *ad limina* visit of the bishops of India, May 1979.

a public opinion influenced by modern communications media. Not without reason did the Second Vatican Council emphasize the indissoluble bond between the *"sensus fidei"* and the guidance of God's People by the magisterium of the Pastors. These two realities cannot be separated. Magisterial interventions serve to guarantee the Church's unity in the truth of the Lord. They aid her to "abide in the truth" in the face of the arbitrary character of changeable opinions and are an expression of obedience to the Word of God.[81]

Who, then, are the *sensus fidelium*? *Donum Veritatis* replies to this question: those faithful who are in profound agreement of spirit and heart with the Church. As Janet Smith puts it, "I believe *sentire cum Ecclesia* means something like 'to think as the Church does,' or that is, that the thoughts of such a thinker flow from the same source as the teachings— they flow from an acceptance of Christ and his teachings and from the guidance of the Holy Spirit."[82]

I turn now to another Catholic theologian who has also compared human experience as a theological source with Scripture and the tradition of the Church, but, like Johnson, accepts a "dialogical authority of Scripture."

AUTHORITY AND EXPERIENCE

Margaret Farley thinks there are four sources for theological ethics: Scripture, tradition, secular disciplines, and contemporary experience.[83] Taken as a descriptive and analytical thesis, and not a purely normative

---

81. *Donum Veritatis*, no. 35.

82. Smith, "*Sensus Fidelium* and *Humanae Vitae*," 284. Congar is right: "But there is more to be said. The loving and believing Church is infallible only when it listens to the teaching Church and this partakes of *the teaching Church's infallibility*; again: the loving and believing Church is infallible through the animation received from the Holy Spirit in her quality as loving and believing Church, which implies organic reference and submission to the magisterium. In the first case, the Holy Spirit makes the hierarch infallible, and the hierarchy, by subjecting the faithful to itself, communicates the benefits of *its* infallibility to them; in the second case, the Holy Spirit makes the Church, as a whole and as such, infallible, and in her each organic part according to what it is—the whole body in order that it may believe and live, the apostolic and magisterial hierarchy in order that it may transmit the apostolical deposit to the body and declare its authentic meaning" (*Lay People in the Church*, 290–91).

83. Farley, *Just Love*, 190. For an incisive critique of Farley's overall position on Christian ethics, see Gardiner, "Catholic Feminist Ethics and the Culture of Death," 19–23.

proposal, I agree with her that a comprehensive and coherent Christian theological ethics must be adequate with reference to those "criteria" (or, in my terms, the sources of "Scripture and Tradition" and the aid that experience may provide to discerning the Word of God). But she means her thesis to be taken as a normative proposal, her so-called "quadrilateral approach," and hence she assumes an absolute equality between these sources. Thus, in my judgment, her normative proposal is incompatible with the dogmatic tradition of the Catholic faith in which Sacred Scripture is the primary and supreme normative source ("the highest authority," in John Paul II words[84]) for faith and practice, and Sacred Tradition is indispensable to the interpretation of the Word of God. This also means that other aids to discernment can be used, such as experience, insofar as they cohere with the primary and normative source of Sacred Scripture and the living Tradition of the Church.

Yet, Farley's "quadrilateral approach" eventually gives way to "experience" as "an authority that modifies the prior norms that would order it."[85] It seems that experience has in some sense priority over Scripture, because in some sense Scripture itself grows out of human experience. Farley says, "Experience is also potentially misleading as a named source for Christian insight, for it is not just one source among many. It is an important part of the content of each of the other sources, and it is always a factor in interpreting the others. Scripture, for example, is the record of some persons' experience of God; tradition is the lived experience of a faith community through time; and secular disciplines, too, are shaped by the experience of those who engage in them."[86] But what criteria does one employ to determine the authority of experience? She explains: "We can identify some guiding criteria for appeals to experience in moral discernment, such as: coherence of the insights from experience with general moral norms; intelligibility of accounts of experience in relation to fundamental beliefs; mutual illumination when measured with other sources of moral insight; harmful or helpful consequences of interpretations of experience; confirmation in a community of discernment and integrity in the testimony of those who present their experience. All of these may be tests for the validity and usefulness of given experiences in a process

---

84. John Paul II, *Ut Unum Sint*, no. 70. I developed this Catholic view of Sacred Scripture and Tradition in chapter 1 of this book.

85. Farley, *Just Love*, 194.

86. Ibid., 190.

of moral discernment."[87] And yet, significantly, experience trumps them all: "experience may challenge its own tests and assert an authority that modifies the prior norms that would order it."[88]

The authority of experience trumps even the Bible's own authority. In particular, women's experience, more accurately, the experience and consciousness of feminists, claims Farley, serves precisely as a "negative limit" in the interpretation of Scripture. This experience and consciousness expresses "deep convictions" and, Farley adds, "whatever contradicts those convictions cannot be accepted as having the authority of an authentic revelation of truth. It is simply a matter of there being no turning back."[89] Thus, on the question of Scripture and experience, it is an understanding of authority that is the basic question. "It is impossible," says Farley, "to separate the question of authority from the question of the content or meaning of what is presented as authoritative." And in order to decide the question of, say, the authority of the Scriptures, whether you ought to accept its claims, the Bible "must 'make sense' to the one who accepts it."[90] Therefore, according to Farley, "The ... authority ... of any source is ultimately contingent on a 'recognition' of the truth it offers.... No source has real and living authority in relation to our moral attitudes and choices unless it can elicit from us a responding recognition."[91] In particular, the Bible "cannot be believed unless it 'rings true' to our deepest capacity for truth and goodness." In that case, however, isn't that to reduce the authority of the Bible "to a measure that is outside of it?"[92] Aren't we dealing here with a subjectification of biblical authority, meaning thereby that the Bible only becomes the authoritative Word of God through acknowledgement? It certainly seems so. For it is within the negative limit established by the deep convictions of feminist consciousness and experience that the "biblical witness as a whole is experienced as authentic," meaning thereby that, according to Farley, "some religious authority is given to Scripture."[93]

---

87. Ibid.
88. Ibid.
89. Farley, "Feminist Consciousness and the Interpretation of Scripture," 56.
90. Farley, *Just Love*, 194.
91. Ibid., 194–95.
92. Ibid., 195.
93. Farley, "Feminist Consciousness and the Interpretation of Scripture," 56.

Does Farley then leave it up to human understanding to decide which biblical texts are authoritative and revelatory? Doesn't this mean that biblical authority is, on her view, founded on human reasoning and the authority of man's own power of conviction, rather than on divine authorship and inspiration, which is the deep foundation of all scriptural faith? Is her view an experiential or existential view that holds the Bible to be authoritative "only in those parts that are existentially engaging and compelling—that give grounding and meaning to existence [?]"[94] Farley is, however, quick to assure us, "This does not mean that sources are completely subjectified, that there is—for example—no revelation in the Bible unless everyone perceives it."[95] Perhaps not, but I am left wondering whether her claim brings with it the very real danger that the authority of biblical truth is tailored to suit human needs. In other words, the claim that biblical truth is authentically authoritative because it elicits from us a responding recognition so easily turns into its opposite, namely, that it is only biblical truth and hence authoritative because it elicits that response from us.[96]

Farley's assurance notwithstanding, I still wonder whether we are dealing with a subjectification of authority in her proposal. Admittedly, the content of Scripture is essential to the proclamation of the Gospel and hence biblical authority cannot be completely severed from man's coming to recognize that content as a revelation of truth. So there is a genuine issue here that I will address below. Still, as John Frame correctly argues, "the content is not the efficient cause of scriptural authority; it is not what makes Scripture the Word of God. What makes Scripture the Word of God is simply the fact that God has spoken it." Put differently, but no less insistent that Holy Scripture *is* the Word of God,[97] Vatican II's

---

94. This is how Dan O. Via, Professor Emeritus of New Testament at Duke University Divinity School, describes his own view of biblical authority in dialogue with Robert A. J. Gagnon, *Homosexuality and the Bible: Two Views*, 2.

95. Farley, *Just Love*, 195, and note 38.

96. Bavinck, *Gereformeerde Dogmatiek*, I, 524 [552–53].

97. *Dei Verbum*, no. 24, "The Sacred Scriptures contain the Word of God, and, because they are inspired, they are truly the Word of God." Elsewhere in *Dei Verbum* we find this teaching reaffirmed: "Since [Sacred Scriptures] are inspired by God and committed to writing once and for all time, they present God's own Word in an unalterable form, and they make the voice of the Holy Spirit sound again and again in the words of the prophets and apostles" (no. 21). Avery Cardinal Dulles rightly argues against Raymond E. Brown that "the position of Vatican II" is "that the whole Bible not only transmits, but is, the Word of God" ("Revelation, Scripture, and Tradition," 48 n. 25).

Dei Verbum teaches: "Those divinely revealed realities [of salvation history] which are contained and presented in Sacred Scripture have been committed to writing under the inspiration of the Holy Spirit. For holy mother Church, relying on the belief of the Apostles (see John 20:31; 2 Tim 3:16; 2 Peter 1:19-20, 3:15-16), holds that the books of both the Old and New Testaments in their entirety, with all their parts, are sacred and canonical because written under the inspiration of the Holy Spirit, they have God as their author and have been handed on as such to the Church herself."[98] Elsewhere in *Dei Verbum* we find the statement that the authority of the Church's teaching office, although exercised in the name of Jesus Christ, "is not superior to the Word of God, but is its servant."[99] That the Church is a servant of the Word of God, subject to its authority, is true of the whole Church and not just the Church's Magisterium. In this light, we cannot fail to make a connection between being a servant of the authoritative Word of God and the "'obedience of faith' (Rom 16:26; cf. Rom 1:5; 2 Cor 10:5-6) [that] must be given to God as he reveals himself [in divine revelation]. By faith man freely commits his entire self to God, making 'the full submission of his intellect and will to God who reveals,' and willingly assenting to the Revelation given by him."[100] Furthermore, regarding the mysteries of faith, such as the Trinity, the Incarnation, the Atoning Work of Christ, the Church, and so forth, the supernatural virtue of faith, which is the beginning of man's salvation, is required. "Whereby," the Dogmatic Decree of Vatican I adds, "inspired and assisted by the grace of God, we believe that the things which he has revealed are true; *not because of the intrinsic truth of the things, viewed by the natural light of reason, but because of the authority of God himself, who reveals them, and who can neither be deceived nor deceive.*"[101]

Now, the question raised by the view of divine authority expressed in this statement of Vatican I, says Berkouwer, is that the assent of faith seems "severed from the content of the message of salvation: it has no inner affinity with this message."[102] Yes, the decree makes clear that there

---

98. *Dei Verbum*, no. 11.

99. Ibid., no. 10.

100. Ibid., no. 5. The quote within the quotation is from Vatican I, 1870, *Decreta Dogmatica Concilii Vaticani de Fide Catholica et de Ecclesia Christi*, chapter 3, *Of Faith*, 242-43.

101. Ibid., italics added.

102. Berkouwer, *De Heilige Schrift*, II, 422 [352]. Berkouwer isn't directing his critical

are motives of credibility showing that the "assent of faith is by no means a blind action of the mind." But those motives only justify the reasonableness of believing *that* something has been revealed; they do not provide, however, an "inner conviction" regarding *what* has been revealed, namely, "the object and content of faith to which man is called."[103] Furthermore, there is also the internal testimony of the Holy Spirit since "no man can assent to the Gospel teaching, as is necessary to obtain salvation, without the illumination and inspiration of the Holy Spirit, who gives to all men sweetness in assenting to and believing in the truth."[104] Therefore, Berkouwer adds, "[t]here is agreement [with the objective content of faith], but there is no biblical trust, even though there is reference to the authority of God, which must be accepted unconditionally."[105] The view represented by Vatican I seems to leave us, he adds, with a "formal authority that can and must be believed no matter what words are spoken."[106]

Let me be clear that Berkouwer is not questioning Vatican I's emphasis on God's authority. In other words, he, too, holds that theological faith is based on that authority as its ultimate motive and formal object. Berkouwer's position on authority and experience does not imply a "subjectification of authority, which might only become reality through acknowledgment."[107] That view, such as we find in Johnson and Farley, is a dialogical view of authority, as I critically discussed earlier in this chapter. Rather, says Berkouwer, "faith is not founded on human reliability but on the explicit authority of God himself, the deep foundation of all apostolic authority."[108]

Let me also make it clear that Berkouwer does not reject a propositional view of faith—as long as we do not understand faith *first and last* to mean holding certain propositions to be true, then Berkouwer has no difficulty taking the act of "faith's assent-function to mean that it must believe and accept certain truths."[109] Says Berkouwer, "There is no reason

---

remarks against Vatican I's view of divine authority. Rather, he is questioning a notion of formal authority.

103. Ibid., 419 [349].

104. *Decreta Dogmatica Concilii Vaticani de Fide Catholica et de Ecclesia Christi*, 244.

105. Ibid.

106. Ibid., 424 [353].

107. Ibid., 418 [348].

108. Ibid., 419 [349].

109. Berkouwer, "Sacrificium Intellectus?" 188. All the English translations of this essay in the text are mine.

to reject the words 'assent,' 'acceptance,' or 'hold to be true.' All these terms are meaningful and legitimate as long as they are maintained in the right framework, which is to say as long as they are not separated from the content of revelation."[110] Put differently, Berkouwer agrees (in my own terms) that theological faith involves holding certain propositions to be true, holding them to be divinely revealed, and holding them because we believe God who reveals them. In short, faith therefore believes what God has revealed, because he has revealed it.

Thus, Berkouwer's problem is not that some men "speak of the authority of God and of the definitive meaning of his revelation, but rather that they separate the formal and material ["content"] authority of revelaton and then place faith in a framework where it is taken to mean acceptance of authority isolated from the content of revelation."[111] Berkouwer, therefore, concludes that this view of biblical authority leaves us with a mere formal authority, a heteronomous power, or as Dietrich Bonhoeffer once put it, a "positivist doctrine of revelation which says, in effect, 'Like it or lump it,'"[112] whereby man is reduced by God's Word ("God has spoken") to passivity, blind submission, and in which a concept of faith is rendered as a sacrifice of the intellect, blind faith, not allowing any insight, understanding, or response on man's part.

Berkouwer is right that this view entails a "dangerous view of faith."[113] "For faith," says Berkouwer, "would then be called to a decision without inner conviction regarding the object and content of the faith to which man is called." Berkouwer seeks to counteract this view of God's authority by arguing that "this authority does not exclude experience and man is freely part of it; but *in* the experience the authority is acknowledged and confessed. Scriptural faith is part of this acknowledgment and is manifested in submission and the obedience of faith."[114] Elsewhere he expresses the correlation between faith and understanding to be such that this correlation is grounded in the unique authority of Scripture rather than in that view in which this authority is made to rest on man's insight and understanding, which

---

110. Ibid.
111. Ibid.
112. Bonhoeffer, *Letters and Papers from Prison*, 157.
113. Berkouwer, *De Heilige Schrift*, II, 422 [352].
114. Ibid., 419 [349].

results in the subjectification of biblical authority.[115] He adds, "It is the deep dynamic of faith in the authority of Scripture that is daily confirmed *in* understanding and *in* listening." This deep dynamic of faith involves "a faithful listening—*ex auditu Verbi*—that more deeply understands what it hears and therein finds rest."[116]

In this biblical vision, faith is never and nowhere portrayed as an irrational acceptance of the objective content of faith on the basis of authority, whereby the emphasis is more on the "that" than the "what" of revelation. Rather, says Berkouwer, "Revelation may never even for a moment be abstracted from the self-revealing God." Indeed, God's gift of himself in revelation involves man "being called to his communion, called to walking in his way, to a faithful listening to his Word. Without this context, faith loses its deepest meaning."[117] In God's calling man to faith, he is called to be "transformed by the renewing of [his] mind" (Rom 12:2). In other words, faith's acceptance of biblical authority means that he "is persuaded [to respond to the Gospel] through the reality of the proclaimed content of the gospel so that he is not led to a sacrifice of the intellect but to renewal of his thought (Rom 12: 2), born in the freedom of faith and issuing in gratitude and adoration. We are dealing here with a faith that is not subject to rational yardsticks and needs no approval of rational verification and yet cannot be separated from insight. . . . This faith is no less full of certainty."[118] But this certainty is based, adds Hans Urs von Balthasar, "not on the human understanding's own power of conviction, but on the manifest evidence of divine truth. In other words, this certainty is founded not on having grasped, but on having been grasped."[119] In other words, it is the Truth itself that, in the power of the Holy Spirit, seizes hold of the human heart. "The heart is the place of decision. . . . It is the place of truth, where we choose life or death. It is the place of encounter, because as image of God we live in relation: it is the place of covenant."[120]

---

115. Berkouwer, "Sacrificium Intellectus?" 198.
116. Ibid.
117. Ibid., 187.
118. Berkouwer, *De Heilige Schrift*, II, 422 [352–53].
119. Balthasar, *Glory of the Lord*, 1:134.
120. *Catechism of the Catholic Church*, no. 2563.

Given this conclusion, there remains to give a brief account of *how the Gospel takes hold of a human life*.[121] I shall answer this question by turning to John Paul II and the then Joseph Cardinal Ratzinger, now Benedict XVI.[122] Let us return to the understanding of faith given in the Dogmatic Decree of Vatican I and in Vatican II's *Dei Verbum*. "By faith man freely commits his entire self to God, making 'the full submission of his intellect and will to God who reveals', and willingly assenting to the Revelation given by him."[123] The supernatural virtue of faith is required in order to make this assent. "Whereby," the Dogmatic Decree of Vatican I adds, "inspired and assisted by the grace of God, we believe that the things which he has revealed are true; *not because of the intrinsic truth of the things, viewed by the natural light of reason, but because of the authority of God himself, who reveals them, and who can neither be deceived nor deceive*."[124]

Now, both John Paul II and Ratzinger draw an analogy between what it is to trust, to have faith in, a human person, to accept the word of another, his testimony, on the one hand, and what is to have faith in God on the other. In this context, John Paul, for one clarifies the pervasive presence of testimony, namely, reliance on the word of others, as a basic belief-producing practice in our ordinary lives. He says, "There are in the life of a human being many more truths which are simply believed than truths which are acquired by way of personal verification. Who, for instance, could assess critically the countless scientific findings upon which modern life is based? Who could personally examine the flow of information which comes day after day from all parts of the world and which is generally accepted as true? Who in the end could forge the treasures

---

121. Berkouwer notes, "We can, in fear of rationalism and intellectual arrogance, refuse to take account of *how* the Gospel takes hold of a human life." "But," he adds, "this is a treacherous route" (Berkouwer, *Half Century of Theology*, 159. This is a translation from the Dutch edition, *Een Halve Eeuw Theologie: Motieven en Stromingen van 1920 tot Heden*, 224: "Het is levensgevaarlijk om uit vrees voor rationalisme en voor de autonomie van de rede zich nauwelijks rekenschap te geven van de wijze, waarop het evangelie het mensenleven binnendringt.").

122. John Paul II, *Fides et Ratio*, nos. 31–33. Ratzinger (Benedict XVI), *Yes of Jesus Christ*, 3–38.

123. *Dei Verbum*, no. 5. The quote within the quotation is from Vatican I, 1870, *Decreta Dogmatica Concilii Vaticani de Fide Catholica et de Ecclesia Christi*, chapter 3, *Of Faith*, 242–43.

124. Ibid., italics added.

of human wisdom and religion?" Of course the obvious answer to these questions is that restricting belief to only those truths that I can discover for myself to be true, a discovery based on my understanding's own power of conviction, would eliminate most of what I know. "This means that the human being—the one who seeks the truth—is also the one who lives by belief."[125] And to live by believing implies that I entrust myself to the knowledge that others have acquired. More accurately, believing involves more than just having an abstract knowledge of the truth declared by others. Although we must not minimize the importance of entrusting ourselves to the truth, believing involves in the first place a personal relationship where trust is needed in the person who asserts the truth of a belief.[126] Believing, then, involves believing in a person as well as believing that something is true. Says John Paul, believing "involves an interpersonal relationship and brings into play not only a person's capacity to know [the truth] but also the deeper capacity to entrust oneself to others, to enter into a relationship with them which is intimate and enduring."[127] What is the meaning here of belief? John Paul explains, "'To believe' means to accept and to acknowledge as true and corresponding to reality the content of what is said, that is, the content of the words of another person ... by reason of his ... credibility. This credibility determines in a given case the particular authority of the person—the authority of truth. So then by saying 'I believe,' we express at the same time a double reference: to the person and to the truth; to the truth in consideration of the person who *enjoys special claims* to credulity."[128] The special claims to credibility enjoyed by the witness' act of stating "that p" is that the witness has the relevant competence or credentials to state truly "that p." Believing, then, involves not only believing that something is true but also believing in a person, the latter characteristically being thought of as trust. "'Faith' then emerges as the appropriate name of those acts of mental consent in which the element of trust is prominent." Benjamin B. Warfield adds,

---

125. John Paul II, *Fides et Ratio*, no. 31. See also, Ratzinger, *Yes of Jesus Christ*, 5–9.
126. Ibid., no. 32.
127. Ibid.
128. John Paul II, *Catechesis on The Creed*, vol. 1, *God Father and Creator*, 31; italics added. See also, *Catechism of the Catholic Church*, no. 177: "'To believe' has thus a twofold reference: to the person and to the truth, by trust in the person who bears witness to it."

"In what we call religious faith this prominent implication of trust reaches its height."[129]

Significantly, we are dealing here with personal relations, and the more intimate, enduring, and life-giving the relationship is, the clearer it becomes that the truth sought is the "truth of the person—what the person is and what the person reveals from deep within." In its higher applications, taking us beyond the cases of interpersonal belief such as with parents, teachers, and doctors, to a marital relationship or friendship, then, the truth that is sought is the truth that brings about ultimate self-fulfillment. "Human perfection, then, consists not simply in acquiring an abstract knowledge of the truth, but in a dynamic relationship of faithful self-giving with others. It is in this faithful self-giving that a person finds a fullness of certainty and security."[130] Acts of entrusting oneself, indeed of total self-giving, to another person are "among the most significant and expressive human acts." In its *highest* application (to borrow a phrase of Warfield), faith, believing, says John Paul, "involves an interpersonal relationship and brings into play not only a person's capacity to know [the truth] but also the deeper capacity to entrust oneself to others, to enter into a relationship with them which is intimate and enduring."[131] Put differently, this search for truth is a personal journey and it, says the pope, "can reach its end only in reaching the absolute."[132] That is, that "ulterior truth which would explain the meaning of life." Indeed, John Paul adds, "Man is able to encounter and recognize a truth of this kind."[133]

Encountering and recognizing a truth of this kind requires self-criticism. That is, says Ratzinger, the fundamental relationship of man to ultimate truth requires understanding that he is in the position of a suppliant rather than a judge. Truth is made manifest to the person aspiring to know the truth given the orientation of his character and state of mind; it shows itself only to the person who is, says Cottingham, "already to some extent in a state of receptivity and trust." Rather than the truth showing itself to an "impartial interrogation of the data," it shows itself,

---

129. Warfield, "On Faith in its Psychological Aspects," 392.
130. John Paul II, *Fides et Ratio*, no. 32.
131. Ibid., no. 13.
132. Ibid., no. 32.
133. Ibid., no. 33.

he adds, "through an inner transformation of the subject."[134] It is precisely this transformation of the subject that Ratzinger has in mind: from being a judge to a suppliant of the truth. Ratzinger explains: "We deceive ourselves by making ourselves the lord of truth . . . It withdraws itself from those who claim self-sufficiency and reveals itself only to those who approach it in an attitude of reverence, of absolute humility."[135] Indeed, adds Ratzinger, "Those who make themselves lords of truth and end by leaving truth on one side when it does not allow itself to be dominated ultimately place power above truth. Their criterion becomes power, ability. But precisely in this way they lose themselves: the throne on which they place themselves is a false throne; what they think is ascending the throne is in reality their fall."[136] But this seems contrary to the "critical mind," that is, says Ratzinger, "[t]o a 'critical' way of thinking that criticizes everything except human being themselves." Regarding this sense of criticism, he puts in its place the character and state of mind of one who has "humility of thought that is ready to bow before the majesty of truth, before which are not judges but suppliants." Truth "reveals itself only to the watchful and humble heart."[137] In a passage worth quoting in full, Ratzinger summarizes the spiritual and intellectual virtues necessary to be grasped by the majesty of truth.

> If it is already true that the great discoveries of science reveal themselves only to long, watchful, and patient labor that is read always to correct itself and let itself be taught, then it is self-evident that the highest truths demand a humble and continuous readiness to listen. . . . [I]t is only to this humility of thought that the majesty of truth reveals itself and thereby grants access to our true dimension. This kind of openness to the infinite and to the One who is infinite has nothing to do with credulity: on the contrary, it demands the keenest self-criticism. It is more open and more critical than that limitation to the sphere of the empirical in which human beings make their desire for mastery the final criterion of knowledge. . . . In this context the Fathers of the Church have continually referred to Christ's saying: "Blessed are the pure in heart, for they shall see God" (Matt 5:8). The "pure" heart is the one that is open and humble. The impure heart according to this is the opposite,

---

134. Cottingham, *Spiritual Dimension, Religion, Philosophy and Human Value*, 139.
135. Ratzinger, *Yes of Jesus Christ*, 17.
136. Ibid., 17.
137. Ibid., 19.

the presumptuous heart that is shut in on itself, thus is completely filled up with itself and incapable of finding room for the majesty of truth that demands reverence and ultimately worship.[138]

Thus far we've been describing this journeying search for truth as if it is a purely human ascent. And yet, we must bring to attention a turn-about in understanding here regarding the search for the Absolute. As Os Guinness puts it, "the secret of the search is not our 'great ascent' but the 'great descent'—of God toward us."[139] John Paul clarifies Guinness' point admirably well:

> History therefore becomes the arena where we see what God does for humanity.... In the Incarnation of the Son of God we see ... the Eternal enters time, the Whole lies hidden in the part, God takes on a human face. The truth communicated in Christ's revelation is therefore no longer communicated to a particular place or culture, but is offered to every man and woman who would welcome it as the word which is the absolutely valid source of meaning for human life. Now, in Christ, all have access to the Father, since by his death and resurrection Christ has bestowed the divine life that the first Adam had refused (cf. Rom. 5:12–15). Through this revelation, men and women are offered the ultimate truth about their own life and about the goal of history. As the Constitution *Gaudium et Spes* [no. 22] puts it, "only in the mystery of the incarnate Word does the mystery of man take on light."[140]

And so John Paul turns this search for the truth, and for the person to whom total self-giving is given, all around, re-describing the journey now in terms of God drawing close to us in Christ, and not only completing our journey but elevating us into the condition of grace. "Christian faith comes to meet [men and women who are on a journey of discovery], offering the concrete possibility of reaching the goal which they seek." "Moving beyond the stage of simple [natural human] believing," adds John Paul, "Christian faith immerses human beings in the order of grace, which enables them to share in the mystery of Christ, which in turn offers them a true and coherent knowledge of the Triune God. In Jesus Christ, who is the Truth, faith recognizes the ultimate appeal to humanity, an appeal made in order that what we experience as desire and nostalgia [for

---

138. Ibid., 19–21.
139. Guinness, *Long Journey Home*, 190.
140. John Paul II, *Fides et Ratio*, no. 12.

God] may come to its fulfillment."[141] At this stage then in our personal journey, we discover that trusting Jesus Christ with a trust that involves a total self-giving can occur only from within a living relationship with him. Indeed, we discover that "the *preparation of man* for the reception of grace [in Christ and through the Holy Spirit] is already a work of grace."[142]

So in divine faith, that is, by a total giving of the self to God, we respond by grace to the personal relationship that God initiates by revealing himself to us in Jesus Christ. This response involves *knowledge, conviction, and trust*.[143] We know who Jesus Christ is and accept his claim to be the way, the truth, and the life. We know that we cannot find, reach or satisfy God without him, who is the way to God that God himself has made for us (see John 14:6). We are convinced that he is the way, the truth, and the life, because we are sure of Christ's truth claim. Lastly, this response of faith includes trust, being drawn into a personal relationship with Christ, which involves a total giving of the self. Thus, to have faith in God implies our whole life's dependence on God because we acknowledge his divinity, transcendence, supreme freedom, and faithfulness. Furthermore, says John Paul, "By the authority of his absolute transcendence, God who makes himself known is also the source of the credibility of what he reveals. By faith, men and women give their assent to this divine testimony. This means that they acknowledge fully and integrally the truth of what is revealed, because it is God himself who is the guarantor of that truth."[144] Moreover, the truth that the believer receives in faith is a pure gift of God, which we receive within the personal relationship where God makes himself known and invites us to an intimate sharing in his life, and so we can make no claim upon this truth. "This is why the Church has always considered the act of entrusting oneself to God to be a moment of fundamental decision which engages the whole person. In that act, the intellect and the will display their spiritual nature, enabling the subject to act in a way which realizes personal freedom to the full."[145] Without the gift of truth conferred by revelation, that is, without God's descent to us in

---

141. Ibid., no. 33.

142. *Catechism of the Catholic Church*, no. 2001. On this, see also Giussani, *At the Origin of the Christian Claim*.

143. Guinness, *Long Journey Home*, 174–75.

144. John Paul II, *Fides et Ratio*, no. 13.

145. Ibid.

the Incarnation, there is no human ascent and hence no fulfillment of the truth-seeker's quest for meaning.

FAITH AND CRITICISM

But if what is required is the attitude of a suppliant rather than a judge before the majesty of truth revealed in the Word of God, then in what sense, if at all, may one approach Scripture critically if he "may only be engaged in the activity of listening [to Scripture] with an attentive heart because of the normative 'is' ["Holy Scripture *is* the Word of God"]." The brief answer to this question here must be that a sharp distinction needs to be drawn "between criticism *of* the word and *by* the Word."[146] The distinction here is crucial since it isn't possible to exalt oneself above God's Word, nor to criticize it. In faith, we are subject to God's Word, servants of that Word.[147] Thus: "We are called precisely in that situation to a 'readiness' to hear God's Word on its own terms and to understand the point it is making. True simplicity excludes 'prejudice', that is, the placing of an opinion or decision ahead of the reading (1 Tim 5:21; Jas 2:1–9), so that one already knows his decision before God's Word is truly heard. A particular frame of reference has been established, and man, in fact rules God's Word and judges it consciously or unconsciously, shaping ideas according to his 'prejudgment' (2 Pet 3:16). This prejudice is judged by God's Word, which itself discerns the thoughts and intentions of the heart (Heb 4:12; Jn 12:48)."[148] Berkouwer gives several examples of "prejudgments" that dangerously inhibit one's faithful reading of Scripture.

> For the dangers of prejudice, which acquire large proportions in any method, cannot be localized in the light of this written Word, for they are present in all reading of Scripture. Scripture itself shows these dangers in an unmistakable manner, even though it does not deal with modern scientific problems. [1] It is possible to read Scripture in a frame of reference whereby a method—though unscientific—or a prejudice deprives human understanding of the mystery of Scripture. [2] It is possible to read and use Scripture out of context and coherence, to isolate and atomize it, and to abandon it to arbitrariness and literalistic exegesis. [3] It is pos-

---

146. Berkouwer, *De Heilige Schrift*, 2:426–27 [355].

147. *Dei Verbum*, no. 10, states that the teaching office of the Church "is not above the word of God, but serves it." Of course this is equally true for all Christian believers.

148. Berkouwer, *De Heilige Schrift*, 2:427 [355].

> sible to malign Scripture without realizing its dimensions, thus losing all contact with the focused command of God's witnessing to the mystery which was kept secret for long ages but is now disclosed (Rom 16:25–26). [4] It is possible to discover 'Bethlehem' in Scripture without going the way to Bethlehem (Mt 2:4f.), to search the Scripture without coming to Christ (Jn 5:39f.), and to read the Scripture and yet err by not knowing it (Mt 22:29, 31). The words may be accessible, yet knowledge of the secret is not thereby guaranteed.[149]

The upshot of this conclusion is that, according to Berkouwer, "God's Word can only have one subjective correlative, namely, faith."[150] In other words, the light of faith is an activity of God, indeed, the work of the Holy Spirit, within the believer such that the witness of Scripture is made intelligible to him.[151] Yet, faith's own dynamic seeks understanding (*fides quaerens intellectum*), on this classical Christian view, and hence it incorporates rationality into its quest for understanding the content of revelation, the objective content of faith (*fides quae*). As Francis Martin correctly notes, however, "The light of faith is an integrating and transforming factor [here] and the light of reason is the integrated and transformed factor."[152] Thus, seeking understanding of the content of revelation is undertaken in the light of faith, which includes disciplined exploration, research, analysis, questioning, but without relativizing biblical authority or attributing greater value to reason than is biblically warranted. Of course, "a method may degenerate into hyper-criticism," adds Berkouwer, "clearly showing with what presuppositions Scripture is approached." When this happens, the method, not biblical scholarship in general, is suspect. "A plea must be made for increased rather than less scientific earnestness and resolution." Berkouwer explains, "Only in this way may we guard against arbitrariness whereby an apparently open approach perishes in the prejudice during this process of analysis. The struggle over the authority of Scripture does not originate in the dilemma of whether Scripture is or is not [open to] scientific [study], but centers in the *method* of science—its earnestness,

---

149. Ibid., 443–44 [363].
150. Ibid., 427 [356].
151. Martin, *Feminist Question*, 72.
152. Ibid., 173.

openness, and its limits."¹⁵³ The Church is indeed served by faithful biblical scholarship.

> Just as with education which helps to show the way to growth and insight, [biblical] research can fulfill a corrective function, as the history of the church often indicates.... The methodological attention to the words of Scripture ... is no obstacle to the way of listening. It must rather be said that close attention to its meaning may result in the protection of the Bible reader against all arbitrariness, whereby the words of Scripture are violated through prejudices. Attention to goal and tendencies, to literary style and interpretation, may sharpen the eyesight and so may become meaningful for the understanding of the specific contours of the message. A dike is thus erected against preconceived notions and postulates. Hence, every analysis and method is a responsible activity. But they may and must be accompanied by critical warnings; for the words themselves are at stake, resisting any human violence (2 Pet 3: 16), words with the unique purpose to bless life with the power and the majesty of the Spirit.¹⁵⁴

Returning now to the dialogical view of authority of Johnson and Farley, there remains to ask, if the normative Scriptures and the dogmatic tradition is countercultural, or seems no longer meaningful, by the standards of contemporary human experience, then are the Scriptures and/or doctrinal tradition to be abandoned, adulterated, or radically reinterpreted? I think Johnson's answer to this question is clear: we reject the straightforward commands of Scripture or radically reinterpret Scripture's themes (say, love, equality, freedom, and justice) so that the fresh revelation in human experience will now be consonant with those themes, even when their concrete application brings one into open conflict with biblical commandments.

Now, positions like Johnson's and Farley's are entirely unsustainable from the standpoint of a Catholic doctrine of revelation. Their position represents "an excessive privileging of Christian experience over against

---

153. Berkouwer, *De Heilige Schrift*, 2:444 [364].

154. Ibid., 441–42 [361–62]. Elsewhere Berkouwer writes, "When the arresting fact that God's Word challenges us to research is understood and honored, the church will be kept from prejudice, from dogmatic exegesis and traditionalism, from the dictatorship of a method, and from neutrality. For the Scripture of the Spirit interprets to the church the great mystery and keeps the church 'dependent' in a very particular way, so that its listening will never become a matter of the past" (*De Heilige Schrift*, 2:445 [365]).

the witness of Scripture and tradition, and over against the Church's magisterium as their interpreter."[155] In Christian theology, experience is an *aid* to discernment of revealed truth as found in revelation's sources, Scripture and tradition, rather than being itself a living *source* of enlightenment. The basic theological reason for this distinction is stated by Aidan Nichols:

> For Catholic theology, after the apostles, more precisely with the death of the last apostle, revelation is closed. In terms of Scripture this means that the canon of the New Testament is completed in the moment when the apostolic Church understands herself as the Church of these Scriptures and no other. In terms of Tradition, it means that the *regula fidei* and *institutio christiana* of the Church are constituted in all essentials in the apostolic period, all else being crystallization and reformation. *But does this mean that from that point on, experience can provide no elements of novelty to an understanding of specifically Christian revelation?*[156]

The brief answer to the question in the last sentence of this quotation is, "not at all." Although not a source of revelation, there is another kind of experience that counts. As Richard B. Hays nicely puts it, "experience must be treated as a hermeneutical lens for reading the New Testament rather than as an independent, counterbalancing authority."[157] That experience is a *corrective* of an already established understanding of revelation, such as the view of some Christians on slavery. But the authority that experience has lies not in the experience itself but in the truth of revelation it lays hold of more fully. In other words, our increased experience of the brotherhood of all men—guided by the revelation that we are all made in the image and likeness of God—was instrumental in changing our thinking of slavery. Our increased experience of the abilities of women has led us to admit women to more kinds of influence and authority. I think experience does help us interpret Scripture but that experience must be one that accords with objective truth, not subjective distortions, such as the experiences had by many homosexuals and even by women who claim to be called to the priesthood. In other words, in this kind of faith-experience the individual is changed *not* by the experience itself, but through becoming united with Truth itself. Thus, in order to determine whether an experience is authoritative, we "must appeal in the last analy-

---

155. Nichols, *Shape of Catholic Theology*, 241.
156. Ibid., 240 (italics added to last sentence).
157. Hays, *Moral Vision of the New Testament*, 399.

sis to some sort of discernment of spirits."[158] And without revealed truth, propositional revelation, which is God's verbal revelation, consisting in the disclosure of truths about himself and his redemptive acts in history, there would be no way to ensure that our faith-experience in fact unites us to the True God, the God who is our happiness and salvation. This last point needs developing.

REVELATION AND EXPERIENCE

Earlier in chapter 1, I argued—following the lead of the Catholic Francis Martin and the Calvinist Herman Bavinck—that objective revelation, which consists in acts, in the events of history culminating in the person and work of Christ, but also in words, verbal revelation, in the communication of truth, *exists independently* of the believer's personal appropriation of those realities. This is the *principium cognoscendi externum*. In addition, Fr. Martin correctly insisted on an internal revelation or illumination of the Spirit in subjective experience. As Bavinck explained, "objective revelation in Christ is not sufficient, but there needs to be added a working of the Spirit in order that human beings may acknowledge and accept that revelation of God and thereby become the image of the Son." Most significant, Bavinck adds, "[S]o external and objective revelation demands an internal revelation in the subject. . . . But it can come into its own only if it is positioned in relation to the objective revelation granted in Christ. Detached from or elevated above this revelation, it loses its criterion and corrective and opens the door to all sorts of arbitrariness and fanaticism. Even the very concept of subjective revelation is determined and controlled by that of objective revelation."[159] In order to avoid opening that door we must insist on holding Word and Spirit fast together.[160]

I now want to argue that it is in the context of the second dimension, of the *principium cognoscendi internum*, of God's active self-presence as the Holy Spirit, of subjective revelation, that we can see a positive role for "experience": this is the context within which we hear Scripture, and hence the context in which the Scripture exercises its normative authority over us (*principium cognoscendi externum*). What sorts of experience? Well, the experience that creates the need to the respond to the Gospel of

---

158. Nichols, *Shape of Catholic Theology*, 237.
159. Bavinck, *Gereformeerde Dogmatiek*, 1:320 [347–48].
160. Congar, *Word and the Spirit*, 21–41.

Jesus Christ in the first place. There is also the experience of conversion or coming to faith. "In conversion, the life, death, and resurrection of Jesus Christ are experienced as throwing light on my life." This is the experience of the self-revealing God made possible by faith. Following that experience there is "postconversion experience of life in the Church: an experience of life in faith, of sacramental life, of life within a specific fellowship of persons." "We can call this," adds Nichols, "the experience of Christian existence, experience of a new quality of existence ushered in by conversion, which itself provides the Christian reinterpretation of pre-Christian experience." Lastly, there is the experience of conscious communion with Father, Son, and Holy Spirit, a communion that has taken hold of my life such that I now know that it is not I who live, but Christ who lives in me. In sum, Christian revelation, in presuming its own intelligibility as an authentic body of knowledge[161], can take hold of my subjective experience.

> Grace modifies the heart and mind, the imagination and the feelings, so that the believing person becomes to some extent a transcription of revelation itself. To the extent that I have faith, hope, and charity, the subjectivity engaged in what I call my experience is affected by revelation [*principium cognoscendi externum*]. As a result, when I come to reflect on my experience, I can find in it an aid to discernment of revealed truth as found in revelation's sources, Scripture and Tradition. To this extent, my experience of the Christian reality provides me with a key to interpreting the Christian sources. And not just me, but anyone, who, by the grace of God, also believes in the Father's sending of his Son and his Holy Spirit to effect the redemption and transfiguration of the world.[162]

So in an act of objective revelation God manifests and communicates something of himself and his plan of salvation. Through faith, revelation is way of knowing and experiencing the divine realities themselves, and reflection on that experience can be an aid to discernment of the sources of Christian revelation. Furthermore, the experience of these divine realities is not a totally subjective event. "It is God who is known in the act by which he reveals himself. The self-revealing aspect of God can be known and shared, because it is not merely the modification of the subject that is known, but God who is known. He is incomprehensible but not indeterminate."[163]

161. John Paul II, *Fides et Ratio*, no. 66. See also, Nichols, *Epiphany*, 62.
162. Nichols, *Shape of Catholic Theology*, 245.
163. Martin, *Feminist Question*, 194.

There is more: knowing and experiencing the divine realities of God's self-revelation can only occur for the subjects who belong to the Church, the new and reborn humanity in Christ, the body of Christ, the communion of the Holy Spirit. The Church is an ordered or structured unity, its hierarchical organs founded, like the community they serve, by Jesus Christ. The implication of this for the appeal to experience should be clear. If the reality of divine revelation and salvation does not come to me except I belong to the Church, "I can never appeal to Christian experience against that Church in order to deny its common faith or disparage its common life. To appeal away from the Church would be to cut off the branch on which I am sitting, to cut myself off from the source of the experience I am claiming, to commit epistemological suicide."[164]

We can surely appreciate Nichols' point by attending to the historical record of theologies based on experience: it offers abundant proof that appeal to "Christian experience" against the Christ's historic Church and its teachings leads to denying her common faith or disparaging her common life. On this view, the object of faith is a subjective principle in its very core, collapsing into individual relativism and historicism. "Since this context is acquired," says Bavinck, "not by the study of Scripture or by reflection but only by personal experience, and this experience is most diverse among Christians, the content of faith will be correspondingly diverse. That which is valid to us need not be valid to others or to people who live in a later period." Most important, appealing to "Christian experience" against the Church's historic Christian teaching "winds up having no Christianity left." "Religious experience is such a subjective and individualistic principle," add Bavinck, "that it opens the door to all sorts of arbitrariness in religion and actually enthrones anarchism: religion as a private thing."[165] Bavinck wrote this statement just over one hundred years ago but its sound like he is describing our times. Religion becomes privately engaging, a personal life-style choice, and nothing more—obviously not about making truth claims regarding the living God who in an act of revelation manifests and communicates something of himself and his plan of salvation, calling us to share in his divine life.

---

164. Nichols, *Shape of Catholic Theology*, 245.
165. Bavinck, *Gereformeerde Dogmatiek*, 1:504, 517 [535, 547].

4

The Phenomenology of the Body

JOHN PAUL II is often said to work out of the phenomenological tradition. I think there is much truth to this statement, but it rarely has received much analysis in an English or American context.[1] To begin, then, I think we can say that the late philosopher-pope construes phenomenology to be complementary rather than contradictory of Thomism.[2] As he himself says in the Author's Preface to the English/American edition of *The Acting Person*, "The author of the present study owes everything to the systems of metaphysics, of anthropology, and of Aristotelian-Thomistic ethics on the one hand, and to phenomenology, above all in Scheler's interpretation, and through Scheler's critique also to Kant, on the other hand."[3] I do not propose in this chapter to explain John Paul's synthesis of a relatively traditional Thomism with contemporary phenomenology,

---

1. An important counter-example to this claim is Kenneth L. Schmitz's study, *At the Center of the Human Drama: The Philosophical Anthropology of Karol Wojtyla/Pope John Paul II*, esp. chapter 3, 58–89. Schmitz gives a very instructive analysis of the integration of phenomenology into the pope's analysis of human action. Some analysis of the pope's phenomenological background is also given by Michael Waldstein, the translator of the new edition of *Theology of the Body*, in his Introduction to the book, but he is mostly concerned with Wojtyla's analysis of Max Scheler, 63–77. A brief analysis of Wojtyla's philosophical background is also given by Rocco Buttiglione, *Karol Wojtyla: The Thought of the Man who became Pope John Paul II*, 270–78. Yet because Buttiglione's book appeared when John Paul II was in the middle of delivering his Wednesday Catecheses on "The Theology of the Body," which ran from September 1979 to November 1984, he provides no analysis of the theology of the body. In the Afterword of the English translation of this book, the translators give a succinct survey-update on the studies that appeared in between the publication of the Italian edition and the English translation. But none of the articles surveyed (323–37) deal with the pope's phenomenological analysis of the body and its bearing on his understanding of revelation. For one such recent attempt, see Kerr, chapter 10, "Karol Wojtyla," *Twentieth-Century Catholic Theologians*, 163–82.

2. Robert Sokolowski, *Introduction to Phenomenology*, 207.

3. Karol Wojtyla, *Acting Person*, xiv.

as it comes to expression in *The Acting Person* and other seminal essays written in the period of the late 1950s to the 1970s.[4] That goes well beyond the scope of this work. Rather, pared down for my purpose here, what I attempt is to show the phenomenological foundation of the pope's theology of the body. In other words, his theology of the body is grounded in a phenomenology of the body that is an "adequate anthropology," as the pope phrases it, having "constitutive elements" and forming "a deep substratum" of that theology (*MWTB*, 26.2). What, then, are these constitutive elements of his adequate anthropology? How do these constitutive elements disclose themselves to us, phenomenologically speaking? To answer these questions, answering the prior question about not only what John Paul understands by phenomenology but also what its relationship is to metaphysics is necessary.[5]

PHENOMENOLOGY AND METAPHYSICS

I have heard it said that the pope adopts phenomenology as a method but not a system. I understand the contrast here between "method rather than system" to express Wojtyla's conviction that no one philosophical system can give a complete understanding of all of reality; indeed, all philosophies give a partial and imperfect view of things.[6] Although this is true, it doesn't tell us either why Wojtyla found phenomenology methodologically significant or what are its limitations. Helpfully, Wojtyla himself gives a glimpse of phenomenology's value at the end of his book on Max Scheler and Christian ethics. He says that the theologian "should not forego the great advantages which the phenomenological method offers his work. It impresses the stamp of experience on works of ethics and nourishes them with the life-knowledge of concrete man by allowing an investigation of moral life from the side of its appearance."[7] For example, Wojtyla draws on the studies regarding the phenomenology of the will

---

4. Many of these essays are collected in Karol Wojtyla, *Person and Community*, Parts I–II.

5. For helping me to see clearly how "besides being a phenomenologist [John Paul II] was also a metaphysician," I am indebted to the late Avery Cardinal Dulles, S.J., "Metaphysical Realism of Pope John Paul II." Also helpful is Deborah Savage's unpublished paper, "Centrality of Lived Experience in Wojtyla's Account of the Person."

6. John Paul II, *Fides et Ratio*, no. 4.

7. As cited by Michael Waldstein in his Introduction to *Man and Women He Created Them*, 75.

of, among others, the German psychologist Narziss Ach (1871–1946) to make the point that in ethical experience the very efficacy of the person self consciously exercising free causal activity is at stake, because we experience ourselves as actually deciding and as the efficient cause of our free actions. He explains:

> The experience upon which ethics is based reveals that persons who experience themselves as the efficient cause of their actions simultaneously experience themselves as subjects of ethical values—moral good and evil. The distinct immanence of ethical experience appears, therefore, in the lived experience of the efficacy of the person, that is, in the phenomenologically apprehended act of will. This is also suggested by the sense of responsibility that accompanies action and is related to ethical value. If the efficacy of the person is the basic element of the experiential whole we call ethical experience, and if the experience of responsibility is connected with it, then ethical value originates, so to speak, between these two elements. Ethical value originates in the lived experience of efficacy, that is, in the act of the will apprehended phenomenologically—and this is what gives us the experiential basis for connecting ethical value with the person as its proper subject.[8]

Though Wojtyla is definitely supportive of the phenomenological method, he stresses its secondary assisting role. Indeed, he claims that "the Christian thinker, especially the theologian, who makes use of phenomenological experience in his work, cannot be a Phenomenologist."[9] Phenomenological analysis of the lived ethical experience of good and evil can only play a subsidiary role because it says "nothing about what is good and what is evil, [and why] but merely asserts that, upon the occasion of a certain thing (some value), 'good' or 'evil' is experienced."[10] Thus,

---

8. Wojtyla, *Person and Community*, "Problem of the Will in the Analysis of the Ethical Act," 9.

9. Again, as cited by Michael Waldstein, Introduction to *Man and Women He Created Them*, 75.

10. Wojtyla, *Person and Community*, "On the Metaphysical and Phenomenological Basis of the Moral Norm," 84–85. It is impossible here to expand on Wojtyla's moral philosophy. Suffice it to quote him: "It seems that the form of ethics that ultimately emerges from the initial and basic questions above will be a *normative* form. When we ask, 'What makes human actions morally good or evil?' we all know that what makes them so is their relation to norms. When we ask the further question, 'Why?' we are then inquiring into the ethical foundation of the norms upon which the moral good or evil of human action rests. To put it another way, we are inquiring into their rightness" (Wojtyla, *Person and Community*, "Problem of the Theory of Morality, 131).

Wojtyla insists that such experiences cannot be divorced from, or be independent of, the existence of an objective hierarchy of goods, which is a normative order grounded in divine reason. "God is the supreme, transcendent measure of all beings through the unconditional perfection of [his] own being, through the unconditional fullness of existence that God is."[11] In Wojtyla's moral epistemology, "cognition does not in any way create 'reality' (cognition does not create its own content), but arises within the context of the different kinds of content that are proper to it; in other words, cognition arises thanks to the various kinds of *esse*, thanks to the enormous richness and complexity of reality." Without this transcendent reality in relation to moral cognition, he adds, "one would thereby rule out the realism of ethics."[12]

A further example of phenomenology's subsidiary use arises from the fact that phenomenology employs Edmund Husserl's *epoché*, which is, says Wojtyla, the methodological discipline of "bracketing the existence, or reality, of the conscious subject." But it is precisely the lived experience of the concretely existing reality of the conscious subject as a real being and a cause of its own activity that Wojtyla seeks to account for philosophically and, therefore, this account can only be accomplished within the framework of a metaphysics of being. Wojtyla is right, therefore, a Christian thinker can never be a phenomenologist *simpliciter* because he requires a realistic metaphysics of the person to ground man as an objective being with his own proper nature. Consider for instance in this connection Wojtyla's efforts to ground the lived experience of agent causation—we experience ourselves as actually deciding and as the efficient cause of our free actions—in the Aristotelian-Thomistic principles of potency and act and hence in a realistic metaphysics of the person. Here, too, Wojtyla shows us the limitations of phenomenological analysis. Let me briefly explain these limitations.

We spoke above of Wojtyla's view that the concrete experience of agent causation and efficacy is the experiential basis for connecting ethical value with the person as its proper subject. Wojtyla explains, "Phenomenologists maintain that this value manifests itself in the person as a subject; they even say that it is a consequence of the efficacy of the

---

11. Ibid., 77.
12. Wojtyla, *Person and Community*, "Problem of Experience in Ethics," 116–17.

person."[13] However true these claims may be, adds Wojtyla, they "do not conceptually apprehend the very essence of this value, for it must be conceded that ethical values reside essentially in the trans-phenomenological order. [That is] If ethical values were only to 'reside' in the person as its phenomenological subject, even as its uniquely proper subject, then despite all else it would not be found in the place where we *de facto* discover it experientially."[14] This conclusion raises the question of who exactly is the *trans-phenomenological* subject of ethical values. "The person," replies Wojtyla, "is not just the uniquely proper phenomenological subject of ethical values but is their *ontic* subject as well."[15] This trans-phenomenological, ontic subject is the substantial existence of the human subject, which is "metaphysical subjectivity ... [and] the guarantor of the identity of this human being in existence and activity."[16] In other words, man is an objective reality, "an individual substance of a rational nature" (as it is phrased by the Boethian definition), a "*suppositum humanum*," which is "subjectivity in the metaphysical and fundamental sense," says Wojtyla, and representing human nature itself in the "metaphysical terrain" of being.[17] In sum, this trans-phenomenological, ontic subject is grounded in a metaphysics of being.

Furthermore, Wojtyla explicitly opposes what he calls the classic phenomenological view of consciousness as an autonomous subject. He writes: "The subject of this state, however, is not consciousness itself but the *human being*, of whom we rightly may say that he is or is not 'conscious', that he has full or limited consciousness, and so on. Consciousness itself does not exist as the 'substantive' subject of the acts of consciousness; it exists neither as an independent factor nor as a faculty."[18] Consciousness has no real existence apart from the person, the man-person, who seen in his "ontological basic structure is the subject of both existence and acting."[19] In other words, the reality of a human being, of a really exist-

---

13. Wojtyla, *Person and Community*, "Problem of the Will in the Analysis of the Ethical Act," 19.

14. Ibid.

15. Ibid., italics added.

16. Wojtyla, *Person and Community*, "The Person: Subject and Community," 223.

17. Ibid., 224.

18. Wojtyla, *Acting Person*, 34.

19. Ibid., 74. Wojtyla also says, "The person is in a way also constituted by and through consciousness (though not 'in consciousness' and not only 'in consciousness'). The con-

ing being, is not constituted by consciousness but instead constitutes it.[20] Wojtyla adds, "This [trans-phenomenological] fact indubitably belongs to experience, which in turn belongs to the general human experience upon which ethics is primarily based. This experience is more fundamental than that so-called phenomenological experience."[21] Here, too, we can understand why phenomenological analysis has a secondary role: it is unable to recognize the substantial existence of the human subject, of the ontic subject, or what Wojtyla elsewhere calls "a structural ontological nucleus that would account for the fact itself of man being the subject or the fact that the subject is a being."[22] There is more: as the metaphysical or ontic subject of his actions, man *transcends* those actions. "The moment of efficacy, the experience of efficacy, brings forth first of all the transcendence of man relatively to his own acting. But then the transcendence proper to the experience has in being the agent of acting passes into the immanence of the experience of acting itself: when I act, I am wholly engaged in my acting, in that dynamization of the ego to which my own efficacy has contributed."[23] Furthermore, man's experience of himself culminates in the experience of the unity and identity of the ego.[24] Moreover, by dynamization Wojtyla is referring to the ethical becoming that is proper to man, which he explains in terms of the Aristotelian-Thomistic philosophy of potency and act, and which is at the heart of the dynamic unity of action and person.

---

tinuity and identity of consciousness reflects and also conditions the continuity and identity of the person" (ibid., 303 n. 15).

20. Wojtyla, *Person and Community*, "The Person: Subject and Community," 226: "Consciousness is always subjectified in the self and . . . its roots are always the *suppositum humanum*. Consciousness is not an independent subject, although by means of a certain abstraction, or rather exclusion, which in Husserlian terminology is called *epoché*, consciousness could be treated as though it were a subject. . . . As long as this type of analysis of consciousness retains the character of a cognitive method, it can and does bear excellent fruit. *And yet because this method is based on the exclusion (epoché) of consciousness from reality, from really existing being, it cannot be regarded as a philosophy of that reality, and it certainly cannot be regarded as a philosophy of the human being, the human person*" (italics added).

21. Wojtyla, *Person and Community*, "The Problem of the Will in the Analysis of the Ethical Act," 19.

22. Wojtyla, *Acting Person*, 72.

23. Ibid., 68.

24. Ibid., 80–81.

In this connection, Wojtyla argues that phenomenological analysis is not only unable to recognize the person as the self-conscious cause of action, as a real being and a cause of its own action, but also the efficacy or causation that is proper to man in his becoming good or bad.[25] In other words, Wojtyla says that "in apprehending and investigating lived [ethical] experience as a phenomenological fact, we focus only on what happens in the person while performing an action. Although we then perceive the lived experience of efficacy and ethical value, these phenomenological elements do not present us with the actual whole [of a concrete human being] so long as we do not apprehend what happens to the person through the act that person consciously performs. What happens to the person is that the person himself . . . *becomes* good or bad depending on the act performed. . . . This becoming of the person also belongs to the totality of experience: the person *experiences* his . . . ethical becoming."[26] Phenomenological analysis of this ethical becoming of the person must be subordinated to metaphysical norms of potency and act as developed by Aquinas in his view that persons actualize themselves through actions.[27] Wojtyla uses the concept of *actualization* to refer to the transition from potency to act. He says, "it indicates some sort of becoming, not in the absolute sense—this is possible only when something comes into being out of nonexistence—but in the relative sense, that is to say, becoming based on an already existing being and from within its inner structure."[28]

In this light we can see why Wojtyla understands man's acts to be the actualization of potentiality, its fulfillment, becoming good or bad depending on the action being performed. He argues: "Fulfillment reaches all the way to the potentiality of the person, as does unfulfillment. In relation to this potentiality essential to the human person, fulfillment is a good and unfulfillment is an evil—the lack of a good to which the person is 'by nature' disposed. In any case, the fulfillment of oneself in action, or self-realization, is also the attainment of the end proper to a human being as a person (a human being as a human being), and herein lies the essence of moral good. The essence of evil, on the other hand, consists in failing to achieve this end that is proper to a human being as a person (a human

---

25. Ibid., 79, 98.

26. Wojtyla, *Person and Community*, "The Problem of the Will in the Analysis of the Ethical Act," 20.

27. Wojtyla/John Paul II, *Acting Person*, 63–64, 98–99.

28. Ibid., 64.

being as a human being)."²⁹ Wojtyla distinguishes Aquinas' view from a phenomenological one. "A conscious human act is for St. Thomas not merely a stage upon which ethical experience is enacted."³⁰ Aquinas does not divorce ethical becoming from the objective human *being*. Wojtyla explains this point—persons are actualized through actions—in a passage worth citing in full:

> The statement that moral value is also an end for human beings and human actions is verified even more fully when we take a different concept of end, when we view it not simply as the object of a particular aim but as that which fulfills—is conductive to the fulfillment of—the subject and its activity. I should add that the concept of fulfillment perhaps most properly corresponds to the Latin *actus*. We know how important *actus* is in Aristotelian and Thomistic philosophy and ethics. In this regard, it seems that moral value determines the fulfillment of actions proper to persons and also determines the fulfillment of the persons themselves in such actions. In acting, we either fulfill ourselves or do not fulfill ourselves. This depends precisely on moral value. Moral good is that through which we fulfill ourselves in action, and evil the opposite. In this view, morality appears as something proper to the human person, corresponding to the person's dynamic sphere of fulfillment and unfulfillments.... As can be seen, the teleological interpretation is a dynamic development of the proper meaning of moral value. We have grasped this meaning in strict connection with the human being as a human being—as a person—becomes and is good, and moral evil that through which the human being as a human being—as a person—becomes and is evil. The teleological interpretation refers directly to this becoming, this *fieri*, [which is] proper to the human being as person. In this *fieri* is also contained the whole dynamic of auto-teleology that corresponds to the human being by reason of being a person.³¹

Let us pick up the thread of our discussion before we illustrated the subordinate place of phenomenological analyses to metaphysics in Wojtyla's view. In a more critical vein, Wojtyla argues that Husserlian analyses conducted within the realm of "pure consciousness" and not on the basis of the concrete experience of man as a real being and a causal agent have been criticized as idealistic and subjectivistic. Says Wojtyla,

29. Wojtyla, *Person and Community*, "The Problem of the Theory of Morality," 149.
30. Ibid., 20.
31. Ibid., 148–49.

"This [criticism] only served to strengthen the line of demarcation in philosophy and the opposition between the 'objective' view of the human being, which was also an ontological view (the human being as a *being*), and the 'subjective' view, which seemed inevitably to sever the human being this [objective] reality."[32] Still, this opposition is in fact breaking down, adds Wojtyla, on the basis of the experience of the subject as a real being and a causal agent of its own activity. "This experience automatically frees us from pure consciousness as the subject conceived and assumed *a priori* and leads us to the full concrete existence of the human being, to the reality of the conscious subject."[33] This breakdown does not, however, mean renouncing either phenomenological analyses or a metaphysics of being, that is, a metaphysical realism of the person.

Indeed, on the one hand, "with all the phenomenological analyses in the realm of that assumed subject (pure consciousness) now at our disposal, we can no longer go on treating the human being exclusively as an objective being, but we must also somehow treat the human being as a subject in the dimension in which the specifically human subjectivity of the human being is determined by consciousness. And that dimension would seem to be none other than *personal* subjectivity."[34] On the other hand, what Wojtyla calls the cosmological understanding of the human being, which expresses "the individuality of the human being as a substantial being with a rational (spiritual) nature," marks out the "'metaphysical terrain'—the dimension of being—in which personal human subjectivity is realized, creating, in a sense, a condition for 'building upon' this terrain on the basis of experience."[35] In short, "this personal human subjectivity is a determinate *reality*: it is a reality when we strive to understand it within the *objective totality* that goes by the name *human being*."[36] Otherwise, without this metaphysical terrain, the focus on personal human subjectivity, degenerates into a subjectivism. Thus, personal human subjectivity is understood in a metaphysical realist sense when it is connected with the person's being as its subject. Subjectivity divorced from the being of the

---

32. Ibid., 210.
33. Ibid.
34. Ibid.
35. Ibid., 212.
36. Ibid., 216.

person and treated as an autonomous subject of activity is understood as a version of subjectivism.

WHAT, THEN, IS THE IMPORT OF PHENOMENOLOGICAL REFLECTION?

What then is the import of phenomenological reflection on the late pope's understanding of the meaning, nature, and action of the human person *qua* person, and hence on his theology of the body? There are three areas that I will single out where one can clearly see the impact of phenomenology: lived experience, the relationship between action and the person, and the personal nature of man's human body, of his bodily existence, as the dimension in and through which man reveals himself. I turn now to say something about each of these areas.

First, Wojtyla regards man to be a unique and unrepeatable person, that is, that each human creature is "the one and ontically unique person" (as Wojtyla phrases it[37]), and given this irreducibility, Wojtyla says that the category of lived experienced takes on greater significance and hence so, too, does a method he refers to as "*pausing at the irreducible.*"[38] In his essay, "Subjectivity and the Irreducible in Man," Wojtyla distinguishes the more personalist focus of his phenomenology from the cosmological focus of the Aristotelian-Thomistic metaphysics of human nature—which studies man in terms of cosmological categories like substance, potentiality, rationality—which he unequivocally accepts but which has its own limits, such as failing to do justice to that which makes man irreducibly a person and hence threatening to reduce man to a cosmological type (i.e., species).[39] Of course man does hold a place in the cosmic order of things and hence John Paul II does make use of the "Aristotelian tradition in logic and in anthropology" to analyze man's nature in terms of a "proximate genus" and "specific differentia" (*MWTB*, 5.5, and note 10). Elsewhere he writes, "The usefulness of the Aristotelian definition [man is a rational animal or an individual substance of rational nature] is unquestionable."[40]

---

37. Wojtyla, *Acting Person*, 186.

38. In *Analecta Husserliana*, 7:107–14. This essay has been retranslated by Theresa Sandok, OSM, with a slightly altered title, "Subjectivity and the Irreducible in the Human Being," in *Person and Community*, 209–17.

39. Ibid.

40. Wojtyla, *Acting Person*, 73.

Still, without severing the person from his objective nature, the objectivity of the *suppositum humanum*, adds Wojtyla, "*a belief in the primordial uniqueness of the human being, and thus in the basic irreducibility of the human being to the natural world*, seems just as old as the need for reduction expressed in Aristotle's definition. This belief stands at the basis of understanding the human being as a *person*, which has an equally long tenure in the history of philosophy; it also accounts today for the growing emphasis on the person as a subject and for the numerous efforts aimed at interpreting the personal subjectivity of the human being.... *Subjectivity is, then, a kind of synonym for the irreducible in the human being*."[41] Wojtyla hastens to remind us, however, "that we must not forget that the subjectivity of the human person is also something objective."[42] Thus, Wojtyla also enriches his understanding of phenomenology as an approach that is concerned with man's lived experience as a concrete self, a self-experiencing subject. This experience is something irreducibly subjective, personal, defying reduction, and so we must pause cognitively before man's lived experience. Wojtyla explains:

> The irreducible signifies that which is essentially incapable of reduction, that which cannot be reduced but can only be *disclosed* or *revealed. Lived experience essentially defies reduction*. This does not mean, however, that it eludes our knowledge; it only means that *we must arrive at the knowledge of it differently*, namely, *by a method or means of analysis that merely reveals and discloses its essence*. The method of phenomenological analysis allows us to pause at lived experience as the irreducible. This method is not just a descriptive cataloging of individual phenomena (in the Kantian sense, i.e., phenomena as sense-perceptible contents). When we pause at the lived experience of the irreducible, we attempt to permeate cognitively the whole essence of this experience. We thus apprehend both the essentially subjective structure of lived experience and its structural relation to the subjectivity of the human being. Phenomenological analysis thus contributes to trans-phenomenal understanding; it also contributes to a disclosure of the richness proper to human existence in the whole complex *compositum humanum*. Such a disclosure—the deepest possible disclosure—would seem to be an indispensable means for coming to know the human being as personal subject. At the same time, this personal

---

41. Wojtyla, *Person and Community*, "Subjectivity and the Irreducible in the Human Being," 211.

42. Ibid.

human subjectivity is a determinate *reality*: it is a reality when we strive to understand it within the *objective totality* that goes by the name *human being*.... How [then] is the philosophy of the subject to disclose the *objectivity* of the human being in the personal *subjectivity* of this being?[43]

The sum and substance of this passage is that pausing at the irreducibility of the human person is a synonym for giving an account of the subjectivity and lived experience of the human person. But the question might be raised as to whether Wojtyla's methodological orientation to the lived experience of the human being as a personal subject condemns him to subjectivism. In reply, Wojtyla claims that "so long as in this interpretation [of lived experience] we maintain a firm enough connection with the integral experience of the human being, not only are we not doomed to subjectivism, but we will also safeguard the authentic personal subjectivity of the human being in the realistic interpretation of human existence."[44] At this point, let me provide some explanation of Wojtyla's claims.

The phenomenological attitude has an anti-reductionist approach to reality because its "prime concern," says Wojtyla, "is *to allow experience to speak for itself as best it can and right to the end.*"[45] The concept of experience in a phenomenological perspective comes fully into its own, according to Wojytla. "Following Husserl," he says, "we do not have reason to accept a restrictive interpretation of experience." Wojtyla explains:

> Experience should be considered as the source and the basis of all knowledge about objects, but this does not mean that there is one and only one kind of experience and that this experience is the so-called "sense" perception".... In general, for phenomenologists "experience" means immediate givenness or every cognitive act in which the object itself is given directly—"bodily"—or, to use Husserl's phrase, is *liebhaft selbstgegeben*. Opposing the empiricistic reductionism[i.e., that all knowledge is derived from sense experience] there are, then, many different kinds of experience in which individual objects are given to be taken into account, as the experience of the individual psychical facts of other selves, the aesthetic in which works of art are given, and so forth.[46]

43. Ibid., 215–16.
44. Ibid., 213.
45. Wojtyla, *Acting Person*, 133.
46. Ibid., 301 n. 1.

It may be helpful to contrast briefly Wojtyla's notion of lived experience with a few other views. Whereas a phenomenalist approach, as one finds in David Hume, confines the knower to the mere appearances of things in sense experience, which are subsequently ordered by the mind,[47] a transcendental idealist approach, as some interpreters of Edmund Husserl find in his understanding of phenomenology, regards objects to be constituted by consciousness. Wojtyla has in mind here Husserl's turn to transcendental idealism because of the "subjectivistic and idealistic character—or at least overtones—of analyses conducted within the realm of 'pure consciousness.'"[48] He regards Kant as a phenomenalist as well. "Phenomenalism assumes that the essence of a thing is unknowable; phenomenology, on the other hand, accepts the essence of a thing just as it appears to us in immediate experience. Phenomenology is therefore *intuitionistic*."[49] Two points must be made here in clarification.

The first point that needs clarification is Wojtyla's claim that experience can grasp the essence of a thing. Now, regarding the claim that "experience ... reveals the phenomenological essence of objects and the relations and connections occurring between them,"[50] Wojtyla explains that the essence of a thing here does not mean essence in the metaphysical sense, namely, some further *substratum* or *substance* underneath the phenomena. "Phenomenologists do not have the kind of cognitive ambitions that Aristotelians and Thomists have—they do not give priority to the philosophy of being; but then, on the other hand, they also differ from Kantians, who sever experience from the noumenal essence of a thing."[51] Consequently, Wojtyla rejects a Humean or Kantian (albeit transcendental) phenomenalism, wherein the essence of a thing is unknowable, or a Berkelian idealism, or a transcendental idealism, wherein consciousness is absolutized and there is nothing to the external world except our experience and its patterns (*esse est percipi*), or where the world is lost, as in Husserlian idealism, because constituted by absolute consciousness.

---

47. Ibid., 3.

48. Wojtyla, *Person and Community*, "Subjectivity and the Irreducible in Man," 209–10.

49. Wojtyla, *Person and Community*, "The Problem of the Separation of Experience from the Act in Ethics," 33; italics added.

50. Ibid.

51. Ibid.

Well, if not a metaphysical essence, then, what kind of essence does experience grasp? Knowledge is, for example, first-off treated "as a certain whole known from experience"; it is a "highly complex and intricate cognitive process,"[52] involving sensory data and the intellect as well as "direct cognitive encounters with objective reality." Says Wojtyla, "The nature of the whole set of cognitive acts directed at man, both at the man I am and at every man other than myself, is empirical as well as intellectual. The two aspects interpenetrate, interact, and mutually support each other."[53] This experience is, above all, cognitive, because "every experience is also a primordial understanding," says Wojtyla, serving "as a point of departure for subsequent understandings and as a kind of provocation toward them."[54] Wojtyla adds, "The tendency toward truth is essential for intellectual cognition, and this tendency is realized by way of increasingly more mature understanding."[55] Given that "the dynamism of the human intellect [toward truth] and the structure of human cognition are evident already in experience,"[56] it is clear that for Wojtyla what is experienced is not limited to the purely sensory contents of the object, but also includes, he says, "the particular structure and essential contents of that perception."[57] Yet, there is more: Wojtyla emphasizes the "indispensable role played by the intellectual element [mental discrimination and classification] in the formation of the experiential acts, [i.e.,] those direct encounters with objective reality."[58] In Wojtyla's account its role is especially important in connection with what he calls the "stabilization of experiential objects."[59]

In addition, human cognition rises from the multiplicity of data manifested to one's experience to what Wojtyla calls the "essential sameness" or "unity of meaning" grasped from among the multiplicity and complexity of phenomena.[60] The process of grasping their unity of meaning is achieved through induction. What kind of induction? "Induction in this case, however, does not have the meaning ascribed to it by Mill

52. Wojtyla, *Acting Person*, 5.
53. Ibid., 8.
54. Wojtyla, *Person and Community*, "The Problem of Experience in Ethics," 117.
55. Ibid.
56. Ibid.
57. Ibid., 115.
58. Wojtyla, *Acting Person*, 6–7.
59. Ibid.
60. Ibid., 14.

and the positivists, but the meaning ascribed to it by Aristotle: it is not a method of generalizing a certain thesis, but simply a method of directly grasping a general truth in particular facts."[61] Wojtyla explains:

> The whole wealth and diversity of "factual" data accumulated from individual details is retained in experience, while the mind disengages from their abundance and grasps only the unity of meaning. In order to grasp this unity the mind, so to speak, allows experience to predominate without, however, ceasing to understand the wealth and diversity of experience. The grasping by the mind of the unity of meaning is not equivalent to a rejection of experiential wealth and diversity. . . . While comprehending the action person on the ground of experience of man, of all the "factual" data of "man-acts," the mind still remains attentive in this essential understanding to the wealth of diverse information supplied to experience.[62]

Moreover, not only induction, but also what Wojtyla calls "reduction" is indispensable to explaining or interpreting the data of experience as it is *given to us* in experience.[63] "After all," says Wojtyla, "we are not concerned with the abstract but seek to penetrate something that actually exists." Explaining or interpreting "this existence [has] to correspond to experience." Reiterating his earlier point that "understanding is intrinsic to human experience but also transcends it," Wojtyla adds, "[t]o experience is one thing and to understanding and interpret (which implies understanding) is quite another."[64] Therefore, "experience and understanding together constitute a whole, and interpretation is interchangeable with comprehending."[65] And as Deborah Savage summarizes, "By way of this inductive and reductive process, which is grounded in the on-going ex-

---

61. Wojtyla, *Person and Community*, "The Problem of Experience in Ethics," 121. Later in *Acting Person*, Wojtyla writes, "Phenomenologists speak of the cognition of what is essential (in this case it would be cognition of the essence inherent in the event 'man-acts'. In their opinion this kind of cognition is *a priori*, remains correlative with a specific intuition, and is consequently not to be reached inductively. . . . This one-sided emphasis is, however, one more reason why it seems absolutely necessary to bring forth again the role of induction as conceived by Aristotle (in contrast with the conception of induction in the positivists)" (301 n. 5).

62. Wojtyla, *Acting Person*, 15.

63. Ibid., 17.

64. Ibid.

65. Ibid., 136.

perience of the person, the apprehension of the object is progressively enriched and extended such that the wealth of its being is more and more fully realized."[66]

The second point that requires clarification is Wojtyla's claim that phenomenology is *intuitionistic*. By this claim he means that phenomenology approaches reality as things that are given to us in experience first-off as whole configurations and hence in their integrity as identifiable wholes prior to any abstractions. This focus on the *integral* experience of the human being is clearly, in Wojtyla's account of lived experience, one of phenomenology's most important features. Furthermore, phenomenology has a realist orientation to the world and hence, properly understood, "*phenomenon* signifies something that 'manifests itself to us, something that affects our cognitive powers in a perceptible way.'"[67] Two elements are constitutive of the "dynamic structural whole" (as Wojtyla phrases it) of experience and they are "intimately united into one organic whole," namely, a "sense of reality" and a "sense of knowing." Explains Wojtyla, "The first element of experience can be defined as a 'sense of reality,' placing the accent on *reality*—on the fact that something exists with an existence that is real and objectively independent of the cognizing subject and the subject's cognitive act, while at the same time existing as the object of that act. Because of this, the structural whole of experience also contains a second element, which can be defined as a 'sense of knowing.' This is a sense of a distinctive kind of relation to what exists in a real and objective way, together with a sense of a distinctive kind of contact or union with what exists and exists in such a way."[68] Wojtyla clearly describes here the noetic/ontic correspondence, or the mutual orientation to each other of the knower and the known, in that dynamic structural whole of experience.

In the passage that follows, Wojtyla makes clear his commitment to epistemological realism: "the sense of knowing differs from the sense of reality, while at the same time intimately corresponding to it. The latter is a sense of reality in and through knowing—and the former is a sense of knowing through reality, through what really and objectively exists with an existence independent of the cognitive act and, at the same time, in

---

66. Savage, "Centrality of Lived Experience in Wojtyla's Account of the Person."
67. Wojtyla, *Person and Community*, "The Problem of Experience in Ethics," 114.
68. Ibid., 115.

contact with that act. It is in just such contact and in just an orientation that the sense of knowing ultimately manifests itself as a tendency toward that which really and objectively exists—a tendency toward an object—as true."[69] In sum, the dynamic structural whole that is experience consists of these two elements, or senses, as Wojtyla puts it, and they define the nature of cognition as well as provide an account of the sense of reality, which he tells us must be seen "as transcendent in relation to every act of cognition. This must be the case, adds Wojtyla, for "if reality were identical with cognition . . . then the necessity of cognition to tend toward the truth would be completely unintelligible. *One could say that it would have no 'assignment.'*" That is, it would not be ordered to knowing the truth. Rather, the only way to explain to explain the tendency or orientation of the intellect to seek the truth "is through the ultimate transcendence of *esse* in relation to *percipi*. Cognition must go beyond itself because it is realized not through the truth of its own act (*percipi*) but through the truth of a transcendent object—something that exists (*esse*) with a real and objective existence independently of the act of knowing."[70]

Turning now to the second area of phenomenological import, I want to address the question of how philosophical reflection on the subject discloses the *objectivity* of the human being in the personal *subjectivity* of this being. Wojtyla gives us his perspective on this question in the Preface to *The Acting Person* explaining the significance of his anti-Cartesian starting point. Rather than start with the *cogito*, Wojtyla begins his study of man "by approaching him through action." In other words, Wojtyla's study of the "acting person" is concerned with the "discovery of the person through his actions."[71] He does not begin here because he identifies the human being with his actions, without any remainder that might admit a person distinct from his actions. On the contrary, Wojtyla distinguishes two complementary principles of the dynamic person-action reality: the "'integration of the person in the action,' which is complementary to the notion of the 'transcendence of the person in the action.'"[72] I shall return to these complementary principles below.

---

69. Ibid.
70. Ibid., 116.
71. Wojtyla, *Acting Person*, viii, xiv, respectively.
72. Ibid., 190.

Put differently, rather than beginning with human nature and its existence, Wojtyla begins with human action, in order to understand the relation between existence and activity. Says Wojtyla, "This relation is expressed in the philosophical adage: *operari sequitur esse*."[73] This principle is methodologically fundamental in Wojtyla's *magnum opus*, *The Acting Person*. He explains, "In its basic conception, the whole of *The Acting Person* is grounded on the premise that *operari sequitur esse*: the act of personal existence has its direct consequences in the activity of the person (i.e., in action). And so action, in turn, is the basis for disclosing and understanding the person."[74] In other words, it means that we can come to know more about *esse* by way of *operari*. He explains: "the form of human *operari* that has the most basic and essential significance for grasping the subjectivity of the human being is *action*: conscious human activity, in which the freedom proper to the human person is simultaneously expressed and concretized." "Thus," adds Wojtyla, "remaining always within the context of the *suppositum* (the *suppositum humanum*, of course), or subjectivity in the metaphysical and fundamental sense, we can arrive at a knowledge and explanation of subjectivity in the sense proper to the human being, namely, subjectivity in the personal sense."[75] Of course Wojtyla's claim regarding the dynamic person-action reality raises the question precisely what is an action.

In this dynamic reality, Wojtyla distinguish two essential forms that "cut across the phenomenological field of experience, but . . . join and unite together in the metaphysical field."[76] This statement requires a brief explanation. First, these two forms provide the basis for his analysis of human action. "The structure of 'man-acts,'" that is "*I* act," on the one hand, "as well as the structure of 'something-happens-in-man,'" on the other, "constitutes the concrete manifestation of the dynamism proper to man."[77] The former notion has to do with the very efficacy of the person, self-consciously exercising self-governance as the efficient cause of his free actions. The latter has to do with the experience of something that happens in man but is not accompanied by efficacy but rather involves what Wojtyla

---

73. Wojtyla, *Person and Community*, "The Person: Subject and Community," 223.
74. Ibid., 260 n. 6.
75. Ibid., 224.
76. Wojtyla, *Acting Person*, 74.
77. Ibid., 65.

calls *activation*. "There is activation whenever something happens only in man and the something that happens is derived from the inner dynamism of man himself."[78] An example of this dynamism is the "somato-vegetative dynamism," meaning thereby that "form of the dynamism proper to man which is vital to the human body as an actual organism and, moreover, so far as the organism conditions the various psychical functions."[79] This physico-organic functioning of man is only the bloody-fleshly base of the human person and, significantly, in and of itself it can only be designated a structure of the *human* body in light of "the *whole that is man, that is, . . . recognizing that he is a person.*"[80] Nevertheless, Wojtyla takes the experiential difference between "man-acts" and "something-happens-in-man" as the starting point of his argument. He explains:

> It is thus that in the dynamism of man there appears the essential difference arising from having the experience of efficacy. On the one hand, there is that form of the human dynamism in which man himself is the agent, that is to say, he is the conscious cause of his own causation; this form we grasp by the expression, "*man acts*." On the other hand, there is that form of human dynamism in which man is not aware of his efficacy and does not experience; this we express by "something happens in man."[81]

Now, these two forms of dynamism "combine together as if they issued from a common root." Indeed, adds Wojtyla, "[t]he synthesis of acting and happening . . . takes place on the ground of the human basic structure," which is the man-person.[82] "In principle, man 'underlies' all his actions and everything that happens in him insofar as they are but his manifestations. And yet we still need to differentiate in man a structural ontological nucleus that would account for the fact itself of man being the subject or the fact that the subject is a being."[83] In other words, "Ultimately, the synthesis not only has its foundation but also occurs actually through the mechanism of the basic ontological structure, that is to say, in the ontic subject. This is the reason why the human being, even while he is

---

78. Ibid., 69.
79. Ibid., 89.
80. Ibid., 203.
81. Ibid., 66.
82. Ibid., 72.
83. Ibid.

the agent in acting, still remains its [metaphysical] subject. He is both the actor and the [transcendent] subject."[84] This conclusion brings us back to the earlier distinguished complementary principles of the "integration of the person in the action" and the "transcendence of the person in the action." The point of the latter distinction is to make clear that the human being is not completely identified with his actions, that is, without any remainder that might admit a person distinct from his actions, but also that the structural nucleus of the transcendent subject functions simultaneously as "both the basis and the source of the two different forms of dynamism."[85]

Yet, there remains to say something about the integration of the person in the action. In setting forth Wojtyla's notion of integration it is best to deal with the whole man, which includes his human body, in that dynamic person-action reality. This brings us to the third area of phenomenological import.

A basic example of an identifiable whole, or a dynamic structural whole, is Wojtyla's treatment of the body-person as not merely an abstract material body, but rather as the whole of man's temporal existence. In fact, Wojtyla says, "It is the body that gives man his concreteness, meaning thereby "the one and ontically unique person."[86] This requires a brief—all too brief—explanation before we can go forward to the *theology* of the body.

The third section of chapter 5 of *The Acting Person* is entitled, "The Person's Integration in the Action is the Key to the Understanding of Man's Psychosomatic Unity."[87] Wojtyla makes clear that by psycho-*somatic* he does not mean psycho-*physical*. He does not actually say why, but I think we can surmise that he regards man's *physico-chemical* dynamism as well as the dynamisms he calls the somato-vegetative and the psycho-emotive, as being in and of themselves structures of the human body only when they are *bound in form* or integrated within "*a new and superior type of dynamism*, from which the others receive a new meaning and a new quality that is properly *personal*." He adds, "They do not possess this meaning and this quality on their own account and, insofar as they are but the

84. Ibid., 75.
85. Ibid.
86. Ibid., 186.
87. Ibid., 196.

natural dynamisms of the psyche and the soma, they attain these only in the *action of the person*."[88] These dynamisms, in sum, "take an active part in integration, not at their own levels but *at the level of the person*."[89] Significantly, Wojtyla distinguishes a "static" understanding of the relation between these dynamisms and the human person. We can call this static relation a "part/whole" relation in which we are just adding level upon level to the whole man. Wojtyla distinguishes, I think, this static relation from a more dynamic one, which I will call an *enkaptic* structural whole,[90] in which these dynamisms receive a new and superior meaning derived from the higher level of unity that is the acting person. Wojtyla does not think of integration at this higher level as merely the sum total of the parts, as if the personal is just another level that with together with the individual atoms and molecules, etc., add up to the human being. Rather, the dynamisms that are parts of the whole that is man receive new meaning and hence are thoroughly qualified by virtue of the one and ontically unique person.

Furthermore, although I cannot argue the point fully here, Wojtyla's point regarding the structural whole that is the body-person is really a contemporary expression of Aquinas' anthropology, namely, the soul is the form of the body (*anima forma corporis*), and of the Church's teaching on the unity of the human person as body and soul.[91] The then Joseph Cardinal Raztinger explains, "the material elements from out of which human physiology is constructed receive their character of being 'body' only in virtue of being organized and formed by the expressive power of soul. Distinguishing between 'physiological unit' and 'bodiliness' now becomes possible.... The individual atoms and molecules do not as such add up to the human being.... The physiology becomes truly 'body' through the heart of the personality. Bodiliness is something other than a summation of corpuscles."[92] That is, in light of considering the human

---

88. Ibid., 197. Wojtyla uses the Greek word *sōma* for body throughout chapter 5 of *Acting Person*.

89. Ibid., 198.

90. Dooyeweerd, *New Critique of Theoretical Thought*, 3:627–784.

91. John Paul II develops the moral and anthropological significance of the unity of the human person as body and soul is *Veritatis Splendor*, nos. 46–50.

92. Joseph Ratzinger, *Eschatology, Death and Eternal Life*, 179–81. Ratzinger is persuaded that Aquinas' philosophical understanding of the "formula *anima forma corporis*: the soul is the form of the body" embodies a "complete transformation of Aristotelianism."

person as a unity of body and soul, we can understand why the body is personal. Rather than bodily existence being a mere instrument or extrinsic tool of man's personal self-realization, the body is the indispensable medium, argues Wojtyla, in and through which I reveal myself. Human bodily existence has the character of a subject. In other words, given man's anthropological unity of body and soul, he exercises the capacity for ethical self-determination as a whole man, meaning thereby in and through his body.[93] This implies, as Schockenhoff rightly argues, that "the body is freedom's boundary." That is, he explains, "We can respect each other as subjects capable of moral action only when we respect each other in the expressive form of our bodily existence. Only so do we make it possible for each other to unfold a personal existence which is a goal in itself."[94] Respecting another person's bodily life unconditionally is to respect that person himself because the "representation of his person . . . is accessible to us . . . only in the medium of its unity as body and soul."[95] In the last chapter of this book, I will show that the bodiliness of the human person is a key to understanding Catholic sexual ethics.

Yet, there is now more to say about the dynamic person-action reality and man's bodily existence. John Paul II writes, "*The structure of this body is such that it permits him to be the author of genuinely human activity. In this activity, the body expresses the person*" (*MWTB*, 7.2). Elsewhere the pope develops the moral significance that the human person is bodily, namely, that his body is not extrinsic to who he really is, and hence to his moral acts. "*The person, including the body, is completely entrusted to himself, and it is in the unity of body and soul that the person is the subject of his*

He writes, "Thomas' twofold affirmation that the spirit is at once something personal and also the 'form' of matter would simply have been unthinkable for Aristotle.... And so we come at last to a really tremendous idea: the human spirit is so utterly one with the body that the term 'form' can be used of the body and retain its proper meaning. Conversely, the form of the body is spirit, and this is what makes the human being a person.... What seemed philosophically impossible has thus been achieved.... The soul belongs to the body as 'form', but that which is the form of the body is still spirit. It makes man a person and opens him to immortality. Compared with all the conceptions of the soul available in antiquity, this notion of the soul is quite novel. It is a product of Christian faith, and of the exigencies of faith for human thought" (ibid., 148–49).

93. Eberhard Schockenhoff, *Natural Law and Human Dignity*, 208.
94. Ibid.
95. Ibid.

own actions."⁹⁶ The moral and anthropological significance of the thesis that the human person is bodily will be developed later in our analysis of the morality of homosexuality. For now, I want to develop Wojtyla's basic point that the body and bodily action is in some sense communicative activity that reveals the person as a whole.

As John Paul says in *The Acting Person*, "For us action *reveals* the person, and we look at the person through his action."[97] Later he says, "man manifests himself ... through his body.... It is generally recognized that the human body is in its visible dynamism the territory where, or in a way even the medium whereby, the person expresses himself."[98] And in the theology of the body, we find a sample of statements expressing the same point. "The body reveals man," "the body is an expression of man's personhood," and "the body *manifests* man and, in manifesting him, acts as an intermediary that allows man and woman, from the beginning, to 'communicate' with each other according to the that *communio personarum* willed for them in particular by the Creator" (*MWTB*, 9.4; also note 18, and 12.5). In sum, "In this sense, the body is the territory and in a way the means for the performance of action and consequently for the fulfillment of the person."[99] Dooyeweerd nicely puts this point, "The human body is man himself in the structural whole of his temporal appearance."[100]

Thus, on the one hand, Wojtyla emphasizes the inalienable unity of the person in his bodily existence. Yet, on the other hand, this inalienable unity of the person with his body does not mean that "the person is to be identified solely with the body as such." Yes, says Wojtyla, "the person ... finds in the human body the territory and the means of expression."[101] Still, Wojtyla says, "man *is not* the body, he only *has* it." What does this distinction mean as far as the ability man has to take up distance vis-à-vis his own body? What is he suggesting with the distinction between "being" and "having" a body? "I *am* my *Leib*, which I also *possess* as *Körper*."[102] Wojtyla clarifies this difference. "To 'have' his own body leads

---

96. John Paul II, *Veritatis Splendor*, no. 48.
97. Wojtyla, *Acting Person*, 11.
98. Ibid., 203–4.
99. Ibid., 205.
100. Dooyeweerd, *New Critique of Theoretical Thought*, 3:89.
101. Wojtyla, *Acting Person*, 205.
102. Schockenhoff, *Natural Law & Human Dignity*, 209.

to its objectification in actions and at the same time it is in this objectification that it expresses itself. Man has his body in a special way and also in a special way he is aware of his 'possession,' when in his acting he employs *his* body as a compliant tool to express his self-determination."[103] Wojtyla, in an effort to explain the "special way" in which man has his body, cites Dutch phenomenologist Wilhelmus Luijpen.[104] He says that Luijpen "criticizes views that treat the body as an object of having (he is of course speaking of 'having' in the literal sense of the word)." Says Luijpen, "My Body is not the Object of 'Having.' . . . I 'have' a car, a pen, a book. In this 'having' the object of the 'having' reveals itself as an exteriority. There is a distance between me and what I 'have.' What I 'have' is to a certain extent independent of me." Thus, if my body is not the object of having, then I may not conceive of either sperm or eggs, either penis or vagina, in impersonal terms. For thinking of my body in impersonal terms is to think of it as a mere instrument or extrinsic tool of man's personal reality. Therefore, Luijpen continues, "My body is not something external to me. I cannot dispose of my body or give it away as I dispose of money. . . . All this stems from the fact, that my body is not 'a' body, but *my* body . . . in such a way that my body *embodies* me."[105] In short, the lived body is myself ("I") in my many activities; my subjectivity.

Any concrete act of man, the pope seems to be arguing, is a bodily expression of the person given the unity of the person as body and soul. Thus, the body grounds human subjectivity, so that all knowledge and thought has bodily roots. It is impossible to pause here to give an account of the sense in which all knowledge and thought has bodily roots. Michael Polanyi will serve here as a clear development of this important claim:

> Our body is the only assembly of things known almost exclusively by relying on our awareness of them for attending to something else. Parts of our body serve as tools for observing objects outside and for manipulating them. Every time we make sense of the world, we rely on our tacit knowledge of impacts made by the world on our body and the complex responses of our body to these impacts. Such is the exceptional position of our body in the universe. Phenomenology contrasts this feeling of our body with

---

103. Ibid., 206.
104. Ibid., 313–14 n. 64.
105. *Existential Phenomenology*, 187–88.

> the view of the body seen as an object from outside. The theory of tacit knowing regards this contrast as the difference between looking *at* something and attending *from* it at something else that is its meaning. Dwelling in our body clearly enables us to attend *from* it to things outside, while an external observer will tend to look *at* things happening in the body, seeing it as an object or as a machine. He will miss the meaning these events have for the person dwelling in the body and fail to share the experience the person has of his body.... I have shown how our subsidiary awareness of our body is extended to include a stick, when we feel our way by means of the stick. To use language in speech, reading and writing, is to extend our bodily equipment and become intelligent human beings. We may say that when we learn to use language, or a probe, or a tool, and thus makes ourselves aware of these things as we are of our body, we *interiorize* these things and *make ourselves dwell in them*. Such extensions of ourselves develop new faculties in us; our whole education operates in this way; as each of us interiorizes our cultural heritage, he grows into a person seeing the world and experiencing life in terms of this outlook.[106]

Furthermore, the body is then as such an expression or disclosure of the person, particularly in conscious human acts such as the sincere gift of self, which is the fullest unfolding of the "spousal meaning of the body" (*MWTB*, 15.5).[107] Says John Paul, "Here we mean freedom above all as *self-mastery* (self-dominion). Under this aspect, self-mastery is indispensable *in order for man to be able to 'give himself,'* in order for him to become a gift, in order for him (referring to the words of the Council) to be able to 'find himself fully' through 'a sincere gift of self' [*Gaudium et Spes*, 24:3]" (*MWTB*, 15.2). We have now crossed the philosophical threshold into the theology of the body proper.

THEOLOGY OF THE BODY

Now, reminiscent of the distinction Wojtyla draws between the cosmological focus of Aristotelian-Thomistic metaphysics of human nature and the more personalist focus of phenomenology, John Paul writes, "[T]heology has built *the overall image of man's original innocence and justice before original sin* by applying the method of objectivization specific to metaphysics and metaphysical anthropology. In the present analysis [of

---

106. Polanyi, "Logic of Tacit Inference," 147–48); idem., *Tacit Dimension*, 3–25.
107. Martin, *Feminist Question*, 385.

the theology of the body], we are trying rather to take into account the aspect of human subjectivity; subjectivity, moreover, seems to be closer to the original [biblical] texts, especially to the second creation account [of Genesis 2], that is, the Yahwist text" (*MWTB*, 17.1). At several points in the early parts of *MWTB*, John Paul uses the concept of "adequate anthropology," referring to "an understanding and interpretation of man in what is essentially human." "'Adequate' anthropology relies on essentially 'human' experience" (*MWTB*, 178–79, note 23; see also, 5.2). The anthropology that he is referring to is the phenomenology of the body that I discussed in the last section.

He distinguishes this "adequate anthropology" from the "theology of the body," but it is nevertheless "strictly linked with the . . . the essential characteristics of personal existence" (*MWTB*, 186 n. 25). These essential characteristics, or what Wojtyla calls as we saw in *The Acting Person*, the essential meaning or unity of meaning derived from the wealth of diverse data supplied to experience, consist of the *triadic* structure of human subjectivity, namely, solitude-unity-nakedness. John Paul II's refers to these "constitutive elements" as the "deep substratum" of man's "original pre-fall experience." But he clearly says that when speaking of these "original human experiences, we have in mind not so much their distance in time, as rather their foundational significance." In other words, they are foundational in respect of their grounding in the order of creation. Therefore, adds John Paul, "*The important thing . . . is not that these experiences belong to man's prehistory (to his 'theological prehistory'), but that they are at the root of every human experience*" (*MWTB*, 11.1; italics added). Again, they can be at the root of every human experience because they are the ontological foundation of that experience.

I turn now to give an overview of that triadic structure: solitude-unity-nakedness. To begin, solitude refers to several things. First, the actual man as he stands in relation to God is a "*subject of the covenant*, that is, a subject constituted as a person, constituted according to the measure of "*partner of the Absolute*" [God-Yahweh] inasmuch as he must consciously discern and choose between good and evil, between life and death." Again: "[H]e finds himself alone before God, above all to express, through a first self-definition, his own self-knowledge as the first and fundamental manifestation of his humanity." I take this self-knowledge to be such that man's relation to God is not something added to his self-enclosed nature, a *donum superadditum*, but that relation is essentially constitutive of man's subjectivity, and he cannot be understood apart from this relation.[108] In other words, "This divine act underlines man's subjectivity" (*MWTB*, 5.6, and 4, and 6.2, respectively).

There is a corollary to this self-knowledge, namely, "*man at the same time reveals himself to himself in all the distinctiveness of his being*." That is, "solitude also signifies man's subjectivity, which constitutes itself through self-knowledge. Man is alone because he is 'different' from the visible world, from the world of living beings." Man *qua* man is a "human *person*, with the proper subjectivity that characterizes the person" (*MWTB*, 5.6). And this proper subjectivity is grounded in man's bodily existence and awareness of the meaning of the body, through which he distinguishes himself from other living beings, and "*through which* he is a *person*" (*MWTB*, 6.3). In sum, man's subjectivity is such that he possesses self-knowledge in his relation to God, but also a self-knowledge of being unique among all living beings. In addition to man's self-knowledge, there is the power of self-determination. This power, says Wojtyla, "emerges precisely from the fact that it is man's task to 'cultivate the earth' and to 'subdue it'. [T]his would be impossible without the typically human intuition of the meaning of one's body" (*MWTB*, 7.1). That meaning is this: "*The structure of this body is such that it permits [man] to be the author of genuinely human activity. In this activity, the body expresses the person*" (*MWTB*, 7.2). If this meaning reminds you of Wojtyla's phenomenology of the body, as I presented earlier in this chapter, then your memory serves you well. It is precisely in this context that the fundamental perception of the meaning of one's own body in the Yahwist text, argues the pope, "reveals itself not on the basis of some primordial metaphysical analysis, but [rather] on the basis of man's sufficiently clear concrete subjectivity" (*MWTB*, 7.2).

Second, the structure of human subjectivity is such that man's unity—the original unity of the man and woman in humanity, "their unity denoting above all the identity of human nature" (*MWTB*, 9.1)—is at the same time a bi-unity: male and female. Put differently, unity-in-*difference*, man as male and female; totally different, yet totally human. This, too, is grounded in the body-subject that is man, sexually differentiated, that is, bodily-sexual difference: "Masculinity and femininity express *the twofold aspect of man's somatic constitution* ('this time she is flesh from my flesh and bone from my bones') and *indicate*, in addition, through the same

---

108. On this, see Berkouwer, 346–89. ET: *Man: The Image of God*, 310–48.

words of Genesis 2:23, *the new consciousness of the meaning of one's body.*" They are two complementary ways of being conscious of the meaning of the body-subject. That is, adds the pope, "This meaning, one can say, consists in *reciprocal enrichment.*"

I understand this reciprocity to be grounded, as John Paul succinctly states elsewhere, in the fact that "*the other is constituted similarly,* that *he is* also a certain "*I.*"[109] For John Paul II, this unity-in-difference is understood as a *communio personarum,* that is, a communion of persons in which the subjectivity that is proper to each person *qua* man and woman is recognized, affirmed, and, subsequently, deepened and fulfilled in the conjugal act. "When they unite with each other (in the conjugal act) so closely so as to become 'one flesh', man and woman rediscover every time and in a special way the mystery of creation, thus returning to the union in humanity ('flesh from my flesh and bone from my bones') that allows them to recognize each other reciprocally and to call each other by name, as they did the first time" (*MWTB*, 10.2). "This union," in and through which the consciousness of the meaning of the body unfolds, the pope adds, "*carries within itself a particular of the meaning of that body in the reciprocal self-gift of the persons*" (*MWTB*, 10.4).

Furthermore, when he develops the implications of the theology of the body for understanding the sacrament of marriage, John Paul regards the "two-in-one-flesh" unity of man and woman to "*constitute the full and real visible sign* of the sacrament itself" (*MWTB*, 103.4). In fact, he argues that the words of the sacrament—"I take you as my wife/as my husband"—"would not of themselves constitute the sacramental sign if the human subjectivity of the . . . man and woman and at the same time the consciousness of the body linked with the masculinity and femininity of the bride and the bridegroom did not correspond to them." In other words, and here the pope links his reflection on the sacrament of marriage to the order of creation, "the structure of the sacramental sign remains, in fact, in its essence the same as 'in the beginning'. What determines it is *in some sense 'the language of the body,'* inasmuch as the man and the woman, who are to become one flesh by marriage, express in this sign [two-in-one-flesh-unity] the reciprocal gift of masculinity and femininity as the foundation of the conjugal union of the persons" (*MWTB*, 103.4). In short, this two-in-one-flesh union is constitutive of the communion of

---

109. Karol Wojtyla, "Participation or Alienation," 64.

persons, man and woman, in becoming a reciprocal gift for each other. And as if to emphasize the constitutive nature of this two-in-one-flesh union in the communion of persons that is marriage, John Paul stresses that man, as male and female, is unable to express that communion "*without the body.*" "He is constituted in such a way from the 'beginning' that the deepest words of the spirit—words of love, gift, and faithfulness—call for an appropriate 'language of the body.' And without this language, they cannot be fully expressed" (*MWTB*, 104.7).

Thus far we have considered solitude and unity as the first two elements of the triadic structure. The third element of that structure is "nakedness." We read in second chapter of Genesis: "And the man and his wife were both naked and were not ashamed" (Gen 2: 25). Nakedness is an "interior" vision of the other person, not merely an "exterior" perception of the other's physical nakedness. "One cannot identify the meaning of original nakedness by considering only man's share in the exterior perception of the world; one cannot determine it without going down into man's innermost [being]" (*MWTB*, 12.4). "Nakedness" signifies the original goodness of the communion of person, seeing each other with the interior gaze that has the perspective of the good creation, reciprocally communicating with each other in the fullness of their humanity, which is precisely the fullness of the intimacy of persons in becoming a mutual gift for each other, in and through the bi-unity of male and female in the marriage bond.

In this connection, we find the fuller meaning of their bodies unfolding in the reciprocal exchange of the gift of the body, as male and female, as the gift of the person. "In reciprocity, they reach in this way a particular understanding of the meaning of their own bodies. The original meaning of nakedness corresponds to the simplicity and fullness of vision in which their understanding of the body is born from the very heart, as it were, of their community-communion. *We will call this meaning 'spousal'*" (*MWTB*, 13.1; italics added). "Spousal" here has the meaning of being a creational given at "*the very heart of that unity that had from the beginning been formed by man and woman*, [when they were] created and called to become 'one-flesh' (Gen 2:24)" (*MWTB*, 20.1). "The spousal meaning of the body," adds John Paul, is integrally inscribed in the very [creational] structure of the masculinity and femininity of the personal subject" (*MWTB*, 105.5). The fullest unfolding of the spousal meaning of the body, of the two-in-one-flesh marital bond, that is, of a covenant of mutual love, is realized in the *generative*, that is, procreative meaning of the body in the spouses' act of reciprocal knowledge given with the reciprocal self-gift of the persons. In sum, although the marital communion of the persons, male and female, is good in itself, procreation and the raising of children together is the intrinsic meaning, indeed, the fulfillment of the spousal meaning of the body.

Three brief points need to be made here with respect to the generative meaning of the body. First, there is a "somatic homogeneity of man and woman, which found its first expression in the words 'this . . . is flesh from my flesh and bone from my bones' (Gen 2:23)." The pope here is referring to the biological unity and organic complementarity of the reproductive organs that make possible the two-in-one-body communion. There are two bodies, "but they function as the complementary parts of a single procreative organism."[110] Patrick Lee explains this point clearly.

> Genuine marriage is in fact a multi-leveled relationship that encompasses the bodily, emotional, volitional, and intellectual aspects of the spouses. In genuine marriage the bodily sexual acts *are part of* the marital union, not just extrinsic symbols. In sexual intercourse between a man and a woman (whether married or not), a *real* bodily union is established. Human beings are organisms, albeit of a particular type. In most actions—digesting, sensing, walking, and so on—individual male or female organisms are complete units. However, with respect to reproduction, the male and the female are incomplete. In reproductive activity the bodily parts of the male and the bodily parts of the female participate in a single action, coitus, which is oriented to procreation (though not every act of coitus actually reproduces), so that the subject of the action is the *male and female as a unit*. Sexual intercourse is a unitary action in which the male and the female complete one another, and become really biologically one, a single organism. In marital intercourse, this bodily unit is an aspect of, a constitutive part of, the couple's more comprehensive, marital communion.[111]

---

110. Budziszewski, "Illusion of Gay Marriage," 46. This article is part of an eight-article discussion on same-sex marriage that was published in the same issue of *Philosophia Christi*.

111. Lee, "Reasons Why Marriage Is Inherently Heterosexual." See also, George, "What Marriage Is—And What It Isn't." More extensively, see Lee and George, *Body-Self Dualism in Contemporary Ethics and Politics*, 182–83.

The point that the *subject* of the action in marital sexual intercourse is the male and female as a unit, becoming really biologically one, a single organism, and that this two-in-one-flesh bodily unit is a constitutive part of the comprehensive entity that is marriage, is absolutely fundamental for refuting the claim that ethical criteria alone rather than the bodies of the participants in a same-sex relationship is the morally decisive factor. I shall return to this point later in my analysis of the normative implications of the bodily nature of the human person, especially with respect to homosexual practice where that two-in-one-flesh unity and, in consequence, male and female complementarity are lacking.

Second, "the 'knowledge' about which Genesis 4:1 speaks is *the act that* originates being, or, *in union with the Creator, establishes a new human being in existence*" (*MWTB*, 21.7). The bi-unity marital bond is a "procreative partnership," to use a term from J. Budziszewski, because "marriage is the unique source of families, the unique way in which we participate in the continuation of the species."[112]

And third, the biological dynamism is an integral part of the man and woman being united as complementary, bodily persons, but that biological basis is sublated into the higher level functioning of the person-action unity that is properly man's personal subjectivity.[113] By sublation I mean: "What sublates goes beyond what is sublated, introduces something new and distinct, yet so far from interfering with the sublated or destroying it, on the contrary needs it, includes it, preserves all its proper features and properties, and carries them forward to a fuller realization within a richer context." This meaning gives the precise difference between a static parts/whole relation where integration is merely the sum total of the parts in the totality of the person and the enkaptic structural whole. The pope explains the latter enkaptic relation as follows: "In *everything* that is determined by both body and sex, 'knowledge' inscribes a living and real content. Consequently, 'knowledge' in the biblical sense signifies that man's 'biological' determination, on the part of his body and his sex, is no longer something passive but reaches a level and content specific to self-conscious and self-determining persons; therefore, it brings with a particular consciousness of the meaning of the human body bound to fatherhood and motherhood" (*MWTB*, 21.4; italics added).

---

112. Budziszewski, "Illusion of Gay Marriage," 46.
113. Lonergan, *Method in Theology*, 241.

Returning now to the pope's analysis of nakedness, it is helpful to note that he draws on the concept of "boundary" situation, in particular, the "boundary" experience of shame in which is manifested, however haltingly, the original meaning of nakedness, its dimension of human interiority. The "boundary" experience of shame is a limit-to our mutual experience of each other. That experience brings about an experience of our own human limits such that there is a *"radical change in the meaning of the original nakedness* of the woman before the man and of the man before the woman" (*MWTB*, 11.5). But in such an experience we both experience not only our human limits (limits-to) as our own but also recognize some disclosure of the original experience of nakedness, which is a limit-of our experience.[114] That is, the original meaning of nakedness shows itself by making possible the experience of shame. "In the experience of shame, the human being experiences fear in the face of the 'second I' (thus, for example, woman before man), and this is substantially fear for one's own 'I.' With shame, the human being manifests 'instinctively,' as it were, the need for the affirmation and acceptance of this 'I' according to its proper value. He experiences this at the same time within himself and toward the outside, in the face of the 'other.' One can thus say that shame is a complex experience in the sense that, while distancing one human being from another (woman from man), as it were, it seeks at the same time their personal approach toward each other, creating a suitable basis and level for such an approach" (*MWTB*, 12.2).

Finally, the dimension of gift, what the pope calls the "hermeneutics of the gift," is the essential truth and depth, the fullest meaning of the body-subject, of original solitude-unity-nakedness. That dimension is reflected in the spousal meaning of the body, and is *"the power to express love: precisely that love in which the human person becomes a gift* and—through this gift—fulfills the very meaning of his being and existence" (*MWTB*, 15.1).

It is precisely this "adequate anthropology"—with the triadic structure of solitude-unity-nakedness—which is a "deep substratum" (to use

---

114. I'm making use of David Tracy's analysis of the concept of limit-situations, a familiar concept in the existentialist philosophy and theology of the first half of the twentieth-century, and the corresponding concepts of "limits-to" and "limits-of" as a way of understanding John Paul's "boundary" experience of shame. The pope's use of this concept is clearly indebted to existentialist thought. For Tracy's analysis, see *Blessed Rage for Order*, 105–9.

the pope's own words) of the theology of the body. This anthropology pertains to the objective totality that is man, and which is grounded in the structures of creation. That is why personal human subjectivity is a determinate reality, and not a reality constituted by man's subjectivity. "Genesis 2 presents the creation of man especially in the aspect of his subjectivity. When we compare the two accounts [of Genesis 1 and 2], we reach the conviction that this subjectivity corresponds to the objective reality of man created 'in the image of God'" (*MWTB*, 3.1). The pope is a realist about the structures of human subjectivity; he regards them as part of God's creational design. But as a phenomenologist he seeks to shows how those objective structures present themselves to us in and through the essential human experience of solitude-unity-nakedness. "This experience also seems to rest on an ontological depth that is so great that man does not perceive it in his own daily life, even if at the same time he presupposes it in some way and postulates it as part of the process of the formation of his own image" (*MWTB*, 11.1).

These are the structures of creation of the full concrete existence of man, his subjectivity, which is bodily, constituting the man's corporeality. In short, man is a body-subject. Alternatively put, the human person is bodily. "That body is authentically human and thus [is] that which determines man as a person, that is, as a being that is, also in all its bodiliness," created in God's image. But "man is a subject not only by his self-consciousness and by self-determination, but also based on his own body." It is the body that gives man his concreteness, says Wojtyla, and this concrete corporeal existence is a multi-layered unity of the whole person, of the one same, individual subject. This body, *my* body, bodiliness as I experience it, is *not* merely a "thing" looked at and described from the outside, abstracted and objectified in terms of aspects, what Wojtyla calls the whole psychosomatic complexity, consisting of the spatial, kinematic, physical, organic, or sensory aspects. This is contrary to experienced fact. Rather, the multiple aspects of each human creature, who is "only one, a whole one" (as Calvin Seerveld phrases it[115]), are indeed tacitly present in my pre-scientific lived experience. In addition to the aspects of the man's psychosomatic complexity, there are a number of others: logical, historical, linguistic, social, economic, aesthetic, legal, ethical, and fiduciary aspects of this unique multi-layered unity that is the body-subject.

---

115. Seerveld, "Christian Tin-Can Theory of Man."

Seerveld eloquently describes the seamless unity, or integrity, of man's many-sided, or multi-leveled, activity. "A human creature is . . . of a piece, whose single existence manifests itself in all sorts of ways—a man is so big, with such a shape, moves, has weighted mass, breathes, feels, forms, can play imaginatively, talks, thinks, socializes, saves possessions and spends them, fights, loves, prays—all these ways of concrete existence, which constitute the man's corporeality, are all manifestations of the one same, individual thing."[116] Yet, there is more. Man's multi-layered complexity is not such as if these various dimensions are ontologically separate compartments; rather these dimensions of integral human experience, says Wojtyla, constitute a "system of . . . interrelations and *mutual conditioning* that allow the functioning of each sphere in the specifically human manner."[117] In Seerveld's words, these spheres are "interpenetrating, intra-related moment of [a man's] concrete existence." He adds,

> There is power not only in a fist action but also reverberating within a man's desires and speech and loyalties. While a woman's feelings are not her thinking, there is always emotional content inside thought, and there is a creational pressure to have emotions thoughtful. There are analogies of vitality in activity beyond one's muscles, in a woman or man's conversation, occupational routines or church life. And there are elements of economy anticipated in one's physical acts, aesthetic response, and social relation. In fact . . . this cohering pattern of ordered, enduring activities is the proper meaning corporeality.[118]

Of course, these aspects can be distinguished, and are certainly open to analysis. But in that lived experience of the concrete corporeal subject, the experience is still "systatic," to use a term of Dooyeweerd's, which refers to the natural coherence of our integral experience of reality, including our body.[119] "Systatic" is another way to refer to the dynamic structural whole (as Wojtyla calls it) of human experience. Says Wojtyla, "Obviously, we cannot discuss the human body apart from *the whole that is man*,

---

116. Ibid.
117. Wojtyla, *Acting Person*, 202.
118. Seerveld, "Christian Tin-Can Theory of Man."
119. Dooyeweerd, *New Critique of Theoretical Thought*, 2:429. The adjective "systatic" derives from Dooyeweerd's neologism, "systasis," which refers to the wholeness or integrality with which the various aspects of reality present themselves in ordinary or "pretheoretical" experience.

that is, without recognizing that he is a person. Neither can we examine the understanding and potentialities proper to the human body without understanding the essentials of action and its specifically personal character."[120] We have already shown that to be the case in the previous section. Yet, in this "systatic" experience, what Wojtyla calls the ontic unity of man, the integrity of the body-subject, the pope recognizes the higher level functioning of the person-action unity, which tacitly relies on the whole psychosomatic complexity below it as its biotic base, even while sublating this complex into the multiple dimensions of the higher level unity of human existence at the level of the person.[121] Wojtyla explains this "systatic unity" of man:

> The dynamism itself of the human body does not depend on the self-determination of the person. It is instinctive and spontaneous. The body as an organism constitutes its dynamic source, that is, its effective cause; the will is not its cause, for the dynamism of the body does not proceed from the person's self-determination. This is why we do not disclose it directly and immediately in the experience "man-acts," which reveals the efficacy of the person, but it is to be found in the experience "something-happens-in-man," where the efficacy of the person is absent.... It is because of the autonomy of the body with its instinctive dynamism with respect to the self-determination of the person that in the totality of the personal structure of man his body is in a way a basis, an underlayer, or a substructure for what determines the structure of the person; of course the substructure itself forms part of the unity of the human being and thus of the unity of the person....This circumstance, let us reemphasize, by no means contradicts man's personal unity; we thus see that there is, intrinsically built into the personal structure of man's unity, a structure that exists and is dynamized according to nature—in a different way than the way of the person. Obviously, the human body does not constitute a separate subject standing apart from the subject that is the man-person. The unity of the body with the ontic subjectivity of man—with the human ontic support—cannot be doubted.[122]

---

120. Wojtyla, *Acting Person*, 203.

121. I refer the reader again to Lonergan's definition of *sublation*: "What sublates goes beyond what is sublated, introduces something new and distinct, yet so far from interfering with the sublated or destroying it, on the contrary needs it, includes it, preserves all its proper features and properties, and carries them forward to a fuller realization within a richer context" (*Method in Theology*, 241).

122. Wojtyla, *Acting Person*, 210–11.

Most significantly, the pope is arguing that in the totality of the personal structure of man his body is a basis, a substructure forming part of the unity of man and thus of the person. Indeed, the meaning of the human body is an integral part of the structure of the personal subject. Of course the pope doesn't deny that the inner structures and regularities of the human organism, *per se*, require scientific analysis and explanation. But having distinguished the body as a 'physiological unit' and the 'bodiliness' of the human person, John Paul can argue that, "the human body is not only the field of reactions of a sexual character, but [rather] it is at the same time the means of the expression of man as an integral whole, of the person, which reveals itself through the 'language of the body.'" "This 'language' has an important interpersonal meaning," the pope adds, "especially in the area of the reciprocal relations between man and woman."

In addition, our earlier analyses show that in this case the 'language of the body' should *express*, at a determinate level, *the truth of the sacrament*," namely, a one-flesh union (*MWTB*, 123.2). Therefore, "In this reflection [the human body is an integral part of the structure of the personal subject] we gain a vantage point that we must necessarily place at the basis of the whole contemporary science about human sexuality in the biophysical sense. This is not to say that must give up this science or deprive ourselves of its results. On the contrary, if these results are to be useful in teaching us something about the education of man in his masculinity and femininity, and about the sphere of marriage and procreation, we must always arrive—through all the single elements of contemporary science—at what is fundamental and essentially personal, both in every individual, man or woman, and in their reciprocal relations" (*MWTB*, 23.4). Elsewhere John Paul II expands on the relation between the theology of the body and the scientific analysis of bio-physiology and bio-medicine, namely, the relation between the integral vision of man and the study of certain aspects that constitute man. He writes:

> The *theology* of the body . . . takes on particular importance for contemporary man, whose science in the fields of bio-physiology and bio-medicine is very advanced. Yet, this science deals with man under a certain 'aspect' and is thus partial rather than comprehensive. We know well the functions of the body as an organism, the functions linked with the masculinity and femininity of the human person. But in and of itself such *science does not yet develop* the consciousness of the body as a sign of the person, as

> a manifestation of the spirit. The whole development of contemporary science of the body as organism has rather the character of biological knowledge, because it is based on the disjunction between what is bodily and what is spiritual in man. When one uses such one-sided knowledge of the body's functions as an organism, it is not difficult to reach the point of treating the body more or less systematically as an *object of manipulations*; in this case, man no longer identifies himself subjectively, so to speak, with his own body, because it is deprived of the meaning and dignity that stem from the fact that this body is proper to the person. Here we touch problems that often need fundamental solutions, which are impossible without an integral vision of man. (*MWTB*, 59.3)

The sum and substance of the pope's point is that the *body is personal*. Michael Polanyi's distinction between subsidiary and focal awareness/knowledge is helpful here in thinking about the sense in which the body is personal. These two elements in his theory of knowledge describe the way in which "we comprehend a particular set of items as parts of a whole." In this case the body is the part of the comprehensive whole that is the acting person. How are we aware of our body in terms of the whole? In other words, what is the particular manner in which we are aware of the particulars in "terms of the whole on which we have fixed our attention [?]" Polanyi replies: "I shall call this a *subsidiary awareness* of the particulars, by contrast to a *focal awareness* which would fix attention on the particulars in themselves, and not as parts of a whole. I shall also speak correspondingly of a *subsidiary* knowledge of such items, as distinct from a *focal* knowledge of the same items."[123] He elaborates:

> We use instruments as an extension of our hands and they may serve as an extension of our senses. We assimilate them to our body by pouring ourselves into them. And we must realize then also that our own body has a special place in the universe: we never attend to our body as an object in itself. Our body is always in use as the basic instrument of our intellectual and practical control over our surroundings. Hence in all our waking hours we are subsidiarily aware of our body within our focal knowledge of our surroundings. And, of course, our body is more than a mere instrument. *To be aware of our body in terms of the things we know and do, is to feel*

---

123. Polanyi, *Study of Man*, 29–30. See also, Polanyi, *Personal Knowledge*, 55–63.

alive. This awareness is an essential part of our existence as sensuous active persons.[124]

This Polanyian analysis of the sense in which the body is an integral part of the personal subject is crucial to John Paul's integral vision of man and it will be extremely significant later in the analysis of the theology of the body and homosexuality (see chapter 6). For the pope's view here is that the body is personal, not impersonal. To quote Robert George: "neither sperm nor eggs, neither penises nor vagina, are properly conceived in ... impersonal terms. Nor are they 'used' by persons considered as somehow standing over and apart from these and other aspects of their biological reality. The biological reality of persons is, rather, part of [rather than a mere instrument or extrinsic tool of] their personal reality."[125]

There remains to mention two things that are fundamental to the pope's phenomenology of the body, his adequate anthropology that is the substratum of the theology of the body. One, this anthropology can be justified by one's own human experience, John Paul claims, because the structures of human subjectivity, of bodily man, show themselves to us above all in lived experience. "In the interpretation of the revelation about man, and above all about the body, we must, for understandable reasons, appeal to experience, because bodily man is perceived by us above all in experience" (*MWTB*, 4.4). What is perceived experientially—meaning thereby the lived experience that I have given a full account of earlier in this chapter—are "constitutive elements of an adequate anthropology and a deep substratum of the theology of the body" (*MWTB*, 26.2). Although a philosophical account of that justification is missing in *Man and Women He Created Them*, it is present in *The Acting Person*, as I have tried to show in this chapter. Given that the pope offers *catecheses* in *Man and Women He Created Them*, it wouldn't have been appropriate to give a philosophical account in his Wednesday audience talks.

Two, John Paul II, if I understand him correctly, is opposed, most significantly, to pitting revelation against experience by arguing that the authority of God's Word revelation "does not exclude experience," as Berkouwer rightly says, but rather it is "*in* the experience itself that the authority is acknowledged and confessed."[126] This is how I understand the

---

124. Polanyi, *Study of Man*, 31.
125. George, *Clash of Orthodoxies*, 85–86.
126. I owe this insight to Berkouwer, *De Heilige Schrift*, 2:419 [349], "De autoriteit sluit de ervaring niet uit en de mens wordt er tenvolle bij betrokken, maar *in* de ervaring

pope's claim that "*our human experience is in some way a legitimate means for theological interpretation* and that, in a certain sense, is an indispensable point of reference to which we must appeal in the interpretation of the 'beginning,'" that is, the revelation about man, and above all the body, grounded in the normative orders of creation (*MWTB*, 4.4). These two points actually belong together because the pope's fundamental aim in the theology of the body is to give a biblical and theological justification for that theology as grounded in the Word of God, divine revelation. I turn now to give an account of that theology's foundation in a Catholic theological understanding of nature, sin, and grace.

---

wordt het *gezag* erkend en beleden" (This authority does not exclude experience and man is freely a part of it; but *in* the experience the authority is acknowledge and confessed).

5

Creation, Fall, Redemption, and Fulfillment

IN A COUPLE OF places earlier in this book, particularly chapters 1 and 2, I briefly addressed the question of the relation of Christ's redemptive work to creation, of the relation of nature (read: structures of reality), sin and grace. In the theological interpretation that follows, that relation is the hermeneutical context for my understanding of John Paul II's *Theology of the Body*.

Now, as I understand the pope's theology of nature and grace, the redemption accomplished through Jesus Christ's saving work—His life, passion, death, resurrection, and ascension, in short, the Christ event—does not (a) stand opposed to, and hence replace altogether, created reality, as if to say that the structures of reality need to be by-passed or suppressed because they are hopelessly corrupt as a consequence of the fall into sin, meaning thereby the replacement of one nature by another. But nor does his redemptive work merely (b) supplement or (c) parallel that reality, which would leave nature untouched by grace, and thus nature and grace would have only an *extrinsic* relation to each other. Furthermore, nor does his redemptive work merely involve (d) acceptance of created reality, of humanity, *as it is*, for that would deny created reality's structures' fallen state, which would, as Guarino puts it, "overlook God's judgment on the world rendered dramatically in the cross of Christ."[1] Rather, the structures of reality, in short, nature, stand in need of being reconsecrated to its Maker, and hence Christ's redemption (e) seeks to penetrate, restore, and renew *from within* the fallen order of creation.[2] These various pos-

---

1. Guarino, *Foundations of Systematic Theology*, 20.
2. I owe this succinct way of formulating the various possibilities of relating nature, sin and grace to Albert Wolters, "What is to be done?" For an introduction to his thinking, see *Creation Regained*. For my own analysis of these various possibilities with respect to a Catholic theology of culture, see *Slitting the Sycamore: Christ and Culture in the*

sibilities of conceiving the relation of nature, sin and grace require some explanation.

NATURE, SIN, AND GRACE

Three quarters of a century past, Jacques Maritain significantly remarked regarding the question of the relation of nature and grace that it is erroneous to ignore both the distinction between nature and grace as well as their union.[3] There are five types of ways in which that relation has been understood.

The first type understands grace and nature to be opposed to each other. Nature has been rendered a corrupt vessel by the fall into sin, needing to be replaced altogether with something new by grace. One influential account of this relation sees human nature to be completely closed to God and hence as capable of nothing but sin, with the accompanying loss or destruction of the natural power of the will. The will itself, as a consequence of the fall and man's fallen state, is "capable of nothing except . . . malicious, empty self-seeking . . . possessing an insuperable bent toward evil."[4] The fall eliminates all natural inclination to goodness in man's will, on this view, and also tempts us to disparage natural virtue as well as our natural capacity for contrary moral choice between good and evil—that is, the will's power to choose good over evil, or vice-versa. In short, on this view of the relation between nature and grace, the very nature of the will as God created it is disparaged in order to magnify grace. In this sense, nature would be the very opposite of grace, and hence cannot be united with grace; rather nature has to struggle against grace and be replaced altogether with something new by grace, meaning thereby a supernatural life of faith and a consequent supernaturalized freedom. Thus, supernatural freedom is to be construed as a "superstructure" added to natural freedom, rather than as determining and elevating our whole being, including

---

New Evangelization. Especially influential not only in my own thinking but also that of Wolter's on the relation between nature and grace are the writings of Dutch neo-Calvinist philosopher Herman Dooyeweerd (1894–1977). For a brief introduction to his thinking, see *In the Twilight of Western Thought*.

3. Jacques Maritain states, "There is one error that consists in ignoring [the] distinction between nature and grace. There is another that consists in ignoring their union," *Clairvoyance de Rome*, 222. Cited in De Lubac, "Apologetics and Theology," *Theological Fragments*, 103 n. 28.

4. See Scheeben, *Nature and Grace*, 308.

our natural, but fallen, will. In short, on this view the Christian withdraws from the corrupt vessel that is human nature and seeks a salvation that is separate from it because human nature in its fallen condition is, essentially, *irreclaimable*. Against this view, John Henry Newman put it just right. He writes,

> [The Church] does not teach that human nature is irreclaimable, else wherefore should she be sent? [N]ot that it [human nature] is to be shattered and reversed, but to be extricated, purified, and restored; not that it is a mere mass of evil, but that it has the promise of great things, and even now has a virtue and a praise proper to itself. But in the next place she knows and she preaches that such a restoration, as she aims at effecting in it, must be brought about, not simply through any outward provision of preaching and teaching, even though it be her own, but from a certain inward spiritual power or grace imparted directly from above, and which is in her keeping.[5]

The second and third types understand the relation between nature and grace to be such that grace is a "plus factor," a mere "add on" to the natural level. Consider, say, the relationship between the natural virtues and the supernatural virtues of faith, hope and charity in light of these types. The *Catechism of the Catholic Church* teaches that "The theological virtues are the foundation of Christian moral activity; they animate it and give it its special character. They inform and give life to all the moral virtues" (no. 1813). Now, I want to show that neither of these types can make sense of what the *Catechism* claims here, namely, the grace of the supernatural virtues directs and orders nature from *within* rather than alongside of or above nature as if those virtues merely add on to the excellencies of virtuous man.[6] The Anglican neo-Thomist Eric L. Mascall critically remarks on what it means to think that grace is simply alongside of or above nature—a mere superstructure erected on top of nature. "The Thomist maxim 'Grace does not destroy nature but perfects it' has been interpreted as if it means simply that it is better for man to enjoy grace *in addition* to nature, although nature would be perfectly complete without it."[7] Mascall correctly rejects this interpretation of the Thomist maxim, giving us a right reading of two complementary principles in Aquinas'

---

5. Newman, *Apologia Pro Vita Sua*, 222.
6. Sokolowski, *God of Faith and Reason*, 72.
7. Mascall, *Openness of Being*, 151, italics added.

thought. He adds, "'Grace does not destroy nature but perfects it,' because nature always lies open to God. 'Grace presupposes nature,' not in the sense that grace is a mere superstructure erected on top of nature and needing nature only to prevent it from falling through the floor, *but that nature is the very material in which grace works and for whole ultimate perfection grace itself exists.*"[8]

Therefore, the reason why neither type can make sense of the Thomist maxim, and hence of the *Catechism of the Catholic Church's* teaching regarding the relation between the natural and supernatural virtues is because they view the relationship between the natural and supernatural virtues in a dualistic and hence extrinsic fashion. In short, thinking in terms of "two-tiers," we can say that, on these types, the upper-level of grace was lost because of original sin, leaving the lower-level relatively intact and integrally unaffected by sin. Thus, both types view the redemption accomplished through the saving work of Christ as something that merely *supplements* or *parallels* our created nature. On this "two-tier" relationship between nature and grace, the latter is merely added (*donum superadditum*) to a nature that has not been integrally affected by sin, and hence human nature requires little or no internal healing and restoration.

The chief problem with these types is that by limiting the scope of man's fallen condition, they in turn limit the scope of Christ's redemptive work. The dualism between faith and life is, for example, one of the practical implications of this limitation and it is well expressed by Vatican II. "This split between the faith which many profess and their daily lives deserves to be counted among the more serious errors of our age." In critical response to this bifurcation, the council Fathers teach, "Since they have an active role to play in the whole life of the Church, laymen are not only bound to penetrate the world with a Christian spirit, but are also called to be witnesses to Christ in all things in the midst of human society."[9] The Fathers add to this, "The good news of Christ continually renews the life and culture of fallen man."[10] Years later the newly established Pontifical Council for Culture states in the same vein, "[This view] gives Christ, the redeemer of man, center of the universe and of history, the scope of

---

8. Ibid., 153. These two maxims are derived from St. Thomas Aquinas, *Summa Theologiae*, I, q. 1, art. 8 *ad* 2, and I, q.2. art. 2 *ad* 1, respectively.

9. *Gaudium et Spes*, no. 43.

10. Ibid., no. 58.

completely renewing the lives of men 'by opening the vast fields of culture to His saving power.'"[11] Rather than those vast fields which make up the whole human cultural enterprise—the sciences, arts, such as music, literature, the work of civilization, as in pursuing a culture of life—being by-passed or suppressed by grace as in the first type; and rather than that grace being just a "plus factor," or mere "add on" to that enterprise; the Pontifical Council has correctly understood the two complementary principles of "grace does not destroy nature but perfects it" and "grace presupposes nature."[12] In sum, the whole human cultural enterprise, nature, as it were, "is the very material in which grace works and for whose ultimate perfection grace itself exists" (to quote Mascall again).[13]

The fourth type I mentioned above understands the relation between nature and grace in such as way that it conflates human nature and divine grace, threatening, as Romanus Cessario puts it, "to confuse God's creative presence to the human creature with the realization of the same person's call to beatitude."[14] This statement requires explanation. God's creative presence refers to man having been created by God and for God. Man is a creature of God such that he is "totally dependent for his existence on the incessant creative activity of the self-existent God."[15] And the importance of this is that, having been created for God, the meaning of man's existence is such that his relation to God is constitutive of his existence. The *Compendium of the Social Doctrine of the Church* expresses well this first principle of Christian anthropology. "This is a relationship that exists in itself, it is therefore not something that comes afterwards and is not added from the outside.... The human being is a personal being created by God to be in relationship with him; man finds life and self-expression only in [that] relationship, and tends naturally to God."[16] The *Compendium's* formulation here avoids the dualistic and hence extrinsic construal of the relation of nature and grace (in which grace is a "plus factor" or an "add-on") discussed above.

---

11. *Towards Pastoral Approach to Culture*, no. 6. The quotation inside this quotation is from John Paul II, "Homily of the Enthronement Mass."
12. Mascall, *Openness of Being*, 153.
13 Ibid.
14. Cessario, *Christian Faith and The Theological Life*, 28.
15. Mascall, *Openness of Being*, 150.
16. *Compendium of the Social Doctrine of the Church*, no. 109.

Now, one of the fundamental implications of this constitutive relationship is that man has, by nature, that is, by virtue of being created, a "capacity for God" ("*homo est Dei capax*").[17] Put differently, "man has, by nature, some *potential oboedientialis*, some receptive capacity ... for the supernatural"; otherwise, "God will be unable to communicate with man because, even if God speaks, man will be unable to hear him."[18] This "capacity for God" is a matter of divine grace; not the special grace of redemption but rather the universal gift due to God's grace resulting in our having been created with this capacity. It is argued, moreover, that man cannot actualize this capacity by his own powers. Thus, he has been endowed by God with a "supernatural existential," which is the offer of God's grace, a supernatural gift not given in and with man's nature.[19] As a consequence of God's universal saving will this offer is, nonetheless, universally bestowed so that man might respond to God, given that he is powerless to save himself. Cessario is right, however, that the "danger here is the risk of emphasizing the pervasive and inclusive character of divine grace in a way that practically eliminates the need for a real grace of justification—one that effectively transforms an impious person into a holy one."[20] Or as Pius XII was to state this risk, "Others destroy the gratuity of the supernatural order, since God, they say, cannot create intellectual beings without ordering and calling them to the beatific vision."[21] Put differently, entirely missing from this picture is, as the *Compendium* pointedly states, the fact that "this relationship with God can be ignored or even forgotten or dismissed"—even if "it can never be eliminated."[22]

Thus, because of original sin, indeed human sinfulness, man is wounded in the sense that at the very core of his being there is an act of separation from God, resulting in alienation and estrangement "not only from God but also from [man] himself, from other men and from the world around him."[23] Man's "capacity for God" has, then, been defectively and frustratedly hindered because of his sinful human condition. We can,

---

17. Ibid.
18. Mascall, *Openness of Being*, 143.
19. Nichols, *Catholic Thought Since the Enlightenment*, 142–43.
20. Cessario, *Christian Faith and the Theological Life*, 28. idem., *Introduction to Moral Theology*, 29–31.
21. Pius XII, 1950 Encyclical Letter, *Humani Generis*, no. 26.
22. *Compendium of the Social Doctrine of the Church*, no. 109.
23. Ibid., no. 116.

therefore, understand why "the New Testament makes it exceedingly difficult to glide over the fact that the justification won by the blood Christ really involves a movement from our being 'by nature children of wrath, like everyone else' to our being 'alive together with Christ—by grace you have been saved' (Eph 2:3–5)."[24] Therefore, we must avoid conflating human nature and divine grace because created reality's structures are in a fallen state and in need of redemption; otherwise, we run the risk of "overlook[ing] God's judgment on the world rendered dramatically in the cross of Christ."[25]

We come now to the fifth way of thinking of the relation between nature, sin and grace. By "nature" here this type understands the deepest foundations of human nature that remain in place after the fall, a nature that has been savagely wounded by the fall, but still remains what God originally made them to be. These foundations are not totally corrupted, destroyed. Rather, sin corrupts God's good creation but the order of creation persists. The good news is that God's salvation in Christ restores the whole fallen creation from *within*. Consider, for example, the *Catechism's* teaching on marriage in light of creation, fall into sin, and redemption. Marriage is grounded in the order of creation: "'The intimate community of life and love which constitutes the married state has been established by the Creator and endowed by him with its own proper laws. . . . God himself is the author of marriage.'" Yet, marriage as it actually functions in its fallen state is under the regime of sin and hence no longer properly functioning. Significantly, the *Catechism* applies an Augustinian principle, namely, "the natures in which evil exists, in so far as they are natures, are good. And evil is removed, not by removing any nature, or part of a nature . . . but by healing and correcting that which had been vitiated and depraved."[26]

In this light, we can easily understand the teaching of the *Catechism* on the relation between sin and nature: "According to faith the disorder we notice so painfully does not stem from the *nature* of man and woman, nor from the nature of their relations, but from *sin*. . . . Nevertheless, the order of creation persists, though seriously disturbed. . . . In his mercy God has not forsaken sinful man. . . . After the fall, marriage helps to overcome

---

24. Cessario, *Christian Faith and The Theological Life*, 28–29.
25. Guarino, *Foundations of Systematic Theology*, 20.
26. St. Augustine, *City of God*, Book XIV, Chapter XI. Online: http://www.ccel.org/ccel/schaff/npnf102.iv.XIV.11.html.

self-absorption, egoism, pursuit of one's own pleasure, to open oneself to the other, to mutual aid and to self-giving." Furthermore, "In his preaching Jesus unequivocally taught the original [i.e., creational] meaning of the union of man and woman as the Creator willed it from the beginning. ... By coming to restore the original order of creation disturbed by sin, [Jesus] himself gives the strength and grace to live marriage in the new dimension of the Reign of God."[27]

On this view, then, of the relation between nature and grace, the relation is such that grace penetrates and transforms and perfects fallen nature from within, and thus nature is redeemed in its own domain. In this connection, let me cite several key passages on the relation between nature and grace from a remarkable book by Etienne Gilson, *Christianity and Philosophy*, written in 1931. "The true Catholic position consists in maintaining that nature was created good, that it has been wounded, but that it can be at least partially healed by grace [here and now] if God so wishes. This *instauratio*, that is to say, this renewal, this re-establishment, this restoration of nature to its primitive goodness, is on this point the program of authentic Catholicism." As Gilson also rightly says elsewhere, "To say that grace is necessary to restore nature is quite other than to suppress that nature to the profit of grace: it is to confirm it by grace. Grace presupposes nature, whether to restore or to enrich it. When grace restores nature, it does not substitute itself for it, but re-establishes it; when nature, thus re-established by grace, accomplishes its proper operations, they are indeed natural operations [now transformed] which it performs." Finally, as Gilson also says later in this book, "Catholicism teaches that before everything the restoration of wounded nature by the grace of Jesus Christ. The restoration of nature: so there must be a nature, and of what value, since it is the work of God, Who created it and re-created it by repurchasing it at the price of His own Blood! Thus grace presupposes nature, and the excellence of nature which it comes to heal and transfigure."[28] Thus, grace restores and transforms nature from within its own domain.

Indeed, this is how the late philosopher-pope John Paul II describes the Church's mission of evangelization and, in fact, "the purpose of the Gospel," namely, "'to transform humanity from within and to make it new.' Like the yeast which leavens the whole measure of dough (cf. Mt 13:33),

---

27. All the quotations in this paragraph, except the quotation from St. Augustine's *The City of God*, are from the *Catechism of the Catholic Church*, nos. 1603, 1606–9, 1614–15.

28. Gilson, *Christianity and Philosophy*, 21, 24, and 111, respectively.

the Gospel is meant to permeate all cultures and give them life from within, so that they may express the full truth about the human person and about human life."[29] In sum, *grace restores or renews nature*, meaning thereby that God's grace in Christ *restores all life to its fullness, penetrating and perfecting and transforming the fallen creation from within its own order*, bringing creation into conformity with His will and purpose.

As John Paul II himself states, "*Redemption* means, in fact, a '*new creation*', as it were, it means *taking up all that is created* to express in creation the fullness of righteousness, equity, and holiness planned for it by God and to express the fullness above all in man, created male and female 'in the image of God'" (*MWTB*, 99.7). God who created all things in and through Christ (Col 1:16), has restored his fallen creation, which was savagely wounded by sin, by re-creating it in Christ. "Therefore, if anyone is in Christ, he is a new creation; the old has passed away, behold the new has come" (2 Cor 5:17). How does the pope understand the "*living forms of the 'new man'*" to which Christ calls man? He replies: "In the ethos of the redemption of the body, the original ethos of creation was to be taken up anew.... In this way a connection is formed, even a continuity, between the 'beginning' and the perspective of redemption" (*MWTB*, 49.4). I turn now to give a systematic account of John Paul's thought in the theology of the body of the relation of creation, fall, redemption, and fulfillment/consummation.

CREATION/FALL/REDEMPTION/CONSUMMATION

Shortly before his death, John Paul II published his final book, leaving the Church, indeed the whole of humanity, the beautiful gift of his reflections entitled, *Memory and Identity*. Relevant to the question of the indivisible unity of nature, sin and grace is the following passage from this work:

> The resurrection of Christ clearly illustrated that only the measure of good introduced by God into history through the mystery of Redemption is sufficient to correspond fully to the truth of the

---

29. John Paul II, *Evangelium Vitae*, no. 95. The quote within this quote is from Paul VI, *Evangelii Nuntiandi*, no. 18. Paul VI adds, "The purpose of evangelization is therefore precisely this interior change, and if it had to be expressed in one sentence the best way of stating it would be to say that the Church evangelizes when she seeks to convert, solely through the divine power of the message she proclaims, both the personal and collective consciences of people, the activities in which they engage, and the lives and concrete milieu which are theirs" (ibid.).

human being. The Paschal Mystery thus becomes the definitive measure of man's existence in the world created by God. In this mystery, not only is eschatological truth revealed to us, that is to say the fullness of the Gospel, or Good News. There also shines forth a light to enlighten the whole of human existence in its temporal dimension and this light is then reflected onto the created world. Christ, through his Resurrection, has so to speak "justified" the work of creation, and especially the creation of man. He has "justified" it in the sense that he revealed the "just measure" of good intended by God at the beginning of human existence. This measure is not merely what was provided by him in creation and then compromised by man through sin; it is a superabundant measure, in which the original plan finds a higher realization (cf. Genesis 3:14–15). In Christ, man is called to a new life, as son in the Son, the perfect expression of God's glory.[30]

At the core of John Paul's understanding of the Christian worldview, as the passage above expresses it, is an interlocking set of life-orienting beliefs regarding the Creation, the Fall into sin, and Redemption (i.e., the Incarnation, Passion, Resurrection, and Ascension of Jesus Christ). How then does the pope understand each of these beliefs and their interrelationship in his theology of the body?

First, God created the world good. Of all the beings God created, man is "'the only creature on earth that God has willed for its own sake' [*Gaudium et Spes*, no. 25], and he alone is called to share, by knowledge and love, in God's own life."[31] Furthermore, man was created in the image of God and, as such, that image consists in possessing human dignity, self-knowledge, self-possession, and "freely giving himself and entering into communion with other persons."[32] Moreover, and particularly important for the theology of the body, "the human body shares in the dignity of 'the image of God': it is a human body precisely because it is animated by a spiritual soul, and it is the whole human person [a living, human body] that is intended to become, in the body of Christ, a temple of the Spirit."[33] As I showed in the last chapter, man's subjectivity is such that he is capable of self-knowledge in his relation to God, but also a self-knowledge of being unique among all living beings. In addi-

---

30. John Paul II, *Memory and Identity*, 25.
31. *Catechism of the Catholic Church*, no. 356.
32. Ibid., no. 357.
33. Ibid., no. 364.

tion to man's self-knowledge, there is the power of self-determination. This power is at the root of man's task to cultivate the earth. Indeed, given the cultural mandate to subdue and have dominion over created reality, God's goodness in creating man extends to the work of man's hands when accomplished in the light of "the truth about ourselves and about the world."[34] Indeed, the totality of creation, especially man who is its crown, actually manifests God's goodness, being created in the image and likeness of God. This manifestation of goodness is God's thesis, his affirmation, His *Yes* to the creation (Gen 1:31).

In this connection, we should note that from the outset the pope distinguishes and contrasts the order of creation and the order of the fall in order to make clear the essential difference between the state of man's original innocence and the state of his sinfulness. "In these two antithetical situations, systematic theology was to see two different states of human nature, '*status naturae integrae*' (state of integral nature) and '*status naturae lapsae*' (state of fallen nature)." The pope adds, "All of this emerges from the Yahwist text of Genesis 2 and 3, which contains in itself the most ancient word of revelation and evidently has a fundamental significance for the theology of man and the theology of the body" (*MWTB*, 3.3). Thus, having made this distinction, John Paul grounds his reflections on the theology of the body, in the first place, in God's original order of creation, and for that reason he concentrates his catecheses on the creative narrative of Genesis 1–2. In short, the biblical anthropology of the pope's theology of the body is grounded in the biblical concept of creation, and thus the deep substratum, which is the triadic structures of solitude-unity-nakedness, of the body-subject is grounded in the order of creation.

So when Christ quotes in summary form Genesis 1:27 and 2:24 in reply to a question about divorce, and the indissolubility of marriage, he refers his listeners back to the "beginning," namely, to God's original plan of creation, his intent for marriage grounded in the creation order, and its normative implications for the present situation of fallen humanity and sin ("hardness of hearts"). "Jesus Christ confirm[s] the eternal law formulated and instituted by God from the 'beginning' as man's creation." "It could also seem that the Teacher," the pope adds, "by confirming this primordial law of the Creator, does nothing else than establish its

---

34. John Paul II, *Memory and Identity*, 81.

proper normative meaning, appealing to the very authority of the first Legislator. Yet, that significant expression, 'from the beginning', repeated twice, clearly leads the interlocutors to reflect about the way in which, in the mystery of creation, man was formed precisely as 'male and female', in order to understand correctly the normative meaning of the words of Genesis. And this is no less valid for interlocutors today than for those then" (*MWTB*, 1.4).

The upshot of this conclusion is that God's original plan for marriage, that is, the indissoluble union of one man and one woman, of sexual complementarity, is still normative for the Church, indeed, for all humanity, expressive of a permanent creation order "established by the Creator and endowed by him with its own proper laws."[35] The order of creation is the work of the wisdom of divine providence. "[W]isdom denotes a teleological principle, viz., one that moves every being toward its proper end or goal through the attractiveness of the end."[36] Being an expression of divine wisdom, the creation order finds its origin in God's eternal law. This foundational truth is expressed by John Paul II in *Veritatis Splendor*: "The supreme rule of life is the divine law itself, the eternal, objective and universal law by which God out of his wisdom and love arranges, directs and governs the whole world and the paths of the human community." Furthermore, the pope adds, "God has enabled man to share in this divine law, and hence man is able under the gentle guidance of God's providence increasingly to recognize the unchanging truth"[37] This is nothing less than Aquinas' view that man rationally participate in God's eternal law for human existence, and that this participation is called natural law.[38] In addition, John Paul calls this participation in God's eternal law a "participated theonomy," meaning thereby the state in which "man's free obedience to God's law discloses that human reason and human will participate in God's wisdom and providence."[39] Moreover, says Romanus Cessario, "Eternal law represents how God knows the world to be, how he effectively conceives the ordering of everything that exists within creation."

---

35. *Catechism of the Catholic Church*, no. 1602.

36. Cessario, *Introduction to Moral Theology*, 54.

37. John Paul II, *Veritatis Splendor*, no. 43. This is actually a quotation from the Second Vatican Council's Declaration on Religious Freedom, *Dignitatis humanae*, no. 3.

38. See Aquinas, *Summa theologiae*, I–II, q. 91, a. 2.

39. John Paul II, *Veritatis Splendor*, no. 41.

In sum, it "represents the exemplar of God's wisdom and power actually directing and moving all that exists toward perfection."[40]

DIVINE WISDOM AND CHRIST

Now, one must ask whether "to affirm the transcendence of divine wisdom, which when applied to creation and its divine government is called the eternal law, does not depreciate the central and indispensable importance of the incarnate Word for Christian living [?]"[41] Well, we have already seen that Jesus Christ reconfirms and recapitulates, says John Paul, "the eternal law formulated and instituted by God from the 'beginning' as man's creation" (*MWTB*, no. 1.4). But we must ask where else is Jesus Christ, the Logos and second person of the Trinity, in that picture of creation order? In short, how should we understand Christ's relation to the creation order? Put differently, in what sense does the Incarnation of the eternal Logos furnish the "ultimate *logos* or intelligibility which undergirds and directs the created order [?]"[42]

The brief answer to this question here must take as its starting point St. Paul's teaching that Jesus Christ, the Eternal Son of God, is "the power of God and the wisdom of God" (1 Cor 1:24). In this regard, St. Paul associates divine wisdom personally with the incarnate Son. Furthermore, he explicitly refers to the pre-existent Christ, the divine Word, as the divine Prototype, in other words, as the true pattern by which "all things in heaven and on earth were created, things visible and invisible" (Col 1:16). In addition, when Aquinas discusses the eternal law, he identifies the second divine Person of the Trinity with the eternal law. He writes: "Therefore, regarding divine things, we speak of the Word itself, which the Father's understanding conceives, as the Second Person of the Trinity, and this Word expresses everything in the Father's knowledge, whether things proper to God's essence or things proper to each Person or things created by God, as Augustine makes evident in his work *On the Trinity*. And among other things so expressed, the Word itself also expresses the eternal law itself."[43] Therefore, given his divine status as the Logos/Son, Christ,

---

40. Cessario, *Introduction to Moral Theology*, 59, 56, respectively.

41. Ibid., 57.

42. Ibid., 56. I am heavily indebted to Fr. Cessario for my understanding and expression of Christ's relationship to the creation order.

43. Aquinas, *Summa theologiae*, I–II, q. 93, a. 1, ad 2.

"the image of the invisible God, the first born of all creation" (Col 1:15), that is, "he who is before all things, and in whom all things hold together" (Col 1:17), this Logos/Son "embodies and displays the definitive shape or form that the order of human existence should take in the world."[44] This conclusion echoes the teaching of the Second Vatican Council: "Only in the mystery of the incarnate Word does the mystery of man take on light." As the Council Fathers make clear:

> For Adam, the first man, was a type of him who was to come, Christ the Lord, Christ the new Adam, in the very revelation of the mystery of the Father and of his love, fully reveals man to himself and brings to light his most high calling.... He who is the "image of the invisible God" (Col 1:15), is himself the perfect who has restored in the children of Adam that likeness to God which has been disfigured ever since the first sin. Human nature, by the very fact that it was assumed, not absorbed, has been raised in us also to a dignity beyond compare.[45]

SEXUAL COMPLEMENTARITY AND THE CREATION ORDER

We need to turn now to discuss the question whether sexual complementarity is divinely intended in the order of creation. That is, does Scripture teach the necessity of sexual complementarity, especially but not only, of the male and female sex organs? It would be wrong to think that complementarity is restricted in the historic Christian teaching to the anatomical fit of the organs. The *Catechism of the Catholic Church* teaches that same-sex acts lack the full complementarity that is a foundational prerequisite for the bi-unitary marriage bond. Of course "full complementarity" means that the spouses are united not only in their bodily dimension—biological unity and organic complementarity—but also in every other dimensions—sense, emotion, reason, will, and heart.[46] I want to fill out

---

44. Cessario, *Introduction to Moral Theology*, 56. John Paul II makes the same point in *Dominum et Vivificantem*. He argues that the Word of God, that is, Jesus Christ, is not only the mediator of redemption but also the mediator of creation. The pope writes, "This Word is the same Word who was 'in the beginning with God,' who 'was God,' and without whom 'nothing was made that was made,' since 'the world was made through him' [John 1:1, 2, 3, 10]. He is the Word who is also the eternal law, the source of every law which regulates the world and especially human acts" (no. 33).

45. *Gaudium et Spes*, no. 22.

46. *Catechism of the Catholic Church*, no. 2357.

Creation, Fall, Redemption, and Fulfillment 219

John Paul's account by developing the point that sexual complementarity is biblically normative: the two, male and female, by being united in the conjugal act, become a "two-in-one-flesh-unity" (Gen 2:24). That is, the marital bond is heterosexual—a union of complementary opposites, as John Paul II argues in *MWTB*. In fact, this understanding of the marital bond is grounded not only in the order of creation but also in the Church's sacramental theology that informs the pope's understanding of the sacrament of marriage. He writes in a passage worth quoting in full:

> *From the words* ["I . . . take you . . . as my wife"; "I . . . take you . . . as my husband"] with which the man and the woman express their readiness to become "one flesh" according to the eternal truth established in the mystery of creation, we pass *to the reality* that corresponds to these words. Both the one and the other element are important *with regard to the structure of the sacramental sign.* . . . The words of new spouses are part of the integral structure of the sacramental sign, not only *by what* they signify, but also in some sense *with what* they signify and determine. . . . Consequently, the [visible] sign of the sacrament of Marriage is constituted by the words of the new spouse inasmuch as the "reality" that they themselves constitute ["one flesh"] corresponds to them. *Both of them, as man and woman,* being ministers of the sacrament at the moment of contracting marriage, at the same time *constitute the full and real visible sign* of the sacrament itself. *The words spoken by them would not of themselves constitute the sacramental sign if the human subjectivity of the engaged man and woman and at the same time the consciousness of the body linked with the masculinity and the femininity of the bride and bridegroom did not correspond to them* [italics added to this last sentence]. Here one must call to mind again the whole series of analyses of Genesis 1–2 [solitude-unity-nakedness] carried out earlier. The structure of the sacramental sign remains, in fact, in its essence the same as "in the beginning." What determines it is *in some sense "the language of the body,"* inasmuch as the man and the woman, who are to become one flesh by marriage, express in this sign the reciprocal gift of masculinity and femininity as the foundation of the conjugal union of the persons. (*MWTB*, 103.3.4)

In other words, the words "I . . . take you . . . as my wife"; "I . . . take you . . . as my husband" not only signify the one flesh union but, in the sacramental theology of the Church, the sacrament actually accomplishes what it symbolizes in the visible one flesh union of the man and woman. That is, their "two-in-one-flesh-unity" is the full and real visible sign of the sacrament itself, for a *real* bodily union has been sacramentally established. Most significant, and put differently, their sexual complementarity constitutes the necessary precondition for actually accomplishing what the sacrament signifies. What this means is that sexual complementarity—the limitation of conjugal sex to intercourse between male and female—is the foundational biblical norm for defining marriage, and hence for opposing same-sex marriage. The historic faith of the Church affirms the teaching that sexual difference is morally and sacramentally significant for a Catholic theology of marriage. Most recently, the Congregation for the Doctrine of the Faith reaffirms that historic teaching:

> The Church's teaching on marriage and on the complementarity of the sexes reiterates a truth that is evident to right reason and recognized as such by all the major cultures of the world. Marriage is not just any relationship between human beings. It was established by the Creator with its own nature, essential properties and purpose [*Gaudium et Spes*, no. 48]. No ideology can erase from the human spirit the certainty that marriage exists solely between a man and a woman, who by mutual personal gift, proper and exclusive to themselves, tend toward the communion of their persons. In this way, they mutually perfect each other, in order to cooperate with God in the procreation and upbringing of new human lives.[47]

Some critics of this historic Christian teaching, such as Dan O. Via, reject it because male-female complementarity, they allege, "does not cover all the complexities of human interaction." These critics allege, more fundamentally, that this exegesis is not the literal sense of biblical texts, such as Gen 1:27, 2:24 and Rom 1: 24–27. These texts do not speak of the anatomical complementarity of sexual organs, and hence, these critics conclude, that intercourse contrary to creation/nature is a violation of that complementarity.[48]

In response to these critics, let's begin by asking what the basis of Jesus' amendment is of the Mosaic practice that allowed divorce because of the hardness of man's heart, which is recorded in Mark 10:6–9 and Matt 19:4–6? Jesus refers to God's creational intent ("In the beginning"),

---

47. *Considerations Regarding Proposals to Give Legal Recognition to Unions between Homosexual Persons*, no. 2.

48. A critic representative of this position is Via, *Homosexuality and the Bible*, 35, 95, respectively.

to the order of creation, citing Gen 1:27 and 2:24 as his justification, namely, God's creation of male and female and the marital standard of a "man" and his "woman" ("This [woman] at last is bone of my bones and flesh of my flesh") being joined together. Jesus' teaching takes these verses as normative for marital monogamy and indissolubility. Most significant, Robert Gagnon rightly argues, these verses imply "that an acceptable sexual bond before God entails as its first prerequisite (after the assumption of an intra-human bond) a man and a woman." "In other words," he adds, "the 'twoness' or duality of a sexual bond is predicated on the 'twoness' or duality of the sexes."[49] Since Jesus takes Gen 1:27 and 2:24 as normative, as prescriptive and not just descriptive, then same-sex intercourse violates God's intentional creation of humans as "male and female" and the definition of marriage as a union between a man and a woman. Gagnon explains:

> Scripture rejects homosexual behavior because it is a violation of the gendered existence of male and female ordained by God at creation. Homosexual intercourse puts males in the category of females and females in the category of males, insofar as they relate to others as sexual beings.... God intended the very act of sexual intercourse to be an act of pluralism, embracing a sexual "other" rather than a sexual "same."... Same-sex intercourse represents a suppression of the visible evidence in nature regarding male-female anatomical and procreative complementarity. Complementarity extends also to a range of personality traits and predispositions that contribute to making heterosexual unions enormously more successful in terms of fidelity, endurance, and health than same-sex ones.[50]

Before going on with Gagnon's argument that the Bible condemns homosexual practice, let us consider the objection that the approach to issue of homosexuality that I'm defending in this book is driven by a biblical fundamentalism or an inerrantist position. Regarding fundamentalism, I argued early on that a fundamentalist operates with a hermeneutic in his appeal to Scripture that presupposes *biblicism*. In short, that presupposition leads exegetes to use Bible texts in an atomistic (isolated) way by lifting them out of their immediate contexts or out of the whole context of Scripture. I called this appeal to Scripture the bad sense of us-

---

49. Gagnon, *Case Not Made*, 6.
50. Gagnon, *Bible and Homosexual Practice*, 487–88.

ing proof-texts. But there is a good sense of using biblical proof-texts, exegetically and scripturally. Otherwise, every appeal to Scripture to support ones theological position would be biblicistic. Now, the biblical hermeneutic I sketched in chapter 2 is not biblicistic precisely because it assumes the hermeneutical golden rule, as Nichols calls it, "interpret every text of Scripture on the understanding that it forms part of a larger whole."[51] Gagnon, too, works with this rule.

I am an inerrantist, however. I accept the following teaching of *Dei Verbum* as normative for my approach to Scripture. "Therefore, since everything asserted by the inspired authors or sacred writers must be held to be asserted by the Holy Spirit, it follows that the books of Scripture must be acknowledged as teaching solidly, faithfully and without error that truth which God wanted put into sacred writings for the sake of salvation."[52] Significantly, Gagnon rejects inerrancy, but he nonetheless still affirms Scripture "as the single most important authority for faith and practice." Affirming the primacy of Scripture for the Church, he argues that affirming that primacy in ones biblical hermeneutic means that Scripture has certain "core values." What is a core value in Scripture, asks Gagnon?

Briefly, as I explained earlier in chapter 2, he replies, "Scripture's core values are values that are held (1) pervasively throughout Scripture (at least implicitly), (2) absolutely (without exceptions), and (3) strongly (as a matter of significance). This applies all the more in instances where: such values emerged in opposition to prevailing cultural trends and (5) prevailed in the church for two millennia. *The limitation of acceptable sexual intercourse to sexually complementary partners and the strong abhorrence of same-sex intercourse is just such a value.*"[53] If one rejects this core value that reflects Scriptural authority, one has to meet an extraordinary burden of proof, says Gagnon. "The evidence adduced [in rejecting this core value] must not only be strong and unambiguous that it makes the strong and unambiguous witness of Scripture pale by comparison; it must also directly refute the reasons for the Bible's position." What does this mean?

Well, suppose we hold, as some do, that the primary expression of homosexuality in antiquity was inherently exploitative because either it

---

51. Nichols, *Shape of Catholic Theology*, 155.
52. *Dei Verbum*, no. 11. I discussed a Catholic view of inerrancy in chapter 1.
53. Gagnon, "Authority of Scripture in the 'Homosex' Debate."

was pederasty or cult prostitution. Furthermore, suppose we hold, as again many do, that homosexuality is a genetic matter—we are born homosexuals, and think that modern science has shown this to be the case. Gagnon is right about the status of these two claims, namely, they are dubious. But his main point is that the person who rejects biblical authority for these alleged reasons must meet an extraordinary burden of proof. He must "also prove that the Bible condemned homosexual practice *primarily* on the grounds of the exploitative mismatch created by pederasty or on the grounds that homosexual behavior was a willfully chosen rejection of God's design for sexuality. Otherwise, even if these claims were valid (*and they are not*), they would still have little relevance for ascertaining the deficiencies in the Bible's reasons for condemning homosexual behavior."[54] Gagnon argues that neither of these points can be substantiated.

First, "the Bible's critique of same-sex intercourse is not aimed primarily at typically exploitative features." Rather, it is aimed at the absence of the foundational male-female requirement for sexual relations. Second, "there were non-exploitative models for same-sex intercourse in antiquity (by ancient standards)," and they were condemned by St. Paul in Rom 1:26–27. Gagnon cites Louis Crompton, a scholar who is a homosexual, who acknowledge this very point. "However well-intentioned," the interpretation that "Paul's words were not directed at 'bona fide' homosexuals in committed relationships ... seem strained and unhistorical. Nowhere does Paul or any other Jewish writer of this period imply the least acceptance of same-sex relations under any circumstance. The idea that homosexuals might be redeemed by mutual devotion would have been wholly foreign to Paul or any other Jew or early Christian."[55] Third, modern science has not substantiated the claim that people are born homosexuals. Fourth, "the notion of a *partially innate* character to homoerotic desires fits quite well with a number of ancient theories *and Pauline perspectives on sin generally.*"[56] Regarding the Pauline perspective on sin, John Finnis has developed the point that even if homosexuality is a condition, not a choice, it doesn't follow that the condition is something other than a reflection of the state of man's fallen nature (*status naturae lapsae*), that is, his inner spiritual woundedness. In other words, theologically the ultimate origin

---

54. Ibid., italics added.

55. Louis Crompton, *Homosexuality and Civilization*, 114, as cited in Gagnon, "Authority of Scripture in the 'Homosex' Debate."

56. Gagnon, "Authority of Scripture in the 'Homosex' Debate," italics added.

of this condition is the fall. Says Finnis, according to William E. May: "I suggest that we might consider the inclination as a specific manifestation of the concupiscence that comes from sin (original sin) and leads to sin but is itself not sin."[57] St. Thomas Aquinas agrees with this assessment of the homosexual condition, according to Janet E. Smith. "Original sin alone makes every human being disordered; many of us have acquired more specific disorders through our genetic heritage, our upbringing, our choices. Many of these make it difficult for us to avoid disordered and sinful actions. For Aquinas, homosexuality is simply one more of those disordered conditions."[58] I shall return to the matter of the condition and practice of homosexuality in the next chapter of this book.

In an earlier passage I quoted from Gagnon, he referred to same-sex intercourse as a matter of suppressing the visible evidence of nature and reminded us of St. Paul's indictment of same-sex intercourse in Rom 1:24–27. St. Paul treats homosexual practice as a matter of idolatry: the truth about God and the way he made us, which is evident in the material structures of creation/nature, is suppressed. There is a close connection between the failure to accept the truth about God visible in creation and homosexual practice that is, among other things, "contrary to, against nature." "Those who denied the obvious truth about God transparent in material structures intact since creation and 'exchanged' the truth about God went on to deny the obvious truth about themselves transparent in their embodied sexuality and 'exchanged' natural (other-sex) intercourse for unnatural (same-sex) intercourse. In both instances there is a suppression of truth accessible through observation of material structures in creation or nature."[59] In Rom 1:20, St. Paul speaks of the "creation of the world." By creation he means the way God's initial act of creating structured the world. Regarding the creation of man, St. Paul clearly thinks that the material structures of creation are manifested here in the complementary embodied character of maleness and femaleness, which of course includes but is not restricted to anatomical complementarity. "Both the truth about God 'since the creation of the world' and the truth about male-female complementarity in nature can be visually seen and

---

57. May, "On the Impossibility of Same-Sex Marriage."

58. Smith, "Thomas Aquinas on Homosexuality," 139.

59. Gagnon, "Rejoinder to Dan O. Via's Response in *Homosexuality and the Bible*." This rejoinder is Gagnon expanded response to his shorter response in the book they co-published.

mentally apprehended 'by means of the things that have been made,' so that humans are 'without excuse' (Rom 1:20)."[60] Those structures of creation give clear evidence of God's will that bodily (sexual) union is the typical foundation of the multi-leveled union—full complementarity—that is marriage, which includes bodily, emotional, intellectual, volitional, and spiritual union. Hence, biblically speaking, same-sex intercourse is structurally incompatible with embodied existence since the body is intrinsically part of the personal reality that is the human being, and hence the sexual act in which the husband and wife become biologically one is the typical biotic substratum and constituent of the multi-leveled union of marriage.

REDEMPTION OF THE BODY

Earlier in chapter 4, I set forth John Paul II's phenomenology of bodily existence as an account of the structures of creation. We have been developing his position on the universally valid truth about man, his being male and female, the two-in-one-flesh-unity expressed in the words of Christ that refer us back to the order of creation, the creational ground in Genesis 1–2. "The *'body' signifies* (according to Genesis) the visible aspect of man and his belonging to the visible world" (*MWTB*, 86.4). And yet, there is more, this truth must be interpreted, says John Paul, in light of another situation, namely, "the situation that came to be through the breaking of the first covenant with the Creator, that is, through original sin. One must see this truth about man—male and female—in the context of his hereditary sinfulness" (*MWTB*, 58.3). Furthermore, sin has both an anthropological and cosmic dimension, indeed, the "whole visible creation, the whole cosmos, carries the effects of man's sin. Therefore, the "redemption of the body has its anthropological dimension: it is the redemption of man. At the same time, it irradiates in some way on all creation, which has from the beginning been tied to man in a particular way and subordinated to him (see Gen 2:28–30). The redemption of the body and, therefore, the redemption of the world, has a cosmic dimension" (*MWTB*, 86.2). Moreover, this already accomplished redemption in Christ has been not only confirmed in him but also "*re-opened anew* to its definitive eschatological fulfillment" (*MWTB*, 86.3).

---

60. On this, see Gagnon in Via and Gagnon, *Homosexuality and the Bible*, 76–81.

Now, in order to understand the profound transformation that is involved in the "redemption of the body," we need to see that, according to Romans 8:23, says John Paul, "the 'redemption of the body' also has a 'cosmic' dimension (with respect to the whole of creation), but at its center stands man: man constituted in the personal unity of spirit and body" (*MWTB*, 52.1). In this light we must understand that all creation (i.e., nature, culture, history, society) is fallen through original sin. Says John Paul, as a consequence of the fall, "man ... was deprived of the supernatural and preternatural gifts that were part of his 'endowment' before sin; in addition, he suffered damage in what belongs to nature itself, to humanity in the original fullness 'of the image of God'" (*MWTB*, 27.2). In other words, human nature as a whole has lost its original harmony, and man is wounded at the very root of his being, estranged from God, from himself, and from his fellow man. His humanity exhibits the marks of being sinful, prone to sin, with sin being a violation of God's will and purpose. This sinfulness denies God's thesis and has its beginnings in Genesis 3. God's response to man's sin is *Yes*, but also *No*. *Yes*, because God, full of love, mercy and grace, does not abandon the fallen creation. Indeed, Genesis 3:15 contains the first proclamation of the Messiah, the *proto-evangelium*. But also *No*, because God, judging man in the light of His perfect justice and holiness is the author of the antithesis, of the sign of contradiction between good and evil, between the seed of the woman and the seed of the serpent., between the Word and the anti-Word, as the pope says elsewhere. "Here, in the third chapter of Genesis, at the very beginning of the bible, it becomes clear that the history of mankind, and with it the history of the world with which man is united through the work of divine creation, will both be subject to rule by the Word and the anti-Word, the Gospel and the anti-Gospel."[61]

In particular, the antithesis between the Gospel and the anti-Gospel is felt in the "spousal meaning of the body": man and wife were intended by God to become "two in one flesh," but this meaning has been distorted and debased by sin, resulting in lust and concupiscence, male domination of women, inter-personal hostility between male and female. "By violating the dimension of the mutual gift of the man and the woman, concupiscence also casts doubt on the fact that each of them is willed by the Creator 'for himself'. The subjectivity of the person gives way in some

---

61. Wojtyla/John Paul II, *Sign of Contradiction*, 29. For an analysis of the key themes of this book, see my article, "Living Truth for a Post-Christian World."

sense to the objectivity of the body. Because of the body, man becomes an object for man: the female for the male and vice versa. Concupiscence signifies, so to speak, that the personal relations of man and woman are one-sidedly and reductively tied to the body and to sex, in the sense that these relations become almost incapable of welcoming the reciprocal gift of the person" (*MWTB*, 32.5). In sum, concupiscence is the inclination or desire to sin found in fallen man as a result of original or inherited sin.

According to the *Catechism of the Catholic Church*, "Etymologically, 'concupiscence' can refer to any intense form of human desire. Christian theology has given it a particular meaning: the movement of the sensitive appetite contrary to the operation of the human reason. The apostle St. Paul identifies it with the rebellion of the 'flesh' against the "spirit" [see Gal 5:16, 17, 24; Eph 2:3]. Concupiscence stems from the disobedience of the first sin. It unsettles man's moral faculties and, without being in itself an offense, inclines man to commit sins."[62] It is precisely this concupiscence, adds William Kurz, that is "the most extreme rejection of God's design [which] comes in the newly contrived circumstance of state-sanctioned male-male and female-female 'marriages.'"[63] Furthermore, as a consequence of sin, which is a fruit of man's becoming a covenant breaker with God in the human heart, a threefold concupiscence takes hold of man. The heart in its biblical sense is the root and center of our whole human existence, in other words, the whole man. Says Wojtyla, "The 'heart' is the dimension of humanity with which the sense of the meaning of the human body, and the order of this sense, is directly linked" (*MWTB*, 25.2).

The heart is, in the words of the *Catechism of the Catholic Church*, "the depth of one's being, where the person decides for or against God." "The heart is the dwelling-place where I am, where I live; according to the Semitic or biblical expression, the heart is the place 'to which I withdraw.' The heart is the hidden center, beyond the grasp of our reason and of others; only the Spirit of God can fathom the human heart and know it fully. The heart is the place of decision, deeper than our psychic drives. It is the place of truth, where we choose life or death. It is the place of encounter, because as image of God we live in relation: it is the place of covenant . . . relationship between God and man in Christ."[64] Concretely speak-

---

62. *Catechism of the Catholic Church*, no. 2515.
63. Kurz, "Scriptural Foundations of *The Theology of the Body*," 40.
64. *Catechism of the Catholic Church*, nos. 2563–64.

ing, then, man's concupiscence is expressed in a three-fold way: "All that is in the world, the concupiscence of the flesh, the concupiscence of the eyes, and the pride of life, comes not from the Father but from the world" (1 John 2:16-17). Given the heart's fundamental core meaning, we can understand why "Concupiscence is to be explained as a lack, however, that plunges its roots into the original depth of the human spirit" (*MWTB*, 27.2). The man of concupiscence reveals "a certain constitutive fracture in the human person's interiority, *a breakup, as it were, of man's original spiritual and somatic unity*" (*MWTB*, 28.3).

Indeed, the man of concupiscence is no longer integrated within himself; his body does not express his reality as a person, something which is fundamental to the meaning of the acting person *qua person*. Consequently, because he is no longer in integral self-possession and self-dominion, he has difficulty not only identifying himself with his own body, or better, his own personal subjectivity, but also he is unable to relate to the subjectivity of the other human being in conformity with God's original plan of creation, and hence his very humanity is threatened. Still, the normativity of God's good creation "in some measure continue[s] to permeate and shape the love born in the human heart. The spousal meaning of the body has not become totally foreign to that heart; *it has not been totally suffocated in it by concupiscence, but only habitually threatened*." The pope adds, "That *reciprocal communion in humanity itself through the body* and through its masculinity and femininity, which had such a strong echo in the earlier passage of the Yahwist narrative (see Gen 2:23-25), *is overturned* at this moment, as if the body in its masculinity and femininity ceased to be 'free from suspicion' as the substratum of the communion of persons, as if its original function were 'called into doubt' in the consciousness of the man and the woman" (*MWTB*, 29.2; see also 29.4 and 32.1). Eloquently, the pope expresses his conviction, "The 'heart' has become a battlefield between love and concupiscence. The more concupiscence dominates the heart, the less the heart experiences the spousal meaning of the body, and the less sensitive it becomes to the gift of the person that expresses precisely this meaning in the reciprocal relations of man and woman" (*MWTB*, 32.3).

In this connection, the pope reminds us that the theology of the body is not just a theory, but rather a specific "evangelical pedagogy of the body" (*MWTB*, 122.5), helping us to overcome concupiscence. In other words, says the pope, "in its theological essence, the evangelical and

Christian ethos [of the theology of the body] is *the ethos of redemption
. . . even better, an ethos of the redemption of the body*. Redemption becomes at the same time the basis for understanding the particular dignity of the human body, which is rooted in the personal dignity of man and woman. The reason for this dignity is precisely what stands at the root of the indissolubility of the conjugal covenant" (*MWTB*, 100.3). This ethos of redemption takes root in the heart of every man, male and female, exhorting them to gain mastery over concupiscence. In this connection, John Paul refers us to Christ's statement in the Sermon on the Mount regarding "purity of heart," which "signifies being free from *every kind* of sin or guilt, not only from the sins that concern the 'concupiscence of the flesh'" (*MWTB*, 58.4).[65] Still, John Paul focuses on "one of the aspects of that 'purity', namely, the contrary of adultery 'committed in the heart'" (ibid.).

> Hence the question: what truth valid for every human being is contained in Christ's words [regarding "purity of heart"]? We must answer that what is contained in them is *not only an ethical truth, but also* the essential truth about man, *the anthropological truth*. This is precisely the reason why we return to these words in formulating the theology of the body, in strict relation with, and so to speak, in the perspective of, the earlier words in which Christ appealed to the "beginning." One can affirm that with this expressive evangelical eloquence these words recall the man of original innocence to the conscience of the man of concupiscence. Yet, Christ's words are realistic. They do not attempt to make the human heart return to the state of original innocence, which man left behind in the moment in which he committed the original sin; rather, they point out to him *the path toward a purity of heart* that *is possible and accessible* for him even in the state of hereditary sinfulness [original sin]. It is the purity of the "man of concupiscence," who is nevertheless inspired by the word of the Gospel and open to "life according to the Spirit" (in conformity with St. Paul's words), that is, the purity of the man of concupiscence who is completely enveloped by the "redemption of the body" achieved by Christ. This is precisely why we find in the words of the Sermon of the Mount

---

65. Given John Paul's claim in this quote, then, Luke Timothy Johnson is mistaken in his charge that the pope "leaves the impression that Matthew's 'blessed are the pure of heart' (5:8) refers to chastity, when in fact he knows very well that the beatitude does not have that restricted sense" ("A Disembodied 'Theology of the Body': John Paul II on love, sex and pleasure"). In short, the pope does not do what Johnson alleges.

the appeal to the "heart," that is, to the inner man. The inner man must open himself to life according to the Spirit, in order to share in the evangelical purity of heart: in order to find again and realize the value of the body, freed by redemption from the bonds of concupiscence. *The normative meaning of Christ's words is deeply rooted in their anthropological meaning, in the dimension of human interiority.* (*MWTB*, 58.5; italics added to last sentence)

Intriguingly, the pope asks whether we should distrust the heart of man. Is the "heart" under total suspicion? Do Christ's words in the Sermon on the Mount (Matt 5:27–28) simply accuse the human heart of the concupiscence of the flesh? Should Christians be "masters of suspicion" like Freud, Marx, and Nietzsche? Should we just add "concupiscence" to the trio of sex-economics-power that is the "hidden basis and the orientation of each [of these masters] in understanding and interpreting the *humanum* itself [?]" John Paul replies in a passage that repays meditation:

It seems necessary to take at least a brief look at this basis and orientation. We should do so to discover, on the one hand, a significant convergence with, and, *on the other hand, also* a fundamental *divergence* from, the hermeneutics that has its source in the Bible and that we are attempting to express in our analyses. In what does the convergence consist? It consists in the fact that the thinkers mentioned above [Freud, Marx, and Nietzsche], who have exercised and still exercise a great influence on the way of thinking and evaluating of people of our time, seem in substance also to judge and accuse the human "heart." Even more, they seem to judge and accuse it *due to what* biblical language, especially Johannine language, *calls concupiscence, the threefold concupiscence*. One could distribute the roles as follows. In Nietzschean hermeneutics, the judgment and the accusation of the human heart correspond in some way to what biblical language calls "pride of life"; in Marxist hermeneutics to what it calls "concupiscence of the eyes"; in Freudian hermeneutics, by contrast, to what it calls "concupiscence of the flesh." The convergence of these conceptions with the hermeneutics of man based on the Bible consists in the fact that when we uncovered the threefold concupiscence in the human heart, we too could have limited ourselves to putting this heart in a state of continual suspicion. *Yet the Bible does not allow us to stop here. Although Christ's words in Matthew 5:27–28 show the whole reality of desire and concupiscence, they do not allow us to turn such concupiscence into the absolute principle of anthropology and ethics or into the very nucleus of the hermeneutics of man* [italics added]. *In the Bible the threefold concupiscence does not constitute the fundamental* and certainly not the only absolute *criterion* of anthropology and ethics, although it is without doubt *an important coefficient for understanding man, his actions*, and their *moral value*. (*MWTB*, 46.1.2; italics added)

This passage raises the fundamental question regarding the basis of a Christian hermeneutics of anthropology and ethics. If such a hermeneutics does *not* stop at the accusation of the human heart, casting it into a state of continual suspicion, what then is the fundamental and absolute criterion of anthropology and ethics? In reply to this question, John Paul says that "the human 'heart' is not so much 'accused and condemned' by Christ because of concupiscence (*concupiscentia* carnis [the concupiscence of the flesh], but first of all 'called'" (*MWTB*, 107.1). In other words, "*God calls man first.*"[66] That is, "Although man can forget God or reject him, He never ceases to call every man to seek him, so as to find life and happiness."[67] A Christian hermeneutics appeals, therefore, to the heart of man that in the very deep-structure of his created humanity still bears witness to "*the original power* (and thus also the [common] grace) *of the mystery of creation.*"[68] "This concerns the very 'nature,' the very substrate

66. *Catechism of the Catholic Church*, no. 2567.
67. Ibid., no. 30.
68. I'm distinguishing here between the common grace of creation and the particular (or special) grace of redemption: the former is a restraining grace, which holds back and blocks the effect of sin; the latter is a saving grace, which reconciles God and man, and which in the end abolishes sin and completely undoes its consequences in and through the whole creation. I'm appealing here to Abraham Kuyper's notion of common grace in order to make the pope's point clearer. Abraham Kuyper gives the first constructive theological analysis of the Reformed doctrine of common grace in his three volume work, *De Gemeene Gratie* ["Common Grace"]—published 1902, 1903, and 1904, respectively by Höveker & Wormser in Amsterdam. For selections from these volumes, see *Abraham Kuyper: A Centennial Reader*, "Common Grace," 165–201. These two forms of grace, special and common grace, have a common origin in Christ, which Abraham Kuyper explains as follows. "If we consult Scripture we will find it clearly spelled out that the . . . the self-same Christ is simultaneously two things: the root of the life of creation as well as the root of the life of the new creation. First we read that Christ is "the first-born of all creation, for in him all things were created, in heaven and on earth," so that he is "before all things and in him all things hold together" [Colossians 1:15–17]. It could hardly be stated more plainly and clearly that Christ is the root of the creation and therefore of common grace, for it is common grace that prevents things from sinking into nothingness. (Does not the text say that all things *hold together* in him?) But we immediately note in the second place that the same Christ is "the *Head of the Body* and the first-born from the dead" [Colossians 1:18], hence also the root of the life of the new creation or

of the humanity of the person, the deepest impulses of the 'heart.' Does man not sense, together with concupiscence, a deep need to preserve the dignity of the reciprocal relations that find their expression in the body thanks to its masculinity and femininity? Does he not feel the need to impregnate them with everything that is noble and beautiful? Does he not feel the need to confer on them the supreme value, which is love" (*MWTB*, 46.5; see also, 46.4)? An affirmative answer to these questions bears witness to the normative power of creation. Says John Paul, "Here we find a decisive divergence between the anthropology (or anthropological hermeneutics) of the Gospel and some influential representatives of the contemporary hermeneutics of man ([Marx-Nietzsche-Freud] the so-called masters of suspicion)" (*MWTB*, 107.1).

Yet there is more: we must make an appeal to the heart of man such that he knows himself called by God "to rediscover, or even better, to realize, the spousal meaning of the body and to express in this way the interior freedom of the gift, that is, the freedom of that spiritual state and power that derives from mastery over the concupiscence of the flesh." And that appeal to rediscover the meaning of the whole of existence, of the meaning of life, including the spousal meaning of the body, draws its very power from the ethos of redemption, namely, from the Pauline "redemption of the body" (Rom 8: 23), which testifies to *the power* (that is, the [saving] grace) *of the mystery of redemption*." Says the pope, "Redemption is a truth, a reality, in the name of which man must feel himself called, and

---

special grace. The two things are even stated in parallel terms: he is the root of common grace for he is *the first born of all creation* [v. 15], and simultaneously the root of special grace, for he the *first-born from the dead* [v. 18]. There is thus no doubt whatever that common grace and special grace come most intimately connected from their origin, and this connection lies in Christ" (*Abraham Kuyper*, 186–87 [*De Gemeene Gratie*, 2:645; see also 183]). I am reminded here of John Paul II who in his 1998 Encyclical Letter, *Fides et Ratio*, makes a similar point about the selfsame Christ. "The unity of truth is a fundamental premise of human reasoning, as the principle of non-contradiction makes clear. Revelation renders this unity certain, showing that the God of creation is also the God of salvation history. It is the one and the same God who establishes and guarantees the intelligibility and reasonableness of the natural order of things ... and who reveals himself as the Father of our Lord Jesus Christ. This unity of truth, natural and revealed, is embodied in a living and personal way in Christ, as the Apostle [Paul] reminds us: 'Truth is in Jesus' (cf. Eph 4:21; Col 1:15–20). He is the *eternal Word* in whom all things were created, and he is the *incarnate Word* who in his entire person reveals the Father (cf. John 1:14, 18). ... [W]hat is revealed in him is 'the full truth' (cf. John 1:14–16) of everything which was created in him and through him and which therefore in him finds its fulfillment (cf. Col 1:17)" (no. 34).

'called with effectiveness.' He must become aware of this call [by faith] in Christ's words." "So faith comes from hearing, and hearing through the word of Christ" (Rom 10:17). This Christian hermeneutics is the antithesis of the "hermeneutics of suspicion." For it is only through the redemption won by Christ that these effects of sin can be overcome and that man can realize his humanity in accordance with God's original plan of creation.

> Such a *hermeneutics* [of suspicion] is very different; *it is radically different* from the one we discover *in Christ's words* in the Sermon on the Mount. These words bring to light not only another ethos, but also another vision of man's possibilities. It is important that precisely in his 'heart' he does not feel himself irrevocably accused and given up to the concupiscence of the flesh, but that in the same heart he feels himself called with energy. Called precisely to this supreme value, which is love. Called as a person in the truth of his humanity, and thus also in the truth of his masculinity and femininity, in the truth of his body. Called in that truth which has been his inheritance "of the beginning," the inheritance of his heart, which is deeper than the sinfulness inherited [original sin], deeper than the threefold concupiscence. Christ's words, set in the whole reality of creation and redemption, re-activate that deepest inheritance and give it real power in human life. (*MWTB*, 46.6)

Significantly, the pope refers us back to God's original plan of creation in order to understand the nature and extent of historical man's fallen nature. "*Thus, historical man is rooted, so to speak, in his revealed theological prehistory* [man's original state of innocence]; and for this reason, every point of his historical sinfulness must be explained (both in the case of the soul and of the body) with reference to original innocence . . . While in every historical man this sin signifies a state of lost grace, it also carries with itself a reference to that grace, which was precisely the grace of original innocence." Two implications follow from using the order of creation as the prism through which we should understand fallen man as he actually and historically is.

The first implication: the fallen human condition has not overcome the goodness of creation. The grace of redemption opposes man's sinfulness, not the created body of man, and hence ontological evil is not constitutive of the human body. Man's sinfulness, and hence his need for the redemption of the body, pertains to that which "*he lost, among other things, the clear sense of the spousal meaning of the body*, in which the interior dominion and freedom of the spirit expresses itself" (*MWTB*, 45.2). Thus: the light of God the Creator shines in the darkness, and the darkness has not overcome it (cf. John 1:5). Hence, says the pope, "It is all the more necessary, however, to penetrate deeply into the mysterious structure, theological and at the same time anthropological, of this 'beginning.' In fact, in the whole perspective of his own 'history', man will not fail to confer a spousal meaning on his own body. Even if this meaning does undergo and will undergo many distortions, *it will always remain the deepest level, which demands that it be revealed in all its simplicity and purity and manifested in its whole truth as a sign of the 'image of God.'* Here we also find the road that goes from the mystery of creation to the 'redemption of the body'" (*MWTB*, 15.5). This last point is fundamental to understanding an essential continuity in man and a link between creation, sin, and redemption. "The Christian ethos [worldview] is characterized by a *transformation of the human person's conscience and attitudes,* both the man's and the woman's, *such as to express and realize the value of the body and of sex* according to the Creator's original plan, placed as they are at the service of the 'communion of persons,' which is the deepest substratum of human ethics and culture" (*MWTB*, 45.3).

Second, Christ refers us to the normative order of creation, and hence the redemption of man "must consist in *retrieving [man's] dignity,* in which the true meaning of the human body, its meaning as personal and 'of communion,'" namely, the spousal meaning of the body, of the reciprocal self-gift of the persons-in-communion, which fully unfolds the hermeneutics of the gift in the conjugal act.

Now, we come to third point regarding the relation between nature, sin and grace, and the key idea that grace restores or renews nature. Central to nature's restoration or renewal, says John Paul is that "Man must rediscover the lost fullness of his humanity" (*MWTB*, 44.1). "In the Sermon on the Mount," the pope adds, Christ does not invite man to return to the state of original innocence, because humanity has left it irrevocably behind, but *he calls him to find*—on the foundation of the perennial and, one might say, indestructible meanings of what is 'human'—the *living forms of the 'new man.'* In this way a connection is formed, even continuity, between the 'beginning' and the perspective of redemption. In the ethos of the redemption of the body, the original ethos of creation was to be taken up anew" (*MWTB*, 49.4). The Redemption of life accomplished through the mystery of the Incarnation and Christ's finished work—His life, passion, death, resurrection, and ascension—abrogate the antithesis between sin and creation. Put differently, the Incarnation, Passion, and Resurrection in Jesus Christ means that his grace restores an original good creation. God's original thesis is reasserted and reestablished, but also, as John Paul II asserts in the above quote, enriched, fulfilled, and perfected. This Redemption restores the very heart of human nature, causing the rebirth of the human self in Christ (Col 2:13; 2 Cor 5:17). "Christ alone, through his humanity, reveals the totality of the mystery of man ... The key to his self-understanding lies in contemplating the divine Prototype, the Word made flesh, the eternal Son of the Father." "Without the Gospel," John Paul adds, "man remains a dramatic question with no adequate answer. The correct response to the question about man is Christ, *Redemptor Hominis*."[69] This rebirth manifests itself in the integral redemption of the whole man in Christ through the fellowship of the Father, Son and Holy Spirit, and with one another in them, which has been given to us in grace (Rom 5:5). Indeed, says the pope, Paul sees the "redemption of the body" (Rom 8:23) "in *an anthropological*, and simultaneously *a cosmic, dimension*." "The whole visible creation," in the pope's words, "the whole cosmos, carries the effects of man's sin" (*MWTB*, 86.1).

Thus, the redemption in Christ becomes a vision of cosmic redemption for the whole creation, including the life of culture. Indeed, God's grace in Christ *restores all life to its fullness, penetrating and perfecting and transforming the fallen creation from within its own order*, bringing creation into conformity with His will and purpose.[70] In this temporal life there is substantial healing ("the first fruits of the Spirit") because the redemption of the body has already been completed in Christ. "In him, the *hope* in which 'we were saved' has been *confirmed*." "At the same time," John Paul adds, "that hope *has been re-opened anew* to its definitive eschatological fulfillment." This renewal is ongoing because it is caught in the eschatological tension between the present ("the now") and future ("not yet") dimensions of the Kingdom of God until its culminating fullness at the end of time. "'The revelation of the sons of God' in Christ has been definitively directed toward that 'freedom and glory' that is to be definitively shared in by the 'children of God'" (see Rom 8:19–21) (see *MWTB*, 86.3).

---

69. John Paul II, *Memory and Identity*, 110, 114.

70. Portions of these three paragraphs were originally published in my article, "Living Truth for a Post-Christian World."

Now, however briefly, in order to do justice to the complexity of the pope's theology of the body in the context of creation/fall/redemption/consummation, I must bring out the essential elements of his subtle theological discourse on the eschatological meaning of the "redemption of the body." With the *Compendium of the Social Doctrine of the Church*, I will speak here of an "*eschatological relativity*, in the sense that man and the world are moving towards their end, which is the fulfillment of their destiny in God."[71]

How, then, are we to think of the order of creation that is redemptively reaffirmed in the cross and resurrection of Jesus Christ when set in an eschatological horizon? More to the point, how does John Paul II understand the redemption of the body in the light of that horizon? Does appealing to the order of creation for determining what is "natural," that is, creationally given, in other words, need qualification in light of the "new creation," of the redemption of the body, realized by the Resurrection of Jesus Christ (*MWTB*, 66.5) and consummated in the eschatological drama of redemption? John Paul II set the stage for his answer to this question in the following,

> One can say that St. Paul sees the future resurrection as a certain *restitutio in integrum*, that is, as the reintegration and at the same time as the attainment of the fullness of humanity. It is not only a restitution, because in this case the resurrection would be, in a certain sense, a return to the state the soul shared in before sin, outside the knowledge of good and evil (see Gen 1–2). Yet, such a return does not correspond to the inner logic of the whole economy of salvation, to the deepest meaning of the mystery of redemption. *Restitutio in integrum*, linked with the resurrection and the [eschatological] reality of the "other world," can only be *an introduction to a new fullness*. It will be a fullness that presupposes man's whole history, formed by the drama of the tree of the knowledge of good and evil (see Gen 3) and at the same time permeated by the mystery of redemption. (*MWTB*, 72.3)

What, then, is that reintegration as well as the attainment of the fullness of humanity in the eschatological drama of redemption? Fundamental to the pope's answer to this question is the Church's teaching that the whole person will be transformed by the resurrection. John Paul distinguishes his own Thomistic position on this teaching from Platonism. "In

---

71. *Compendium of the Social Doctrine of the Church*, no. 48.

Creation, Fall, Redemption, and Fulfillment   237

fact, the resurrection attests, at least indirectly, that in the whole of the human composite, the body is not, contrary to Plato, only temporarily linked with the soul (as its earthly 'prison,' as Plato maintained), but that together with the soul it constitutes the unity and integrity of the human being." Therefore, the pope adds, "the truth about the resurrection clearly affirms that man's eschatological perfection and happiness cannot be understood as a state of the soul alone, separated (according to Plato, liberated) from the body, but must be understood as *the definitively and perfectly 'integrated' state of man* brought about by such a union of the soul with the body that it definitively qualifies and assures this perfect integrity" (*MWTB*, 66.6).

Against this background, the pope distinguishes two features of the fullness of humanity in the eschatological drama. On the one hand, the redemption of the body, which already has taken root in the man who belongs to Christ, will perfect bodiliness, that is, says John Paul, "the meaning of being male or female in the body." But the fullness of humanity, on the other hand, "will be *constituted and understood differently* in the 'other world' than it had been 'from the beginning' and then in its whole earthly dimension" (*MWTB*, 66.4).

In connection with the reality of the "other world," the pope is referring to the passage in the three Synoptic Gospels where Jesus is speaking to the Sadducees about the resurrection conforming to the power of the living God. For instance, "When they rise from the dead, they take neither wife nor husband" (Mark 12:25). The biblical teaching, John Paul says, holds that marriage and procreation do not constitute man's eschatological future. As the pope puts it, "In the [future] resurrection [of the body] they [marriage and procreation] lose, so to speak, their *raison d'etre*.... The words 'neither wife nor husband' [Luke 20:35] ... allows us to deduce that the dimension of masculinity and femininity—that is, being male and female in the body—will be newly constituted in the resurrection of the body in that 'other world'" (*MWTB*, 66.4).

Furthermore, the pope adds, we cannot speak of resurrection unless there is an identity of a psychosomatic nature between the man who existed at some point in the past and his resurrected body. "If it were otherwise, it would be meaningless to speak about the resurrection" (*MWTB*, 66.5). Moreover, "Resurrection means restoration to the true life of human bodiliness, which was subjected to death in its temporal phase.... One must suppose that in the resurrection ... [there is not a] disincarnation of man, but [rather a] spiritualization of his somatic nature, that is, by another 'system of powers' within man. The resurrection signifies a new submission of the body to the spirit" (*MWTB*, 56.4). What, then, does John Paul mean by the "spiritualization" of the body if not the transformation of man's nature into a loss of bodiliness rather than its perfection?

Now, spiritualization means "not only that the spirit will master the body," but, the pope says, "that *it will also fully permeate the body and the powers of the spirit will permeate the energies of the body*" (*MWTB*, 67.1). In addition, "This new spiritualization will thus be a *fruit of grace*, that is, *of God's self-communication in his very divinity*, not only to the soul, but *to the whole of man's psychosomatic subjectivity*" (*MWTB*, 67.3). In other words, spiritualization signifies the fullness of grace transforming the whole man from within in a definitively and perfectly integrated state of being. Says John Paul II, it is "a new formation of man's entire personal subjectivity according to the measure of union with God in his trinitarian mystery and of intimacy with him in the perfect communion of persons" (*MWTB*, 67.3; see also 68.2.3).

This conclusion brings us back to the question as to how the one-flesh communion of marriage will endure and be perfected within the greater one-flesh communion of the blessed in and with Trinitarian communion, Father, Son and Holy Spirit? In other words, the one-flesh communion of marriage, conjugal, procreative and generative, does not endure forever within the limits of the whole earthly dimension. How then will it endure without these limits in the resurrection of the body? I'll let the pope's answer to this question conclude this chapter.

> We should think of the reality of the "other world" in the categories of the rediscovery of a new, perfect subjectivity of each person and at the same time of the *rediscovery* of a new, *perfect intersubjectivity of all*. In this way this reality means the true and definitive fulfillment of human subjectivity and, on this basis, the definitive fulfillment of the "spousal" meaning of the body. The total concentration of created, redeemed, and glorified subjectivity on God himself will not take man away from this fulfillment, but—on the contrary—will introduce him into it and consolidates him in it. One can say, finally, that in this way the eschatological reality will become the source of the perfect realization of the "trinitarian order" in the created world of persons. (*MWTB*, 68.4)

6

The Theology of the Body and Homosexuality

SEX, THE BODY, AND HOMOSEXUALITY

IN THIS CHAPTER, I will draw out the normative implications of John Paul II's theology of the body for sexual ethics, particularly the ethics of homosexuality. I begin by presenting a composite portrait of the Church's most recent teaching about homosexuality: a synthesis from several sources, namely, the two major documents of the Congregation for the Doctrine of the Faith (CDF), *Persona Humana* (1975) and *Homosexualitatis problema* (1986),[1] the *Catechism of the Catholic Church* and, of course, John Paul's theology of the body. His theology is a further deepening and enrichment of the Church's theology of creation, anthropology, and sexual ethics. I shall make clear his theology's implicit critique of homosexuality, especially the normative implications of the pope's anthropological, as well as, theological claim that the body expresses or reveals the person.

John Paul's theology of the body is central to understanding the basic issues in sexual ethics, in my judgment, because that theology emphasizes the bodily nature of the human person, meaning thereby that the body is intrinsic to human beings as bodily persons.[2] Given that my body is intrinsic to myself, there is a unitary activity such that, as the pope says, "[t]he *person, including the body, is completely entrusted to himself,*

---

1. These documents have a different English title: the former is *Declaration on Certain Questions Concerning Sexual Ethics*; the latter is *Letter to Bishops of the Catholic Church on the Pastoral Care of Homosexual Persons.*

2. I am immensely indebted to the writings of Germain Grisez, John Finnis, Robert George, and Patrick Lee in my theological and philosophical understanding that the human person is bodily and the development of that understanding for sexual ethics, in particular, regarding the ethics of homosexuality.

and it is in the unity of body and soul that the person is the subject of his own moral acts."[3] In short, since the human person is bodily, then sexual moral choices are exercised in and through an act in which my bodily "activity is as much the constitutive subject of what one does as one's act of choice is."[4] Therefore, in light of the theology of the body, I will argue that in order for a sexual act to be morally right, the person's integrity, namely, the intrinsic good of self-integration, must be respected. That is, the sexuality of the person must be integrated with the person as a whole, meaning thereby thus "the inner unity of man in his bodily and spiritual being,"[5] so that the bodily union of sexual intercourse, of the mutual gift of a man and a woman, will be a communion of persons, as marital intercourse is. Real bodily union is a necessary but not sufficient condition to bring about that communion; what is also needed is "marital consent which conjugal intercourse fulfills."[6] Otherwise, sexual immorality—and all non-marital sexual acts, especially but not only homosexual acts, are morally wrong—involves in some way a self-*dis*integration, which is an alienation of the body from the consciously experiencing self, because the body is used as a mere instrument in the service of that self. By contrast, only marital sexual acts expressing marital union and procreative openness, according to John Paul, "recognize both the spiritual and corporal character of conjugal communion." He then adds: "In this way sexuality is respected and promoted in its truly and fully human dimension and is never 'used' as an 'object' that, by breaking the personal unity of soul and body, strikes at God's creation itself at the level of the deepest interaction of nature and person."[7]

Now, magisterial teaching regarding homosexuality has often been misunderstood even by its supporters,[8] or misrepresented, at times, by

---

3. John Paul II, *Veritatis Splendor*, no. 48.

4. Finnis, "Personal Integrity, Sexual Morality and Responsible Parenthood," 177.

5. *Catechism of the Catholic Church*, no. 2337.

6. Grisez, *Way of the Lord Jesus*, 2:651.

7. John Paul II, *Familiaris Consortio*, no. 32.

8. The most common misunderstanding is represented in, for example, the 1998 USCCB document, *Always Our Children*, A Pastoral Message to Parents of Homosexual Children and Suggestions for Pastoral Ministers. Twice the pastoral states that the homosexual condition is not sinful or immoral in itself, because it is not freely chosen. This leaves us with the impression that it is, therefore, morally neutral. But this is clearly not the case. For example, an infertile woman did not freely choose that condition, but no one suggests that infertility is a good. Similarly, the Church explicitly rejects the inference

those who do not expressly deny the Church's teaching about either homosexual tendencies or homosexual practice, but whose understanding of this teaching is such that they cannot consistently assert it. Representative of this misunderstanding, indeed, misrepresentation[9] is the statement ("Homosexuality and Sexual Orientation: Common Questions") by the "Core Council for Gay and Lesbian Students" at the University of Notre Dame. In reply to the question, "What does the Catholic Church say about homosexuality?" the Council replies: "Homosexual orientation in and of itself is morally neutral, but genital homosexual relations are sinful, in the same way that genital heterosexual relations outside marriage are immoral." There are several things wrong with this answer, according to the Church's teaching on homosexuality.

First, homosexual tendencies are not morally neutral, but rather objectively disordered, as such, because they incline a man to homosexual practice that is itself intrinsically immoral. Something can be bad in some sense other than being morally sinful, for instance, the condition of infertility, or being born blind, without it being something that is knowingly and explicitly chosen. Second, the claim that heterosexual and homosexual sexual relations are sinful *in the same way* because they manifest sins against chastity fails to recognize that homosexuality, unlike heterosexuality, is a fundamental problem because homosexual tendencies are objectively disordered. As two critics of the view represented by the Notre Dame Council recently wrote, "if homosexual activity itself is always intrinsically immoral, and homosexual tendencies are therefore always objectively disordered because they incline to what is always intrinsically immoral, then it makes good sense to say that his sexual affections, as such, are not good. They do not bear on the feminine, which is the target of mature male psychosexual desire."[10] Third, the Council is, therefore,

---

that the homosexual condition is morally neutral because it was not freely chosen; rather it states that the condition itself is objectively disordered because it inclines to what is always intrinsically wrong. The pastoral refrains from speaking of the condition itself as objectively disordered.

9. The website of the Core Council for Gay and Lesbian Students at the University of Notre Dame does not post magisterial documents of the Catholic Church's teaching on homosexuality, such as *Persona Humana* (1975), *Homosexualitatis problema* (1986), and the relevant paragraphs from the *Catechism of the Catholic Church* on sexual ethics (nos. 2331–2400). It only posts the 1998 document, *Always Our Children*s, as well as interpretations of that teaching. http://corecouncil.nd.edu/church_response/index.shtml.

10. Mansini and Welch "In Conformity to Christ."

mistaken in claiming that "the Church does not say that the *homosexual orientation* is wrong; rather, it is *sexual activity between same sex persons* that is 'objectively disordered' and therefore sinful." But this statement is inaccurate, giving us only a half-truth. Actually, the Church says that the source of objectively disordered homosexual activity is the homosexual condition that is itself therefore always objectively disordered because it inclines to what is always intrinsically immoral. And although the Notre Dame Council is right to insist that the homosexual inclination is not a disease, nonetheless, it is an objective disorder, a sexual deviance, as it were, because it is unable to meet the natural goods of sexuality, of the body-soul person's creational ordering to the sexual "other."[11]

So, to say that the condition itself is not sinful is not to say, or to imply, moral neutrality. Homosexual desires are wrong in the sense of not being good, and this is not the same thing as making a moral judgment about the personal moral guilt of an individual who engages in homosexual activity. He is morally blamable for such activity only if the act was freely and knowingly chosen. Furthermore, homosexual and heterosexual

---

11. Levering, "Knowing What is 'Natural,'" 135. According to Ashley and O'Rourke, "sexual deviances are to be distinguished from sexual dysfunctions in that the object or action in which sexual satisfaction is sought is abnormal" (*Health Care Ethics*, 389). Is the same-sex attraction narcissistic or self-deceptive because of "a desire for the essential sexual self that one shares in common with one's same-sex partner: males for essential maleness, females for essential femaleness" [?] According to Gagnon, "From a theological perspective, the core problem with any attempted homosexual bond is not merely that it is structurally incongruous. It is also, *by definition*, sexually narcissistic or at least sexually self-deceptive.... If one is conscious of being strongly aroused by the distinctive features of one's own sex, it is case of sexual narcissism. If one is not conscious of this sameness but thinks instead of a same-sex partner as completing what is lacking in one's own sex (probably the common scenario), then it is a case of sexual self-deception.... Notice here that I am not asserting that two or more persons in a homoerotic relationship can never exhibit genuine compassion toward one another. Such a claim would be absurd for virtually any proscribed form of human sexuality. Rather, *so far as the erotic dimension is concerned*, homoerotic desire is sexual narcissism or sexual self-deception. In a sexual bond between persons of the same sex, the extremes of one's sex are not moderated and true gaps are not filled. It is this reality that contributes markedly to the disproportionately high rate of problems associated with homosexual practice: high number of sex partners and high rates of sexually transmitted disease, especially among male homosexuals, as well as a dearth of long-term relationships and high incidence of major depression and substance abuse, especially among female homosexuals" ("Scriptural Perspectives on Homosexuality and Sexual Identity," 300). Gagnon provides the scientific sources for these claims in *Bible and Homosexual Practice*, 425–60, 471–85; idem., *Immoralism, Homosexual Unhealth, and Scripture*.

genital relations are not morally wrong *in the same way*, as if to say that those engaging in both types of relations have similarly failed to be chaste. This equates the problem of homosexuals and heterosexuals sexual activity, leaving us with the impression that the homosexual condition itself is not a moral problem in any sense whatsoever, which suggests parity between homosexuality and heterosexuality on the order of creation. But heterosexuality is not in itself objectively disordered because it does not incline, unlike homosexual tendencies, to intrinsically wrong sex acts. The orientation/act distinction implies, as it is used by the Notre Dame Council, that there exists parity between heterosexual and homosexual orientation on the order of creation, and the Church's teaching on human sexuality rejects that claim.

Still, the understanding expressed in the Notre Dame Council statement is taken by many to be the correct view of the Church's teaching. In reaction to this (mis)understanding, critics of the Church's teaching accuse the teaching of being inconsistent. For example, Andrew Sullivan claims that the Church is caught in a dilemma because she claims that the homosexual condition is morally neutral because it is not knowingly and freely chosen: "how [could] something that seemed to occur naturally . . . still be profoundly unnatural, and against the end of God's creation [?]" Regarding the condition in and of itself to be a creational given, such that homosexuality is a natural variety of sexuality, critics like Sullivan, Farley, Johnson, and others, then argue that the only way to be freed from this inconsistency is to regard homosexual activity itself as morally right.[12] Now, I shall argue that this view is profoundly wrong, not only about Church teaching, but also the morality of homosexual practice. So, it is important that we get this teaching right in order to deal with objections to that teaching. I will address six important objections that have been raised in criticism of the Church's teaching: five in this chapter and the last objection in a brief concluding chapter.

12. Sullivan, "Catholicism and Homosexuality," 317–19. This chapter is a short excerpt from Sullivan's book, *Virtually Normal*. See also, Farley, *Just Love*. I wish that theologians like Farley would give as much careful and sustained attention to magisterial Catholic teaching on sexual morality, particular John Paul II's theology of the body, as well as the writings of orthodox Catholic philosophers and theologians, such as G. Grisez, J. Finnis, R. George, P. Lee, W. May, J. E. Smith, et al., as she does to non-Christian thought and thinkers. Rather, what I find in Farley's book is passing critical remarks on Catholic thought with no sustained effort to understand it or respond to its exceptionally articulate defenders.

First, some critics of the normative significance of humanity's sexual difference in creation, after the fall, in redemption, and in the eschaton, argue that, as James Olthuis says, "the ethical quality of a same-sex relationship, rather than the gender of its participants, be the morally decisive factor."[13] This, too, is Luke Timothy Johnson's position. Johnson's objection to connecting homosexuality to porneia, that is, sexual immorality, presupposes an understanding of the body's place such that "the moral quality of sexual behavior is not defined biologically in terms of the use of certain body parts." Rather, it is defined, he suggests, in terms of personal commitment and attitudes."[14] This view raises several questions. By assuming the insignificance of sexual difference for making a sexual act morally right, does this view fail to grasp the unified totality that is the body-person and hence the human meaning of the body?[15] Does the view Olthuis and Johnson represent do justice to the embodiment of human persons as man and woman and hence to sexual differences between them? Does it properly express the intrinsic place of the body in interpersonal unity or does the body remain extrinsic to personhood? If the later, does that view satisfactorily deal with the human meaning as well as moral status of the human body?

Second, some critics have raised the so-called "sterility objection" against the Church's teaching. They argue that same-sex relations are similar to a sterile heterosexual marriage inasmuch as both are not open to procreation, and hence, since the latter lacks pro-creative potential, this analogy justifies the moral character of homosexual love and mutual self-giving. Stephen Macedo argues this point: "If there is no possibility of procreation, then sterile couples are, like homosexuals, incapable of sex acts 'open to procreation.' What is the point of sex in an infertile marriage? Not procreation; the partners (let us assume) know that they are infertile. If they have sex, it is for pleasure and to express their love, or friendship, or some other shared good. It will be for precisely the same reasons that committed, loving gay couples have sex. Why are these good reasons for sterile or elderly married couples but not for gay and lesbian couples?"[16]

13. Olthuis, "When is Sex Against Nature?" 201.

14. Johnson, "Debate & Discernment."

15. John Paul II, *Veritatis Splendor*, no. 50.

16. Stephen Macedo, "Homosexuality and the Conservative Mind," as cited in Lee and George, *Body-Self Dualism*, 198. See also, Matthews, *Body in Context, Sex and Catholicism*, 161–62.

Is this a good analogy? What are the significant points of difference between these analogates such that they render arguments like Macedo's invalid?

Third, other critics argue that the Church's teaching is inherently contradictory in not recognizing the homosexual condition as a natural condition. Arguing that the Church teaches that the homosexual condition is not chosen, that individuals in that condition are morally blameless, that this condition is unalterable and thus constitutive of their emotional and sexual identity, they ask how these individuals can be blamed for acting on that condition. The Church seems to be pulling us in two directions at the same time—or so at least the objector claims. But we'll need to ask whether the Church actually teaches that same-sex attraction is natural, meaning thereby a creational given. In responding to this question, I shall criticize the root assumption of this objection, namely, that Scripture's condemnation of homosexuality pertains only to outward acts rather than to the inward condition, to homosexual actions rather than to the homosexual condition itself. This assumption is biblically untenable since, according to the Scriptures, it is not only actions that are wrong, but also the desire to do such actions (see Matt 5:27–29; Rom 13:14; Col 3:5–6; 1 Pet 2:11).[17] I will also criticize the logical corollary of this assumption, namely, that homosexuality is a normal variant of sexuality, in accord with the creation order rather a disordered relationship resulting from the fall.

Fourth, the Church teaches that the individual in a homosexual condition is a person of dignity as such, created in God's image, and that he should be shown respect, compassion, and sensitivity.[18] But if my sexual identity is constituted by the homosexual inclination itself, and hence it is at the core of my personal identity, as these critics of the Church's position claim, how then can my dignity be honored if that inclination or condition is objectively disordered, and is regarded as an objective evil? Isn't then the affirmation of being in God's image just an abstraction that is undercut, as one objector put it, "if not by logic, then by psychological experience [?]."[19] This objection raises the general question: does my fallen human nature undercut the *imago Dei* and, if so, in what sense? Put differ-

---

17. For example, says the *Catechism of the Catholic Church*, "Christ condemns even adultery of mere desire" (no. 2380).

18. Ibid., no. 2358.

19. Pope, "Vatican's Blunt Instrument."

ently, how are we to understand the central question of man's humanity *in* his sinfulness? Does the Fall literally dehumanize man, depriving him of his essential nature?

Fifth, I will answer Luke Timothy Johnson objection to the Church's teaching on creation order and sexual ethics regarding that teaching's alleged essentialism. This objection amounts to doubting whether we can take the order of creation to be an ethical norm. What is taken to be "natural" is often just a cultural construction, he says, and must always be challenged on the basis of actual human experience. The chief objection here is that the Church does not take seriously the historical and cultural construction of gendered and bodily realities, and hence of human nature, but rather grounds them in biology, claiming a creational complementarity, which includes a biological complementarity, between a man and a woman. This objection raises the question of whether human nature as such is changing and, if so, in what sense. Furthermore, to say the least, isn't a union of complements, the union of a man and a woman, founded in that one function in which the male and the female are not complete, namely, reproduction? As Lee and George argue, "In reproductive activity the bodily parts of the male and the bodily parts of the female participate in a single action, coitus, which is oriented to reproduction (though not every act of coitus actually reproduces), so that the subject of the action is the male and the female as a biological unity. Coitus is a unitary action in which the male and the female become really biologically one. In marital intercourse, this bodily unity is an aspect of, the biological matrix of, the couple's more comprehensive, marital communion."[20] Doesn't the denial of this literal biological, and thus personal, unit imply either a resurrection of ancient Gnosticism in its common denial of the created order[21] or the reduction of that biological matrix to a difference between the male and the female that is merely biological and not really personal, a reduction that fails to grasp the specifically human meaning of the body?[22] But is either alternative consistent with the bodily nature of the human person? Moreover, is Johnson right that making judgments about what is "natural"

---

20. Lee and George, *Body-Self Dualism*, 182–83.

21. The charge of Gnosticism, or a "quasi-Manichaeism," is made against those theologians, such as Graham Ward, who hold to the insignificance of sexual difference for marriage by Christopher C. Roberts in his fine study, *Creation & Covenant*, 240.

22. John Paul II, *Veritatis Splendor*, no. 50.

from the "order of creation" is really a form of essentialism that doesn't take seriously actual human existence?[23]

Sixth, critics of the Church's pastoral practice in responding to self-professed homosexuals inside the Church, such as Dominican theologian Timothy Radcliffe, O.P., claim that the Church must be "with people where they are, not telling them where they ought to be."[24] "It is no good telling people that they should not be divorced or remarried or living with a partner or gay. We begin where they are now."[25] But then how does a person become virtuous? How does Radcliffe propose to help a person build a virtuous self? Moral choices are the fruit of complex histories, he says, and if the Church is to respect an individual's freedom to discover what is right, rather than telling him from a position of authority what he must do, Radcliffe adds, the Church must be prepared to enter into his life, accompanying him in his moral exploration, sharing what she knows in friendship.[26] "Even when Christian teaching seems clear and unambiguous," says Radcliffe, "we must still be prepared to enter into the complexity of people's lives as they struggle to discover what is right."[27] What is Fr. Radcliffe's pastoral aim for dealing with Catholics who reject the Church's teaching on sexual ethics, in particular, homosexuality? Does his pastoral proposal underestimate the seriousness of sin's power to enslave us and the power of the death and resurrection of Jesus Christ to liberate us from its stranglehold?

THE ETHICS OF SEX

A key to understanding Catholic sexual ethics is the truth that the human person is bodily.[28] On the bodily dimensions of a moral act, Farley is right in stating that the basic issue in sexual ethics "is the question of whether, or to what extent, our bodies provide a basis, or even small clues, for determining acceptable practices of human sexuality."[29] Gagnon's an-

---

23. Johnson, "Homosexuality & the Church."
24. Radcliffe, *What's the Point of Being a Christian?* 42.
25. Ibid.
26. Ibid., 39.
27. Ibid., 38.
28. Lee and George, "Sex and the Body," in *Body-Self Dualism*, 176–217. See also, May, *Catholic Sexual Ethics*.
29. Farley, *Just Love*, 111.

swer to this question is right and consistent with the Catholic tradition of sexual ethics: "Because sexual intercourse is about sexual completion it requires complementary sexual others. Anatomy and physiology provide two transparent clues to a *broad* range of discomplementary features in homoerotic union."[30] As I argued in the last chapter, the human body is not only good, but also it is intrinsic to being human—in creation, after the fall, in redemption, and in the eschaton. A human person's body is not a mere extrinsic tool, an instrument, to be used for providing him with subjective states of consciousness, such as giving and obtaining pleasure. Rather, the body is intrinsic to one's self as a unified bodily person; in other words, as a unified whole. This implies that the subject of one's own moral actions is the unified bodily person so that "bodily activity ... is," as John Finnis says, "as much the constitutive subject of what one does as one's act of choice is."[31] This emphasis on the body being intrinsic to one's own self is rooted in the Church's teaching on the unity of the human person. As John Paul says, "In fact, *body and soul are inseparable*:

---

30. *Homosexuality and the Bible*, 65. One such transparent clue is the health risks that follow from the fact that the human body was not physiologically made to accommodate anal intercourse, which is the preferred sexual act for many male homosexuals, according to the study by Gabriel Rotello, himself an active homosexual, in *Sexual Ecology: AIDS and the Destiny of Gay Men*. On these health risks, John R. Diggs, MD, writes: "The rectum is significantly different from the vagina with regard to suitability for penetration by a penis. The vagina has lubricants and is supported by a network of muscles. It is composed of a mucus membrane with a multi-layered stratified squamous epithelium that allows it to endure friction without damage and to resist the immunological actions caused by semen and sperm. In comparison, the anus is a delicate mechanism of small muscles that comprise an 'exit-only' passage. With repeated trauma, friction, and stretching, the sphincter loses its tone and its ability to maintain a tight seal. Consequently, anal intercourse leads to leakage of fecal material that can easily become chronic. The potential for injury is exacerbated by the fact that the intestine has only a single layer of cells separating it from highly vascular tissue, that is, blood. Therefore, any organisms that are introduced into the rectum have a much easier time establishing a foothold for infection than they would in a vagina.... Furthermore, ejaculate has components that are immunosuppressive. In the course of ordinary reproductive physiology, this allows the sperm to evade the immune defenses of the females.... The end result is that the fragility of the anus and rectum, along with the immunosuppressive effect of ejaculate, make anal-genital intercourse a most efficient manner of transmitting HIV and other infections. The list of diseases found with extraordinary frequency among male homosexual practitioners as a result of anal intercourse is alarming: anal cancer, chlamydia trachomatis, cryptosporidium, giardia lamblia, herpes simplex virus, human immunodeficiency virus, human papilloma virus, microsporidia, gonorrhea, viral hepatitis types B and C, syphilis" ("Health Risks of Gay Sex," 3).

31. Finnis, "Personal Integrity, Sexual Morality, and Responsible Parenthood," 177.

in the willing agent and in the deliberate act *they stand or fall together*."[32] Therefore, he adds, we can easily understand why separating "the moral act from the bodily dimensions of its exercise is contrary to the teaching of Scripture and Tradition."[33]

Such a separation occurs when the biological dimension of the human person is reduced to a "raw datum, devoid of any [intrinsic] meaning and moral values until freedom has shaped it in accordance with its design."[34] That freely chosen design confers on sexual union the personal meaning of causal fun, of spousal commitment, or of procreative openness, and so forth. Significantly, any one of these meanings may be conferred by persons, as well as revoked by them. For sexual union as such does not by its very nature have any definite personal meaning.[35] "Consequently," John Paul adds, "human nature and the body appear as [mere] *presuppositions or preambles*, materially *necessary*, for freedom to make its choice, yet extrinsic to the person, the subject and the human act."[36] On this view, given that sexual union is devoid of any intrinsic meaning, not having by its very nature any definite personal meaning, and because we can in freedom confer on it an instrumental meaning that is more than merely physiological, sexual union is, therefore, an extrinsic sign or symbol of personal communion, fostering marital love and friendship by signifying it. But on John Paul's view, the sexual act is much more than a natural bodily symbol; indeed, it embodies marital union, becoming bodily, or organically complete, and thus one, expresses total self-giving and makes it bodily present in the sense that, as Lee says, "this expression is not extrinsic to what it expresses, but is the visible and tangible embodiment of it."[37] Put differently, adds Lee, "this real bodily oneness *actualizes*—not just extrinsically signifies—their total marital unity."[38] He elaborates:

> Sexual intercourse is a real, biological unity, and if it is loving and respectful sexual intercourse within marriage, it is the substratum or constitutive element of marriage: a joint act, not just a gesture,

---

32. John Paul II, *Veritatis Splendor*, no. 49.
33. Ibid.
34. Ibid., no. 48.
35. Crosby, "Estrangement of Persons from their Bodies," 130–31.
36. John Paul II, *Veritatis Splendor*, no. 48.
37. Lee, "Human Body and Sexuality in the Teaching of Pope John Paul II," 114.
38. Ibid.

in which the two become co-subjects and thus become one. Thus, it is fundamentally a real act, and a real unification, and *because of that*, it is a gesture with profound significance or meaning. So, when John Paul speaks of sex as a "language of the body," he is not regarding the sexual act as a mere extrinsic sign. Nor is he saying only that the sexual sign is a *gesture* or a natural bodily *symbol*.[39]

In light of this truth, namely, that the sexual act is the bodily constituent or substratum of that multi-leveled union we call marriage, we can understand the profound significance of John Paul II's theology of the body for the ethics of sex. Given that the human person is a unity of body and soul, it follows that the body is personal. Rather than the body being "extrinsic to the person, the subject and the human act,"[40] says the pope, or bodily existence being a mere instrument or extrinsic tool in the service of man's consciously experiencing self, the body is the indispensable medium in and through which I reveal myself. Human bodily existence has the character of a subject in and through which my actions are realized as bodily persons. In other words, given man's anthropological unity of body and soul, he exercises the capacity for ethical self-determination as a whole man, meaning thereby in and through his body.[41] This implies, as Schockenhoff rightly argues, that "the body can be called the concrete limit of freedom." That is, he explains, "the body and physical life are not 'goods' external to human personal realization, standing in a purely instrumental relation to the person's authentic determination as a subject. The body is rather the irreducible means of expression in which human persons in all their acts ... are represented."[42] Respecting another person's bodily life unconditionally is to respect that person himself because a person shows himself only in and through his own body. So, "respect for the personal worth of persons relates not only to their inner convictions or moral values but must also include the inviolability of their bodily existence."[43] If the body is, then, freedom's boundary, such that respecting one's own body as well as others' bodies is both to respect our own person and other persons, this raises the question regarding the conditions under which a sexual act is morally right.

39. Ibid., 115.
40. John Paul II, *Veritatis Splendor*, no. 48.
41. Schockenhoff, "Consistent Ethic of Life," 249.
42. Ibid.
43. Ibid.

I now argue that unless the sexual act embodies or actualizes a real union of persons, it will involve the objectification and use of one's own body and of the other as a means of satisfaction. This instrumentalizing of the body as a vehicle of satisfaction occurs in non-marital intercourse, especially but not only homosexual conduct. Thus, only marital intercourse can constitute a real union of persons, because such intercourse is a real bodily unity, a constitutive element or substratum, a necessary condition, of marriage, which along with marital consent that conjugal intercourse fulfills, succeeds in realizing the fundamental but complex human good of marital communion: the good of marriage itself, of intimate human friendship ("person-uniting"), of procreation ("life-giving"), and the good of personal integrity, which "entails one's own bodily integrity, for one's body is integral to one's being as a human person."[44] In sum, John Paul II expresses the general argument for the basic principle in sexual ethics that I am defending in this chapter:

> Consequently sexuality, by means of which man and woman give themselves to one another through the acts which are proper and exclusive to spouses, is by no means something purely biological, but concerns the innermost being of the human person as such. It is realized in a truly human way only if it an integral part of the love by which a man and a woman commit themselves totally to one another until death. The total physical self-giving would be a lie if it were not the sign and fruit of a total person self-giving, in which the whole person including the temporal dimension, is present: If the person were to withhold something or reserve the possibility of deciding otherwise in the future, by this very fact he or she would not be giving totally.[45]

I said above that non-marital intercourse, especially but not only homosexual, mistreats sexuality in that the body is treated as an instrument to gain satisfaction, that is, the pleasure of arousal and orgasm. Someone may raise several questions about this claim, especially in regard to homosexual conduct.[46] First, surely it is the case that "in itself the use of the body for pleasure is not wrong; it's a creational gift to us." Second, he adds, "to the extent that homosexual sex may be selfish, it is a sin often shared

---

44. May, *Catholic Sexual Ethics*, 16.

45. John Paul II, *Familiaris Consortio*, no. 11.

46. These questions were put to me by my colleague, Hans Boersma, of Regent College, in a private email.

by heterosexuals: who is without erotic selfishness in sexual activity?" Third, there is also the issue that "homosexuals often seek true intimacy (more than sexual) in their relationships." Therefore, even if we say that same-sex desire is a misdirected desire, it is more complex that simply a desire for sexual gratification (even though, of course, all ill-directed erotic desire is unfaithfulness to God and others, and to that extent selfish)." These questions deserve a brief reply.

First, although pleasure is a good, it is not just by itself a genuine good such that, say, sex just for pleasure is morally right. Why not? Quite simply, adulterous pleasures, or sadistic pleasures, or the pleasures of pedophilic sex, are all bad, but one wouldn't say, "Well, at least he enjoyed himself." In other words, as George and Lee rightly state, "when one takes pleasure in an inappropriate object, the pleasure itself is bad. So, bodily pleasure is not *of itself* a good."[47] Rather, in order for pleasure to be a good it must be connected to an "*appropriate* object," they add, "an object or activity really good and worthy of pursuit." Such an object or activity is good and worthy of pursuit because it is really fulfilling or perfective of our human nature. Thus, in the case of sexual conduct "our choices ought to be in accord with a respect and love for real human goods, precisely because such goods are intrinsic aspects of the well-being and fulfillment of human persons—ourselves and others."[48] In that case, since the pleasure is attached to an activity that is already fulfilling and perfective, it adds to the goodness or fulfillment of the object or activity. "We can see this point when we consider that it is better, for example, to have learning with pleasure than without it."[49] Therefore, treating the body, one's own or another's body, as a mere object of pleasure involves not only divorcing, or alienating, the bodily from the personal but also regarding it as a *sub*personal object.

Second, for different reasons both homosexual and heterosexual sex is selfish. That is because in each case a body is used as an instrument to bring about subjective satisfaction in the conscious self. This results in the failure to respect the integration of the bodily and the personal, but that is because they are *non-marital* sexual acts, intrinsically incapable of participating in, actualizing, the common good of marriage with its two

---

47. Lee and George, *Body-Self Dualism in Contemporary Ethics and Politics*, 187.
48. Ibid., 187–88.
49. Ibid.

aspects: marital communion itself, which is unitive in its significance, and procreation, and hence of what is genuinely fulfilling or perfective for the persons involved in those acts.[50] In short, says Finnis, "sexual acts are not unitive in their significance unless they are marital (actualizing the all-level unity of marriage) and (since the common good of marriage has two aspects) they are not marital unless they have not only the generosity of acts of friendship but also the procreative significance, not necessarily of being intended to generate or capable in the circumstances of generating but at least of being, as human conduct, acts of the reproductive kind—actualizations, so far as the spouses then and there can, of the reproductive functions in which they are biologically and thus personally one."[51] In other words, non-marital sexual acts involve the instrumentalization of one's own and another's body. Whether heterosexual or homosexual, such non-marital acts cannot realize a real common good in the sexual act. Although heterosexuals may be united as one organism in reproductive type acts, and hence they are biologically one, the latter is only a necessary condition, an aspect, but not a sufficient condition for actualizing a real union of persons that is genuinely fulfilling. Say Lee and George, "If they are united as one organism, but are not united in other aspects of their lives or selves, then they are treating their bodies as extrinsic instruments. ... Only if they *are* married, only if they (publicly) consent to marriage, does their becoming biologically one actualize (initiate or renew) marriage. So, only if they have a truly marital relationship can their sexual act embody their personal communion."[52] Regarding homosexual sexual acts, their acts are intrinsically incapable of bringing about real unity of persons because the bodies of the same sex cannot become biologically one, one complete organism, and so cannot contribute to a communion of persons in and by their bodily union. So, since they are not "the subject of a single biological act and so do not literally become 'one flesh,'"[53] their act is self-alienating or depersonalizing.

Third, homosexual sex is often much more that self-gratification, involving sincere mutual affection, intimacy, self-giving, love, and so forth. So, such sex wants to bring about not only subjective satisfaction but also

50. Finnis, "Law, Morality, and 'Sexual Orientation,'" 8.
51. Ibid., 9–10.
52. Lee and George, *Body-Self Dualism*, 196–97.
53. Ibid., 194.

interpersonal unity, and even partnership in a common life.[54] Suppose we grant this claim to be true. The problem is that bodily coupling of same-sex partners does not in truth actualize, as do husbands and wives, one complete reproductive couple, because they cannot engage in reproductive type acts, and hence the good of marriage.[55] Marital acts, which are in principle unrealizable by same-sex intercourse, "presupposes bodily union as the biological actuation of the multi-level (bodily, emotional, intellectual, and volitional) marital relationship."[56]

HOMOSEXUALITY

Magisterial teaching about homosexuality is expressed in two ways: both as a *condition* (or inclination or attraction) and as an *activity*.[57] The Church rightly understands that Holy Scripture's condemnation of homosexuality pertains not only to outward acts but also to the inward condition, to homosexual actions as well as to the homosexual condition itself. First, as condition, "Homosexuality refers to relations between men or between women who experience an exclusive or predominant sexual attraction toward persons of the same sex."[58] Same-sex attraction may come "from a false education, from a lack of normal sexual development, from habit,

---

54. Grisez, *Way of the Lord Jesus*, vol. 2, *Living a Christian Life*, 653–54.

55. May, *Catholic Sexual Ethics*, 26.

56. Finnis, "Law, Morality, and 'Sexual Orientation,'" 20–21.

57. I refrain from using the term "orientation" in order to avoid the implication that some persons are "constitutionally" homosexual in a biological or genetic sense. On the question of whether same-sex attraction is genetically determined before birth, and on the possible causes of that attraction, see the document of the Catholic Medical Association, *Homosexuality and Hope*. Furthermore, Ashley and O'Rourke are, in my judgment, right: "Even if it is eventually proven that homosexuality is genetic in origin, this defect, like other genetic defects, would not excuse aberrant behavior, but would call for continuing efforts to find a remedy. It remains probable that homosexuality has multiple causes of which the principal are a dysfunctional family and early masturbatory or homosexual experiences. Thus the popular stereotype of genetically gay and lesbian persons is a social construct developed in recent years that greatly distorts the historical, biological, psychological, and social facts (Catholic Medical Association, 2004). The Church urges health professionals to treat homosexuals with respect and compassion and to encourage them to get help from psychiatrists and psychologists who regard this condition as a disorder that may be remediable. It strongly encourages objective scientific research to gain greater certainty about its etiology and possible methods of treatment" (*Health Care Ethics*, 68).

58. *Catechism of the Catholic Church*, no. 2357.

from bad example, or from other similar causes."⁵⁹ Some homosexuals experience their condition as a short-term disability ("transitory"), or at least not immutable, whereas others are such that they judge their condition to be immutable. The condition itself is intrinsically disordered, that is, it is an objective evil, and not, necessarily, a moral evil, so long as it is not knowingly chosen by the willed act of some individual moral agent.

Second, homosexuality, as activity, includes homosexual conduct that "refers to bodily acts, on the body of a person of the same sex, which are engaged in with a view to securing orgasmic sexual satisfaction for one or more of the parties."⁶⁰ Now, according to the *Catechism of the Catholic Church*, same-sex acts lack the full complementarity of the man-woman relationship as well as a procreative openness to new life.⁶¹ Of course "full complementarity" means that the spouses are united not only in their bodily dimension—biological unity and a real organic complementarity union—but also in every other dimension—sense, emotion, reason, will, and heart. Such acts are contrary to the objective moral order, the Church teaches, inasmuch as they lack the ability to realize *qua* sexual acts their essential and indispensable ends, the *procreative* and *unitive* ends of the sexual act, and hence are intrinsically disordered.⁶² Those who freely and knowingly perform such acts are immoral, and hence are guilty of sin, of a blamable action, of an offense against chastity. Says the *Catechism*, "Chastity means the successful integration of sexuality within the person and thus the inner unity of man in his bodily and spiritual being. Sexuality, in which man's belonging to the bodily and biological world is expressed, becomes personal and truly human when it is integrated into the relationship of one person to another, in the complete and lifelong mutual gift of a man and a woman." In sum, "The virtue of chastity therefore involves the integrity of the person and the integrality of the gift."⁶³ The *integrity of the person* pertains to the intrinsic good of self-integration, of a person's sexuality, or body, being integrated with the person as a unified totality; the *integrality of the gift* pertains to the mutual self-giving of a man and a woman to participate in the real and basic good of marriage, of the real

---

59. *Persona Humana*, no. 8.
60. Finnis, "Law, Morality, and 'Sexual Orientation,'" 3–4.
61. *Catechism of the Catholic Church*, no. 2357.
62. *Persona Humana*, no. 8.
63. *Catechism of the Catholic Church*, no. 2337.

experience of interpersonal unity that consummates or renews the two-in-one-flesh unity of a man and a woman.

Regarding magisterial teaching, Margaret Farley claims to see changes in the teaching that "should not be underestimated." She explains: "Although homosexual genital actions are still judged to be intrinsically disordered, and hence 'objectively' immoral, they can be 'subjectively' moral depending on the state of mind and intentions of an individual person. Also, homosexual orientation in persons is not condemned; it is even accepted."[64] Clarity is much needed here regarding Farley's statement. In what sense, if any, may homosexual acts be subjectively moral? Furthermore, having made the act/orientation distinction, does the Church actually accept same-sex orientation?[65]

In answering the first question, we may properly distinguish between objective and subjective morality.[66] Consider the example of an honestly mistaken conscience. My conscience may be subjectively good but objectively mistaken in the case in which I honestly, but mistakenly, believe that a certain action is moral. The question here is not whether an objective evil may become subjectively good for some individual in the case of an honestly mistaken conscience. If that is what Farley is suggesting, then she is mistaken. Rather, the question of subjective morality is whether a person's conscience is either invincibly (non-culpably) erroneous—"an ignorance of which the subject is unaware and which he is unable to correct by himself"[67]—or vincibly (culpably) erroneous, that is, whether he is blamable or blameless given his state of mind and intentions.[68] For

---

64. Farley, *Just Love*, 279.

65. Farley probably has in mind paragraph 2358 of the *Catechism of the Catholic Church*: "Men and women who have deep-seated homosexual tendencies . . . must be accepted with respect, compassion, and sensitivity." But this statement is followed by the Church urging us to avoid "every sign of unjust discrimination" regarding such men and women. Furthermore, our acceptance, compassion and sensitivity, as Christians, derive from recognition of the cross they bear from "the difficulties they may encounter from their condition." In short, "These persons are called to fulfill God's will in their lives and, if they are Christians, to unite [their difficulties] to the sacrifice of the Lord's Cross."

66. Ashley, *Living the Truth in Love*, 118–19.

67. John Paul II, *Veritatis Splendor*, no. 62.

68. Regarding homosexuality, "the Church's wise moral tradition is necessary since it warns against generalizations in judging individual cases. In fact, circumstances may exist, or may have existed in the past, which would reduce or remove the culpability of the individual in a given instance; or other circumstances may increase it. What is at all costs to be avoided is the unfounded and demeaning assumption that the sexual behavior of

instance, we may impute blame when an individual is mistaken because he was imprudent by not taking "serious care to inquire whether what [he is] about to do is morally right and to follow what [his] reason tells [him] is right."[69] But even when blame is not imputed that does not eliminate the objective morality of an action. As John Paul II argues, "It is possible that the evil done as the result of invincible ignorance or a non-culpable error of judgment may not be imputable to the agent; *but even in this case it does not cease to be an evil, a disorder in relation to the truth about the good.*"[70] Furthermore, the pope adds, "It is never acceptable to confuse a 'subjective' error about moral good with the 'objective' truth rationally proposed to man in virtue of his end, or to make the moral value of an act performed with a true and correct conscience equivalent to the moral value of an act performed by following the judgment of an erroneous conscience."[71] Thus: "If acts are intrinsically evil, a good intention or particular circumstances can diminish their evil, but they cannot remove it. They remain 'irremediably' evil acts; *per se* and in themselves they are not capable of being ordered to God and to the good of the person. . . . Consequently, circumstances or intentions can never transform an act intrinsically evil by virtue of its object into an act 'subjectively' good or defensive as a choice."[72] John Paul II's much needed clarification on the distinction between objective morality and subjective morality avoids any confusion generated by Farley's statement that an objectively immoral act may be subjectively moral depending on the state of mind and intentions of an individual person.

---

homosexual persons is always and totally compulsive and therefore inculpable. What is essential is that the fundamental liberty which characterizes the human person and gives him his dignity be recognized as belonging the homosexual person as well. As in every conversion from evil, the abandonment of homosexual activity will require a profound collaboration of the individual with God's liberating grace" (*Homosexualitatis problema*, no. 11).

69. Ashley, *Living the Truth in Love*, 119. See also, *Catechism of the Catholic Church*, nos. 1779–1785. In regard to judgments about sexual acts, such as masturbation, that are offenses against chaste sexual intercourse, the *Catechism* states: "To form an equitable judgment about the subject's moral responsibility and to guide pastoral action, one must take into account the affective immaturity, force of acquired habit, conditions of anxiety, or other psychological or social factors that lessen or even extenuate moral culpability" (no. 2352).

70. John Paul II, *Veritatis Splendor*, no. 62.

71. Ibid., no. 63.

72. Ibid., no. 81.

In addition, regarding Farley's claim that so-called "homosexual orientation" is not only not condemned but also accepted, *Homosexualitatis problema* explicitly rejects the kind of "overly benign interpretation" that some theologians, like Farley, give to the "homosexual condition itself, some going so far as to call it neutral or even good." The Church's teaching on homosexuality does not accept the homosexual condition itself. How could she accept that condition when embedded in that condition "is a more or less strong tendency ordered toward an intrinsic moral evil [?]" Since the Church regards the "inclination itself . . . as an objective disorder," then it is not solely homosexual acts that are intrinsically disordered and thus objectively evil, but the inclination itself is equally disordered as the source of man's sinful homosexual activities.[73] In other words, as Mansini and Welch correctly state the teaching of the Church in *Homosexualitatis problema*, "if homosexual activity itself is always intrinsically immoral, and homosexual tendencies are therefore always objectively disordered because they incline to what is always intrinsically immoral, then it makes good sense to say that his [homosexual's] sexual affections, as such, are not good. They do not bear on the feminine, which is the target of mature male psychosexual desire. And therefore, since they are deep seated, they prevent 'affective maturity,' which means, if it means anything, having good desires rightly ordered."[74] Clearly, then, the act/orientation distinction is morally relevant only insofar as it allows us to distinguish between culpable homosexual acts and the source of those acts in an individual's same-sex attraction for which he may not be morally culpable. But it should be abundantly clear that the act/orientation distinction as the Church understands it explicitly rejects the interpretation of that orientation as morally neutral—rather the homosexual desire itself is an objectively disordered inclination or propensity to evil. What, then, is the origin of that inclination if not the choices that men make?

Theologically, the ultimate origin of this condition, and hence those homosexual tendencies that incline an individual to what is always intrinsically immoral, is the Fall. John Finnis, Aidan Nichols,[75] Helmut

---

73. *Homosexualitatis problema*, no. 3.

74. Mansini and Welch, "In Conformity to Christ." This article is an exposition and interpretation of the November 29, 2005, instruction concerning the admission of men with homosexual tendencies to seminaries released by the Congregation for Catholic Education in Rome.

75. Nichols, *Epiphany*, 423.

Thielicke,[76] and others are right that the intrinsically disordered inclination of this condition, which reflects the brokenness of our sinful world, the disordered creation that exists since the Fall, should be seen as a specific manifestation of the concupiscence that comes from original sin and leads to sin but is itself not, necessarily, consciously chosen sin. I will return to this point later.

MARRIAGE

Furthermore, both the condition and the acts of homosexuality are contrary to God's original plan for creation, the Creator's sexual design for marriage, which is necessarily a bi-unitary bond of a man and a woman, that is, a two-in-one-flesh covenantal union of mutual love. Why necessarily bi-unitary? Briefly, the male and female must become complementary parts of a single organism making them a two-in-one-flesh in which the real good of marriage is realized or participated. That is, the marriage bond is essentially a bi-unity of husband and wife, united as complementary, *bodily* persons, in a two-in-one-flesh communion. Given that a man and a woman complete each other, they become an organic and thus personal unit. It is literally true that "they become one flesh" (Gen 2:24). The inner unity and identity of this bond is typically founded in the conjugal bi-unity of the marital act of sexual intercourse that is realized by bodily communion. This bodily union is founded on biological unity and organic complementarity, in short, the biological matrix (to use a term of Robert George's), of the persons united in this bond, and hence this matrix is the foundational requirement, necessary but not sufficient condition, of the inner structure of marriage.[77] This biological matrix is part of, not merely an instrument of, their personal subjectivity, focusing on acts of a reproductive kind creating a complementary biological unity. Acts of a reproductive kind are acts that consist in the bodily union of reproductive organs of husband and wife, regardless of whether or not reproduction is *actually* possible. John Finnis has carefully explained the concept of "reproductive-type acts."

---

76. Thielicke, *Ethics of Sex*, 282.

77. Real bodily union is a necessary but not sufficient condition to bring about that communion; what is also needed is, as Grisez correctly notes, "marital consent which conjugal intercourse fulfills" (*Way of the Lord Jesus*, 2:651).

> Sexual acts which are marital are "of the reproductive kind" because in willing such an act one wills sexual behavior which is (a) the very same as causes generation (intended or unintended) in every case of human *sexual* reproduction, and (b) the very same as one would will if one were intending precisely sexual reproduction as a goal of a particular marital sexual act. This kind of act is a "natural kind," in the morally relevant sense of "natural," not . . . if and only if one is intending or attempting to produce an *outcome*, viz., reproduction or procreation. Rather it is a distinct rational kind—and therefore in the morally relevant sense a natural kind—because (i) in engaging in it one is intending a *marital* act, (ii) its being of the reproductive kind is a necessary though not sufficient of its being marital, and (iii) marriage is a rational and natural kind of institution. One's reason for action—one's rational motive—is precisely the complex good of marriage.[78]

Same-sex relations are incapable of being acts of a reproductive kind because their reproductive organs do not create a complementary biological, and thus personal, unit. So without being one organism, their sexual act does not actually effect interpersonal unity. In other words, "the coupling of two bodies of the same sex cannot form one complete organism and so cannot contribute to the bodily communion of persons."[79] Without then the organic unity of male and female in conjugal sex as the foundational function of the structural whole that is marital union, homosexual partners cannot become one and hence they cannot manifest a unity of action, that is, an action sharing in a real, common good of their actions that is performed jointly.[80] And therefore without the unity of action, the unity of persons is unrealized.

> In the case of the sexual act of a married couple, their acts of physically or organically becoming one (organic unity) is the common good, the shared pursuit of which (unity of action) also brings about or enhances their interpersonal unity (unity of persons). But if the participants in a sexual act do not become physically or organically one, then, whatever goods [e.g., intimacy of friendship] they have as ulterior ends, the immediate goal of their act can only be either mere pleasure or an illusory experience. There is in such an act no common good, the common pursuit of which

---

78. Finnis, "Law, Morality, and 'Sexual Orientation,'" 18.
79. Grisez, *Way of the Lord Jesus*, 2:653.
80. Lee and George, *Body-Self Dualism*, 195.

> makes them one. There is no real unity of action to effect or enhance their interpersonal unity. So in that case, although they may intend or wish otherwise, their act is in reality a using of their own and each other's bodies-as-sexual as a means of obtaining a pleasurable experience, which might include the illusory experience of a union which they are not by this action promoting or effecting in any way.[81]

Of course the spousal union is more than biological. Indeed, as the *Catechism of the Catholic Church* expresses this important point, "Sexuality, by means of which a man and woman give themselves to one another through the acts which are proper and exclusive to spouses, is not something simply biological, but concerns the innermost being of the human person as such."[82] Thus, spousal union is a multi-leveled union expressive of personal complementarity. As Robert Gagnon puts it, "anatomical complementarity serves as an important heuristic springboard for grasping the broad complementarity of maleness and femaleness," namely, "physiological, psychological, interpersonal, distinctive arousal, etc." Put differently, that multi-facetted union is expressive of a real communion of persons that is the experience and actualizing of the body's spousal meaning, meaning thereby "*the power to express love: precisely that love in which the human person becomes gift* and—through this gift—fulfills the very meaning of his being and existence" (*MWTB*, 15.1).

So in the structural whole that is the bi-unitary marriage bond, marriage is founded in the biological matrix that is intrinsic to the unitary activity of self-giving. This bodily act of self-giving, which is not extrinsic to the subject's emotional, intellectual and spiritual unity, but rather is a foundational level of a unitary, multi-leveled personal communion, is necessary for actualizing and hence experiencing the common good of marriage with its two-fold ends, the *unitive* and *procreative* ends of conjugal love. These are intrinsic meanings of the marital act as an act of self-giving, constituting a communion of bodily persons, and the fullest unfolding of the spousal meaning of the body.

Furthermore, rather than the bi-unitary marital bond being merely an instrumental good in which it is only thought of as a necessary means for attaining the extrinsic purpose of having children, that bond is good-in-itself with procreation being the fullest internal unfolding of the mu-

---

81. Ibid., 196.
82. *Catechism of the Catholic Church*, no. 2361.

tual gift of self. Since marriage is in itself good, and not a mere means to the extrinsic end of having children, it follows that even sterile married couples can become a union of complements, an interpersonal unity called marriage. Of course that union is, normally, naturally fulfilled by bearing and raising children. "This openness to procreation, as the community's natural fulfillment, distinguishes this community from other types of community." As the Dutch neo-Calvinist Dooyeweerd puts it:

> The marriage bond, as such, is typically founded in the *institutional* (and not in an incidental) sexual union of husband and wife, which is undoubtedly made serviceable for the propagation of the human race. It is according to the order of the creation that normally marriage leads to the formation of a family. In other words, the typical foundational relation between the family and the conjugal bond implies *the natural disposition of the latter to procreation. In this sense marriage may be called the 'germ-cell' of the family-relationship*. Both communities remain most intensely interwoven during the time of their actual existence. Yet marriage, as a love-communion, maintains its own structure notwithstanding its interwovenness with the family.[83]

Like Grisez, Finnis, George, et al., Dooyeweerd holds that "marriage, as a love-communion, maintains its own structure notwithstanding its interwovenness with the family."[84] Elsewhere he writes:

> After having gained a sufficient insight into the inner structure of the marriage bond [as a bi-unitary love-communion founded on the organic unity of biotic complementarity] we shall now try to deepen our insight into its inner coherence with the family. *According to the divine order of creation marriage is intentionally adapted to the family relationship.* [T]his means that marriage is enriched and deepened by its natural interweaving with the family relationship, and conjugal love is deepened and enriched in parental love.... When the marriage bond has expanded into a family relationship the former is enriched and deepened in its meaning by its close interweaving with the latter, because its bi-unity in conjugal love has produced a unity in plurality. In the conjugal union, as such, the expression of the personality in the temporal existence of each of the married persons is enriched, enlarged and completed by that of the other. A woman becomes "wife" in the

---

83. Dooyeweerd, *New Critique of Theoretical Thought*, 3:307; italics added.
84. Ibid.

full sense of the word only in the conjugal union with her husband, and *vice versa*. And the expression of the personality in the bi-unitary bond assumes a wider and deeper perspective in the multi-unitary bond of the family.[85]

Dooyeweerd wishes to affirm marriage's intrinsic value, an interpersonal union that is in itself good, rather than to see marriage as a mere instrumental good for the extrinsic purposes of having and raising children. Dooyeweerd correctly understands that the internal meaning-structure of married love may not be detached from "its biotic foundation in the organic difference between the sexes."[86] In short, like Grisez, Finnis, George, and Lee, Dooyeweerd also holds that the marriage bond, as a love-communion, is typically founded in sexual difference: the organic unity of male and female in conjugal sex is the foundational function of the structural whole that is marital union. In the above passage, on the one hand, he makes it clear that that this union is naturally fulfilled by bearing and raising children. Thus, he does not displace parenthood as an *integral* part of the communion of married life.

Still, Dooyeweerd insists, on the other hand, "[I]t is not possible to deduce the essential internal structure of the marriage-bond from the 'cosmic purpose of propagation,' as was done by Thomas Aquinas." "This traditional universalistic construction," adds Dooyeweerd, "necessarily results in an eradication of the boundaries between the marriage union and the family relationship."[87] The eradication of the boundaries between marriage and family is, he argues, implied by Aquinas' attempt to deduce the essential internal structure of the marriage-bond from the "cosmic purpose of propagation." He writes:

> This is evident from Thomas' statement that posterity is essential to the marital bond [4 *Sent*. Dist. 31, q. I, a. 3, c]. Such a construction must naturally restrict itself to a deduction of the general *institution* of marriage from the purpose of procreation. . . . [But] in its application to the factual relationships [of marriage] Thomas' view leads to constructions of a very artificial and internally contradictory character. We need only mention his explanations of the relation between the individual act of sexual uniting and the "objective procreative purpose." Thomas concedes that sexual intercourse in

---

85. Ibid., 322–23; italics added.
86. Ibid., 320.
87. Ibid., 323.

a barren marriage, or in general such which is not carried on with a concrete procreative intention, is morally permissible. *But then it will not do to seek the inner essence of the conjugal institution in the aim of propagation.* Then the internal structure of the marriage bond, in its difference from the family relationship, irresistibly forces itself upon us.... The marriage bond ... normally embraces husband and wife for life, independent of the natural procreative end. No "rational procreative purpose" can justify the sexual consummation of marriage in an ethical sense, but only married love sanctified in Christ. This love (and not a utilitarian kind of thought) is the true regulator and educator of married life towards temperance and chastity. In the divine order of creation, marriage is the only ordered *way* to form a family; marriage and family are mutually adapted to each other. But they retain their own peculiar internal structure and value. If this is ignored or misinterpreted, our marital morality will result in a labyrinth of contradictions of our own creating, and the lucid simplicity of the divine ordinance [of marriage] will be obscured.[88]

In one sense, Dooyeweerd's main point is right: marriage isn't merely for having children, as if to say that it is merely a means to the procreative end. Indeed, it is precisely for this reason that, in 1936, Dooyeweerd already expressed his appreciation for the work of Catholic philosopher Dietrich von Hildebrand on marriage, *Die Ehe* (1929). Hildebrand affirms the primacy of love in marital communion.[89] Hildebrand says, "No other

---

88. Ibid., 323–24; italics added. For an alternative, and I judge, more correct, interpretation of Aquinas than Dooyeweerd's, see Finnis, "Law, Morality, and 'Sexual Orientation,'" 14–21. For Finnis' fuller treatment of Aquinas' sexual ethics, see his *Aquinas*, chapter VII.2.

89. Dooyeweerd is referring to Hildebrand's 1929 book, *Die Ehe* (ET: *Marriage*, 1942). For this very same reason, Dooyeweerd also values Pius XI's 1930 Encyclical Letter, *Casti Connubii*. Pius writes: "This mutual molding of husband and wife, this determined effort to perfect each other, can in a very real sense, as the Roman Catechism teaches, be said to be the chief reason and purpose of matrimony, provided matrimony be looked at not in the restricted sense as instituted for the proper conception and education of the child, but more widely as the blending of life as a whole and the mutual interchange and sharing thereof" (no. 24). Although Pius explained the blessings of marriage in terms of the three goods of marriage, namely, offspring, conjugal faith, and the sacrament, it is clear from this passage that husband and wife should seek to realize these goods according to the ultimate meaning of marriage, which is conjugal love. Dooyeweerd remarks: "This encyclical frankly assigned 'primary of honor' (*principatus nobilitatis*) to married love in a Christian marriage. All this was in striking contrast with what happened in Protestant circles two years later, when the moral theologian Emil Brunner, published his book *Das Gebot und die Ordnungen*, in which love, if viewed as the basis of marriage, was called a

earthly community is constituted so exclusively in its very substance by mutual love."[90] Significantly, he advances the thesis that the meaning of the sexual act in marriage, given that marriage is in itself, principally, a communion of love, may not be restricted to being a mere means to procreation. So, the meaning of marriage, conjugal love, in its interpersonal and unitive aspect is a good in itself.[91] "Its meaning is primarily the realization of the sublime communion of love in which, according to the words of our Savior, 'They shall be two in one flesh'" (Matt 19:5).[92] Of course, Hildebrand has no intention of detaching the bodily union of married love from the essential unfolding of this act in the primary end of procreation. Indeed, the "general connection between procreation and the communion of love must always be maintained even subjectively, at least as a general possibility of this act."[93] He adds, "Love is the *primary meaning* of marriage *according to the creation* [Schöpfungssinn der Ehe], just as its *primary end according to the creation* [Schöpfungszweck] is the begetting of new human beings."[94] Although Hildebrand leaves unexplained here the relation between "meaning" and "end," it is clear throughout the book that the relationship is such that this end and others are to be realized on the basis of marital love. Put differently, marital love is the intimate interpersonal two-in-one-flesh union in which husband and wife reciprocally complement one another in their mutual self-donation, bringing to fulfillment the meaning of marriage in and through these ends.[95]

'sandy ground' and marital love was identified with erotic inclination!" (*New Critique of Theoretical Thought*, 3:322).

90. Hildebrand, *Marriage*, 3.

91. Ibid., 24: "[Marriage] exists in the first place for its own sake and not exclusively for the sake of any result that it produces."

92. Ibid., 21.

93. Ibid., 23. In a general critique of contraceptive sex, Hildebrand adds: "It is difficult to imagine a greater lack of reverence toward God than interfering with this mystery with desecrating hands in order to frustrate this mystery. How terrible to think of man wanting to destroy this unity which God has established so mysteriously, deeming those united in the highest earthly union of love worthy to take part in His creative power. To go against God's purposes through a desecrating interference, perhaps even thus to throw back into the void a being that God has intended to exist—what sacrilegious presumption!"

94. I am citing here the original German: "Die Liebe ist der primäre Schöpfungssinn der Ehe, wie die Enstehung neuer Menschen ihr primärer Schöpfungszweck" (*Die Ehe*, 7). The English translation leaves out, inexplicably, the emphasis on the creation.

95. Hildebrand, *Marriage*, 12, 15.

In response, Dooyeweerd gratefully acknowledges that "[Hildebrand] voices the Biblical-Christian conception of the conjugal bond as a typical and incomparable institutional love-union between husband and wife, [and] as the expression of the eternal love of Christ towards the Church as His Bride."[96] Karol Wojtyla, too, rejects the idea that marriage is a means to an end, and hence he agrees with Dooyeweerd's point as well as Hildebrand's. In his 1960 work, *Love and Responsibility*, Wojtyla rejects what he calls the "rigorist" interpretation of the conjugal life and sexual intercourse that sees the latter as instrumental goods serving the purpose of procreation."[97] Wojtyla then adds: "The Creator, then, does not utilize persons merely as the means or instruments of his creative power but offers them the possibility of a special realization of love. It is for them to put their sexual relations on the plane of love, the appropriate plane for human persons, or on a lower plane. The Creator's will is not only the preservation of the species by way of sexual intercourse but also its preservation on the basis of a love worthy of human persons."[98] So, Wojtyla's claim here is no different than Dooyeweerd's point that the inner essence

---

96. Dooyeweerd, *New Critique of Theoretical Thought*, 3:320. Not entirely taken with Hildebrand's book, however, Dooyeweerd also claims that Hildebrand "detaches the inner meaning-structure of married love from its temporal biotic foundation in the organic difference between the sexes." But this is simply not the case. Hildebrand explicitly asserts the contrary: "The special character of conjugal love is, furthermore, marked by the fact that this love can only come into being, between men and women and not between persons of the same sex, as is the case with friendship, parental love, or filial love" (*Marriage*, 25).

97. Wojtyla, *Love and Responsibility*, 58-59. Dooyeweerd raises a similar objection to what he calls the "rationalistic conception of married love as essentially a 'blind passion'. ... When this individualistic rationalism found its way in Protestant ethics there was of course no longer any possibility of a really Christian notion of married love as the most intense moral bi-unity. Symptomatic is the utterance recorded by P. Kluckhohn of the Methodist preacher William Whitefield (1714-1770), who boasted that in his proposal of marriage there had been no question of love: 'God be praised, if I know my own heart a little I am free of that foolish passion which the world calls love.' This shows how far the rationalistic utilitarian spirit of the Enlightenment had penetrated under the guise of Puritan piety" (*New Critique of Theoretical Thought*, 3:316). Hildebrand follows up his citation of the Methodist Whitefield with an old Catholic prayer that speaks of marriage as "the mystery of love": "O God, at the creation of mankind, making woman from man Thou hast already ordained that there should be a union of the flesh and of sweet love. ... Lord our God, Thou has created man pure and immaculate and still Thou wishest that in procreation of the generations one be made from the other by the *mystery of love*" (*Marriage*, 22).

98. Wojtyla, *Love and Responsibility*, 60.

of marriage may not be sought in the purpose of having children; rather, absolutely peculiar about the meaning of the marital bond is the constant love-union between husband and wife. Furthermore, like Hildebrand, Wojtyla regards procreation to be the primary end of marriage because "procreation is objectively, ontologically, a more important purpose than that man and woman should live together, complement each other and support each other (*mutuum adiutorium*), just as this second purpose is in turn more important that the appeasement of natural desire."[99] But, significantly, for Wojtyla, just as it is for Hildebrand, love is not an end of marriage; rather, love is the single but complex meaning of marriage that is expressed and fulfilled in each of these ends, though most essentially and fully in procreation, which is the primary end of marriage.[100]

Affirming marriage's intrinsic value is significant, but unfortunately Dooyeweerd seems to express himself in a way that he does so at the expense of displacing parenthood from its central position. I need to make my point carefully, however, because Dooyeweerd does say, "It is according to the order of the creation that normally marriage leads to the formation of a family. In other words, the typical foundational relation between the family and the conjugal bond implies the natural disposition of the latter to procreation. In this sense marriage may be called the 'germ-cell' of the family-relationship." This passage makes clear that he sees the bearing and raising of children to be the natural fulfillment of the interpersonal unity of marriage. In other words, having and raising children fulfills marriage intrinsically rather than accidentally.[101]

And yet, in order to avoid getting entangled in one of the contradictions in that labyrinth he speaks of in the above passage, Dooyweerd thinks, correctly, that this marital unity is good in itself even in a sterile marriage. But he makes this point in such a way that he sounds as if he is displacing the integral position of parenthood in marriage, and hence severing the link as such between marriage and children. But I think we can put Dooyeweerd's point more clearly by saying that even a sterile marriage is fully a marriage, remains good in itself, even if it lacks it natural fulfillment or unfolding in the bearing and raising of children. "The communion of married life is actualized and experienced not only in chaste

99. Ibid., 68; see also, 66.

100. Wojtyla says, "There is no question of opposing love to procreation nor yet of suggesting that procreation takes precedence over love" (ibid.).

101. Grisez, *Way of the Lord Jesus*, 2:570.

marital intercourse but also, when intercourse is fruitful, in having and raising children, and in domestic life as a whole."[102] Put differently, in light of the Church's teaching, according to the divine order of creation, the sexual act is intrinsically ordered to the good of marriage and marriage itself is intentionally ordered to the family relationship, to the procreation and education of children.[103]

Whatever may actually be the case here about the relation between marital union and parenthood in Dooyeweerd's view, what is most significant for our purpose in my discussion of homosexuality, is that severing the link between marriage and children from an essential to an accidental one is by now, some more than seventy years after Dooyeweerd made his case against an instrumentalist view of marriage, become the typical way that, even some Christians, use to justify same-sex marriage: if a sterile marriage is fully a marriage in the true sense, without the couple having children, why can't same-sex couples, who are by definition sterile couples, be genuinely married.[104] Rebutting this point brings us back to the notion of reproductive-type acts. As Lee and George describe this act:

> In sexual intercourse between a man and a woman (whether married or not), a *real* organic union is established. This is a literal, biological point. Human beings are organisms, albeit of a particular type.... For most actions, such as sensation, digestion, and walking, individual male or female organisms are complete units.... However, with respect to one function the male and the female are *not* complete, and their function is reproduction. In reproductive activity the bodily parts of the male and the bodily parts of the female participate in a single action, coitus, which is oriented to reproduction (though not every act of coitus actually reproduces), so that the subject of the action is the male and the female as a biological unit. Coitus is a unitary action in which the male and the female become really biologically one. In marital intercourse, this

---

102. Ibid., 556 n. 3.
103. *Gaudium et Spes*, no. 50.
104. For a critical discussion of proposals regarding the insignificance of sexual difference for a Christian ethics of sex and marriage, see Roberts, *Creation and Covenant*. For a defense of same-sex marriage on the grounds that the "good of marriage is not tied directly to the rearing of children ... to propagate the species, nor to establish a seal of sexual union," see Jensen, "God's Desire for Us: Reformed Theology and the Question of Same-Sex Marriage."

bodily unity is an aspect of, the biological matrix of, the couple's comprehensive, marital communion.[105]

But how can the sexual acts of a sterile couple be oriented toward procreation, when either one or the other of them lacks the internal resources to procreate? In short, how can we still speak of reproductive type acts, let alone of reproductive organs in that case? In sum, are only *actually* reproductive acts genuinely reproductive? The brief answer to this question here must be as follows. Even if a reproductive organ is defective in some manner, making it such that that organ does not possess the immediate present capacity to result in actual reproduction, it still remains a reproductive organ in fact, not just nominally, because it possesses the basic inherent capacity to be a reproductive organ.[106] That is, it is this organ *qua* organ that is suitable for reproduction. And regarding a reproductive-type *act*, I now argue that the process of reproduction has two parts. First, a reproductive act is the inseminatory union of male genital organ with female genital organ; a biological union in which the male and the female act as a single unit. Second, even if the act does not result in actual reproduction, the male and the female "still continue (biologically) to act as a unit." Say Lee and George, "A condition, or even a defect, which prevents the second part of the [reproductive] process cannot change the fact that the make and the female did become organically one by engaging in the first part of the process."[107] So it is a mistake to think that "only acts that have the power to reproduce are genuinely reproductive in kind." In fact, "the orientation of the sexual acts toward procreation belongs to the set of sexual acts, not directly to each act.... Many sexual acts are reproductive in kind which will not actually succeed in reproducing and are known to be impossible of succeeding. So these are acts in which the male and the female become a single unit."[108]

THE GOOD OF SELF-INTEGRATION

I said above that the biological matrix that is a foundational to bringing about or deepening interpersonal unity is part of, not merely an instrument of, man's personal subjectivity, of the unified bodily person. What

---

105. Lee and George, *Body-Self Dualism*, 182–83.
106. Ibid., 202.
107. Ibid., 203.
108. Ibid.

difference does it make if we treat the human body as an intrinsic part of the personal subject rather than as a mere instrument?[109] To treat our bodies as an instrument is to treat one's own body or others' bodies as a sub-personal object, as an extrinsic instrument that is outside me, as it were, rather than rightly treating the body as intrinsic to the person, as a unitary activity in which "bodily activity is as much the constitutive subject of what one does as one's act of choice is."[110] In doing so, we lay ourselves open to an existential "dis-integration of the self as bodily and the (same) self as personal," which is a violation of the good of self-integration and which is "attendant upon a reduction of one's bodily self to the level of an extrinsic instrument."[111]

How do we affirm the good of self-integration, that is, the self-integration of the person as bodily with the person as intentional agent? In short, how does the body participate in the unitary, multi-leveled personal communion that is conjugal love? Suppose we think in a Polanyian way of the conjugal act as a comprehensive entity.[112] "We can see then two complementary efforts aiming at the elucidation of a comprehensive entity. One proceeds from a recognition of a whole towards an identification of its particulars; the other from the recognition of a group of presumed particulars towards the grasping of their relation in the whole."[113] Let's take the second approach. What then is the relation of particulars like the body within that entitary whole that is the conjugal act? It's important to note that these particulars can be noticed in two different ways.

Polanyi's theory of tacit knowing is helpful here to gain conceptual clarity regarding these two ways. The theory comprises two kinds of awareness, *subsidiary awareness* and *focal awareness*, which are fundamental to the tacit comprehension of coherence, of a comprehensive entity.[114] Thus, we may be aware of the particulars *focally*; alternatively, we may be aware

109. Although I am following here the argument of Patrick Lee and Robert P. George ("What Sex Can Be"), I will show in the text that their argument is actually developing one of the chief claims of John Paul II's theology of the body, namely, that "the body reveals man" (*MWTB*, 9.4).

110. Finnis, "Personal Integrity, Sexual Morality, and Responsible Parenthood," 177.

111. Lee and George, "What Sex Can Be," 141, 139, respectively.

112. Polanyi, "Knowing and Being," 124–37. Earlier in chapter 4 of this book (187, 200–201) I explained how Polanyi's theory of tacit knowing is helpful in explaining the claim that the body is personal.

113. Ibid., 125.

114. Polanyi, "Logic of Tacit Inference," 138–58.

of them *"subsidiarily in terms of their participation in a whole."*[115] In the latter case of awareness, "we are subsidiarily aware of the elements that we integrate inside our body and where our body touches things outside it. This is how we are usually aware of our body." So, we are subsidiarily aware of one's body when one works and plays, when one communicates verbally in using the tongue to speak, and our finger to point. Significantly, we are also subsidiarily aware of our genitals when engaging in marital intercourse. As Polanyi argues, the body functions subsidiarly as part of the totality that is the unified, bodily person, such that the body serves the whole and participates in the resulting benefit. Therefore, Polanyi says, "Our internal parts are focally felt only when we are in pain." Or, as Grisez similarly points out, "in choosing to masturbate, one does not choose to act for a goal which fulfills oneself as a unified, bodily person. The only immediate goal is satisfaction for the conscious self; and so the body, not being part of the whole for whose sake the act is done, serves only as an extrinsic instrument. Thus, in choosing to masturbate one chooses to alienate one's body from one's conscious subjectivity."[116] Rather, normally speaking, adds Polanyi, "the external appearance of our body is rarely observed by us; people having no large looking glasses know very little of their body externally. It is the subsidiary sense of our body that makes us feel that it is *our* body. This is *the meaning our body normally has for us.* ... And hence we can say that in this sense all subsidiary elements are *interior to the body* in which we live. To this extent we dwell in all subsidiarily experienced things."[117]

However, it is possible to concentrate our focal attention on the particulars of the body in the biophysical sense, but doing so, says John Paul II, "is based on the disjunction between what is bodily and what is spiritual in man." That is, doing so ignores the phenomenological contrast between the interior experience of the body as my own and the "view of the body seen as an object from outside."[118] In other words, the study of the body in that sense *"does not yet develop* the consciousness of the body as a sign of the person, as a manifestation of the spirit." He adds, "When one uses such one-sided knowledge of the body's [biophysical] functions

---

115. Polanyi, "Knowing and Being," 128.
116. Grisez, *Way of the Lord Jesus*, 2:650.
117. Polanyi, "Sense-Giving and Sense-Reading," 183.
118. Polanyi, "Knowing and Being," 148.

as an organism, it is not difficult to reach the point of treating the body more or less systematically as an *object of manipulations*; in this case, man no longer identifies himself subjectively, so to speak, with his own body, because it is deprived of the meaning and dignity that stem from the fact that this body is proper to the person" (*MWTB*, 59.3). How then should we think of the meaning that is proper to the bodily person?

Tacit knowing then regards the phenomenological contrast described above "as the difference between looking *at* something and attending *from* it as something else that is its meaning." In other words, in tacit knowing we always attend from the subsidiary to the focal. Says Polanyi, "tacit knowing *is directed from the first to the second*." Thus: "Dwelling in our body clearly enables us to attend *from* it to things outside, while an external observer will tend to look *at* things happening in the body, seeing it as an object or as a machine. He will miss the meaning these events have for the person dwelling in the body and fail to share the experience the person has of his body."[119] Therefore, the body reveals the person because it is internally related to the entitary whole that is the conjugal act, but it does so when we attend *from* the particulars, the biological matrix, *to* the whole which they form. "In view of this, we may be prepared to consider the act of comprehending a whole *as an interiorization of its parts*, which makes us dwell in the parts. We may be said to live in the particulars which we comprehend."[120] Because of this interiorization, we can affirm the good of self-integration and, therefore, do justice to the first principle of the theology of the body, namely, that the "body *manifests* man" (*MWTB*, 12.5).

The Church teaches that marriage is part of God's plan of Creation. According to the order of creation, the marital act, which is an act of self-giving, consists of two inseparable meanings that enrich and deepen as well as express the spousal meaning of the body. But this meaning has been obscured by original sin as well as actual sin. "There inevitably follows a loss of awareness of the covenantal character of the union these persons had with God and with each other. The human body retains its 'spousal significance,' but this is now clouded by sin."[121] How in particular does sin effect "*the human essentiality of one's own body*, a difficulty man had not experienced in the state of original innocence" (*MWTB*, 28.2) [?]

---

119. Polanyi, "Logic of Tacit Inference," 141, 148, respectively.
120. Polanyi, "Knowing and Being," 148.
121. *Homosexualitatis problema*, no. 6.

The influence of sin shows itself in the "dimension of human interiority and, at the same time, it refers to the 'other.'" Regarding the former, man now experiences "an almost constitutive *difficulty in identifying oneself with [his] own body.*" But this difficulty is "not only in the sphere of one's own subjectivity, but even more so *in regard to the subjectivity of the other human being*, of woman for man and man for woman" (*MWTB*, 29.4). In other words, says the pope,

> [There is] a certain constitutive fracture in the human person's interior, *a breakup, as it were, of man's original spiritual and somatic unity*. He realizes for the first time that his body has ceased drawing on the power of the spirit, which raised him to the level of the image of God.... The body is not subject to the spirit as in the state of original innocence, but carries within itself a constant hotbed of resistance against the spirit and threatens in some way man's unity as a person, that is, the unity of the moral nature that plunges its roots firmly into the very constitution of the person. The concupiscence of the body is a specific threat to the structure of self-possession and self-dominion, through which the human person forms itself....
>
> Concupiscence in general—and the concupiscence of the body in particular—attacks precisely this "sincere gift": *it deprives man, one could say, of the dignity of the gift, which is expressed by his body through femininity and masculinity,* and in some sense "depersonalizes" man, making him an object "for the other." Instead of being "together with the other"—a subject in unity ... man becomes an object for man, the female for the male and vice versa....
>
> The human body in its masculinity and femininity has almost lost the power of expressing this love in which the human person becomes a gift, in conformity with the deepest structure and finality of his or her personal existence ... If we do not formulate this judgment here in an absolute way, but add the adverb "*almost (quasi)*," we do so because the dimension of gift—*that is, the power to express the love by which man, through his femininity or masculinity becomes a gift for another*—has in some measure continued to permeate and shape the love born in the human heart. The spousal meaning of the body has not become totally foreign to that heart: *it has not been totally suffocated in it by concupiscence, but only habitually threatened.* The "heart" has becomes a battlefield between love and concupiscence. The more concupiscence dominates the heart, the less the heart experiences the spousal meaning of the body, and the less sensitive it becomes to the gift of the person that

expresses precisely this meaning in the reciprocal relations of man and woman. (*MWTB*, 28.3, 32.4, 32.3, respectively)

I take what the pope is saying to be this: the fracture in the self as bodily and the (same) self as personal (spiritual) is a consequence of original sin, of the state of fallen human nature. This fracture, a self-disintegrity, or existential self-alienation, is such that it renders the person unable to act as an integrated, bodily being, alienating him from his own body or another person's body, an alienation that results in a choice to use his own body, or another person's body, as an object, as an extrinsic instrument. This choice unavoidably violates the basic human good of self-integration, damaging the body's capacity to function as an integral part of oneself in an act of self-giving, and hence to realize a one-flesh communion of bodily persons, which is the good of marriage.[122] This assessment also applies to homosexual sex: the partners do not unite biologically, as a single organism, and hence their sexual act does not actually effect unity, and so they do not become "one flesh." Because each person's self is fractured, he is self-alienated from his own body and treats his body and the other's body as an instrument in order to obtain subjective satisfaction, say, pleasurable experience of sexual arousal and orgasm. Due to the continuing hold exercised on man by the objective structures of creation, including the structures of the body, however tacit and muffled that may sometimes be because of sin, the spousal meaning of the body still shows itself in the aspiration of homosexuals to satisfy sexual intimacy, caring, and interpersonal love in the ongoing partnership of a common life—all of which are aspects of the good of marriage. Nonetheless, Grisez rightly argues:

> The coupling of two bodies of the same sex cannot form one complete organism and so cannot contribute to a bodily communion of persons. Hence, the experience of intimacy of the partners in sodomy cannot be the experience of any real unity between them. Rather, each one's experience of intimacy is private and incommunicable, and is no more a common good than is the mere experience of sexual arousal and orgasm. Therefore, the choice to engage in sodomy for the sake of that experience of intimacy in no way contributes to the partners' real common good as committed friends . . . At the same time, in choosing to act for an experience which they know cannot fulfill that capacity, they act on their inclination toward one-flesh communion in a self-defeating way. The

---

122. Grisez, *Way of the Lord Jesus*, 2:650–51.

preceding explanation has shown what is characteristic of sodomy: an experience of intimacy which cannot be the experience of a real communion of persons inasmuch as the coupling of two bodies of the same sex cannot form one complete organism.[123]

OBJECTIONS AND REPLIES

I turn now to consider several objections to the Church's teaching on the condition of homosexuality and homosexual genital acts.

Is There a Distinctive Sexual Ethics?

Regarding same-sex relationships, is the ethical quality of that relationship, rather than the body/gender of its participants, as Olthuis claims, the morally decisive factor? Olthuis explains: "That would mean, from a moral viewpoint, that the gender of the lovers in a committed relationship is less germane than we may think." That doesn't mean that anything goes. Rather, "moral norms—troth, justice, integrity, mutuality, choice, non-coercive consent, etc.—remain clear and undiluted. Violence of any kind in sexual relations is condemned; rape, incest, abuse of children, battering of women or children stand judged. The relevance of this call for normativity in our contemporary world plagued with violence and antinormative behavior needs no argument. We have clear normative guidelines for everyone regardless of sexual orientation."[124] The view expressed by Olthuis, sometimes called the "responsible-relational"[125] position, claims that the morally decisive factors in a sexual relationship are none other than conformity to general moral norms governing relationships as such. Norms that prohibit lying, deception, and exploitation are sufficient to render sexual acts morally good. This is how Margaret Farley describes the norms for what she calls sexual justice: refusal to do unjust harm, free consent, mutuality, equality, commitment, fruitfulness, and social justice.[126]

---

123. Ibid., 653–54.
124. Olthuis, "When is Sex Against Nature?" 201.
125. Lawler, Boyle, and May, *Catholic Sexual Ethics*, 14.
126. Farley, *Just Love*, 231: "Sex should not be used in ways that exploit, objectify, or dominate; rape, violence, and harmful uses of power in sexual relationships are ruled out; freedom, wholeness, intimacy, pleasure are values to be affirmed in relationships marked by mutuality, equality, and some form of commitment; sexual relations like other profound interpersonal relations can and ought to be fruitful both within and beyond

But this view assumes that the moral norms that make sexual acts morally right are no different than general moral norms governing relationships as such, namely, norms that prohibit lying, deception, coercion, exploitation, and so forth. In other words, the "responsible-relational" view, whatever its undeniable merits—surely all interpersonal relationships should be free of deception, noncoercive, and nonexploitative—leaves us without a specific *sexual* ethics. Aren't there "special moral responsibilities that flow from concern for the human goods [the interpersonal unity that is marital communion and its natural fulfillment in procreation] toward which sexuality itself is ordered [?]."[127] In other words, there can only be special moral responsibilities if sexual acts are uniquely distinct from other bodily acts because they are ordered to real human goods that are intrinsic aspects of the well-being and fulfillment of human persons. Patrick Lee rightly states, "It seems that there is something special about sex, and it seems that we can be aware of this point whether we accept revelation or not. For example, it seems clear to most people that a punch in the nose is far less serious than rape, although both involve violence. And it seems that this can be true only if sexual acts have some feature or features making them significantly different from other bodily acts."[128] Lee offers some examples that I will adapt to illustrate this difference.

Consider two scenarios. In one, I buy a colleague an expensive dinner with the mutual understanding that he will take over teaching my class when I am out of town visiting family. In another, I buy a woman I know an expensive cruise with the mutual understanding that she will have sex with me. In both cases, the individuals seek to back out of the agreement with me. Our reaction would be different in each case. On the one hand, we wouldn't hesitate to say that my colleague owes it to me to comply with our agreement. On the other hand, we wouldn't hesitate to say that it was bad for this woman to agree to such a deal with me in the first place; in addition, and most important, we don't think that I am entitled to the fulfillment of the agreement against the wishes of this woman. Isn't the disparity in these scenarios suggestive of the difference between sex and other bodily acts? Consider some other examples:

---

the relationship; the affections of desire and love that bring about and sustain sexual relationships are all in all genuinely to affirm both lover and beloved."

127. May, *Catholic Sexual Ethics*, 14.

128. Lee, "Human Body and Sexuality in the Teaching of Pope John Paul II," 108.

> A and B could enter a contract involving physical therapy, dental work, hair cutting, and so on, all actions which B might perform on A's body. And with respect to such acts we have no hesitation about their being commercialized, and the relevant contracts being enforced. A may hire B wholly or in part because B is a skillful physical therapist. Moreover, B's continuing to provide that service may quite properly be a condition of his or her continued employment. But most of us would at least balk at saying that C could hire D wholly or in part because of her sexual skills and make her continued employment conditional upon her continuing to provide those services. Moreover, we do not hesitate to say that bodily actions such as physical therapy are appropriate actions to perform with anyone, including one's parents, one's children, or even lower animals (as in veterinary). Yet sexual actions are not appropriate with our children or parents, or with animals.[129]

Significantly, insisting that voluntary and informed consent would be sufficient to render these actions different from immoral manipulation seems incorrect. For, Lee adds, "if this were true, then our different reactions to the different scenarios described above would be groundless."[130] What then is it about sexual acts that make them different from other bodily acts? And if they are uniquely distinct, because they are ordered by their very nature to marital communion and procreation, marital love and children, doesn't that mean that there is a distinctive sexual ethics?

There is another major point to consider in rejecting the view represented by Olthuis and Farley. This view seems to presuppose a dualistic view of the human person—"dualistic in the sense of viewing the self as something which *has* or *inhabits* a body, rather than being a living, bodily entity."[131] But if the "human person is essentially a bodily being, a unity of body and soul, and that therefore the masculinity or femininity of the human being is internal to his or her personhood (rather than just interesting external 'equipment')," as John Paul II has argued, then it seems likely that this view does not do justice to the embodiment of human persons as man and woman and hence to sexual differences between them. By assuming the *in*significance of sexual difference for making a sexual act morally right, this view fails to grasp the unified totality that is the body-person and hence the human meaning of the body, especially but

129. Ibid.
130. Ibid.
131. Ibid., 107.

not only for sexual acts.[132] Says John Paul, "The body can never be reduced to mere matter: it is a *spiritualized body*, just as man's spirit is so closely united to the body that he can be described as *an embodied spirit*."[133] Intriguingly, this, too, is the view of Farley:

> We usually think of freedom as a capacity of the spirit, and free choice as an act of the spirit, with the body being simply the object or the instrument of our choice in some way. Yet choice is always of an action, and although action may sometimes seem to be wholly interior (as when we choose to accept a situation about which we can do nothing), it is always action that rises from and is realized by ourselves as embodied spirits, inspirited bodies. As I have been trying to show, our bodies are not purely passive, not appendages, not merely instruments for ourselves; they are intrinsic to our selves. The body, inspirited, is therefore intrinsic to ourselves as subject; we "live" our bodies even when we are using them.[134]

Farley is right that the human person is bodily, but it is not too long before she claims that "Postmodern ways of thinking have so subverted and destabilized notions of the human body and of gender that there is no longer any room for a moral 'law.'"[135] That is, there is no room, on her view, for a moral law, grounded in the one human nature, willed by God, and known as the natural law.[136] The reason for her rejection of a moral law derives from her view that the meaning of the body/gender is no longer rooted in the very nature of man as embodied person; this nature possessing a creational teleology ordering the body-soul person to the sexual "other."[137] In other words, since sex is merely a biological category ("interesting external equipment") and gender is a socially and culturally constructed category, Farley rejects the teaching of the Church, indeed of Vatican II, that "the principles of the moral order . . . spring from human nature itself."[138] Since Farley assumes the *in*significance of sexual difference for making a sexual act morally right, her positions on sexual ethics (e.g., fornication, masturbation, and homosexuality) are al-

---

132. John Paul II, *Veritatis Splendor*, no. 50.
133. John Paul II, *Letter to Families*, no. 19.
134. Farley, *Just Love*, 129.
135. Ibid., 131.
136. Benedict XVI, *Caritas in Veritate*, no. 59.
137. Levering, "Knowing What is 'Natural,'" 135.
138. *Dignitatis Humanae*, no. 14.

most entirely inconsistent with the Church's sexual ethics.[139] And Vatican II adds, particularly now in regard to sexual ethics, "When it is a question of harmonizing married love with the responsible transmission of life, it is not enough to take only the good intention and the evaluation of motives into account; the objective criteria must be used, criteria drawn from the nature of the human person and human action, criteria which respect the total meaning of mutual self-giving and human procreation in the context of true love; all this is possible only if the virtue of married chastity is seriously practiced."[140] In conclusion, given her dualistic view of the body/self relation, the body is just raw material for the meaning-conferring activities of human persons, as John Paul critically remarks throughout his writings.[141] Since sexuality has no definite personal meaning, and can only receive a more-than-physiological meaning from a freedom that is self-designing, this is a personalism that misunderstands embodiment—Crosby calls it "spiritualistic personalism"[142]—and hence it fails to recognize that man lives as the subject of his own moral acts as a body-person. "And since the human person cannot be reduced to a freedom which is self-designing, but entails a particular spiritual and bodily structure, the primordial moral requirement of loving and respecting the person as an end [in the medium of its unity as body and soul] and never as a mere means also implies, by its very nature, respect for certain fundamental goods [toward which sexuality itself is ordered], without which one would fall into relativism and arbitrariness."[143] In sum, given their dualistic view of the human person and all that it entails, Olthuis and Farley reject traditional sexual morality, and hence are unable to do justice, not only to the intrinsic place of bodily sexual difference, indeed of unity-in-difference, in interpersonal unity, but also to the moral status of the human body.

---

139. For a summary statement of the Church's teaching on sexual ethics, see *Catechism of the Catholic Church*, nos. 2331–2400.
140. *Gaudium et Spes*, no. 51.
141. *Veritatis Splendor*, no. 48; *Letter to Families*, no. 19.
142. Crosby, "Estrangement of Persons from their Bodies," 130.
143. *Veritatis Splendor*, no. 48.

The Sterility Objection

Let us now consider the objection that some have called "the sterility objection." The objection focuses on the analogy between sterile heterosexuals and homosexuals and alleges that a "double standard" is at work in opposing same-sex marriage but not marriage "where sterility is certain and even certain to be permanent (as in the case of the marriage of a woman who has been through menopause or has undergone a hysterectomy)."[144] As one objector puts it:

> If there is no possibility of procreation, then sterile couples are, like homosexuals, incapable of sex acts "open to procreation." What is the point of sex in an infertile marriage? Not procreation; the partners (let us assume) know that they are infertile. If they have sex, it is for pleasure and to express their love, or friendship, or some shared good. It will be for precisely the same reason that committed, loving gay couples have sex. Why are these good reasons for sterile or elderly married couples but not for gay and lesbian couples?[145]

This argument from analogy fails.[146] First, this objection overlooks the sameness in what sterile and fertile married couples do, namely, penal-vaginal intercourse ("anatomical fit") in which the organic complementarity of a reproductive-type act enables them truly to become one body, one organism. So there is no difference in what they do. The difference is elsewhere, that is, in the nonbehavioral conditions extrinsic to what they do, but which affect what may result from what they do. Grisez explains: "In most instances, [of infertility] of course, physiological conditions preclude reproduction. However, those conditions are not part of the human act of intercourse, for they are neither included in the couple's behavior nor subject to their choice. So, the appropriateness of their human act of sexual intercourse to realize their organic complementarity depends, not on its being able to cause conception, but only on its being the pattern of behavior which, in conjunction with other necessary conditions, would result in conception."[147] In sum, "their act remains the kind of bodily act

---

144. George, *Clash of Orthodoxies*, 79.

145. Stephen Macedo as cited in Lee and George, "What Sex Can Be," 149.

146. Lee and George, "What Sex Can Be," 149–56. Grisez, *Way of the Lord Jesus*, 2:634–36. George, *Clash of Orthodoxies*, 77–86.

147. Grisez, *Way of the Lord Jesus*, 2:634.

that alone is "apt" for generating human life."[148] What this means is that a heterosexual couple embodies a procreative communion—whether or not the non-behavioral conditions of procreation obtain—when they willingly and lovingly consent to join their lives in an act of itself—a reproductive-type act that realizes their organic complementarity—suited to procreating, and hence "their mutual self-giving actualizes their one-flesh unity."[149] As Robert George and Gerard V. Bradley note in answer to a homosexual apologist's question regarding the point of sex in an infertile marriage: "the intrinsic point of sex in marriage, fertile or not, is . . . the basic good of marriage itself, considered as a two-in-one-flesh communion of persons that is consummated and actualized by acts of the reproductive type. Such acts alone among sexual acts can be truly unitive, and thus marital, and marital acts, thus understood, have their intelligibility and value intrinsically, and not merely by virtue of their capacity to facilitate the realization of other goods."[150]

Second, the difference between any heterosexual couple—sterile or fertile—and a homosexual one is a radical difference: they lack the biological basis of organic complementarity making it impossible for them to perform the kind of reproductive-type act which makes them the one-flesh union of marriage itself. Unlike the sterile heterosexual couple whose physiological conditions preclude conception, the homosexual couple's sexual acts do not unite them biologically—they do not perform with each other a reproductive-type act—but also "homosexual partners cannot form the kind of personal communion with each other which is embodied by reproductive-type acts."[151] This radical difference in what they do is morally significant. This brings me to my third point.

Third, there is a moral difference between treating one's body or another's body as an extrinsic instrument and treating the body as intrinsic to the person, as incorporated into the unitary activity of the person's life. The former treatment instrumentalizes the body. This way of treating the body is in itself wrong because the body is not merely related to the person as something to be manipulated as if it were merely an object. Rather it is related as something to be interiorized into the life of the person,

---

148. May, "On the Impossibility of Same-Sex Marriage."
149. Grisez, *Way of the Lord Jesus*, 2:635.
150. George and Bradley, "Marriage and the Liberal Imagination," 305. This passage is cited in May, "On the Impossibility of Same-Sex Marriage."
151. Lee and George, "What Sex Can Be," 150 n. 29.

for the body manifests man, as John Paul II repeatedly states. Thus, in the bi-unity marital bond the body provides the person with a medium for a deeper and fuller disclosure of himself in a bodily act that springs from the depths of his selfhood and interiority. In short, the human body serves to manifest the supreme self-gift of the person, which is the fullest disclosure of the spousal meaning of the body. Thus: "To regard one's body as an extrinsic instrument is immoral because it involves contempt for the body; it involves treating the body as if it were outside oneself, a sub-personal object. To treat one's body as a mere object is a violation of the basic good of self-integration. Since we are our bodies (and do not merely inhabit them), it is treating a person (ourselves) as a sub-personal object."[152] For the Christian, to treat one's own body or that of another as an object is to do an injustice to the human body, which "shares in the dignity of 'the image of God.'"[153] "Do you not know that your own body is a temple of the Holy Spirit, who is in you, whom you have received from God? You are not your own; you were bought at a price. Therefore honor God with your body" (1 Cor 6: 18–20).

John Paul II speaks of the sexual act as an act of complete self-giving and it is a reciprocal act of giving; it is a giving that helps complete the other. In the sexual act the female rejoices in what is masculine about the male and the male rejoices in what is feminine about the female. The two more perfectly image God in whose image they are made, "male and female he created them" (Gen 1:27).

Is the Church's Teaching on Homosexuality Contradictory?

Is the Church's teaching contradictory, as some allege? The distinction between condition and activity, when first made in *Persona Humana*, was not well understood, especially because the CDF suggested that some people who suffer from the condition are not morally blameworthy. Does this mean that same-sex attraction is unchosen? Hence, is the condition constitutive of the emotional and sexual identity of some people, and, if so, is it unalterable? How can we understand something to be morally wrong if it is not the result of a free choice?

Some clarity was gained with the follow-up document from the CDF, *Homosexualitatis problema*. The CDF there explicitly rejected "an

---

152. Ibid., 155.
153. *Catechism of the Catholic Church*, no. 364.

overly benign interpretation [of] the homosexual condition itself," particularly the view of those "going so far as to call it [morally] neutral, or even good." This interpretation arose particularly because there was reluctance on the part of some, and downright refusal on the part of others, to make a judgment about the homosexual condition itself, especially if it was involuntary. The CDF answered: "Although the particular inclination of the homosexual person is not a sin, it is a more or less strong tendency ordered toward an intrinsic moral evil; and thus the inclination must be seen as an objective disorder."[154] And yet the critics persisted, some, as noted, even urging that the Church's teaching was contradictory. If the homosexual condition itself is morally blameless, they asked, why is an individual morally blameworthy if he acts upon it? As Andrew Sullivan was eventually to ask, "If there is nothing morally wrong, per se, with the homosexual condition or with homosexual love and self-giving, then homosexual persons are indeed analogous to those [heterosexuals] who cannot reproduce.... [The Church] cannot yet see [homosexuals] as it sees sterile heterosexuals: as people who, with respect to procreation, suffer from a clear limiting condition, but who nevertheless have a potential for real emotional and spiritual self-realization.... It cannot yet see them as truly made in the image of God."[155]

Clarity is much needed here. First, as I argued in the last chapter as well as earlier in this chapter, even if homosexuality is a condition, not a choice, it doesn't follow that the condition is something other than a reflection of the state of man's fallen nature (*status naturae lapsae*), that is, his inner spiritual woundedness. Theologically, in other words, the ultimate origin of this condition is the Fall.[156] Furthermore, Scripture's condemnation of sin, including homosexuality, pertains not only to outward acts but also to man's inward condition. Reformed theologian Greg L. Bahnsen correctly argues that this condition is the source of man's sinful activities:

> Scripture teaches that all men inherit a depraved, fleshly nature: a principle of sin operates in their members and captivates them [Rom 7:23], the fleshly nature brings forth fruit unto death [Rom 7:5], and it lusts against the Spirit so that men cannot do the things

154. *Homosexualitatis problema*, no. 3.
155. Sullivan, "Catholicism and Homosexuality," 319.
156. Aidan Nichols makes this very point in *Epiphany*, 423. See also, Smith, "Thomas Aquinas on Homosexuality," 139.

they would [Gal 5:17]. The flesh gives rise to certain forms of evil [Gal 5:19], so that by nature men fulfill the desires of the flesh and mind [Eph 2:3]. It would be hard to understand such teachings apart from some notion of inner disposition and inherited orientation. The same holds for the doctrine that "out of the heart are the issues of life" [Prov 4:23]; the Bible portrays man's heart as stiff, crooked, uncircumcised, deceitful, divided, hard, blind, and darkened [Deut 10:16; Prov 17:20]; Jer 9:26]; 17:9; Hos 10:2; Matt 19:8; Eph 4:18]. Such metaphors demonstrate that biblical writers recognized an inner, spiritual depravity in men—a disinclination to good and a propensity for evil . . . Therefore, we cannot deny that an inner, inherited, irresistible orientation of man's psyche was recognized in Scripture, and this condition was viewed precisely as the source of man's sinful activities. Men are drawn away by their own lusts, which conceive and bring forth sin. As Jesus declared, "Out of the heart proceed evil thoughts, murder, adulteries, fornications, thefts, false witness, [and] blasphemies."[157]

Sullivan is then mistaken in the two conclusions he draws from the CDF claim that the condition itself is not sinful. First, even if the individual in that condition is not blamable for being in that condition, it doesn't follow that there is nothing morally problematic with the condition itself. Rather, it is an expression of man's fallen condition and, being a disordered condition, we should strive, by God's grace, or order, to transform, any disorder that results from sin. But the mere possession of a disorder does not necessarily suggest that one had done something culpable or is morally wrong.

Second, he also misunderstands the CDF when he suggests that *Homosexualitatis problema* is saying that there is nothing wrong with homosexual generosity and self-giving. Actually, the document says, "Homosexual activity is not a complementary union, able to transmit life; and so it thwarts the call to a life of that form of self-giving which the Gospel says is the essence of Christian living. *This does not mean that homosexual persons are not often generous and giving of themselves; but when they engage in homosexual activity they confirm within themselves a disordered sexual inclination which is essentially self-indulgent.*"[158] Whether or not one agrees with the judgment that homosexual sex is self-indulgent, that is, violating the bodily person's capacity for authentic self-giving is

---

157. Bahnsen, *Homosexuality*, 66–67.
158. *Homosexualitatis problema*, no. 7.

not, as such, the point here. I have argued above that homosexual sex violates the good of personal self-integrity and hence damages the partners' ability "to participate in the real and basic good of marital union, rather than to induce in oneself and one's partner(s) a merely illusory experience of interpersonal unity."[159] Rather, the point is that there is no way to claim that the CDF is suggesting that there is nothing wrong with homosexual generosity and self-giving; if anything the CDF is saying that genuine generosity and self-giving is lacking in homosexual sex to participate in the common good of marital union. Admittedly, there would have been no room for misinterpretations like Sullivan's if the CDF had made explicit, in stating that the homosexual condition is objectively disordered, that a fallen human nature is the source of man's sinful acts. In other words, what the CDF did not make as clear as it should of is that even though we may have wounds in our being for which we are not responsible, it is not correct at all to claim that that woundedness is natural and thus a legitimate source for human moral action.

Indeed, the CDF could have avoided altogether the charge of being entangled in contradiction if it had satisfactorily explained its claim that the condition is objectively disordered but that the particular inclination which has its source in that condition is not sinful. To begin with, if homosexual acts are inherently sinful, then the desire for homosexual sex is an inherently sinful desire. This can be said without implying that the individual with those desires is necessarily blameworthy for having them. Furthermore, theologically, if the ultimate origin of the homosexual condition is our fallen human nature, then there would be no justification for seeing homosexuality from the order of creation as a creational given, a normal variant of sexuality, and hence there would be no parity between homosexuality and heterosexuality in light of that order. Of course the CDF does not deny this fundamental teaching. What I am saying is that the CDF could have prevented any confusion from taking root if from the outset it had made clear that Scripture's condemnation of homosexuality pertains not only to outward acts but also to the inward condition itself, to homosexual actions as well as the homosexual condition itself. For, according to the Scriptures, it is not only actions that are wrong, but also the desire to do such actions (see Matt 5:27–29; Rom 13:14; Col 3:5–6; 1 Pet 2:11).

159. Lee and George, "What Sex Can Be," 136.

The CDF could have clarified the difference it was expressing between condition and act by appealing to the necessary distinction between evil (*malum*), sin (*peccatum*), and moral fault or wrong (*culpa*). Evil is a privation, an objective evil, such as being born deaf, blind, or with spina bifida, all of which are contrary to God's will in creation. Furthermore, technically *peccatum* properly translated as sin (but perhaps more properly understood as "mistake" or "wrong") refers to any disordered act even though it is not deliberately willed, such as an emotional outburst of anger, or some abnormal personality structure. If the emotion is inordinate, meaning thereby too strong for the occasion or the person we're angry at, then it's a sin. Still, perhaps we're not at fault if such emotional outbursts are expressions of a personality disorder. Moreover, moral fault or *culpa* (which is commonly referred to as sin) refers to an act done with deliberate will, for which the person is morally culpable, blamable and worthy of being punished. Janet E. Smith is helpful in explaining these distinctions from St. Thomas Aquinas and their import for sexual matters.

> Malum (translated as "evil") is any privation of form or order or due measure either in the subject or in the act; it would be right to speak of this as objective evil. Peccatum (translated as "sin"), a subcategory of malum, is any act lacking due order or form or measure (e.g., limping). And culpa (translated as "fault"), a subcategory of peccatum, is a voluntarily disordered act.... In order to illustrate Aquinas's terms and to show the disparity between them and common English usage, let us apply his distinctions to four sexual matters. 1) If one were infertile, Aquinas would call this condition a malum, since infertility is not the natural or healthy or good condition for an adult person. 2) If one were to undertake an act of sexual intercourse (and here it is irrelevant whether the act is with one's spouse or with one not one's spouse), and were unable to complete the act because of impotence, Aquinas would call this act a peccatum (a kind of malum), not because the act is blameworthy (assuming it is not) but because it is an act that did not achieve its proper completion or fullness. 3) If one were mistakenly (and not culpable for one's ignorance) to have intercourse with a woman one believed to be one's spouse, this act would also be a peccatum, but not a culpa. 4) If one deliberately and willingly had sexual intercourse with someone one knew not to be one's spouse, this act would be a culpa.... [A]gents in instances 3 and 4 would be understood to have committed adultery, an intrinsically

evil act, but only the agent in instance 4 would have committed a blameworthy act.[160]

In light of Smith's explanations of Aquinas' distinction, we can say that the homosexual condition of same-sex attraction is an objective evil, a *malum* resulting from the Fall (as is the *malum* of infertility in Smith's example). The activity itself of same-sex relations is a sin, a *peccatum*, and if deliberately willed, arising from an inherently sinful desire for homosexual sex, a moral fault, a *culpa*. Calling the condition a *malum*, not a *peccatum*, and certainly not a *culpa*, raises the question of the moral blameworthiness of the person in a homosexual condition, particularly one who has the desire for homosexual sex. Although the condition is something else than the desire, it seems to me that the former is what gives rise to the latter by virtue of multiple causative factors for homosexuality—indirect congenital influences, postnatal biological influences, macro- and micro-cultural influences from one's environment, and personal psychological predispositions. All these causes may contribute to the emergence of same-sex desires, particularly when those desires are voluntarily cultivated, becoming stronger and focused, inclining us to act in regarding to something that is inherently wrong. Surely that is consistent with Gagnon's claim that "choices ... involv[ing] responses to socio-cultural stimuli ... may, down the end of a long road, lead to greater or lesser likelihood of homosexual identification."[161] But then isn't an individual with those desires blameworthy for them? Aren't any desires for illicit sexual activity on his part sinful, due to his volition being involved? Again, consider the example in which a married man has adulterous desires for a specific woman. I don't mean so-called unguarded thoughts about another woman for which he quickly prays for healing. I mean the willful cultivation of that adulterous desire that is, biblically speaking, inherently sinful. The *Catechism of the Catholic Church* states that "Christ condemns even adultery of mere desire."[162] Surely, in this case, I am blameworthy for my adulterous desire. Thus, since the desire for homosexual sex is an inherently sinful desire, it is not only a *peccatum*, but also a *culpa*.

We must always keep clearly in mind that the Church has great sympathy for those with the homosexual condition; they possess a disorder

---

160. Smith, "Moral Terminology and Proportionalism," 128.
161. Gagnon, "Sexual Orientation." Email Correspondence.
162. *Catechism of the Catholic Church*, no. 2380.

that makes life difficult (as all human beings possess disorders that make life difficult). Although it is an objective evil, the Church does not consider the homosexual condition in itself to be a culpa or sin; she considers both cultivated desires, due to the individual's volition that is involved, and freely chosen acts, to be susceptible to moral judgment, and hence morally blameworthy.

The Image of God and Man's Sinful Condition

Stephen Pope raises the fourth objection to the Church's position on the homosexual condition and homosexual genital acts succinctly. He maintains that the CDF "implies that homosexuals are internally directed to a form of sexual love that will always be effectively sterile and to relationships that are irredeemably dysfunctional. *The abstract affirmation [by the Church] of the imago Dei is undercut by this way of regarding the core of the person's sexuality—if not by logic, then by psychological experience.*"[163] As I said earlier, critics, such as Pope, claim that the Church is inconsistent. On the one hand, the Church teaches that the individual in a homosexual condition is a person of dignity, created in God's image, and that he should be shown respect, compassion, and sensitivity. On the other hand, if my sexual identity is at the core of my personal identity, as these critics of the Church's position claims, how then can my dignity be honored if that core is objectively disordered, and is regarded as an objective evil? Isn't then the affirmation of being in God's image just an abstraction that is undercut, as one objector put it, "if not by logic, then by psychological experience [?]."

In one sense, this objection is hard to fathom. The fall into sin, original sin, has corrupted the image of God in all men. "The harmony ... thanks to original [holiness and] justice is now destroyed: the control of the soul's spiritual faculties over the body is shattered; the union of man and woman becomes subject to tensions, their relations henceforth marked by lust and domination. Harmony with creation is broken: visible creation has become alien and hostile to man."[164] And so the same ques-

---

163. Pope, "Vatican's Blunt Instrument."

164. *Catechism of the Catholic Church*, no. 400. Furthermore, "Because of man, creation is now subject 'to its bondage to decay' [Rom 8:21]. Finally, the consequence explicitly foretold for this disobedience will come true: man will 'return to the ground' [Gen 3:19], for out of it he was taken. *Death makes its entrance into human history* [see Rom 5:12]" (ibid.) See also, *Catechism*, no. 405.

tion could be asked, indeed, has been asked throughout the history of the Church and Christian theology: does my fallen human nature undercut the *imago Dei* and, if so, in what sense? Put differently, how are we to understand the central question of man's humanity *in* his sinfulness?[165] Does the Fall literally dehumanize man, depriving him of his essential nature?

We are all children of Adam and by virtue of this unity we are all implicated in his sin. St. Paul affirms: "By one man's disobedience many [that is, all men] were made sinners": "sin came into the world through one man and death through sin, and so death spread to all men because all men sinned" (Rom 5:12, 19). This original sin is the state or underlying condition of man's alienation from God that is the source of visible acts of sin. It affects human nature, resulting in a deep flaw in that nature and hence a fallen state. Helmut Thielicke correctly remarks in his gloss on Romans 5:18 ("one man's trespass led to condemnation for all men"): "We are all under the same condemnation and each of us has received his 'share' of it." He then draws this implication: "In any case, from this point of view the homosexual share of that condemnation has no greater gravity which would justify any Pharisaic feelings of self-righteousness and integrity on the part of us 'normal' persons."[166]

Of course God didn't create man flawed. John Paul II rightly says, "The splendor of truth shines forth in all the works of the Creator and, in a special way, in man, created in the image and likeness of God (cf. Gen 1:26)."[167] Thus, we must distinguish between his nature as created by God and the crisis effected by original sin itself. This fallen state affects the whole of man's nature, every aspect of human existence—personal, social, cultural, and the like. In the history of Christian thought sin has been likened to an illness, moral guilt, an enslaving force, as well as the antithesis between two comprehensive ways of living (death and life [Rom 6:3-8], darkness and light [John 1:5; 1 Pet 2:9], flesh and spirit [Gal 5:16-26], being lost and being found [Luke 15]).[168] In sum, then, "Following St. Paul, the Church has always taught that the overwhelming misery which oppresses men and their inclination toward evil and death cannot be understood apart from their connection with Adam's sin and the fact

---

165. Berkouwer, *De Mens het Beeld Gods*, 124-56; ET: *Man: The Image of God*, 119-47.

166. Thielicke, *Ethics of Sex*, 283.

167. John Paul II writes these words in the opening sentence of *Veritatis Splendor*.

168. On this, see McGrath, *Intellectuals Don't Need God*, 134-37.

that he has transmitted to us a sin with which we are all born afflicted, a sin which is the 'death of the soul.'"¹⁶⁹ Man's alienation from God produces man's spiritual death, manifesting itself in "hardness and impenitent heart" (Rom 2: 5), in "ungodliness and unrighteousness" (Rom 1:18), in "vanity and darkness" (Rom 1:21), and "foolishness and uncleanness (Rom 1:22, 24). "Man is flesh, darkness, a slave of sin, lawless, rebellious, [and] full of error. And in all this, he shows his enmity to God—one of Scripture's sharpest and most radical characterizations of sin. The inclination of the flesh is enmity towards God (Rom 8:7; cf. Col 1:21)."¹⁷⁰ This inclination to evil is called concupiscence, as I noted in the last chapter. The sacrament of Baptism imparts new life in Christ, frees us from original sin and reconciles us to God. Nevertheless, man's wounded nature, though renewed in Christ at its root, remains weakened and inclined to evil, and hence is still caught up in a spiritual battle between the old and the new man, the flesh and the spirit (Gal 5:16–26). Thus, those who freely engage in sinful acts, including homosexual acts, are giving in to the desires of the flesh and not disciplining the flesh as Scripture exhorts us to do.

Thus, on the one hand, there is the Church's teaching that the heart of sin is the alienation from God that produces spiritual death. On the other hand, however, the Church also teaches that *in* this alienation from God, man still remains man: man's nature, his fundamental identity, has not been annihilated or extinguished by sin, and since all substantializing of sin is rejected, man's nature after the Fall is still the work and creature of God, intrinsically religious, that is, intrinsically ordered to the knowledge of God, and hence the deepest foundation of human nature is still what God made it. That is, as the *Catechism of the Catholic Church* teaches: "The desire for God is written in the human heart, because man is created by God and for God; and God never cease to draw man to himself." In addition, "Although man can forget God or reject him, He never ceases to call every man to seek him, so as to find life and happiness." Furthermore, "Being in the image of God the human individual possesses the dignity of a person, who is not just something, but someone. He is capable of self-knowledge, of self-possession and of freely giving himself and entering into communion with other persons. And he is called by grace to a covenant with his Creator, to offer him a response of faith and love that

---

169. *Catechism of the Catholic Church*, no. 403.
170. Berkouwer, *De Mens het Beeld Gods*, 152; ET: *Man: The Image of God*, 143–44.

no other creature can give in his stead."[171] Moreover, although the Church calls all men to acknowledge and accept their sexual identity, that is, sexual differentiation and complementarity, a person's sexual identity is grounded in his more fundamental identity, namely, "the creature of God, and by grace, His child and heir to eternal life."[172] Thus, the person who experiences same-sex attractions is made no less in the image of God than any other human being; his same-sex attractions are simply the result of his being a fallen creature, as we all are. The individual in a homosexual condition must accept his maleness (or her femaleness) as a gift from God and that his maleness or her femaleness is a way in which he or she is made in God's image. The experience of homosexual attractions does not obliterate the fundamental maleness and femaleness of our being nor the necessity of embracing and identifying with these fundamental features of our identity.

The Church may speak of man's humanity *in* his sinfulness, within the corruption of man's nature, because the light of divine mercy and common grace, centered in Christ, restrains, holds in check, that is, limits the power of sin and evil from having its full way with us. God's mercy and grace has a conserving effect that keeps man human. Dooyeweerd explains:

> It is all due to God's common grace in Christ that there are still means left in the temporal world to resist the destructive force of the elements that have got loose; that there are still means to combat disease, to check psychic maladies, to practice logical thinking, to save cultural development from going down into savage barbarism, to develop language, to preserve the possibility of social intercourse, to withstand injustice, and so on. All these things are the fruits of Christ's work, even before His appearance on the earth. From the very beginning God has viewed His fallen creation in the light of the Redeemer.... [M]eaning in apostasy remains real meaning in accordance with its creaturely mode of being. [173]

Unlike common grace, however, there is the particular grace of Jesus Christ that renews and regenerates the fallen man from sin, reconciling him to God the Father, in Christ, and through the power of the Holy Spirit. The restorative and saving grace of God, through the saving

---

171. *Catechism of the Catholic Church*, nos. 27, 30, 357.
172. *Homosexualitatis problema*, no. 16.
173. Dooyweerd, *New Critique of Theoretical Thought*, 2:34–35.

death and resurrection of Christ, renews the meaning of God's creation, breaks the power of sin, cancels our moral guilt, and offers us new life in Christ as a gift. "Catholicism teaches before everything the restoration of wounded nature by the grace of Jesus Christ. The restoration of nature: so there must be a nature, and of what value, since it is the work of God, Who created it and re-created it by repurchasing it at the price of His own Blood! Thus grace presupposes nature, and the excellence of nature which it comes to heal and transfigure."[174]

In this light, we can easily understand why the Church is right about reassuring people that they are created in God's image. This foundational Christian truth certainly entails reassuring them of their human worth in God's eyes in Christ. Still, in reply the homosexual avers that the Church's exclusiveness is contrary to the open, inviting, and inclusive message of the gospel.[175]

In response to this charge, two things must be said. First, of course, no sinner is excluded from the Church—not the thief, murderer, adulterer, fornicator, spouse abuser, and so forth. For it is proof of God's own love for us that Christ died for us while we were still sinners (Rom 5:8; Eph 2:4–5). The Church is a body of sinners, and thus it makes absolutely no sense to claim that she excludes anyone, regardless of their sins. As Dominican theologian Benedict Ashley notes, Sinners "are not excluded from the Church's care, since it prays for them and, like Jesus, seeks the lost sheep's return (Luke 15:1–7; cf. St. Paul, 2 Cor 2:1–4 urging love for an excommunicated man)." "The Church is always," Fr. Ashley adds, "ready to receive them into full forgiveness and communion when they are willing to return to the Christian life. The Church is obliged to do this by Jesus' own words about the love to be shown even to enemies (Matt 5:43–48) and the prodigal son (Luke 15:11–32)."[176]

Second, we stand condemned as sinners apart from the saving grace of Christ (Rom 8:1), and so we are called to make a heartfelt act of repentance in responding positively to the invitation of the gospel of salvation. Sometimes I think that people who claim that they are being excluded from the Church deny this basic tenet of Christian faith. They seem to be suggesting that our human nature is pleasing to God and affirmed

---

174. Gilson, *Christianity and Philosophy*, 111.

175. The next two paragraphs are from my article, "There is Wideness to God's Mercy," 54.

176. See also, Ashley, "Compassion and Sexual Orientation," 105–11.

by him *as it is*, without redemption and renewal. But that would deny created human reality's fallen state, which would, as Fr. Thomas Guarino puts it, "overlook God's judgment on the world rendered dramatically in the cross of Christ."[177] In other words, they seem to ignore the truth that unredeemed, fallen human nature is under the judgment of God (Rom 8:1; Eph 2:1–3). They seem to deny the atoning work of God—the cross of Jesus Christ and sanctification by the Holy Spirit alone render life pleasing to God. To quote Ashley again: "The Church does not exclude homosexuals but seeks to help them live in a way that she is convinced will be for their real happiness, rather than to be a facilitator of their denial of their problem. Thus the Church excludes no one from her care; but care, to be genuine, must be based on truth not on making people comfortable."

Surely then it is only half-truth to affirm the dignity of an individual in a sinful condition. It misses the *whole truth* about human nature: the tension in human existence itself between being created good and our actual fallen state, between our human greatness and wretchedness, as Pascal said. In sum, it is precisely the humanity of man in his relation to God that makes the seriousness of his sin fully evident. "The Bible teaches that, though man is hopelessly lost, he is not nothing. Man is lost because he is separated from God, his true reference point, by true moral guilt. But he never will be nothing. Therein lies the horror of his lostness. For man to be lost, in all his uniqueness and wonder, is tragic"[178]

Against this background, we can easily understand why I reject the logic of Pope's position whose aim is to put the Church before a false dilemma: either she continues teaching that both the condition and the activity are "intrinsically disordered," in which case, homosexuals will continue "loathing" themselves, or she must, in accord with her teaching that all men are created in God's image, "fully accept" homosexuals as they are, implying that some homosexual relations are good, indeed holy. But these are false alternatives.

> Persons who experience homosexual desires are like any persons who experience desires to do what God expressly forbids (which, ultimately, takes in everyone). They are welcome in the Church but not to engage unrepentantly in behavior that Scripture treats (and, I might add, Reason confirms) as abhorrent to God—irrespective of whatever intense impulses are experienced. The Church obviously

177. Guarino, *Foundations of Systematic Theology*, 20.
178. Schaeffer, *Escape from Reason*, 90.

should not loathe persons struggling with same-sex attractions either by consigning them callously to hell or by blessing behavior that will put their inheritance in God's kingdom at risk [1 Cor 5–6; Gal 5:16–25]. The Church expresses its love precisely in a refusal to condone homosexual practice, coupled with efforts at meeting intimacy needs short of violating God's clear commands.[179]

The Church views those experiencing homosexual attractions as it views all human beings; as individuals made in the image and likeness of God, wounded by original sin, and in need of the healing graces of Christ. I conclude this fourth point with some wise words from Robert Gagnon:

> I deplore attempts to demean the humanity of homosexuals.... The person beset with homosexual temptation should evoke our concern, sympathy, help, and understanding, not our scorn or enmity. Even more, such a person should kindle a feeling of solidarity in the hearts of all Christians, since we all struggle to properly manage our erotic passions.... Thus a reasoned denunciation of homosexual behavior ... is not, and should not be construed as, a denunciation of those victimized by homosexual urges, since the aim is to rescue the true self created in God's image for a full life.[180]

Natural Law and the Essentialist Objection

The fifth and last objection I will consider in this chapter is raised by Luke Timothy Johnson. It is an often raised objection, but it seems appropriate to return to him at the end of this study since we began with his rejection of the Scripture's explicit teaching regarding homosexuality.

John Paul II's theology of body takes the structures of man's bodily existence to be grounded in the order of creation, God's original creational intent. Johnson raises an objection to this approach. "Along with Scripture, the teaching of the church on sexuality is based on what is called 'natural law.... Determining what is 'natural' or the 'order of creation' is often—as in recent Vatican theology—far removed from the analysis of actual human existence, and instead represents a form of essentialist thinking on the basis of Scripture."[181] What are we, then, to make of Johnson's essen-

---

179. Gagnon, "Case Not Made."

180. Online: http://www.robgagnon.net/articles/homosexGrimsrudTheissenReview.pdf.

181. Johnson, "Homosexuality & the Church." Unfortunately, Johnson overlooks orthodox Catholic scholars, such as Maritain, Grisez, Finnis, May, George, Lee, and J.

tialist objection? Is the opposition, in the Church's natural law thinking, in particular in the teaching of John Paul II, between a normative moral order and actual human existence a straw man? What, then, is essentialist thinking about human nature in regard to the natural law? Johnson doesn't say so, but I think we can surmise that he rejects the teaching of Vatican II that the moral order flows from human nature itself.[182]

Now, Johnson says that he doesn't dismiss the natural law tradition. Indeed, he expresses an appreciation for the natural-law tradition. But what does he understand by natural law? He doesn't say. What he does say is as follows: "Indeed, in its positive dimensions, the natural-law tradition is compatible with my argument that moral thinking should begin with what God discloses to us in creation." This is loose talk about the relation between "moral thinking" and "what God discloses to us in creation." Still, since God discloses himself in experience, according to Johnson, then it's not surprising that he may want to emphasize that moral normativity is experientially grounded rather than being grounded in an objective moral order. Perhaps then Johnson's view of "natural law" is similar to Richard Gula's: "The norms of Christian morality reflect the collective of the Christian community's experience of what it means to be human. As our norms emerge from our experience of what it means to be human, so are they tested by continual experiences of what builds up and promotes the dignity of human life. All this means that our moral theology must pay close attention to what our experience, past and present, is telling us about what it means to be human."[183] Significantly, Gula's view of morality obscures the universality of moral normativity, reducing the latter to its source, he claims, to human experience, albeit man's collective experience throughout the ages. Does Johnson share Gula's view? What, then, of the natural law's universality and immutability? In other words, doesn't the truth of the natural law involve universality and, yes, objectivity, precisely because it is true? This question deserves a brief reply, in light of John Paul II's view of truth.

What, then, is truth, according to John Paul? The pope thinks that the idea of truth is, first, indissolubly linked to that of claims to *univer-*

Budziszewski, as well as the pre-papal and papal writings of John Paul II, where both the ontological and epistemological issues regarding the natural law are addressed with a great deal of thoroughness and sophistication.

182. *Dignitatis Humanae*, no. 14.
183. Gula, *What Are They Saying about Moral Norms?* 46.

sality. "Driven by the desire to discover the ultimate truth of existence, human beings seek to acquire those universal elements of knowledge which enable them to understand themselves better and to advance in their own self-realization."[184] Given the indissoluble link between truth and universality, the pope rejects relativism, or historicism as he calls it, because it "denies the enduring validity of truth."[185] In other words, truth is *universal* in that "if something is true, then it must be true for all people and at all times."[186] It makes no sense to claim that truth varies with epistemic context. As John Paul says elsewhere, "Truth can never be confined to time and culture; in history it is known, but it also reaches beyond history."[187] This, too, is the case about moral truth that grounds universal and permanent, or absolute, moral norms known by practical reason. "The acting subject personally assimilates the truth contained in the law.... The *negative precepts* of the natural law are universally valid. They oblige each and every individual, always and in every circumstance. It is a matter of prohibitions that forbid a given action *simper et pro simper*, without exception, because the choice of this kind of behavior is in no case compatible with the goodness of the will of the acting person, with his vocation to life with God and to communion with his neighbor."[188] So, moral truth is not only universally valid, but also absolute in the sense of being immutable, permanent.

Second, truth is also objective and thus there exists "'objective norms of morality' valid for all people of the present and the future, as for those of the past."[189] This is a second point to make about John Paul's view about truth. This point is already implied by the claim that every truth is both universal and absolute. First, the assertions we make express our beliefs, and having a belief means that I am intellectually committed to the truth of certain propositions, of what I believe. "To believe," says John Paul, "means to accept and to acknowledge as true and corresponding to reality the content of what is said."[190] These assertions are either true or

---

184. John Paul II, *Fides et Ratio*, no. 4.
185. Ibid., no. 87.
186. Ibid., no. 27.
187. Ibid., no. 95.
188. John Paul II, *Veritatis Splendor*, no. 52.
189. Ibid., no. 53.
190. John Paul II, *Catechesis on The Creed*, vol. 1, *God: Father and Creator*, 31.

false, and objective reality is what makes the propositions they express true. In short, John Paul II is a realist about truth. By this I mean that, for a realist, a proposition is true if and only if objective reality is the way that the proposition says it is; otherwise, the proposition is false. So, according to the realist concept of truth, the proposition "God exists" is true if and only if God exists. The second point is this: it is not needed for the belief that God exists to be true, that there is someone who is justified in believing that God exists. Whether or not objective reality is the way that the proposition says it is does not depend on someone having reasons to think it is true. In other words, what makes the proposition is a different matter from how I know the proposition is true. Similarly, the moral proposition "abortion is wrong" is true if and only if it is the case that abortion is wrong; otherwise, the proposition is false. This concept of truth is non-epistemic, transcendent, as it were, because it distinguishes conditions of truth from conditions of epistemic justification.

Given John Paul II realist view of truth, then, we are not surprised that the truth of the natural law involves universality precisely because moral propositions grounded in that law are true. In this light, we can understand the following claim he makes:

> Inasmuch as [natural law] is inscribed in the rational nature of the person, it makes itself felt to all beings endowed with reason and living in history.... [And] inasmuch as the natural law expresses the dignity of the human person and lays the foundation for his fundamental rights and duties, it is universal in its precepts and its authority extends to all mankind. *This universality does not ignore the individuality of human beings,* nor is it opposed to the absolute uniqueness of each person. On the contrary, it embraces at its root each of the person's free acts, which are meant to bear witness to the universality of the true good.[191]

In this passage, John Paul assumes that the moral order flows from human nature itself. That is, he understands a human being as one who possesses a permanent nature or, as Jacques Maritain puts it, "an ontological structure which is a locus of intelligible necessities," meaning thereby, "man possesses ends which necessarily correspond to his essential constitution and which are the same for all."[192] In addition, according to Maritain, "But since man is endowed with intelligence and determines his

---

191. John Paul II, *Veritatis Splendor*, no. 51.
192. Maritain, *Man and the State*, 86.

own ends, it is up to him to put himself in tune with the ends necessarily demanded by his nature. This means that there is, by the very virtue of human nature, an order or a disposition which human reason can discover and according to which the human will must act in order to attune itself to the essential and necessary ends of the human being. The unwritten law, or natural law, is nothing more than that."[193] The ends to which human actions are ordered Maritain, following Aquinas, and John Paul agrees, considers as "goods" to be pursed, realized, and done, and these goods fulfill or perfect human beings because they are constitutive of their flourishing or well-being. Thus, the first principle of practical reason is as follows: "The good is to be done and sought; evil is to be avoided." This principle is fleshed out in the order of ends that is grounded in human nature and that is called by Maritain, a dynamic scheme of inclination and their corresponding goods. These inclinations that serve as principles of practical reason are summed up by William May:

> St. Thomas Aquinas identified a triple-tiered set of such human goods which, when grasped by our reason as ordered to action ("practical reason"), serve as first principles or starting points for practical deliberation—"what am I to do?" Aquinas' first set includes being itself, a good that human persons share with other entities, and since the being of living things is life itself, the basic human good at this level is that of life itself, including bodily life, health, and bodily integrity. His second set includes the sexual union of man and woman and the handing on and educating of human life, a set of goods human persons share with other sexually reproducing species but, of course, in a distinctive human way. His third set includes goods unique to human persons such as knowledge of the truth, especially truth about God, fellowship and friendship with other persons in a human community (friendship and justice, peace), and the good of being reasonable in making choices or what can be called the good of practical reasonableness.[194]

Now, the opposition Johnson draws between natural law and actual human existence isn't clear either. But here too I think we can surmise that Johnson has in mind an opposition between an abstract nature—such as the idea of permanent human nature construed by natural law—and the concrete human nature of an actual historical existence of man which is

---

193. Ibid.
194. May, *Catholic Sexual Ethics*, 9–10.

changing and developing. Of course some thinkers have suggested that nothing can be permanent, that all must be subject to change, including moral norms, because human nature is changeable?[195] Is this Johnson's view?" Is he suggesting that because of historical change and development moral norms must be experientially based in concrete human nature? Is he opposing this historically conscious view of moral norms to the more static view, as he sees it, of moral norms grounded in the unchangeable characteristics of man?

In reply to Johnson, let me begin by making the point that natural-law morality, rightly understood, does not need to choose between permanence and change, between unchangeable principles and ongoing development of insight into their application. Johnson seems to put the Church's teaching in a false dilemma. Indeed, he is criticizing a straw man. John Paul II briefly addresses the very same concern voiced by Johnson regarding actual human existence and natural-law morality in his 1993 Encyclical Letter *Veritatis Splendor*: "The great concern of our contemporaries for historicity and for culture has led some to call into question *the immutability of the natural law* itself, and thus the existence of 'objective norms of morality' valid for all people of the present and the future, as for those of the past. Is it ever possible, they ask, to consider as universally valid and always binding certain rational determinations established in the past, when no one knew the progress humanity would make in it future?"[196]

The pope's answer to this question avoids the horns of the dilemma between permanence and change by arguing that man, although as he actually and historically exists, exists in a particular culture, "is not exhaustively defined by that culture." Indeed, he then explains: "Moreover, the very progress of cultures demonstrates that there is something in man which transcends those cultures. This 'something' is precisely human nature: this nature is itself the measure of culture and the condition ensuring that man does not become the prisoner of any of his cultures, but asserts his personal dignity by living in accordance with the profound truth of his being."[197] In this connection, consider the mandate of Amnesty International.

---

195. Finnis, *Moral Absolutes*, 24.
196. *Veritatis Splendor*, no. 53.
197. Ibid.

> To seek the release of prisoners of conscience, people imprisoned solely for their beliefs, color, ethnic origin, sex, language, or religion, provided that they have neither used nor advocated the use of violence; to oppose the death penalty, torture, or other cruel, inhuman, or degrading punishment of all prisoners; to end extrajudicial executions or disappearances; to oppose abuses by opposition groups' hostage taking, the torture and killings of prisoners, and other arbitrary killings.[198]

This mandate raises the question of the foundation of human rights and the substantive nature of the human person in which these rights inhere. Some anti-foundational human rights skeptics have asked, "How on this earth, with all we know now about human variety and the elusive nature of the self, how in the name of truth can Amnesty reasonably claim that certain actions committed by legitimate states are just plain wrong, regardless of circumstances?"[199] I hear an echo of this very point in Johnson's objection grounding moral norms in the creation order. And the answer to this question is to argue that certain acts like slavery and torture are fundamentally, universally wrong, not just in the USA, but in all places and at all times. Indeed, just 50 years ago the United Nations adopted a Universal Declaration of Human Rights. This document confirmed, as Pope John Paul II puts it in his October 5, 1995 speech to the U.N. General Assembly, that "there are indeed universal rights rooted in the nature of the person, rights that express the objective and inviolable demands of the universal moral law."[200]

This question was specifically addressed in the 1992 Oxford Amnesty Lectures. The lecture by Wayne Booth in this series stands out in my mind because he asks whether the idea of basic and inalienable human rights makes sense if human beings are centerless networks of beliefs and desires determined by historical circumstances. He says,

> Can we not expect that the world's ubiquitous torturers will welcome the rumor that advanced thinkers in the most advanced nations find no solid reality in that victim who cringes and weeps

---

198. From the Amnesty Leadership Group mailing of 5 December 1991, John G. Healey, Executive Director, as quoted in Booth, "Individualism and the Mystery of the Social Self," 70–71.

199. This is the question that Wayne Booth raises and proposes to answer in his essay, "Individualism and the Mystery of the Social Self."

200. John Paul II, *Make Room for the Mystery*, 20.

before their dry eyes? That precise fear was recently expressed to me by a young Chinese woman who had fled China after Tiananmen Square and then found, she said, that postmodernist Western thought seemed to deny her very existence as an individual protester.[201]

In this Chinese woman's plea we see the tragic consequences of denying the idea of human rights—rights inherent in every person and prior to any Constitution and state legislation--and its ground in the transcendent dignity of the human person, of human nature itself.

Now, John Paul sees the permanent structural elements of man's human nature, the dynamic schemes of natural inclinations and their corresponding goods, to be integrally connected with man's own bodily dimensions. This particular spiritual and bodily structure is grounded in God's original plan of creation, the order of creation. Hence the import of *"Jesus' reference to the 'beginning,'"* adds John Paul, "precisely where the social and cultural context of the time had distorted the primordial meaning and the role of certain moral norms (cf. Mt 19:1–9)."[202] Those permanent structural elements of man consist of that triple-tiered set of human goods described above by Aquinas.

On the very question before us, then, Grisez argues, "human nature and natural-law morality are both stable and changing." In what sense is that the case? Human nature and natural-law morality are "stable, in that the givenness and fundamental unalterability of natural inclinations [to the basic human goods] account for the unalterability of the principles of natural law; but also changing, in that the dynamism of the inclinations [to the basic human goods], their openness to continuing and expanding fulfillment, accounts for the openness of natural law to authentic development."[203] Like Maritain, Grisez argues that those permanent structural elements of man's nature are the fundamental dynamic schemes of inclinations to human goods such as "the basic possibilities of human individuals as bodily creatures, endowed with intelligence, able to engage in fruitful work and creative play, psychically complex, capable of more or less completely reasonable action, in need of companionship, capable of love, and open to friendship with God in whose image they are

---

201. Booth, "Individualism and the Mystery of the Social Self," 11.
202. *Veritatis Splendor*, no. 53.
203. Grisez, *Way of the Lord Jesus*, 1:182.

made."[204] These structural elements of man's nature are creational givens, and hence do not change.

On the matter of human nature's unalterability, Finnis notes that "human nature in its basic possibilities of fulfillment, possibilities which are adequately known only by adverting to the basic forms of human flourishing which are understood in our grasp of fundamental reasons for action," does not change. He explains:

> Is there, then, anyone for whom it was not or is not or will not be the case that life and health, knowledge of truth and beauty, excellence in work and play, the harmony in friendship with others, the procreative friendship of marriage with another, personal harmony in interior integrity and peace and outer authenticity, and harmony with the source of all meaning and value, are the basic reasons for actions, the basic forms of the human fulfillment in which he ... would wish to share and outside which no benefit or goal could seem really worthwhile? No. No such human person could be identified, and the talk of human nature's changeability—equivocating between nature as actualized and nature as basic possibilities of fulfillment—fails to impinge on the foundations of morality.[205]

Hence, the moral precept forbidding murder is grounded on man's nature, namely, the basic good of human life, and that precept in its positive sense is meant to protect that good. What this means is that the murder of a human person is incompatible with "the general ends and innermost dynamic structure of [his] rational essence."[206] Maritain adds, "Hence the prohibition of murder is grounded on or required by the essence of man. The precept: thou shalt do no murder, is a precept of natural law."[207] In sum, there is a correlative relationship between the fundamental dynamic schemes of natural inclinations to the basic goods of human nature, on the one hand, and basic precepts of the natural law, corresponding to each natural inclination on the other.

On the one hand, then, human nature in its basic givenness does not change. On the other hand, says John Paul II, "Certainly there is a need to seek out and to discover *the most adequate formulation* for universal

---

204. Ibid., 183.
205. Finnis, *"Historical Consciousness" and Theological Foundations*, 25.
206. Maritain, *Man and the State*, 88.
207. Ibid.

and permanent moral norms in the light of different cultural context, a formulation most capable of ceaselessly expressing their historical relevance, of making them understood and of authentically interpreting their truth."[208] The first principle of the natural law is: we should do and seek good, and shun evil. For example, human life is a good to be sought, and sickness is to be shunned. Thus: "The natural inclination toward health and what protects and promotes it is constant and unchanging. Modern medicine, however, has given 'health' a much richer content for us than people of any previous era. Thus, even with regard to the basic good of life, the possibilities of human fulfillment are only gradually specified as humankind realizes and experiences them, then presses on to expand them further."[209] Because of unchangeable elements of human nature, in particular, the goods at stake in making sexual choices, therefore, there can never be moral approval of homosexual acts. Nonetheless, advances in knowledge of the homosexual condition have refined our approach to our moral judgment of homosexual acts. We recognize that the homosexual condition is not always chosen and that thus some of the culpability for engaging in homosexual acts may be reduced. We have come to recognize that more than sacramental confession is necessary for enabling those prone to homosexual activity to acquire the moral strength to resist temptations. They may well need therapy and further life coaching to be able to acquire the moral strength to be chaste, and, eventually, be transformed to God's normative design for male and female relations. Groups such as Courage and NARTH draw tremendously upon experience for their pastoral and psycho-therapeutic care of those struggling with homosexual attractions.[210]

So the allegation that all natural-law morality of the sort that Church affirms cannot do justice to man's historical actuality is simply not the

---

208. *Veritatis Splendor*, no. 53.

209. Grisez, *Way of the Lord Jesus*, 1:182.

210. The Courage Apostolate is "a support group for men and women with same-sex attractions, dedicated to attaining the virtue of chastity, in accord with the Magisterium's teaching on homosexuality" (http://www.couragerc.net/). Fr. John Harvey, O.S.F.S., the founder of Courage, explains the program of Courage: "Courage: A Chastity Program for Persons with Same Sex Attraction." The National Association for Research and Therapy of Homosexuals "upholds the rights of individuals with unwanted homosexual attraction to receive effective psychological care, and the right of professionals to offer that care" (http://www.narth.com/). On context in which NARTH arose, see Nicolosi, "Removal of Homosexuality from the Psychiatric Manual."

case. For the constancy of human nature and its corresponding unalterable principles of the natural law does not imply that all the possible applications of the natural law are already inscribed in the natural law. Rather, as the *Catechism of the Catholic Church* correctly notes, natural law thinking "can demand reflection that takes account of various conditions of life according to places, times, and circumstances."[211] In other words, the applications of universal and permanent moral norms, their most adequate formulation to existential situations of man, situations unheard of in human history, such as reproductive technologies, stem cell research, cloning, and the like, are not inscribed in the essential structure of human nature, and are known to man. The understanding of the truth of the moral law has unfolded in the interpretation and application of that law down the centuries.

Drawing on the distinction between truth and its formulations, between moral propositions and their linguistic expressions, John Paul explains that the moral norms expressive of moral truths, although taking account of various conditions of life according to places, times, and circumstance, "remain valid in their substance" and hence "must be specified and determined '*eodem sensu eademque sententia*' [keeping the same meaning and the same judgment]" about that moral truth. So, there is growth in the understanding of moral truth, seeking our and discovering "the *most adequate formulation* for universal and permanent moral norms" without changing the substantive truth of morality. Maritain elaborates:

> Men know [natural law] with greater or less difficulty, and in different degrees, running the risk of error here as elsewhere.... That every sort of error and deviation is possible in the determination of these things merely proves that our sight is weak, our nature coarse, and that innumerable accidents can corrupt our judgment. ... Man's knowledge of [natural law] has increased little by little as man's moral conscience has developed.... The knowledge which our own moral conscience has of this law is doubtless still imperfect, and very likely it will continue to develop and to become more refined as long as humanity exists. Only when the Gospel has penetrated to the very depth of human substance will natural law appear in its flower and its perfection.[212]

---

211. *Catechism of the Catholic Church*, no. 1957.
212. Maritain, *Man and the State*, 89–90.

The concluding sentence of this passage from Maritain makes clear that not only the effects of sin upon human nature, but also the deepening of our knowledge regarding the fullest meaning of the natural law must be considered from the perspective of Christ's redemptive work. As I argued earlier in chapter 5, *grace restores or renews nature*, meaning thereby that God's grace in Christ *restores all life to its fullness, penetrating and perfecting and transforming the fallen creation from within its own order*, bringing creation into conformity with His will and purpose. Given this understanding of the relation between nature, sin and grace, we can understand why "'the Church affirms that underlying so many changes there are some things which do not change and are *ultimately founded upon Christ*, who is the same yesterday and today and forever.' Christ is the 'Beginning' who, having taken on human nature, definitively illumines it in its constitutive elements and in its dynamism of charity towards God and neighbor."[213]

---

213. *Veritatis Splendor*, no. 53. The quote within the quote is from *Gaudium et Spes*, no. 10.

7

Caritas in Veritate

> To defend the truth, to articulate it with humility and conviction, and to bear witness to it in life are ... exacting and indispensable forms of charity.[1]

BENEDICT XVI WRITES IN his recent encyclical, "Charity, in fact, 'rejoices in the truth' (1 Cor 13:6)."[2] He adds, "*Only in truth does charity shine forth*, only in truth can charity be authentically lived. Truth is the light that gives meaning and value to charity."[3] Charity in truth: this is the context in which I aim to consider, in the concluding chapter of this book, the last objection to the Church's position on homosexuality. This is the pastoral objection some raise regarding the so-called 'gap' that exists between Catholic sexual ethics and peoples' real lives. I treat, however briefly, this pastoral objection in a separate chapter because, in a sense, it is the most important objection: it deals directly with the eternal significance of the moral choices that people make, indeed, with their eternal salvation. St. Paul consistently urges us to make choices that are worthy of the calling that we have received in Christ (Eph 4:1; Phil 1:27; Col 1:9). In particular, he identifies the risk posed by, especially *but not only*, sexual offenses: "Do you not know that the unrighteous will not inherit the kingdom of God? Stop deceiving yourselves: Neither sexually immoral persons [*pornoi*, i.e., like the incestuous man], nor idolaters, nor adulterers, nor 'soft men' [*malakoi*, i.e., men who feminize themselves to attract male sex partners], nor men who lie with a male [*arsenokoitai*, a term formed from the Levitical prohibition of male homosexual practice]

---

1. Benedict XVI, *Caritas in Veritate*, no. 1.
2. Ibid.
3. Ibid., no. 3.

... shall inherit the kingdom of God (1 Cor 6:9–10)."[4] The *Catechism of the Catholic Church* instructs us that certain choices result "in the loss of charity and the privation of sanctifying grace, that is, of the state of grace." The *Catechism* adds, "If it is not redeemed by repentance and God's forgiveness, it causes exclusion from Christ's kingdom and the eternal death of hell." How is that so? Because, the *Catechism* concludes, "our freedom has the power to make choices for ever, with no turning back."[5] This makes the Church's pastoral practice a life-and-death matter. Clearly, then, our pastoral practice should be informed by the sense of urgency for the lives of people and that of their eternal salvation.

Before turning to consider the objection to the Church's pastoral practice, I think it's absolutely necessary to define the meaning of "pastoral" in the notion of pastoral practice. I know of no better attempt to describe this meaning than the one given by the then Joseph Ratzinger, now Pope Benedict XVI, in his attempt to explain what it means to speak of Vatican II as a pastoral council. He explains: "'Pastoral' should not mean nebulous, without substance, merely 'edifying'—meanings sometimes given to it. Rather what was meant was positive care for the man of today who is not helped by condemnations and who has been told for too long what is false and what he may not do. Modern man really wishes to hear what is true. He has, indeed, not heard enough truth, enough of the positive message of faith for our time, enough of what the faith has to say to our age."[6] The significance of the point that Ratzinger is making here for a pastoral practice that is informed by the theology of the body and its normative implications for sexual ethics is as follows: in an effort to show compassion take care not to dilute the truth of the Gospel regarding the meaning of man's body. "The human body shares in the dignity of 'the image of God': it is a human body precisely because it is animated by a spiritual soul, and it is the whole human person that is intended to become, in the body of Christ, a temple of the Spirit [Cf. 1 Cor 6:19; 15:44–45]."[7] Vice-versa: truth without compassion turns cold, harsh, and

---

4. See also Gal 5:19–21; Eph 5:3–5; 1 Thess 4:2–8. I am using Robert Gagnon's translation of 1 Cor 6:9–11. For a thorough exegetical justification of this translation of the passive and active partners in homosexual acts, see his *Bible and Homosexual Practice*, 303–39.

5. *Catechism of the Catholic Church*, no. 1861.

6. Ratzinger, *Theological Highlights of Vatican II*, 23.

7. *Catechism of the Catholic Church*, no. 364.

ugly, and hence, in short, truth without love is nothing (1 Cor 13:2). Love without truth is, however, blind, sentimental, empty. Says Benedict XVI, "In a culture without truth, this is the fatal risk facing love. It falls prey to contingent subjective emotions and opinions, the word 'love' is abused and distorted."[8] Rather than overlooking truth or love, however, in the context of sketching the Church's practical practice, we need to show the interdependency of love and truth. As Ratzinger say, "Love is of no avail. It serves no purpose if truth is not on its side. Only when truth and love are in harmony can man know joy. For it is truth that makes man free."[9]

What, then, is the objection by some to the Church's pastoral practice regarding homosexuals? Fr. Timothy Radcliffe put this objection succinctly as follows: the Church must be "with people where they are, not telling them where they ought to be." "It is no good telling people that they should not be divorced or remarried or living with a partner or gay. We begin where they are now."[10] This is Radcliffe's strategy even where the teaching is unambiguous, which is the case in the realm of sexual ethics and, "there is an abyss between what the Church teaches and the way many members of the Church live."[11] So Radcliffe isn't talking about Church moral teaching that is unclear and open to varying interpretation. What is then the point that he is making here?

On the one hand, is he saying that the Church must be sensitive to a man's moral progress, namely, that he is striving to become good by stages of moral growth? The former is, according to John Paul, "the law of gradualness" or a step-by-step moral advance in becoming good and realizing the standard of Christian holiness.[12] In this context, we may speak of a man's moral immaturity. Here, too, we may understand St. Paul pastoral admonition, "Brothers, if anyone is caught in any transgression, you who are spiritual should restore him in a spirit of gentleness" (Gal 6:1). John Paul II explains the pastoral implications of the "law of gradualness":

---

8. Benedict XVI, *Caritas in Veritate*, no. 3.

9. Ratzinger (Benedict XVI), *Principles of Catholic Theology*, 80. On the corollary of love and truth, see also, John Paul II, "Canonization of Edith Stein and Homily," no. 6: "St. Benedicta of the Cross says to us all: Do not accept anything as the truth if it lacks love. And do not accept anything as love which lacks truth! One without the other becomes a destructive life."

10. Radcliffe, *What's the Point of Being a Christian?* 42.

11. Ibid., 95.

12. John Paul II, *Familiaris Consortio*, no. 34.

"In this context, appropriate allowance is made both for *God's mercy* towards the sin of the man who experiences conversion and for the *understanding of human weakness*."[13] Notwithstanding this compassion, he adds, "Such understanding never means compromising and falsifying the standard of good and evil in order to adapt it to particular circumstances."[14] "In fact," the pope adds, "genuine understanding and compassion must mean love for the person, for his true good, for his authentic freedom. And this does not result, certainly, from concealing or weakening moral truth."[15] Therefore, "It is quite human," the pope explains, "for the sinner to acknowledge his weakness and to ask mercy for his failings; [but] what is unacceptable is the attitude of one who makes his own weakness the criterion of the truth about the good, so that he can feel self-justified, without even the need to have recourse to God and his mercy."[16] Significantly, the "law of gradualness" presupposes St. John's teaching, which is vitally important here: "If we say we have no sin, we deceive ourselves, and the truth is not in us. If we confess our sins, he is faithful and just to forgive us our sins and to cleanse us from all unrighteousness. If we say we have not sinned, we make him a liar, and his word is not in us" (1 John 1:8–10).

On the other hand, is Fr. Radcliffe suggesting something else entirely, namely, that there are "in divine law various levels or forms of precept for various persons and conditions."[17] The latter is described (and rejected) by John Paul as the "gradualness of the law."[18] What this law means, according to Grisez, is that there are "gradations of the law," namely, "the whole of Christian morality—or, at least, many norms traditionally received as binding precepts—is [such] that willful violations are acceptable provided one looks forward to living according to the norm at some time in the

---

13. John Paul II, *Veritatis Splendor*, no. 104.

14. Ibid.

15. Ibid., no. 95. Indeed, the pope adds, "The Church can never renounce 'the principle of truth and consistency, whereby she does not agree to call good evil and evil good'; she must always be careful not to break the bruised reed or to quench the dimly burning wick (cf. Is 42:3). As Paul VI wrote: 'While it is an outstanding manifestation of charity toward souls to omit nothing from the saving doctrine of Christ, this must always be joined with tolerance and charity, as Christ himself showed by his conversations and dealings with men. Having come not to judge the world but to save it, he was uncompromisingly stern towards sin, but patient and rich in mercy towards sinners'" (ibid.).

16. Ibid.

17. Grisez, *Way of the Lord Jesus*, 1:687.

18. John Paul II, *Familiaris Consortio*, no. 34.

future."[19] But this is ruled out by Radcliffe. He insists that the Church must be "with people where they are, not telling them where they ought to be." "It is no good telling people that they should not be divorced or remarried or living with a partner or gay. We begin where they are now."[20] So by his own account the "gradualness of the law" cannot even mean that "received moral norms characterizing various kinds of acts as grave matter merely mark out an ideal to be achieved in the future."[21]

If the Church's teaching is clear, unambiguous, and absolute (i.e., exceptionless)—as is her teaching regarding adultery, same-sex intercourse, rape, murder, incest, for example—then the moral law is not an "ideal" that is realized in varying degrees in various persons and under differing conditions. For if morally obligatory then only one moral choice is the right one. Of course, "man is sometimes confronted by situations that make moral judgments less assured and decision difficult. But he must always seriously seek what is right and good and discern the will of God expressed in divine law."[22] Yet, the presumption is that when the Church has made her moral teaching clear, then it *isn't* a question of discovering what is right for me here and now, but rather of *doing* the right thing. So "the process of gradualness has no place unless one accepts divine law with a sincere heart and seeks the goods which protected and promoted by the moral truth clarified in Jesus and proposed to us in the Church's moral teaching."[23]

I'm not sure Radcliffe agrees with the last sentence of the preceding paragraph. Indeed, the tenor of his pastoral proposal is such regarding those Catholics whose lives do not conform to the moral teaching of the Church that they are left in their sinful condition. Of course we should compassionately "enter into" the lives of people struggling *to do* the right thing. But does that mean that we should devise pastoral programs, such as Helmut Thielicke and others suggest, in which "the homosexual has to realize his optimal ethical potentialities *on the basis* of his irreversible situation."[24] Unlike Radcliffe, Thielicke, first, clearly explains that,

19. Grisez, *Way of the Lord Jesus*, 1:687.
20. Radcliffe, *What's the Point of Being a Christian?* 42.
21. Ibid., 687.
22. *Catechism of the Catholic Church*, no. 1787.
23. Grisez, *Way of the Lord Jesus*, 1:687.
24. Thielicke, *Ethics of Sex*, 285. See also, for a similar pastoral strategy, Bordeyne, "Homosexuality, Seen in Relation to Ecumenical Dialogue."

biblically speaking, "homosexuality cannot simply be put on the same level with the normal created order of the sexes, but that it is rather a habitual or actual distortion or deprivation of it.... The homosexual must therefore be willing to be treated or healed so far as this is possible; he must, as it were, be willing to be brought back into the 'order.'"[25] But what about the homosexual who is incurable, that is, whose condition is judged to be "constitutional" (as Thielicke puts it). In this case, Thielicke asks whether there is an "*ethically responsible* way" to live with homosexuality and "achieve an acceptable partnership."[26] In the end, Thielicke's pastoral strategy dovetails with Radcliffe's own, and hence it suffers from the same limitations.[27]

St. Paul wouldn't say to the person in a homosexual condition, with same-sex attraction: "We implore you on behalf of Christ, 'be *reconciled to what is possible.*'" Of course not. Nor would he say, "We implore you on behalf of Christ, 'achieve the optimal ethical potential of sexual self-realization.'" Of course not. Otherwise, we would deny that our sinful condition is open to radical transformation. Indeed, St. Paul says, "We implore you on behalf of Christ, *be reconciled to God*" (Eph 5:20; italics added). Elsewhere he proclaims, "My grace is sufficient for you, for my power is made perfect [or: brought to full measure] in weakness" (2 Cor 12:9).

John Paul II correctly understands one of the implications of the "gradualness of the law": "An attitude of this sort corrupts the morality of society as a whole, since it encourages doubt about the objectivity of the moral law in general and a rejection of the absoluteness of moral prohibitions regarding specific human acts, and it ends up by confusing all judgments about values."[28] Now, I think Radcliffe's position will lead, indeed, to moral laxity, indeed, to the sort of moral corruption the pope describes, and it is a matter of concern for the whole Church. St. Paul tells us that the Church must not succumb to a lax attitude toward sin (see 1 Cor 5:6: "a little leaven leavens the whole lump"). He urges the believers at Corinth to take action against a man's sexual sin (i.e., incest) by removing him from

---

25. Ibid., 283.
26. Ibid., 285, 287.
27. In all fairness to Thielicke, I should add that he sees the homosexual subject to certain temptations that are so great that he does not "venture to credit the "minimal chances of being able to live ethically with homosexuality and achieve an acceptable partnership ... with anything more than being a possible exception" (*Ethics of Sex*, 287).
28. John Paul II, *Veritatis Splendor*, no. 104.

the community. The community should mourn for him rather than become inflated with pride (5:2). As St. Paul says elsewhere in 1 Corinthians, we must "not rejoice at wrongdoing, but rejoice with truth" (13:6). *The truth being that we in the Church are all sinners who are saved by grace*: "For all have sinned and fall short of the glory of God, and are justified by his grace as a gift, through the redemption that is in Christ Jesus, whom God put forward as a propitiation by his blood, to be received in faith" (Rom 3:23–25).

Nevertheless, says St. Paul, the Church should take a stand against all sorts of sexual sin by warning the offending believers that if they continue in sexual immorality they will not inherit the Kingdom of God. Against this Pauline background, we should also ask Radcliffe how he proposes to help these offending believers to be "saved" from judgment "on the day of the Lord" (1 Cor 5:5). What about St. Paul's teaching that serial and unrepentant immoral sexual practices puts one at the risk of not inheriting God's eternal kingdom (1 Cor 6:9–10; 2 Cor 12:21; Gal 5:19–21; Rom 1:24–27; 6:19–23; Col 3:5–10; Eph 5:3–6, 4:17–19; 1 Thess 4:2–8). Furthermore, if "our deepest freedom is to do the will of the Father," as Radcliffe rightly says, how then does a person who is actively and unrepentantly engaged in same-sex practice change his life, radically reorient his whole life, put an end to sin, turn away from evil, "with repugnance toward the evil actions [he has] committed,"[29] if no one, least of all the Church, calls him to interior repentance, conversion, that is, "the conversion of the heart, interior conversion" and a holy life?[30] As the *Catechism of the Catholic Church* teaches, "This endeavor of conversion is not just a human work. It is the movement of a 'contrite heart,' drawn and moved by grace to respond to the merciful love of God who loved us first" (Ps 51:17; John 6:44; 12:32; 1 John 4:10).[31]

Now, then, if we begin where people are, as Radcliffe suggests, that is because we seek to bear witness to the truth of the integrity of the chaste person. "The chaste person maintains the integrity of the powers of life and loved place in him. This integrity ensures the unity of the person; it is opposed to any behavior that would impair it. It tolerates neither a double

---

29. *Catechism of the Catholic Church*, no. 1431.
30. Ibid., no. 1430.
31. Ibid., 1428.

life nor duplicity in speech."[32] We bear witness to this truth in the power of God's love and mercy to and for them, hoping and praying that by his grace he will give them a new heart (see Ezek 36:26–27). Chastity is an infused moral virtue, a gift of God's grace, which takes root in a person's character, and helps him to become virtuous by refining, educating and disciplining his desires. Specifically, virtues properly order our desires to the good, and thus the transformation of morally corrupted desires, like same-sex attraction, takes place through true virtue.

Let us then follow the lead of Robert Sokolowski, who following Aristotle, distinguishes four possibilities of human character. Character has to do with a person's whole moral identity. A moral agent may be (1) virtuous, or (2) self-controlled, or (3) weak in self-control, or (4) vicious.[33] A virtuous man is one who not only knows what is right, but also is inwardly disposed to do it. A self-controlled man is one who knows what is right, but whose inward disposition is in conflict with reason. Says Sokolowski, "He does not exist in the harmony found in the virtuous man; he requires self-control. Since he possesses self-control, he generally masters his inclinations and usually does what is good. . . . Self-control, although good, is not the same as virtue."[34] Echoing Sokolowski, Radcliffe claims that the interior freedom, or spontaneity, that characterizes virtue, is "the fruit of a deep travail or rebirth."[35] This interior freedom is ordered to the gift of the self.

A weak man is one who knows what is right but he often cannot do it. His inclinations are in conflict with reason but, unlike a person who has self-control, exhibiting self-mastery, he is not able to master his inclinations. "His reason is disposed correctly but it is often overcome by inclination; this kind of man," Sokolowski adds, "often repents for what he does." Finally, "a vicious man is one whose mind and inclinations both move toward what is bad."[36] There is no internal struggle with a vicious man; he is not overcome by his desires, doing what he knows to be wrong.

---

32. Ibid., no. 2338.
33. Sokolowski, *God of Faith and Reason*, 57–58.
34. Ibid., 57.
35. Radcliffe, *What's the Point of Being a Christian?* 42.
36. Sokolowski, *God of Faith and Reason*, 58.

Unlike the weak person, a vicious person "chooses what is wrong and consequently is not likely to repent."[37]

We all should strive to be virtuous persons. "It is not easy for man, wounded by sin, to maintain moral balance. Christ's gift of salvation offers us the grace necessary to perservere in the pursuit of the virtues."[38] And pursuing the virtues in order to become virtuous, that is, to develop a habitual and firm interior disposition to do the good, involves, in the wonderful words of the *Catechism*, "an apprenticeship in self-mastery which is training in human freedom."[39] This training is required because our desires or feelings can be unruly, possessing of life of their own, as it were, resulting in an inner struggle between what we know to be right and the sway of disordered emotions. "The alternative is clear: either man governs his passions and finds peace, or he lets himself be dominated by them and becomes unhappy."[40]

St. Paul expressed this interior struggle pointedly, "For I do not do the good I want, but the evil I do not want is what I keep on doing" (Rom 7:19). The solution to this interior struggle, he urges, is only union with the person of Christ, governed by moral guidelines—the authentic moral life flowing from the transformed life in Christ. This personal relationship with Christ through the work of the Holy Spirit effects a real transformation from within, establishing a harmony between what is right and my inclinations. "[P]ut off your old man, which belongs to your former manner of life and is corrupt through deceitful desires, and . . . be renewed in the spirit of your minds, and . . . put on the new man, created after the likeness of God in true righteousness and holiness" (Eph 4:22–24). Wouldn't Radcliffe agree? Isn't this what he means when says, "Christ in us makes all our actions ours."[41]

Radcliffe's proposal seems to pull him in another direction. Central to his proposal is urging the Church to take the stance of "friendship and proximity" so that she "can be with us as we face moral dilemmas and make choices."[42] He adds, "The Church will only be a cradle of gospel free-

---

37. Ibid.
38. *Catechism of the Catholic Church*, no. 1811.
39. Ibid., no. 2339.
40. Ibid.
41. Radcliffe, *What's the Point of Being a Christian?* 42.
42. Ibid., 40.

dom if we are seen to stand beside people, supporting them as they make moral decisions *within the range of what is possible*, rather than making decisions for them."⁴³ Within the range of what *is possible*? *Possible for whom*? John Paul II pointedly asks, "Of man *dominated* by lust or of man *redeemed by Christ*?" "This is what is at stake," he adds, "the *reality of Christ's redemption. Christ has redeemed us! . . . Only in the mystery of Christ's Redemption do we discover the 'concrete' possibilities of man. . . .* This means that he has given us the possibility of realizing the *entire truth* of our being; he has set our freedom free from the *domination* of concupiscence. And if redeemed man still sins, this is not due to an imperfection of Christ's redemptive act, but to man's will not to avail himself of the grace which flows from that act."⁴⁴

Doesn't Radcliffe's pastoral proposal underestimate the seriousness of sin's power to enslave us and the power of the death and resurrection of Jesus Christ to liberate us from its stranglehold? Doesn't his proposal deny that human nature is truly renewed by the redemptive power of Jesus Christ's finished work? St. Paul describes his own experience of sin trapping him, of a power at work within him, from which he is unable to break free (see Rom 7:13–23). "Wretched man that I am! Who will deliver me from this body of death?" His answer: "Thanks be to God, through Jesus Christ our Lord!" (Rom 7:24–25).⁴⁵ "For this is the will of God, your sanctification" (1 Thess 4:3). So urges Vatican II in its timely and challenging presentation of the call to holiness of the whole Church.⁴⁶ "The Lord Jesus, the divine Teacher and Model of all perfection, preached holiness of life to each and every one of His disciples, regardless of their situation: 'You therefore must be perfect, as your heavenly Father is perfect' (Mt 5:48). He Himself stands as the Author and Finisher of this holiness of life." At the head of all biblical motivations for holiness there is God's love. "God's love has been poured into our hearts through the Holy Spirit who has been given to us" (Rom 5:5). The Council Fathers add, "For He sent the Holy Spirit upon all men that He might inspire them from within to love God with their whole heart and their whole soul, with all their

---

43. Ibid., 37; italics added.

44. John Paul II, *Veritatis Splendor*, no. 103.

45. On sin being like an enslaving force, see McGrath, *Intellectuals Don't Need God*, 136.

46. *Lumen Gentium*, no. 39–42. See also, Webster, *Holiness*, 91.

mind and all their strength (cf. Mark 12;30) and that they might love one another as Christ loved them (cf. John 13:34; 15:12)."[47]

But, as Fr. Raniero Cantalamessa rightly notes, "there is no sanctity without obedience," and thus "to say that all those baptized are called to holiness," which Vatican II does, "is to say that all are called to obedience." He adds, "St Paul speaks of obedience to faith (Rom 1:5; 16:26), of obedience to the teaching (Rom 6:17), of obedience to the Gospel (Rom 10:16; 2 Thess 1:8), of obedience to truth (Gal 5:7), of obedience to Christ (2 Cor 10:5)."[48] There is no sanctity without obedience, and there is no obedience without the gift of faith in Jesus Christ as Lord, trusting fully in his saving work, following him, dying to self, and living for him who loved me and gave himself for me on the Cross (Gal 2:20; cf. Mark 8:34–36).

Radcliffe's pastoral strategy is missing the call to holiness, to conversion, repentance, and the forgiveness of sins. But there is no sanctity without obedience, and no obedience without interior conversion of the heart. Of course the Church consists of sinners who are saved by grace. Nevertheless, there is a spiritual battle being waged in our lives (see Eph 6:10–20). "This is the struggle of conversion directed toward holiness and eternal life to which the Lord never ceases to call us."[49] Jesus calls us to conversion. This is not only the initial response to the Gospel, which is the fruit of the regenerating grace of Baptism, of the new birth and gift of the Holy Spirit. This is "Christ's call to conversion [that] continues to resound in the lives of Christians."[50] "This second conversion is," the *Catechism* adds, "the movement of a 'contrite heart,' drawn and moved by grace to respond to the merciful love of God who loved us first [in Christ]."[51] In short, this movement is "the conversion of the heart, interior conversion."[52] Indeed, that should be the aim of the Church's pastoral practice regarding the sexual sin of homosexuality.[53] I conclude with the words of the *Catechism of the Catholic Church*:

---

47. *Lumen Gentium*, no. 40.
48. Cantalamessa, *Obedience*, 30–31, 34, respectively.
49. *Catechism of the Catholic Church*, no. 1426.
50. Ibid., no. 1428.
51. Ibid.
52. Ibid., no. 1430.

53. Helpful in drawing out Scriptural principles for clinical practice is Gagnon, "Scriptural Perspectives on Homosexuality and Sexual Identity."

In the formation of conscience the Word of God is the light for our path. We must assimilate it in faith and prayer and put it into practice. We must also examine our conscience before the Lord's Cross. We are assisted by the gifts of the Holy Spirit, aided by the witness or advice of others and guided by the authoritative teaching of the Church.... This is how moral conscience is formed.[54]

---

54. *Catechism of the Catholic Church*, nos. 1785, 1802.

Bibliography

Agnes, Mario, editor. *Christian Anthropology and Homosexuality*. Vatican City: L'Osservatore Romano Reprints, 1997.
Anglican-Roman Catholic International Commission. *The Gift of Authority*. Joint Statement of the ARCIC. Online: http://www.prounione.urbe.it/dia-int/arcic/doc/e_arcicII_05.html.
Aquinas, Thomas. *Commentary on Saint Paul's Epistle to the Galatians*. Translated by F. R. Larcher. Albany, NY: Magi, 1966.
———. *Commentary on Saint Paul's Second Epistle to the Corinthians*. Translated by F. R. Larcher. Online: http://www.aquinas.avemaria.edu/Aquinas-Corinthians-Sec2.pdf.
———. *Summa Theologiae*. Vol. 1, *Christian Theology*. Translated by Thomas Gilby. New York: McGraw-Hill, 1965.
———. *Summa Theologiae*. Vol. 28, *Law*. Translated by Thomas Gilby. New York: McGraw-Hill, 1966.
———. *Summa Theologiae*. Vol. 30, *The Gospel of Grace*. Translated by Cornelius Ernst. New York: McGraw-Hill, 1972.
———. *Summa Theologiae*. Vol. 31, *Faith*. Translated by T. C. O'Brien. New York: McGraw-Hill, 1975.
———. *Truth*. Vol. 3. Translated by James V. McGlynn, SJ. Indianapolis: Hackett, 1995.
Ashley, Benedict M., OP. "The Bible Gap." *Catholic Dossier*, March-April 1996. Online: https://www.ewtn.com/library/SCRIPTUR/BIBLEGAP.TXT.
———. "Compassion and Sexual Orientation." In *The Vatican and Homosexuality: Reactions to the "Letter to the Bishops of the Catholic Church on the Pastoral Care of Homosexual Persons,"* edited by Jeannine Gramick and Pat Furey, 105–11. New York: Crossroad, 1988.
———. *Living the Truth in Love*. New York: Alba, 1996.
Ashley, Benedict M., Jean DeBlois, and Kevin D. O'Rourke. *Health Care Ethics: A Theological Analysis*. 5th ed. Washington, DC: Georgetown University Press, 2006.
Augustine. *The City of God*. Translated by Marcus Dods. Online: http://www.ccel.org/ccel/schaff/npnf102.iv.html.
Avila, Daniel. "Sexual Difference and Marriage: An Urgent Need for New Studies." *The National Catholic Bioethics Quarterly* 9 (2009) 441–46.
Bahnsen, Greg L. *Homosexuality: A Biblical View*. Grand Rapids: Baker, 1978.
———. "The Theonomic Antithesis to Other Law-Attitudes." Online: http://www.cmfnow.com/articles/pe054.htm.
Baillie, John. *The Idea of Revelation in Recent Thought*. New York: Columbia University Press, 1954.

Balthasar, Hans Urs von. *The Glory of the Lord: A Theological Aesthetics.* Vol. 1, *Seeing the Form.* Translated by Erasmo Leiva-Merikakis. Edited by Joseph Fessio et al. San Francisco: Ignatius, 1982 [1961].

———. *The Von Balthasar Reader.* Translated by Robert J. Daly and Fred Lawrence. Edited by Medard Kehl and Werner Löser. New York: Crossroad, 1982.

Barbeau Gardiner, Anne. "Catholic Feminist Ethics and the Culture of Death: The Case of Sister Margaret Farley." *Fellowship of Catholic Scholars Quarterly* 32 (2009) 19–23.

Barth, Karl. *Church Dogmatics* III/2. Translated by H. Knight et al. Edited by G. W. Bromiley and T. F. Torrance. Edinburgh: T. & T. Clark, 1960.

Bavinck, Herman. *Gereformeerde Dogmatiek* I. 6th unrevised Dutch edition. Kampen: Kok, 1976 [1895]. Translated as *Reformed Dogmatics, Prolegomena*, vol. 1, by John Vriend. Edited by John Bolt. Grand Rapids: Baker Academic, 2003.

———. *Wijsbegeerte der Openbaring* (1908). Princeton Stone Lectures. Kampen: Kok, 1908. Translated as *The Philosophy of Revelation.* London: Longmans, Green, 1909.

———. *De Zekerheid des Geloofs.* Kampen: Kok, 1901. Translated by Harry der Nederlanden as *The Certainty of Faith.* St. Catherines, Ontario: Paideia, 1980. The Dutch version is online: http://www.neocalvinisme.nl/tekstframes.html.

Béchard, Dean P. *The Scripture Documents: An Anthology of Official Catholic Teachings.* Edited and translated by Dean P. Béchard. Collegeville, MN: Liturgical, 2002.

Berkouwer, G. C. *De Algemene Openbaring.* Kampen: Kok, 1951. Translated as *General Revelation.* Grand Rapids: Baker, 1955.

———. *Een Halve Eeuw Theologie: Motieven en Stromingen van 1920 tot Heden.* Kampen: J. H. Kok, 1974. Translated and edited by Lewis B. Smedes as *A Half Century of Theology: Movements and Motives.* Grand Rapids: Eerdmans, 1977.

———. *De Heilige Schrift* I-II. Kampen: Kok, 1966–1967. Translated and edited by Jack B. Rogers as *Holy Scripture.* Grand Rapids: Eerdmans, 1975.

———. *De Mens Het Beeld Gods.* Kampen: Kok, 1957. Translated Dirk W. Jellema as *Man: The Image of God.* Grand Rapids: Eerdmans, 1962.

———. "Sacrificium Intellectus?" *Gereformeerd Theologisch Tijdschrift* 68 (1968) 177–200.

———. *Vatikaans Concilie en de nieuwe theologie.* Kampen: Kok, 1964. Translated by Lewis B. Smedes as *The Second Vatican Council and the New Catholicism.* Grand Rapids: Eerdmans, 1965.

Blackburn, Simon. *Being Good.* Oxford: Oxford University Press, 2001.

Blocher, Henri. *Original Sin: Illuminating the Riddle.* Grand Rapids: Eerdmans, 1997.

Bonhoeffer, Dietrich. *Letters and Papers from Prison.* Translated by Reginald Fuller. Edited by Eberhard Bethge. New York: Macmillan, 1953.

Booth, Wayne. "Individualism and the Mystery of the Social Self." In *Freedom and Interpretation: The Oxford Amnesty Lectures, 1992*, edited by Barbara Johnson. New York: HarperCollins, 1993.

Bordeyne, Philippe. "Homosexuality, Seen in Relation to Ecumenical Dialogue: What Really Matters to the Catholic Church." *New Blackfriars* 87 (2006) 575–76.

Braaten, Carl E. *Mother Church, Ecclesiology and Ecumenism.* Minneapolis: Fortress, 1998.

———. Review of *Mother Church, Ecclesiology and Ecumenism*, by Avery Dulles, SJ. *First Things* 89 (1999) 41–45. Online: http://www.leaderu.com/ftissues/ft9901/reviews/dulles.html.

Brown, Raymond E. *The Sensus Plenior of Sacred Scripture*. Baltimore: St. Mary's University Press, 1955. Reprint, Eugene, OR: Wipf & Stock, 2008.

Budziszewski, J. "The Illusion of Gay Marriage." *Philosophia Christi* 7 (2005) 45–52.

Bultmann, Rudolph. "The Concept of Revelation in the New Testament." In *Existence and Faith, Shorter Writings of Rudolph Bultmann*, selected, translated, and introduced by Schubert M. Ogden, 67–106. London: Collins, 1964.

Buttiglione, Rocco. *Karol Wojtyla: The Thought of the Man Who Became Pope John Paul II*. Translated by Paolo Guietti and Francesca Murphy. Foreword by Michael Novak. Grand Rapids: Eerdmans, 1997 [1982].

Cahill, Lisa Sowle. "Is Catholic Ethics Biblical?" Warren Lecture Series in Catholic Studies 20. University of Tulsa, 1992.

Calvin, John. *Institutes of the Christian Religion*. 2 vols. Translated by Ford Lewis Battles. Edited by John T. McNeil. Philadelphia: Westminster, 1960.

Cantalamessa, Ranier. *Obedience: The Authority of the Word*. Translation by Francis Lonergan Villa. Boston: St. Paul, 1989.

Caputo, John D. *What Would Jesus Deconstruct? The Good News of Post-modernism for the Church*. Church and Postmodern Culture. Grand Rapids: Baker Academic, 2007.

Catechism of the Catholic Church. Online: http://www.vatican.va/archive/catechism/ccc_toc.htm.

Catholic Medical Association. *Homosexuality and Hope: Questions and Answers about Same-Sex Attraction*. CMA, 2008. Online: http://www.cathmed.org/issues_resources/publications/position_papers/homosexuality_and_hope/.

Cavanagh, Lorraine. "Truth and Meaning: Preaching the Gospel from a Church in Conflict." *Expository Times* 116.9 (2005) 289–94.

Cessario, Romanus. *Christian Faith and The Theological Life*. Washington, DC: Catholic University of America Press, 1996.

———. *Introduction to Moral Theology*. Washington, DC: Catholic University of America Press, 2001.

———. "On Bad Actions, Good Intentions, and Loving God: Three Much-Misunderstood Issues about the Happy Life that St. Thomas Aquinas Clarifies For Us." *Logos* 1.2 (1997) 100–24.

Christian Reformed Church. Belief Statement on "Homosexuality." Online: http://www.crcna.org/pages/positions_homosexuality.cfm.

Compendium of the Social Doctrine of the Church. Libreria Editrice Vaticana. Washington, DC: United States Conference of Catholic Bishops, 2005.

Congar, Yves. *The Meaning of Tradition*. Translated by A. N. Woodrow. San Francisco: Ignatius, 2004 [1964].

———. *Tradition and Traditions*. Translated by Michael Naseby and Thomas Rainborough. New York: Macmillan, 1966.

———. *The Word and the Spirit*. Translated by David Smith. London: Chapman, 1986.

Congregation for the Doctrine of the Faith. *Considerations Regarding Proposals to Give Legal Recognition to Unions Between Homosexual Persons*. June 3, 2003. Online: http://www.vatican.va/roman_curia/congregations/cfaith/documents/rc_con_cfaith_doc_20030731_homosexual-unions_en.html.

———. *Donum Veritatis*. ["On the Ecclesial Vocation of the Theologian"] May 24, 1990. Online: https://www.vatican.va/roman_curia/congregations/cfaith/documents/rc_con_cfaith_doc_19900524_theologian-vocation_en.html.

———. *Homosexualitatis problema*. ["Letter to Bishops of the Catholic Church on the Pastoral Care of Homosexual Persons"] October 1, 1986. http://www.vatican.va/roman_curia/congregations/cfaith/documents/rc_con_cfaith_doc_19861001_homosexual-persons_en.html.

———. *Mysterium Ecclesiae*. ["Declaration in Defense of the Catholic Doctrine on the Church against Certain Errors of the Present Day"] June 24, 1973. Online: http://www.saint-mike.org/library/curia/congregations/faith/mysterium_ecclesiae.html.

———. *Persona Humana*. ["Declaration on Certain Questions Concerning Sexual Ethics"] December 29, 1975. Online: http://www.vatican.va/roman_curia/congregations/cfaith/documents/rc_con_cfaith_doc_19751229_persona-humana_en.html.

Copan, Paul. "Is Yahweh a Moral Monster? The New Atheists and Old Testament Ethics." *Philosophia Christi* 10 (2008) 7–37.

Cottingham, John. *The Spiritual Dimension, Religion, Philosophy and Human Value*. Cambridge: Cambridge University Press, 2005.

Crompton, Louis. *Homosexuality and Civilization*. Cambridge: Harvard University Press, 2003.

Crosby, John F. "The Estrangement of Persons from Their Bodies." *Logos* 1.2 (1997) 125–39.

Cullmann, Oscar. "The New Direction: Divine Revelation and the Virgin Mary." In *Vatican Council II: The New Direction*. New York: Harper & Row, 1968.

Davis, Ellen F., and Richard B. Hays, editors. "Nine Theses on the Interpretation of Scripture." In *The Art of Reading Scripture*, 1–5. Grand Rapids: Eerdmans, 2003.

Dawkins, Richard. "Obscurantism to the Rescue." *Quarterly Review of Biology* 72 (1997) 397–99.

Diggs, John R., Jr. "The Health Risks of Gay Sex." Corporate Resource Council, 2002. Online: http://www.corporateresourcecouncil.org/white_papers/Health_Risks.pdf.

Dooyeweerd, Herman. *In the Twilight of Western Thought: Studies in the Pretended Autonomy of Philosophical Thought*. Nutley, NJ: Craig, 1968.

———. *Vernieuwing en Bezinning, Om Het Reformatorisch Grondmotief*. Zutphen: J. B. Van Den Brink, 1963. Tweede Druk. Bewerkt door J. A. Oosterhoff. Translated by John Kraay, and edited by Mark Vander Vennen and Bernard Zylstra as *Roots of Western Culture*. Toronto: Wedge, 1979.

———. *De Wijsbegeerte der Wetsidee*. Vol. 2, *De Functioneele Zin-Structuur der Tijdelijke Werkelijkheid en Het Probleem der Kennis*. Amsterdam: H. J. Paris, 1936. Translated David H. freeman and H. De Jongste as *A New Critique of Theoretical Thought*. Vol. 2, *The General Theory of the Modal Spheres*. Philadelphia: Presbyterian & Reformed, 1955.

———. *De Wijsbegeerte der Wetsidee*. Vol. 3, *De Individualiteits-Structuren der Tijdelijke Werkelijkheid*. Amsterdam: H. J. Paris, 1936. Deel II, Hoofdstuk II, A §4, 249–91. Translated by David H. freeman and H. De Jongste as *A New Critique of Theoretical Thought*. Vol. 3, The Structures of Individuality of Temporal Reality. Philadelphia: Presbyterian & Reformed, 1955.

Douma, Jochem. "Appendix: The Use of Scripture in Ethics." In *The Ten Commandments: Manual for the Christian Life*, translated by Nelson D. Kloosterman, 355–90. Phillipsburg, NJ: Presbyterian & Reformed, 1996.

———. *Responsible Conduct: Principles of Christian Ethics*. Translated by Nelson D. Kloosterman. Phillipsburg, NJ: Presbyterian & Reformed, 2003 [1997].

Dulles, Avery. *The Assurance of Things Hoped For: A Theology of Christian Faith.* Oxford: Oxford University Press, 1994.

———. *Magisterium: Teacher and Guardian of the Faith.* Naples, FL: Sapientia, 2007.

———. "The Metaphysical Realism of Pope John Paul II." *International Philosophical Quarterly* 48.189 (2008) 99–106.

———. *Models of Revelation.* Garden City, NY: Image, 1983.

———. "The Orthodox Imperative." *First Things* 165 (2006) 31–35.

———. "Revelation, Scripture, and Tradition." In *Your Word is Truth: A Project of Evangelicals and Catholics Together,* edited by Charles Colson and Richard John Neuhaus, 35–58. Grand Rapids: Eerdmans, 2002.

———. "Vatican II: The Myth and the Reality." *America* 188 (2003) 7–11.

Echeverria, Eduardo J. *Dialogue of Love, Confessions of an Evangelical Catholic Ecumenist.* Eugene, OR: Wipf & Stock, 2010.

———. "Living Truth for a Post-Christian World: The Message of Francis Schaeffer and Karol Wojtyla." *Religion & Liberty* 12.6 (2002). Online: http://www.acton.org/publications/randl/rl_article_443.php.

———. "The Moral Life in Biblical Perspective." *Homiletic & Pastoral Review* (2001) 28–32, 48–49. Online: http://www.catholic.net/rcc/Periodicals/Homiletic/2001-12.pdf.

———. *Slitting the Sycamore: Christ and Culture in the New Evangelization.* Grand Rapids: Acton Institute, 2008.

———. "There is Wideness to God's Mercy." *Homiletic & Pastoral Review* CI.5 (2001) 50–55.

Erickson, Millard. *Christian Theology.* 2nd ed. Grand Rapids: Baker Academic, 1998 [1983].

Faith and Order. *The Fourth World Conference on Faith and Order, Montreal 1963.* Edited by P. C. Rodger and Lukas Vischer. New York: Association, 1964.

Farley, Margaret A. "Feminist Consciousness and the Interpretation of Scripture." In *From Christ to the World: Introductory Readings in Christian Ethics,* edited by Wayne G. Boulton, Thomas D. Kennedy, and Allen Verhey, 51–57. Grand Rapids: Eerdmans, 1994.

———. *Just Love: A Framework for Christian Sexual Ethics.* New York: Continuum, 2006.

Finnis, John. *Aquinas.* Oxford: Oxford University Press, 1998.

———. "The Good of Marriage and the Morality of Sexual Relations: Some Philosophical and Historical Observations." *American Journal of Jurisprudence* 42 (1997) 97–134.

———. "*Historical Consciousness*" *and Theological Foundations.* The Étienne Gilson Series 14. Toronto: Pontifical Institute of Medieval Studies, 1992.

———. "Law, Morality, and 'Sexual Orientation.'" *Notre Dame Journal of Law, Ethics, and Public Policy* 9 (1995) 11–39. Online: http://www.princeton.edu/~anscombe/articles/finnisorientation.pdf.

———. *Moral Absolutes.* Washington, DC: Catholic University of America Press, 1991.

———. "Personal Integrity, Sexual Morality and Responsible Parenthood." In *Why Humanae Vitae Was Right: A Reader,* edited by Janet E. Smith, 171–92. San Francisco: Ignatius, 1993.

———. "Reason, Faith and Homosexual Acts." *Catholic Social Science Review* 6 (2001) 61–69.

Forell, George Wolfgang. *History of Christian Ethics.* Vol. 1, *From the New Testament to Augustine.* Minneapolis: Augsburg, 1979.

Frame, John. "Rationality and Scripture." In *Rationality in the Calvinian Tradition*, edited by Hendrik Hart et al., 293–317. Lanham, MD: University Press of America, 1983.

Furnish, Victor Paul. *II Corinthians*. Anchor Bible 32A. Garden City, NY: Doubleday, 1984.

Gagnon, Robert, A. J. "Are There Universally Valid Sex Precepts? A Critique of Walter Wink's View on the Bible and Homosexuality." *Horizons in Biblical Theology* 24 (2002) 72–125.

———. *The Bible and Homosexual Practice: Texts and Hermeneutics*. Nashville: Abingdon, 2001.

———. *Case Not Made: A Response to Prof. John Thorp's "Making the Case" for Blessing Homosexual Unions in the Anglican Church of Canada, June 20, 2007*, 6. Online: http://www.robgagnon.net/articles/homosexThorpCanadaResp.pdf.p.

———. *Homosexuality and the Bible: Two Views*. Minneapolis: Fortress, 2003.

———. *Immoralism, Homosexual Unhealth, and Scripture: A Response to Peterson and Hedlund's "Heterosexism, Homosexual Health, and the Church." Part 2: Science*. Online: http://www.robgagnon.net/articles/homo-HeterosexismRespPart2.pdf.

———. "Rejoinder to Dan O. Via's Response in *Homosexuality and the Bible: Two Views*." Online: http://www.robgagnon.net/2Views/homoViaRejoinder.pdf.

———. "Scriptural Perspectives on Homosexuality and Sexual Identity." *Journal of Psychology and Christianity* 24.4 (2005) 293–303.

———. "Sexual Orientation." Email correspondence, July 8, 2009. Online: http://www.robgagnon.net/AnswersToEMails.htm.

———. "What the Evidence *Really* Says about Scripture and Homosexual Practice: Five Issues." March 14, 2009. Online: http://www.robgagnon.net/articles/homosexScripReallySays.doc.pdf.

———. "What Should Faithful Lutherans in the ELCA Do?" September 30, 2009. Online: http://www.robgagnon.net/articles/homosexELCAonWhatToDo.pdf.

———. "Why I Could Not Recommend the Mennonite Book *Reasoning Together: A Conversation on Homosexuality*." November 18, 2009. Online: http://www.robgagnon.net/articles/homosexGrimsrudTheissenReview.pdf.

Gagnon, Robert A. J., and Dan O. Via. "The Authority of Scripture in the 'Homosex' Debate." An expanded version of a presentation made to the Southeastern ELCA synod, June 2002. Online: http://www.robgagnon.net/.

Genderen, J. van, and W. H. Velema. *Concise Reformed Dogmatics*. Translated by Gerrit Bilkes. Edited by M. van der Mass. Phillipsburg, NJ: Presbyterian & Reformed, 2008 [1992].

Geiselmann, Josef Rupert. *The Meaning of Tradition*. Translated by W. J. O'Hara. Quaestiones Disputatae 15. London/Freiburg: Burns & Oates/Herder, 1966.

———. "Scripture and Tradition in Catholic Theology." *Theology Digest* 6 (1958) 73–78.

———. "Scripture, Tradition, and the Church: An Ecumenical Problem." In *Christianity Divided, Protestant and Roman Catholic Theological Issues*, edited by Daniel J. Callahan, Heiko A. Oberman, and Daniel J. O'Hanlon, 39–72. New York: Sheed & Ward, 1961.

George, Robert P. *The Clash of Orthodoxies: Law, Religion and Morality in Crisis*. Wilmington, DE: ISI, 2001.

———. "What Marriage Is—And What It Isn't." *First Things* 195 (2009) 35–38.

George, Robert P., and Gerard V. Bradley. "Marriage and the Liberal Imagination." *Georgetown Law Journal* 84 (1995) 301–20.

Gilson, Etienne. *Christianity and Philosophy.* Translated by Ralph MacDonald. London: Sheed & Ward, 1939.

———. *The Spirit of Mediaeval Philosophy.* Gifford Lectures 1931–1932. Translated by A. H. C. Downes. New York: Scribners, 1940.

Goldingay, John E., Grant R. LeMarquaand, George R. Summer, and Daniel A. Westberg. "Same-Sex Marriage and Anglican Theology: A View from the Traditionalists," and "The Traditionalist Response." In *Same-Sex Relationships in the Life of the Church*, edited by Ellen T. Charry, 1–39, and 68–76, respectively. Online: http://www.collegeforbishops.org/assets/1145/ss_document_final.pdf.

Goldring, Richard. "Changing Our Corporate Mind: Reflections on Paradigm Shift in Ethical Thinking." *Scottish Journal of Theology* 63 (2) 163–84.

Grisez, Germain. "On Interpreting Dogmas: A Preliminary Analysis." *Communio: International Catholic Review* 17 (1990) 120–26.

———. *The Way of the Lord Jesus.* Vol. 1, *Christian Moral Principles*. Chicago: Franciscan Herald, 1983.

———. *The Way of the Lord Jesus.* Vol. 2, *Living a Christian Life*. Chicago: Franciscan Herald, 1993.

Guarino, Thomas G. "Catholic Reflections on Discovering the Truth of Sacred Scripture." In *Your Word is Truth: A Project of Evangelicals and Catholics Together*, edited by Charles Coulson and Richard John Neuhaus, 79–101. Grand Rapids: Eerdmans, 2002.

———. *Foundations of Systematic Theology.* New York: T. & T. Clark, 2005.

———. *Vattimo and Theology.* New York/London: T. & T. Clark, 2009.

Guinness, Os. *Long Journey Home.* Colorado Springs, CO: Waterbrook, 2001.

Giussani, Monsignor Luigi. *At the Origin of the Christian Claim.* Translated by Viviane Hewitt. Montreal: McGill-Queen's University Press, 1998.

Gustafson, James M. *Protestant and Roman Catholic Ethics.* Chicago: University of Chicago Press, 1978.

Hahn, Scott. *Letter and Spirit: From Written Text to Living Word in the Liturgy.* New York: Doubleday, 2005.

Haight, Roger. "Liberal and Catholic." *Union Seminary Quarterly Review* 61.1–2 (2008) 22–29.

Harvey, John. "Courage: A Chastity Program for Persons with Same-Sex Attractions." *Catholic Social Science Review* 6 (2001) 79–85.

Hays, Richard B. *The Moral Vision of the New Testament.* San Francisco: HarperSanFrancisco, 1996.

Harrison, Brian W. "Does Vatican II Allow for Errors in Sacred Scripture?" *Divinitas* LII.3 (2009) 279–304.

———. "The Truth and Salvific Purpose of Sacred Scripture according to *Dei Verbum*, Article 11." *Living Tradition: Organ of the Roman Theological Forum* 59 (1995). Online: http://www.rtforum.org/lt59.html.

Helm, Paul. "Against Ideological Apologetics." *Reformation* 21 (February 2007). The Online Magazine of the Alliance of Confessing Evangelicals. Online: https://newhope2.timberlakepublishing.com/files/Helm%20Against%20Apologetics.pdf.

———. *The Divine Revelation.* London: Marshall Morgan & Scott, 1982.

———. "Revealed Propositions and Timeless Truths." *Religious Studies* 8 (1972).

Hick, John. *Faith and Knowledge: A Modern Introduction to the Problem of Religious Knowledge.* 2nd ed. Ithaca, NY: Cornell University Press, 1966.

Hildebrand, Dietrich von. *Die Ehe*. Munich, 1929. Translated as *Marriage*. London: Longmans, Green, 1942.

Hodge, Archibald A., and Benjamin B. Warfield. *Inspiration*. Grand Rapids: Baker, 1979.

Holwerda, David E. "Jesus and the Law: A Question of Fulfillment." In *Jesus and Israel: One Covenant or Two*, 113–46. Grand Rapids: Eerdmans, 1995.

Hopko, Thomas. *Christian Faith and Same-Sex Attraction*. Ben Lomond, CA: Conciliar, 2006.

Hutchinson, Robert J. *The Politically Incorrect Guide to the Bible*. Washington, DC: Regnery, 2007.

Jeffrey, David Lyle. "Houses of the Interpreters, Spiritual Exegesis and the Retrieval of Authority." *Books & Culture* 8.3 (2002) 30.

Jensen, David H. "God's Desire for Us: Reformed Theology and the Question of Same-Sex Marriage." *Theology* 109 (2006) 12–20.

Jenson, Robert W. "Hermeneutics and the Life of the Church." In *Reclaiming the Bible for the Church*, edited by Carl E. Braaten and Robert W. Jensen, 89–105. Grand Rapids: Eerdmans, 1995.

John Paul II (Karol Wojtyla). *The Acting Person*. Translated by Andrzej Potocki. Edited by Anna-Teresa Tymieniecka. *Analecta Husserliana* 10. Dordrecht: D. Reidel, 1979 [1969].

———. Address by John Paul II during the *ad limina* visit of the bishops of India. May 1979. Online: https://www.vatican.va/holy_father/john_paul_ii/speeches/1979/may/documents/hf_jp_ii_spe_19790531_ad-limina-india_en.html.

———. "Canonization of Edith Stein and Homily." *L'Osservatore Romano* (October 14, 1998). Online: http://ewtn.com/library/papaldoc/jp2stein.htm.

———. *A Catechesis on the Creed*. Vol. 1, *God Father and Creator*. Boston: Pauline, 1996.

———. *A Catechesis on the Creed*. Vol. 2, *Jesus, God and Savior*. Boston: Pauline, 1996.

———. *Centesimus Annus*. Encyclical Letter. May 1, 1991. Online: http://www.vatican.va/holy_father/john_paul_ii/encyclicals/documents/hf_jp-ii_enc_01051991_centesimus-annus_en.html.

———. *Dominum et Vivificantem*. ["On the Holy Spirit in the Life of the Church and the World"] Encyclical Letter. May 18, 1986. Online: http://www.vatican.va/holy_father/john_paul_ii/encyclicals/documents/hf_jp-ii_enc_18051986_dominum-et-vivificantem_en.html.

———. *Evangelium Vitae*. [The Gospel of Life"] Encyclical Letter. March 25, 1995. Online: http://www.vatican.va/holy_father/john_paul_ii/encyclicals/documents/hf_jp-ii_enc_25031995_evangelium-vitae_en.html.

———. *Familiaris Consortio*. ['On the Role of the Christian Family in the Modern World"] Apostolic Exhortation. November 22, 1981. Online: http://www.vatican.va/holy_father/john_paul_ii/apost_exhortations/documents/hf_jp-ii_exh_19811122_familiaris-consortio_en.html.

———. *Fides et Ratio*. ["On the Relationship between Faith and Reason"] Encyclical Letter. September 14, 1998. Online: http://www.vatican.va/holy_father/john_paul_ii/encyclicals/documents/hf_jp-ii_enc_15101998_fides-et-ratio_en.html.

———. "Homily of the Enthronement Mass." *L'Osservatore Romano* (October 22, 1978).

———. *Love and Responsibility*. Translated by H. T. Willets. New York: Farrar, Straus, Giroux, 1981 [1960].

———. *Make Room for the Mystery: Visit of John Paul II to the USA, 1995*. Boston: St. Paul, 1995.

———. *Man and Woman He Created Them: A Theology of the Body*. Translated by Michael Waldstein. Boston: Pauline, 2006 [1986].
———. *Memory and Identity: Conversations at the Dawn of a Millennium*. New York: Rizzoli, 2005.
———. *Mulieris Dignitatem*. ["On the Dignity and Vocation of Woman"] Apostolic Letter. August 15, 1988. Online: http://www.vatican.va/holy_father/john_paul_ii/apost_letters/documents/hf_jp-ii_apl_15081988_mulieris-dignitatem_en.html.
———. "Participation or Alienation." In *The Self and the Other, Analecta Husserliana* 6, edited by Anna-Teresa Tymieniecka, 61–73. Dordrecht: D. Reidel, 1977.
———. *Person and Community: Selected Essays*. Translated by Theresa Sandok. New York: Lang, 1993.
———. "The Pope's Message on Evolution to the Pontifical Academy of Sciences." *Quarterly Review of Biology* 72.4 (1997) 377–83.
———. *Sign of Contradiction*. New York: Seabury, 1979.
———. "Subjectivity and the Irreducible in Man." In *Analecta Husserliana* VII, 107–14. Dordrecht: D. Reidel, 1978.
———. *Ut Unum Sint*. Encyclical Letter. May 25, 1995. Online: http://www.vatican.va/holy_father/john_paul_ii/encyclicals/documents/hf_jp-ii_enc_25051995_ut-unum-sint_en.html.
———. *Veritatis Splendor*. ["Splendor of Truth"] Encyclical Letter. August 6, 1993. Online: http://www.vatican.va/holy_father/john_paul_ii/encyclicals/documents/hf_jp-ii_enc_06081993_veritatis-splendor_en.html.
Johnson, Luke Timothy. "After the Big Chill: Intellectual Freedom & Catholic Theologians." *Commonweal* 133.2 (2006) 10–14.
———. "Debate & Discernment: Scripture & the Spirit." *Commonweal* (January 28, 1994). Online: https://www.encyclopedia.com/printable.aspx?id=1G1:14788234.
———. "A Disembodied 'Theology of the Body': John Paul II on Love, Sex and Pleasure." *Commonweal* 128.2 (2001). Online: http://findarticles.com/p/articles/mi_m1252/is_2_128/ai_71578789/pg_8/.
———. "Homosexuality & the Church." *Commonweal* 134.15 (2007). Online: http://www.commonwealmagazine.org/print_format.php?id_article=1957.
———. "Participating in Revelation (1 Kg. 19: 9-18; Rom. 9: 1-5; Mt. 14: 22-33)." *Christian Century* (August 8–15, 1990) 731. Online: https://www.religion-outline.org/showarticle.asp?title=729.
Johnson, Luke Timothy, and William S. Kurz. *The Future of Catholic Biblical Scholarship: A Constructive Conversation*. Grand Rapids: Eerdmans, 2002.
Journet, Charles Cardinal. *What is Dogma?* Translated by Marx Pontifex. New York: Hawthorn, 1964.
Kaiser, Walter C., Jr. *Mission in the Old Testament: Israel as a Light to the Nations*. Grand Rapids: Baker Academic, 2000.
Kerr, Fergus. "Karol Wojtyla." In *Twentieth-Century Catholic Theologians: From Neoscholasticism to Nuptial Mysticism*, 163–82. Oxford: Blackwell, 2007.
Kimel, Alvin Fr. "Sola Scriptura." April 2, 2004. Online: https://pontifications.wordpress.com/sola-scriptura.
Köstenberger, Andreas J., and Peter T. O'Brien. *Salvation to the Ends of the Earth: A Biblical Theology of Mission*. Downers Grove, IL: InterVarsity, 2001.
Kurz, William S. "The Scriptural Foundations of *The Theology of the Body*." In *John Paul II on The Body: Human, Eucharistic, Ecclesial: Festschrift Avery Cardinal Dulles, S.J.*,

edited by John M. McDermott and John Gavin, 27–46. Philadelphia: Saint Joseph's University Press, 2007.

Kuyper, Abraham. *Abraham Kuyper: A Centennial Reader*. Edited by James D. Bratt. Grand Rapids: Eerdmans, 1998.

———. *De Gemeene Gratie* I–III. Amsterdam: Höveker & Wormser, 1902–1904. Online: http://www.neocalvinisme.nl/tekstframes.html.

Lawler, Michael G. *What Is and What Ought to Be: The Dialectic of Experience, Theology, and Church*. New York: Continuum, 2005.

Lee, Patrick. "The Human Body and Sexuality in the Teaching of Pope John Paul II." In *John Paul II's Contribution to Catholic Bioethics*, edited by Christopher Tollefsen, 107–20. Dordrecht: Springer, 2004. Online: http://www.patrickleebioethics.com/jp2_on_sex_and_the_body.pdf.

———. "The Reasons Why Marriage Is Inherently Heterosexual." Online: http://www.thepublicdiscourse.com/2008/12/102?printerfriendly=true.

Lee, Patrick, and Robert P. George. "What Sex Can Be: Self-Alienation, Illusion, or One-Flesh Union." *American Journal of Jurisprudence* 42 (1997) 135–57. Online: http://www.patrickleebioethics.com/articles.html.

———. *Body-Self Dualism in Contemporary Ethics and Politics*. New York: Cambridge University Press, 2008.

Levering, Matthew. "Knowing What Is 'Natural': Thomas Aquinas and Luke Timothy Johnson on Romans 1–2." *Logos* 12 (2009) 117–42.

Lonergan, Bernard J. F. "The Dehellenization of Dogma." In *A Second Collection*, edited by William J. Ryan, and Bernard J. Tyrell, 11–32. Philadelphia: Westminster, 1974.

———. *Method in Theology*. New York: Herder & Herder, 1972.

———. "The Origins of Christian Realism." In *A Second Collection*, edited by William J. Ryan and Bernard J. Tyrell, 239–61. Philadelphia: Westminster, 1974.

———. *The Way to Nicea: The Dialectical Development of Trinitarian Theology*. Philadelphia: Westminster, 1976.

Lubac, Henri de. "Apologetics and Theology." In *Theological Fragments*. San Francisco: Ignatius, 1989.

———. *A Brief Catechesis on Nature and Grace*. San Francisco: Ignatius, 1984.

———. *Catholicism: Christ and the Common Destiny of Man*. San Francisco: Ignatius, 1988.

Luijpen, Wilhelmus. *Existential Phenomenology*. Pittsburgh, PA: Duquesne University Press, 1965 [1959].

Mansini, Guy, and Lawrence J. Welch. "In Conformity to Christ." *First Things* (April 2006). Online: http://www.firstthings.com/article/2007/01/in-conformity-to-christ---38.

Maritain, Jacques. *Clairvoyance de Rome*. Paris: Spes, 1929.

———. *Man and the State*. Chicago: University of Chicago Press, 1951.

Martin, Francis. "All Israel Will Be Saved." Online: http://hebrewcatholic.org/FaithandTheology/Reflections-Covenant-Mission/allisraelwillbes.html.

———. *The Feminist Question, Feminist Theology in the Light of Christian Tradition*. Grand Rapids: Eerdmans, 1994.

———. "Revelation as Disclosure: Creation." In *Wisdom and Holiness, Science and Scholarship, Essays in Honor of Matthew L. Lamb*, edited by Michael Dauphinais and Matthew Levering, 204–47. Naples, FL: Sapientia, 2007.

———. *Sacred Scripture: The Disclosure of the Word*. Naples, FL: Sapientia, 2006.

———. "Some Aspects of Biblical Studies since Vatican II: The Contribution and Challenge of *Dei Verbum*." In *Sacred Scripture: The Disclosure of the Word*, 227–47. Naples, FL: Sapientia, 2006.

———. "Some Directions in Catholic Biblical Theology." In *Out of Egypt: Biblical Theology and Biblical Interpretation*, edited by Craig Bartholomew et al., 65–87. Scripture and Hermeneutics Series 5. Grand Rapids: Zondervan, 2004.

Mascall, E. L. *The Openness of Being, Natural Theology Today*. The Gifford Lectures, 1970–1971. London: Darton Longman & Todd, 1971.

Mathison, Keith A. *The Shape of Sola Scriptura*. Moscow, ID: Canon, 2001.

Matthews, G.. *The Body in Context, Sex and Catholicism*. London: SCM, 1992.

Mavrodes, George I. *Revelation in Religious Belief*. Philadelphia: Temple University Press, 1988.

May, William E. *Catholic Sexual Ethics*. New Haven: Knights of Columbus Supreme Council, 2001.

———. "On the Impossibility of Same-Sex Marriage." Online: https://www.christendom-awake.org/pages/may/homosex.htm.

May, William E., et al. *Catholic Sexual Ethics: A Summary, Explanation and Defense*. 2nd ed. Huntington, IN: Our Sunday Visitor, 1998.

McConville, Gordon. *Grace in the End: A Study in Deuteronomic Theology*. Grand Rapids: Zondervan, 1993.

McGrath, Alister E. *Intellectuals Don't Need God and Other Modern Myths*. Grand Rapids: Zondervan, 1993.

———. *Reformation Thought: An Introduction*. 2nd ed. Oxford: Blackwell, 1993.

Mouw, Richard J. "Narrative, Character, and Commands." In *The God Who Commands*, 116–49. Notre Dame, IN: University of Notre Dame Press, 1990.

Newman, John Henry. *Apologia Pro Vita Sua*. London: Dent, 1912 [1864].

Nichols, Aidan. *Catholic Thought since the Enlightenment*. Leominster, UK: Gracewing, 1998.

———. *Epiphany, A Theological Introduction to Catholicism*. Collegeville, MN: Liturgical, 1996.

———. *From Newman to Congar, The Idea of Doctrinal Development from the Victorians to the Second Vatican Council*. Edinburgh: T. & T. Clark, 1990.

———. "Reclaiming the Bible." In *Christendom Awake: On Reenergizing the Church in Culture*, 163–74. Grand Rapids: Eerdmans, 1999.

———. "Reviving Doctrinal Consciousness." In *Christendom Awake: On Reenergizing the Church in Culture*, 41–52. Grand Rapids: Eerdmans, 1999.

———. *The Shape of Catholic Theology*. Collegeville, MN: Liturgical, 1991.

Nicolosi, Joseph. "The Removal of Homosexuality from the Psychiatric Manual." *Catholic Social Science Review* 6 (2001) 71–77.

Noriega, José. "Homosexuality: The Semblance of Intimacy." *Communio: International Catholic Review* 35 (2008) 451–64.

Obermann, Heiko. *Forerunners of the Reformation: The Shape of Late Medieval Thought*. London: Lutterworth, 1967.

O'Brien, T. C. "Old Testament." In *Summa Theologiae*, vol. 26, *Original Sin*, translated by T. C. O'Brien, 121–23. New York: McGraw-Hill, 1965.

———. "Thematic Conspectus of Catholic Teaching." In *Summa Theologiae*, vol. 26, *Original Sin*, translated by T. C. O'Brien, 115–20. New York: McGraw-Hill, 1965.

O'Collins, Gerald, and Mario Farrugia. *Catholicism, The Story of Catholic Christianity*. Oxford: Oxford University Press, 2003.

Olthuis, James. "When Is Sex against Nature?" In *An Ethos of Compassion and the Integrity of Creation*, edited by Brian J. Walsh et al., 188–205. Lanham, MD: University Press of America, 1995).

Packer, J. I. "Biblical Authority, Hermeneutics and Inerrancy." In *Jerusalem and Athens: Critical Discussions on the Thelolgy and Apologetics of Cornelius Van Til*, edited by E. R. Geehan, 141–53. Philadelphia: Presbyterian & Reformed, 1971.

———. *Fundamentalism and the Word of God*. Grand Rapids: Eerdmans, 1958.

Paul VI. *Evangelii Nuntiandi*. ["Proclaiming the Gospel"] Apostolic Exhortation. December 8, 1975. Online: http://www.vatican.va/holy_father/paul_vi/apost_exhortations/documents/hf_p-vi_exh_19751208_evangelii-nuntiandi_en.html.

Pelikan, Jaroslav. *Credo: Historical and Theological Guide to Creeds and Confessions of Faith in the Christian Tradition*. New Haven: Yale University Press, 2003.

———. *Interpreting the Bible and the Constitution*. New Haven: Yale University Press, 2004.

Perry, John. "Gentiles and Homosexuals: A Brief History of an Analogy." *Journal of Religious Ethics* 38 (2) 321–47.

Pié-Ninot, Salvador. "Sensus Fidei." In *Dictionary of Fundamental Theology*, edited by René Latourelle and Rino Fisichella, 992–95. New York: Crossroad, 1994.

Pius XII. *Humani Generis*. Encyclical Letter. August 12, 1950. Online: http://www.vatican.va/holy_father/pius_xii/encyclicals/documents/hf_p-xii_enc_12081950_humani-generis_en.html.

Pinckaers, Servais. *The Pursuit of Happiness—God's Way*. Translated by Sr. Mary Thomas Noble. New York: Alba, 1998.

Polanyi, Michael. "Knowing and Being." In *Knowing and Being: Essays by Michael Polanyi*, edited by Marjorie Grene, 124–37. London: Routledge & Kegan Paul, 1969.

———. "The Logic of Tacit Inference." In *Knowing and Being: Essays by Michael Polanyi*, edited by Marjorie Grene, 138–58. London: Routledge & Kegan Paul, 1969.

———. *Personal Knowledge: Towards a Post-Critical Philosophy*. New York: Harper & Row, 1964 [1958].

———. "Sense-Giving and Sense-Reading." In *Knowing and Being: Essays by Michael Polanyi*, edited by Marjorie Grene, 181–207. London: Routledge & Kegan Paul, 1969.

———. *The Study of Man*. Chicago: University of Chicago Press, 1959.

———. *The Tacit Dimension*. Chicago: University of Chicago Press, 1966.

Pontifical Council for Culture. *Towards Pastoral Approach to Culture*. May 23, 1999. Online: http://www.vatican.va/roman_curia/pontifical_councils/cultr/documents/rc_pc_pc-cultr_doc_03061999_pastoral_en.html.

Pontifical Biblical Commission. *The Interpretation of the Bible in the Church*. April 15, 1993. Online: http://www.ewtn.com/library/CURIA/PBCINTER.htm.

Pope, Stephen. "The Vatican's Blunt Instrument." *The Tablet* (August 9, 2003). Online: http://www.clgs.org/marriage/history_pope.html.

Pottmeyer, Hermann. "Tradition." In *Dictionary of Fundamental Theology*, edited by René Latourelle and Rino Fisichella, 1119–26. New York: Crossroad, 1994.

Pronk, Pim. *Against Nature? Types of Moral Argumentation regarding Homosexuality*. Grand Rapids: Eerdmans, 1993.

Radcliffe, Timothy. *What's the Point of Being a Christian?* London: Burns & Oates, 2005.

Rahner, Karl. *Foundations of Christian Faith: An Introduction to the Idea of Christianity.* Translated by William V. Dych. London: Darton Longman & Todd, 1978.

———. "Theological Reflections on Monogenism." In *Theological Investigations*, translated by Cornelius Ernst, 229–96 (Baltimore: Helicon, 1961 [1954]).

Ratzinger, Joseph. (Benedict XVI). "Address of His Holiness Benedict XVI to the Participants in the Plenary Assembly of the Pontifical Biblical Commission." April 23, 2009. Online: http://www.vatican.va/holy_father/benedict_xvi/speeches/2009/april/documents/hf_ben-xvi_spe_20090423_pcb_en.html.

———. "Address of His Holiness Pope Benedict XVI to Swiss Bishops." November 9, 2006. Online: http://www.vatican.va/holy_father/benedict_xvi/speeches/2006/november/documents/hf_ben-xvi_spe_20061109_concl-swiss-bishops_en.html

———. *Caritas in Veritate.* ["On Integral Human Development in Charity and Truth"] Encyclical Letter. June 29, 2009. Online: http://www.vatican.va/holy_father/benedict_xvi/encyclicals/documents/hf_ben-xvi_enc_20090629_caritas-in-veritate_en.html.

———. "The Church's Teaching Authority—Faith—Morals." In *Principles of Christian Morality*, translated by Graham Harrison, 45–73. San Francisco: Ignatius, 1986.

———. "Current Doctrinal Relevance of the *Catechism of the Catholic Church.*" October 9, 2002. Online: http://www.vatican.va/roman_curia/congregations/cfaith/documents/rc_con_cfaith_doc_20021009_ratzinger-catechetical-congress_en.html.

———. *Doctrinal Commentary on the Concluding Formula of the Profession Fidei.* June 29, 1998. This commentary was issued coincident with the promulgation of Ad tuendam fidem by Pope John Paul II, modifying the Oriental and Latin codes of canon law. Online: http://www.ewtn.com/library/CURIA/CDFADTU.HTM.

———. "Dogmatic Constitution on Divine Revelation." In *Commentary on the Documents of Vatican II*, vol. 3, translated by William Glen-Doepel, et al., 155–98. New York: Herder & Herder.

———. *Eschatology, Death and Eternal Life.* 2nd ed. Translated by Michael Waldstein. Edited by Aidan Nichol. Washington, DC: Catholic University Press of America, 2007 [1977].

———. *Jesus of Nazareth.* Translated by Adrian J. Walker. New York: Doubleday, 2007.

———. *Many Religions—One Covenant, Israel, the Church and the World.* Translated by Graham Harrison. San Francisco: Ignatius, 1999.

———. *Principles of Catholic Theology.* Translated by Sister Mary Francis McCarthy. San Francisco: Ignatius, 1987 [1982].

———. "The Question of the Concept of Tradition: A Provisional Response." In *God's Word: Scripture, Tradition, Office,* edited by Peter Hünermann and Thomas Söding, and translated by Henry Taylor, 41–89. San Francisco: Ignatius, 2008.

———. "Revelation and Tradition." In *Revelation and Tradition,* 26–78. Quaestiones Disputatae 17. New York: Herder & Herder, 1966.

———. *The Spirit of the Liturgy.* Translated by John Saward. San Francisco: Ignatius, 2000.

———. *Theological Highlights of Vatican II.* Translated by Henry Traub, Gerard C. Thormann, and Werner Barzel. New York: Paulist, 1966.

———. *The Yes of Jesus Christ.* Translated by Robert Nowell. New York: Crossroad, 1991.

Reformed Ecumenical Council, Athens 1992, *Hermeneutics and Ethics.* Online: www.recweb.org.

Ridderbos, Herman. *Heilsgeschiedenis en Heilige Schrift Van Het Nieuwe Testament.* Kampen: Kok, 1955. Translated by. H. de Jongste as *Redemptive History and the New*

Testament Scriptures. Revised by Richard B. Gaffin Jr. Phillipsburg, NJ: Presbyterian & Reformed, 1963.

———. *Paul: An Outline of His Theology.* Translated by John Richard De Witt. Grand Rapids: Eerdmans, 1975 (1966).

Roberts, Christopher C. *Creation and Covenant: The Significance of Sexual Difference in the Moral Theology of Marriage.* New York: T. & T. Clark International, 2007.

Rush, Ormond. *Still Interpreting Vatican II: Some Hermeneutical Principles.* Mahwah, NJ: Paulist, 2004.

Savage, Deborah. "The Centrality of Lived Experience in Wojtyla's Account of the Person." Unpublished paper.

Schaeffer, Francis. *Escape from Reason.* London: InterVarsity, 1968.

Scheeben, Matthias Joseph. *Natur und Gnade. Versuch einer systematischen, wissenschaftlichen Darstellung der natürlichen und übernatürlichen Lebensordnung im Menschen.* Mainz 1861. Translated by Cyril Vollert, as *Nature and Grace.* London: Herder, 1954.

Schmidt, Thomas E. *Straight & Narrow: Compassion and Clarity in the Homosexuality Debate.* Downers Grove, IL: InterVarsity, 1995.

Schneiders, Sandra M. *The Revelatory Text.* HarperSanFrancisco, 1991.

Schmitz, Kenneth L. *At the Center of the Human Drama: The Philosophical Anthropology of Karol Wojtyla/Pope John Paul II.* Washington, DC: Catholic University of America Press, 1993.

Schockenhoff, Eberhard. "A Consistent Ethic of Life (with a Few Blemishes): Moral-Theological Remarks on *Evangelium Vitae* and on Some Protestant Questions about It." In *Ecumenical Ventures in Ethics, Protestants Engage Pope John Paul II's Moral Encyclicals,* edited by Reinhard Hütter and Theodor Dieter, 237–61. Grand Rapids: Eerdmans, 1998.

———. *Natural Law and Human Dignity, Universal Ethics in an Historical World.* Translated by Brian McNeil. Washington, DC, Catholic University of America Press, 2003.

Schreiner, Thomas R. "A New Testament Perspective on Homosexuality." *Themelios* 31.3 (2006) 62–75.

Seerveld, Calvin G. "A Christian Tin-Can Theory of Man." *Journal of the American Scientific Affiliation* (1981) 74–81. Online: http://www.freewebs.com/seerveld/Seerveld%20_A_Christian_Tin-Can_Theory_of_Man.pdf.

———. *How to Read the Bible to Hear God Speak.* Sioux Center, IA: Dordt College Press, 2003 [1968].

Semmelroth, Otto. "The Community of Mankind." *Commentary on the Documents of Vatican II,* Volume V. New York: Herder & Herder, 1969, 164–201.

Smedes, Lewis. "The Bible and Ethics." Presented at a Conference on "Interpreting an Authoritative Scripture," held June 22–26, 1981 at the Institute for Christian Studies, sponsored by Fuller Theological Seminary, Pasadena, CA, and the Institute for Christian Studies, Toronto, Canada.

———. *Mere Morality.* Grand Rapids: Eerdmans, 1983.

Smith, Janet E. "Moral Terminology and Proportionalism." In *Recovering Nature: Essays in Natural Philosophy, Ethics, and Metaphysics in Honor of Ralph McInerny,* edited by Thomas Hibbs and John O'Callaghan, 127–46. Notre Dame: University Press, 1999. Online: http://www.aodonline.org/aodonline-sqlimages/shms/faculty/SmithJanet/Publications/MoralPhilosophy/MoralTerminology.pdf.

———. "The *Sensus Fidelium* and *Humanae Vitae*." *Angelicum* 83 (2006) 271–97.

———. "Thomas Aquinas on Homosexuality." In *Homosexuality and American Public Life*, edited by Christopher Wolfe, 129–40. Dallas: Spence, 1999.

Sokolowski, Robert. *Christian Faith and Human Understanding*. Washington, DC: Catholic University of America Press, 2006.

———. *The God of Faith and Reason, Foundations of Christian Theology*. Washington, DC: Catholic University of American Press, 1995 [1982].

———. *Introduction to Phenomenology*. Cambridge: Cambridge University Press, 2000.

Stegman, Thomas D. "'Actualization': How John Paul II Utilizes Scripture in *The Theology of the Body*." In *John Paul II on The Body: Human, Eucharistic, Ecclesial, Festschrift Avery Cardinal Dulles, S.J.*, edited by John M. McDermott, and John Gavin, 47–64. Philadelphia: Saint Joseph's University Press, 2007.

Sullivan, Andrew. "Catholicism and Homosexuality." In *Creative Fidelity: American Catholic Intellectual Traditions*, edited by R. Scott Appleby et al., 317–19. Maryknoll, NY: Orbis, 2004.

———. *Virtually Normal: An Argument about Homosexuality*. New York: Knopf, 1995.

Swinburne, Richard. *Revelation*. Oxford: Clarendon, 1992.

Temple, William Archbishop. *Nature, Man and God*. Gifford Lectures, 1932–1933. London: Macmillan, 1960; originally published 1934.

Thielicke, Helmut. *The Ethics of Sex*. Translated by John W. Doberstein. New York: Harper & Row, 1964.

Tracy, David. *Blessed Rage for Order*. New York: Seabury, 1975.

Trimp, Cornelius. "The Witness of the Scriptures." In *Jerusalem and Athens: Critical Discussions on the Theology and Apologetics of Cornelius Van Til*, edited by E. R. Geehan, 172–84. Philadelphia: Presbyterian & Reformed, 1971.

United States Conference of Catholic Bishops. *Always Our Children* (1998). A Pastoral Message to Parents of Homosexual Children and Suggestions for Pastoral Ministers. Online: http://www.usccb.org/laity/always.shtml.

Vanhoozer, Kevin J. *The Drama of Doctrine*. Louisville: Westminster John Knox, 2005.

———. *Is There a Meaning in this Text? The Bible, The Reader, and the Morality of Literary Knowledge*. Grand Rapids: Zondervan, 1998.

———. "Scripture and Tradition." In *The Cambridge Companion to Postmodern Theology*, edited by Kevin J. Vanhoozer, 149–69. Cambridge: Cambridge University Press, 2003.

Vatican Council I. *Decreta Dogmatica Concilii Vaticani de Fide Catholica et de Ecclesia Christi*, 1870, Chapter II, *of Revelation*. In *The Creeds of Christendom*, edited by Philip Schaff, revised by David S. Schaff, vol. 2, *The Greek and Latin Creeds*. Grand Rapids: Baker, 1931.

Vatican Council II. *Dei Verbum*. ["Dogmatic Constitution on Divine Revelation"] November 18, 1965. Online: http://www.vatican.va/archive/hist_councils/ii_vatican_council/documents/vat-ii_const_19651118_dei-verbum_en.html.

———. *Dignitatis humanae*. ["Declaration on Religious Freedom"] December 7, 1965. Online: http://www.vatican.va/archive/hist_councils/ii_vatican_council/documents/vat-ii_decl_19651207_dignitatis-humanae_en.html.

———. *Gaudium et Spes*. ["Pastoral Constitution on the Church in the Modern World"] December 7, 1965. Online: http://www.vatican.va/archive/hist_councils/ii_vatican_council/documents/vat-ii_cons_19651207_gaudium-et-spes_en.html.

———. *Sacrosanctum Concilium*. [Dogmatic Constitution on the Sacred Liturgy"] December 4, 1963. Online: http://www.vatican.va/archive/hist_councils/ii_vatican_council/documents/vat-ii_const_19631204_sacrosanctum-concilium_en.html.

Vos, Geerhardus. "The Idea of Biblical Theology as a Science and as a Theological Discipline." Inaugural address as Professor of Biblical Theology, Princeton Theological Seminary, delivered at the First Presbyterian Church, Princeton on May 8, 1894. Online: http://homepage.mac.com/shanerosenthal/reformationink/gvbiblical.htm.

Ward, Timothy. *Words of Life: Scripture as the Living and Active Word of God*. Downers Grove, IL: IVP Academic, 2009.

Warfield, B. B. "On Faith in its Psychological Aspects." In *Studies in Theology*, 537–66. New York: Oxford University, 1932.

Webb, William J. "A Redemptive-Movement Hermeneutic." In *Discovering Biblical Equality*, edited by Ronald W. Pierce and Rebecca Merrill Groothuis. Downers Grove, IL: InterVarsity, 2005.

Webster, John. *Holiness*. Grand Rapids: Eerdmans, 2003.

———. *Holy Scripture: A Dogmatic Sketch*. Cambridge: Cambridge University Press, 2003.

Williams, Rowan. "The Body's Grace." In *Theology and Sexuality: Classic and Contemporary Readings*, edited by Eugene F. Rogers, 309–21. Oxford: Blackwell, 2002.

———. "Knowing Myself in Christ." In *The Way Forward? Christian Voices on Homosexuality and the Church*, edited by Timothy Bradshaw, 12–19. 2nd ed. Grand Rapids: Eerdmans, 2003 (1997).

Williamson, Peter S. "Catholic Principles for Interpreting Scripture." *Catholic Biblical Quarterly* 65 (2003) 327–49.

Wojtyla, Karol. See John Paul II.

Wolters, Albert M. "Creation Order: A Historical Look at Our Heritage." In *An Ethos of Compassion and the Integrity of Creation*, edited by Brian J. Walsh et al., 33–48. Lanham, MD: University Press of America, 1995.

———. *Creation Regained: Biblical Basics for a Reformational Worldview*. Grand Rapids: Eerdmans, 1985.

———. "What Is To Be Done? Toward a Neo-Calvinist Agenda." Online: http://www.wrf.ca/comment/article.cfm?ID=142.

Wolterstorff, Nicholas. *Reason within the Bounds of Religion*. 2nd ed. Grand Rapids: Eerdmans, 1984.

Wright, N. T. "How Can the Bible be Authoritative?" *Vox Evangelica* 21 (1991) 7–32. Online: https://www.ntwrightpage.com/Wright_Bible_Authoritative.htm.

———. *The Last Word*. San Francisco: Harper, 2005.

Subject/Name Index

Aquinas, Thomas, St., 33–34,
  62n222, 73, 93–94, 105–6,
  119, 120n133, 141, 142n76,
  172–73, 186, 207, 208n8,
  216–17, 224, 263, 264n88,
  286–87, 298, 301, 319
Ashley, Benedict M., OP, xvin2, 6n9,
  72, 74, 75n13, 76n16, 242n11,
  254, 256n66, 257n69, 292–93,
  319
authority, historical and normative,
  97–100

Balthasar, Hans Urs von, xviin5, 152,
  320
Barth, Karl, xvin3, xvin5, 30n93, 320
Bavinck, Herman, xxvn33, 10,
  25n70, 26n72, 28n82, 39n131,
  49–52, 54n202, 55–56,
  57n206, 58, 66–68, 76, 97,
  98n84, 99–100, 123–25,
  148n96, 163, 165, 320
Belief Statement on Homosexuality
  (Christian Reformed
  Church), xix
Berkouwer, G. C., xxvn33, 25, 26n72,
  31n95, 41, 45n158, 47n169,
  99, 149–52, 153n121, 159–60,
  161n153, 192n108, 203,
  289n165, 290n170, 320
Bible, as special revelation, 23–34
  authority of, 50–53, 57–59
  canonicity of, 9, 45–46, 48,
  134

inerrancy of, 59–66
inspiration of, 25, 46–48
teaching office of Church and,
  66–71
Blackburn, Simon, 1n1, 320

Cahill, Lisa Sowle, 114n124, 321
Caputo, John, 4n6, 321
Catechism of the Catholic Church,
  xxiii, xxivn31, 26, 27n76, 29,
  33–34, 59n214, 64n229, 73n7,
  86, 87n54, 90n60, 92n69, 101,
  102n96, 102n97, 111, 113, 142,
  152n120, 154n128, 158n142,
  207, 212n27, 214n31, 216n35,
  218, 227, 231n66, 239, 240n5,
  241n9, 245n17, 254n58,
  255, 256n65, 257n69, 261,
  279n139, 282n153, 287,
  288n164, 290, 291n171, 304,
  307, 310n22, 312, 314n38, 316,
  317n54, 321
Cavanagh, Lorraine, 81–82, 321
Cessario, Romanus, OP, xxiv,
  209–10, 211n24, 216, 217n40,
  218n44, 321
Congar, Yves, 22, 23n64, 33n99,
  35n108, 45–46, 46n164, 47,
  49–50, 52n193, 53n197, 54,
  92, 135n48, 137, 138n61,
  141–42, 143n78, 145n82,
  163n160, 321
Copan, Paul, 2n1, 6n10, 7n12, 16,
  18–19, 96n81, 322

creation, fall, redemption, and fulfillment (theology of the body), 205–38
creation order, xviii, xxiii, xxv*n*33, 26n25, 128, 215–17, 245–46, 300
creation revelation, xxi, xxiv, 13, 26, 57, 127
Crosby, John, xxvi*n*37, 249n35, 279, 322

Dawkins, Richard, 1–3, 322
Dei Verbum, Vatican II, xx*n*15, xxii, 9–10, 23–24, 25n69, 28–29, 31, 35n108, 43n150, 44–45, 46n165, 49n177, 50–52, 53n196, 55n204, 58–61, 62n223, 63n227, 67n240, 70n246, 71n252, 72–74, 82, 87, 88n55, 102, 127, 132–34, 143, 148n97, 149, 153, 159n147, 222, 333
dialogical view of biblical authority, 127–32, 150, 161, 243
Dooyeweerd, Herman
 common grace, 291
 creation, fall and redemption, 111n116
 creation revelation, xviii, xxiii
 ecumenism, xxvi
 Hildebrand, Dietrich von, 264–68
 human body, 188
 integral experience of reality, 199
 marriage, 262–68
Douma, Jochem, xxi, xxii, 16n42, 89n56, 102n95, 104, 114–15, 118–19, 322
Dulles, Avery Cardinal, SJ, 11n27, 12n29, 25n70, 30n93, 31n95, 69–71, 133n37, 148n97, 167n5, 323

ethics, biblical hermeneutics, 96–122

faith and authority, 145–59
faith and criticism, 159–63
Farley, Margaret, xi, 145–47, 147n89, 148, 150, 243, 247n29, 256, 258, 275, 277–79
Fides et Ratio (John Paul II), 77n21, 153n122, 154n125, 157n140, 158n144, 164n161, 167n6, 232n68, 296n184, 326
Finnis, John, xi, 65, 66n236, 223–224, 239n2, 240n4, 243n12, 248, 253, 254n56, 255n60, 258–59, 260n78, 262–63, 264n88, 270n110, 294n181, 299n195, 302, 323
focal and subsidiary awareness (Polanyi), 202–3, 270–72
Frame, John, xxiv, 54n200, 60n217, 64n231, 148, 324
fundamentalism, biblicism, xxi–xxv, 219–20

Geiselmann, Josef R., 34–35, 35n111, 37–38, 40n136, 41, 42n145, 132n31, 135, 140, 324
Gilson, Etienne, xix, 212, 292n174, 325
George, Robert, xi, 65, 66n236, 95n111, 203, 239n2, 243n12, 244n16, 246, 247n28, 252–53, 260n80, 262–63, 268–69, 270n109, 280n144, 281, 285n159, 294n181, 324
Grisez, Germain, xi, 10, 15, 18, 25n70, 28n83, 32n98, 59n213, 60n217, 61n219, 62n223, 65, 66n236, 239n2, 241n6, 243n12, 254n54, 259n77, 260n79, 262–63, 267n101, 271, 274, 280, 281n149, 294n181, 301, 303n209, 309, 310n19, 325

Subject/Name Index   337

Guarino, Thomas G., 29n90, 33n99, 34n105, 84n38, 90n59, 134n41, 205, 211n25, 293, 325

Hahn, Scott, 89, 325
Hays, Richard, xxii, xxiii, 85n42, 128, 162, 325
hermeneutics of suspicion, 230–34
Homosexuality
   Catholic Church, *Persona Humana, Homosexualitatis problema*, 94, 254–59, 261, 272, 282–88
   Farley, Margaret, 247, 256–59, 275–79
   Finnis, John, 223–24, 248, 253, 259–60
   Gagnon, Robert A. J., 5–8, 99, 116–18, 128–32
   George, Robert, 251–54, 259–61, 268–70, 280
   Hays, Richard B., xxii–xxiii, 128
   John Paul II (Karol Wojtyla), 247–50, 270–74, 294–305
   Johnson, Luke Timothy, 2–14, 128–32, 244, 246, 294–305
   Lee, Patrick, 251–54, 259–61, 268–70, 280–82
   Pope, Stephen, 288–94
   Radcliffe, Timothy, 308–17
   Sullivan, Andrew, 243, 283–85
   Thielicke, Helmut, 310–11, 311n27, 333
Helm, Paul, xvin4, 24n66, 29, 30n92, 31n94, 84n40, 94, 98n85, 325
Hermeneutics, Biblical
   canonical sense, xxii, 73–74, 84–85
   literal sense, 72–73, 77–78, 84
   realism, truth, 78–84
   sensus plenior (plenary sense), 74, 94
   spiritual, traditional sense, 85–88, 90–94

unity of Scripture, 88–90
Hildebrand, Dietrich von, 264–67
Hutchinson, Robert J., 5–7, 326

Jenson, Robert W., 83, 326
John Paul II (Karol Wojtyla), x–xi, xiii, xv, xvii, xviiin7, xxi, xxiii, xxv, xxvn34, xxvi, xxviin40, 13, 15n35, 44, 64n229, 75, 77–78, 82n33, 83, 94n75, 95n77, 96, 100–101, 107–8, 115, 119–20, 126, 144, 153, 154n125, 155n130, 157n140, 158n144, 164n161, 166, 175, 186n91, 187, 188n96, 193, 201, 203, 209n11, 212–13, 214n30, 215n34, 216, 218n44, 219, 226n61, 229n65, 232n68, 235–36, 238, 240n3, 244n15, 246n22, 249n32, 250n40, 251, 256n67, 257, 271, 276n128, 277, 278n132, 282, 289, 295, 296n184, 297, 299–300, 302, 308, 309n13, 311, 315, 326
Johnson, Luke Timothy, 1–23, 127–32, 244, 246–47, 294–305
Journet, Charles Cardinal, 34, 327

Kimel Alvin, 76n17, n19, 327
Kurz, William S., xxvn34, 2n3, 23n65, 86n49, 227, 327
Kuyper, Abraham, xxvn33, 231–32n68, 328

Lawler, Michael G., 33, 47n169, 115n124
Lee, Patrick, 65, 66n236, 195, 239n2, 243n12, 244n16, 246, 247n28, 249, 252–53, 260n80, 263, 268–69, 270n109, 276–77, 280n146, 281n151, 285n159, 294n181, 328
Levering, Matthew, 129n18, 242n11, 278n137, 328

Subject/Name Index

Lonergan, Bernard J. F., SJ, 78–80, 82–83, 84n38, 85, 100n92, 196n113, 328

marriage, xvii–xviii, xxi, xxiii, xxv, 16, 26–27, 65–66, 95, 105, 111, 113–14, 116, 119, 193–96, 201, 211–12, 215–16, 218–21, 225, 237–38, 241, 244, 250–51, 253–55, 259–68, 272, 274, 280
Maritain, Jacques, 111, 206, 297–98, 301–2, 304–5, 328
Martin, Francis, xxii*n*6, 5n6, 24n67, 25n70, 26n72, 27n78, 55–56, 87–88, 90n61, 100, 125n7, 160, 163, 164n163, 190n107, 328
Mascall, E. L., 207, 209, 210n18, 329
Mavrodes, George I., 25n70, 27n79, 329

nature and grace, 111–13, 205–13
Nichols, Aidan, OP, xviii, n9, xxii*n*23, 8n18, 32, 33n99, 34, 35n108, 36n117, 37n122, 40–44, 48, 51, 60n217, 62n223, 63–65, 73, 74n11, 75, 78, 86, 91–92, 93n71, 94–95, 108n108, 117n128, 123, 125, 126n8, 135, 136n50, 137n58, 140, 143n78, 162, 163n158, 164–65, 210n19, 222, 258, 283n156, 329
Noriega, José, xxvi, 329
Notre Dame Core Council for Gay and Lesbian Students, 241, 241n9, 242–43

Olthuis, James, 244, 275, 277, 279, 330

Packer, J. I., 23, 24n66, 90n62, 330
Pié-Ninot, Salvador, 142–43, 330
Pinckaers, Servais, OP, 120–21, 330

Polanyi, Michael, xi, 189, 190n106, 202–3, 270–72, 330
Pope, Stephen, xi, 245n19, 288–94,
Pottmeyer, Herman, 28n85, 36n116, 43n147, 51n188, 133n34, 134n38, 330
propositional revelation, 23–24, 30n93, 31–33, 34n105, 81, 113, 114n124, 163

Radcliffe, Timothy, OP, xi, 247, 308–10, 313–14, 330
Ratzinger, Joseph (Benedict XVI), xxi, xxii*n*23, 15n38, 19, 20n55, 21n58, 35–36, 40n138, 43n150, 44, 57, 61, 73n7, 106, 107n105, 112, 136, 153, 154n125, 155–56, 186n92, 307–8, 331
Reformed Christianity, xxv*n*33
Reveal, two senses of, 98
revelation as experience
    Berkouwer, G. C., 149–52
    Farley, Margaret, 145–49
    Johnson, Luke Timothy, 8–14, 127–32
    Nichols, Aidan, 123–27
Revelation, subjective and objective, 24–27, 55–57, 163–65
Ridderbos, Herman, 4n6, 11n25, 22, 25n71, 58, 130n23, 131, 331
Roberts, Christopher C., xvi*n*3, xxi, 246n21, 268n104, 332
Rush, Ormond, 132–39, 144, 332

Schlier, Heinrich, 34n106
Schockenhoff, Eberhard, 187, 188n102, 250, 332
Scripture and Tradition
    Catholic teaching, 35–44
    Protestant critics, 44–53
Seerveld, Calvin, 58n210, 89, 198–99, 200n118, 332
Semmelroth, Otto, xxiii, xxiv, 332

Sensus fidelium, 132–45
sexual complementarity, creation order, 112, 116–18, 218–25
sexual ethics, xix, xxvii, 65–66, 117–18, 130, 187, 239, 246–54, 275–80, 306–8
Smedes, Lewis, 15–16, 18n50, 20n57, 112, 113n121, 114, 332
Smith, Janet E., *Foreword*, 90n59, 139–40, 141n73, 143n78, 145, 224, 243n12, 283n156, 286–87, 323, 333
Sokolowski, Robert, 70, 166n2, 207n6, 313, 333
Stegman, Thomas D., xxv$n$34, 95n77, 96, 333
Sullivan, Andrew, xi, 243, 283–85, 333
Swinburne, Richard, 30, 31n95, 48n171, 333

tacit knowing (Polanyi), 190, 270–72
Thielicke, Helmut, 259, 289, 310–11, 311n27
theology of the body
  adequate anthropology, 190–91
  phenomenological reflection, 175–91
  phenomenology and metaphysics, 166–75
  solitude–unity–nakedeness, 191–204
  triadic structure of human subjectivity, 191, 194, 198

Vanhoozer, Kevin, 39, 40n135, 45, 48n174, 66, 84n38, 85, 86n46, 333
Veritatis Splendor (John Paul II), xxi$n$36, 15n35, 82n33, 109n110, 119n131, 121n136, 186n91, 188n96, 216, 240n3, 244n15, 246n22, 249n32, 250n40, 256n67, 257n70, 278n132, 279n141, 289n167, 296n188, 297n191, 299, 301n202, 303n208, 305n213, 309n13, 311n28, 315n44, 327

Williams, Rowan, xxi, 2, 334
Wojtyla, Karol (John Paul II), xv$n$1, xxvii$n$36, 166n1, 167–92, 193n109, 198–200, 226n61, 228, 266–67, 326
Wolterstorff, Nicholas, 72n2, 334
Wright, N. T., 8n18, 57n208, 334

www.ingramcontent.com/pod-product-compliance
Lightning Source LLC
Chambersburg PA
CBHW071149300426
44113CB00009B/1144